So Help Me God

Mike Pence

Simon & Schuster

NEW YORK   LONDON   TORONTO
SYDNEY   NEW DELHI

Simon & Schuster
1230 Avenue of the Americas
New York, NY 10020

First Simon & Schuster hardcover edition November 2022

SIMON & SCHUSTER and colophon are registered trademarks
of Simon & Schuster, Inc.

For information about special discounts for bulk purchases,
please contact Simon & Schuster Special Sales at 1-866-506-1949
or business@simonandschuster.com.

The Simon & Schuster Speakers Bureau can bring authors to your
live event. For more information or to book an event, contact
the Simon & Schuster Speakers Bureau at 1-866-248-3049
or visit our website at www.simonspeakers.com.

Manufactured in the United States of America

1 3 5 7 9 10 8 6 4 2

Library of Congress Cataloging-in-Publication Data has been applied for.

ISBN 978-1-9821-9033-0
ISBN 978-1-9821-9035-4 (ebook)

For the love of my life, Karen

Contents

*"For I know the plans I have for you," declares
the Lord, "plans to prosper you and not to harm you,
plans to give you hope and a future."*

—Jeremiah 29:11

Prelude

January 6, 2021, United States Capitol, Washington, DC
Shortly after 2:00 p.m. Eastern Standard Time

I had always been loyal to President Donald Trump. He was my president, and he was my friend. Over the past four years we had forged a close working relationship, spending hours together nearly every day in the Oval Office. In those times when we had disagreements, I had always shared my opinion in private. But today things had to be different.

For my first loyalty was to the Constitution of the United States. I had taken an oath here at the Capitol nearly four years ago to support and defend the Constitution, which ended with a prayer, "so help me God." This morning, I told the president one final time that I believed my oath required me to preside over this joint session of Congress and certify the results of the 2020 presidential election—the election we had lost. It had been a difficult conversation.

And now here I was, sitting quietly at the head of the Senate Chamber, with all one hundred of America's senators seated at their desks. We had come to open and count the electoral votes submitted by the states. We had convened as a joint session in the House Chamber earlier that afternoon but had quickly adjourned to the Senate Chamber to hear the debate over objections raised under the Electoral Count Act of 1887.

Republican senator James Lankford of Oklahoma, easily recognizable by his red hair and white temples, had the floor. As he spoke solemnly about vote counts, the Senate parliamentarian, Elizabeth MacDonough, seated just a few feet in front of me, leaned back in her chair and whispered through her face mask, "Mr. Vice President, protestors have breached the building's doors on the first floor. Just informing you."

I glanced across the room where we were gathered. The rich blue carpet covering the floor, the ivory plaster ceiling overhead, the rows of historic mahogany desks arranged neatly in a semicircle. A number of those same desks were replacements for ones burned by the British during their invasion of Washington, DC, in 1814.

This is democracy's sacred ground—not because of its occupants, current or past, but because whenever the American people demanded that we live up to the ideals of the Constitution, whenever we set out to accomplish the seemingly impossible, it ultimately happened here, under this dome.

From here we sent Meriwether Lewis and William Clark on their journey west. Here we ended slavery. From here we launched the United States into victories for freedom in two world wars. Here we fostered the world's largest economy and mustered a national defense that has been the greatest force for good the world has ever known.

For two centuries, it was here that the people's will was honored, that their choice of one fellow citizen to temporarily lead the American government was formally accepted. I was here on January 6 because, for the fifty-ninth time in our nation's history, we would certify the election of the president of the United States.

As Lankford's speech headed toward its conclusion, I could see his colleagues anxiously glancing at their cell phones. Max Millian, one of the men on my Secret Service detail, walked onto the Senate floor and straight to my chair. "Mr. Vice President," he said, "we gotta go."

He told me that protestors were on the move in the Capitol, that we needed to leave the building. I was confident that the US Capitol Police would soon have the situation in hand, so I told him we would just wait in the ceremonial office reserved for my use as president of the Senate.

Since the 1850s, the small, elegantly appointed space a few steps from the Senate Chamber has served as an office of sorts for the vice president. The room is full of history: One vice president, Henry Wilson, died here after suffering a stroke. Another, Harry Truman, became president here. The women's suffrage movement ended triumphantly in this same room when another Hoosier second-in-command, Thomas Marshall, signed the Nineteenth Amendment into law.

The only addition I had made to the decor during my time as vice president was a quiet Hoosier autumn landscape by T. C. Steele titled *Road Through the Woods*. No artist better captured the calm beauty of southern Indiana, a place that had brought our family great comfort through the years.

My senior staff was waiting in the office. My wife, Karen, and daughter Charlotte joined us shortly after. Family has always been among my greatest sources of strength, and it would prove so in that moment. Along with my brother Gregory, an Indiana congressman, we stood together in that cramped room and watched the mayhem unfolding inside and around the Capitol on a small television set.

Soon my lead Secret Service agent, Timothy Giebels, walked through the doors of the office and said, "Sir, we've got to get you out of the building." A large, confident man, Tim informed me that protestors who had smashed their way into the House side of the Capitol were now heading for the Senate Chamber. They had come to protest the result of the election and to prevent Congress from fulfilling its responsibility to open and count the Electoral College votes. And, as I later learned, many had come looking for me.

I have often told our three children that the safest place in the world to be is in the center of God's will. I knew in my heart that we were where we were supposed to be, doing what we were supposed to be doing. I felt resolve and a peace informed by my upbringing in Indiana, my faith, my family, a lifetime of service, and a lifelong love of the Constitution. I felt no fear. I told my detail that we would hold there until the Capitol was secured. I was not leaving my post.

I was not afraid; I was angry. I was angry at what I saw, how it desecrated the seat of our democracy and dishonored the patriotism of millions of our supporters, who would never do such a thing here or anywhere else. To see fellow Americans ransacking the Capitol left me with a simmering indignation and the thought: Not here, not this . . . *not in America*.

Yet from the terrorist attacks of 9/11 to the covid pandemic we had endured over the past year, Americans have faced and overcome threats much graver than rioters in the Capitol. That mob could shatter glass, overturn desks, occupy offices, but they could not stop our democracy. My father, a combat veteran, had instilled into me a deep sense of duty. My faith reminded me that you "keep your oath, even when it hurts." I had made a promise to the American people to support and defend the Constitution, and I was determined to keep it. We would not be deterred. We would finish our work that day. So help us God.

As we heard a muffled roar in the distance, my wife closed the drapes over the large windows facing outside to the north as Tim Giebels returned to make one more urgent plea for us to leave.

The rioters had reached our floor, he said. We had to leave the building at once. I pointed my finger at his chest and said, "You're not hearing me, Tim. I'm not leaving! I'm not giving those people the sight of a sixteen-car motorcade speeding away from the Capitol."

"Okay," he answered in a voice that made it clear that it wasn't. "Well, we can't stay here. This office only has a glass door, and we can't protect you." I asked him what our options were. We could move temporarily, he suggested, to the Capitol's loading dock and garage, a few stories below. I agreed.

The door to the office opened. A path was cleared in the corridor to the stairwell descending to the garage. The steps were secured. "Sir, we have to go now!" Tim shouted. I stood up, placed my hand on Karen's elbow. Charlotte was at our side. I looked at them and said, "Let's go."

We walked out into the hall slowly. I glanced back to make sure my brother Gregory was with us. All around was a blur of motion and chaos: security and police officers directing people to safety, staffers shouting and running for shelter. I could see the intensity in the eyes of the Secret Service detail; it was audible, too, in the voices of the Capitol Police. I could hear the fall of footsteps and angry chanting.

On the wall, in the now-empty office we had left behind, still hung that painting of a lonely road, softly winding its way past a row of barren trees into the southern Indiana horizon.

CHAPTER ONE

Climb Your Own Mountain

From everyone who has been given much,
much will be demanded.
—Luke 12:48

This is where it all began for me.

The town of Columbus, Indiana, sits where the Flatrock and Driftwood Rivers connect, forming the East Fork of the White River, the waterway that cuts across southern Indiana. It's a quietly beautiful part of the world, a patchwork of lush farmland, rolling hills, and forests that turn remarkable shades of gold and burgundy in the autumn. There are towns, too, cut out of the wilderness just decades after America's founding.

The pioneers who populated them built churches, raised families, formed communities. And when the time came, they left their homes to defend a set of ideals on battlefields in places like Buena Vista and Bull Run.

They were Hoosiers.

The root of that word is a mystery and the source of great debate within and beyond our state. Its origin may never be fully revealed. Some say that the term derives from the "Who's there?" pioneers would ask when they heard a knock on their door. Others suggest that the word was a Native American term for "corn." Or did it come from a man named Hoosier who had hired Indiana's workers on the Louisville and Portland Canal? The poet James Whitcomb Riley, a Hoosier himself, offered a less flattering origin story: among the violent backwoods brawling among our state's earliest settlers, "Whose ear?" was often asked after a particularly nasty fight. That then transformed into "Hoosier."

My own theory is that it came from a traveling African American Methodist preacher named Harry Hosier, who established churches along the Ohio River in the early days of the Indiana Territory during the Second Great Awakening in the eighteenth century. His congregants were often referred to as Hoosiers. But who knows? We do know, though, that it is the most widely recognized nickname for the residents of any state in the union. It's not even close. Wherever a Hoosier goes, Hoosiers are known.

And so are their qualities. They are tough and independent, hardworking, creative, and caring. They value faith and family. And as any public servant in our state can testify, Hoosiers have strong hearts and strong opinions but deliver them politely. Usually.

Much of this character comes from the farm, the initial and continuing engine of the state's economy. Agriculture was the driver for Bartholomew County, of which Columbus is the seat. Farmers shipped their crops along the White River and along the railroad that arrived in the 1840s, running between Madison on the Ohio River and the state's new capital, Indianapolis.

By the beginning of the twentieth century, the town was a manufacturing hub. The engines, automotive parts, and radios built there were shipped around the world. The industrial demand of two world wars kicked Columbus's economy into high gear. Between 1940 and 1960, the town's population doubled. Among those who saw in it a vision of the American Dream were my parents.

Edward and Nancy Pence were city kids, from the Irish enclaves of south Chicago. Dad was the oldest son of another Edward Pence, who made a good living at the stockyards but had a hard edge as a parent. When Dad graduated from high school, the story goes, Grampa Pence walked him out the front door of their well-appointed brick home to show him his graduation present. He thought his father had bought him a car. Instead, my grandfather said, "There's the world, Son, go take from it whatever you want." And that was it.

Dad served in the US Army in the Korean War. On April 15, 1953, Second Lieutenant Edward J. Pence was awarded the Bronze Star for having "under withering enemy fire" led the rescue of a combat patrol stranded in a minefield. The medal stayed in a drawer. When we were kids, Dad never spoke of his time in the war, other than that he prayed often. "There weren't any atheists in the foxholes," he'd say.

Only after we became adults, when pressed, did he share the harrowing story of how his platoon had been ordered to withdraw under a major enemy assault only to find their escape hindered by a minefield. Dad told his second that he would lead the platoon across the minefield, stepping heavily, and that they should follow in his footsteps for however far he was able to get. After he reached the other side of the minefield unharmed, the entire patrol was able to safely cross.

A cousin Dad grew up with told me years later that he had been a happy-go-lucky kid but the war had changed him. "I don't think he ever got over the guilt of coming home," he said. In that moment, every faraway look in Dad's eyes when his service in the war came up made sense to me.

Mom was a first-generation American. Her dad, Richard Michael Cawley, had left Ireland to escape the civil war. He went first to England and worked in a coal mine, then returned to Ireland. He sailed from the port at Cobh to Ellis Island in the spring of 1923. He went west and settled in Chicago, where he met Mary Maloney, whose parents had both grown up in a small town in Ireland called Doonbeg. Grampa drove a bus for the Chicago Transit Authority for thirty years and was a proud member of the transportation union.

In America, he prospered. He loved his adopted country and believed dearly in its promise. He belonged, and he raised a family of Americans. He told his children and grandchildren over and over again that in America, anything was possible. His story is not particularly unique. But it is uniquely American.

And so, in its way, was my parents' meeting. It was 1954. Mom noticed Dad, a recently returned serviceman, looking sharp in his uniform in a Chicago bar named Applejacks. He noticed her, too. Through mutual friends, he found out that she was Nancy Cawley, a secretary in a small business agency. He turned up in the agency's office one afternoon in a stylish hat and coat. And that was it. It was St. Patrick's Day. They were married on January 14, 1956.

Dad, who had a degree from Loyola University, began a job as a salesman for the Pure Oil Company, which was headquartered in Chicago. When the offer of a promotion in Indiana came, he followed it to Indianapolis, where they lived in a small apartment off Keystone Avenue. Three years and two little boys (my brothers Gregory and Edward) later, they relocated fifty miles south to Columbus, where Dad took a job as vice president of Kiel Brothers Oil Company. He would ultimately become a minority owner and run the company, which supplied some two hundred gas stations across Indiana and Kentucky. I was born at the Bartholomew County Hospital on June 7, 1959, and named Michael Richard Pence after my Irish maternal grandfather.

Note that each of us were known by our full first names: Gregory, Edward, Michael, Thomas. As my mother always said, "If you want to raise respectable people, you should give them respectable names." To this day each of us is better known by a shorter version of our name. But we all still address one another as our parents did. I'll never be anyone other than Michael to my mother, brothers, and sisters. I'll let you decide how well our mother's theory worked out.

The first Pence home in Columbus was a two-story apartment building not far from downtown. We didn't stay long, though, before moving to a small three-bedroom ranch-style house in a new subdivision named Everroad Park West. My parents watched a truck bring the home up the street and lower it onto the concrete slab at 2744 31st Street in the summer of 1960.

It was the setting for an idyllic youth. Every home on the block had children our age. There was a cornfield in our backyard, and just a short walk away was Haw Creek, where we spent every waking hour of those hot summer days splashing in the shallow water, which seemed so much deeper then. The four Pence boys—now including my little brother, Thomas, who arrived in 1961—would walk out the front door of that house every summer morning and not be back until sundown. There was a sandlot for baseball games and always enough friends around to play army. The memories of those days are some of my happiest.

It wasn't all Huck Finn, though. The Pence boys were rambunctious. Dad was on the road four days of the week, meeting clients around the Midwest, and the phrase "Wait till your father gets home" still sends a shiver down my spine. Mom usually had a list detailing our misbehavior for him when he walked through the door. Truth be told, my mother never needed much assistance keeping her kids in line and at eighty-eight years young still doesn't. My parents raised us with love and discipline, although when our two sisters came along years later, the rules seemed to change. Annie and Mary had Dad wrapped around their little fingers, and that never changed.

Our family ran like Dad's old platoon. It was up early, school or chores, home for dinner, saying grace, and Mass on Sunday. We were a devout Catholic family, and all four of us boys were routinely called into service as altar boys whenever Father Gleason had a need. And attending church was mandatory. Faith was always a central part of our lives.

Dad was involved with the local chapter of the Society of St. Vincent de Paul, a Catholic organization that helps those struggling with hunger or poverty. Every week leading up to Christmas, he would fill our station wagon with groceries and presents. We would pile into the car, not knowing where he was taking us. He would then drive us to the poor part of town, park the car in front of a house, get out, and knock on the door, my brothers and I behind him, our arms full of bags and boxes. I have never forgotten walking into those homes and seeing those hurting families, many with small children who had little to eat and no chance to celebrate Christmas. I thought back then that Dad had brought us along as help to carry the gifts and groceries, but the reason he took us was to see, as the Bible says, that faith without works is dead.

Mom grew up during the Great Depression. We heard stories of how her grandmother, whom she called Nana, would cook more food for dinner than their family needed. Poor souls would walk up the alley behind their brick house and wait outside the back door, knowing that my great-grandmother would give them a bowl of soup. This quiet charity is part of who my mom is. Over and over again I saw my parents' generosity; there was never any fanfare about it, it was not done for other people to see; they just lived out their faith. And growing up around it impacted me in a real way, laying a foundation for my own faith. As I told my dad years later, "I have the faith I have because of the faith you have."

Catholics were a minority in Columbus. We never minded it or felt like outsiders. After my parents moved to town, one of my mom's dearest friends, who was Baptist, offered her a good-natured suggestion. "Nancy," she said, "we would appreciate it if you didn't refer to us as non-Catholics."

Southern Indiana has long been considered part of "tornado alley," and tornadoes touch down often during the spring and summer. When one was spotted near our house in Everroad Park West, Mom would round us kids up in the living room—we didn't have a basement—and proceed to douse us and much of the living room in holy water from a small bottle from the local Catholic church. My brothers and I were convinced that we would have been drier outside in the driving rainstorm. We gave her a hard time about it for years, but point of fact, the tornado did not hit our house.

Dad was not a native Hoosier, but his beliefs were right at home in Indiana. If Ed Pence gave you his word, you could count on it. And he did not mince those words. He was loving but tough. One Mother's Day, we tried to get him to help us with a surprise for Mom. He wouldn't participate. "She's not my mother," he told us. "I'm going golfing; you figure it out." Music was a constant in the Pence house. Dad loved Frank Sinatra. One song in particular encapsulated my father's philosophy of life. In the song "That's Life," he sang, "I've been up and down and over and out/And I know one thing/Each time I find myself/Flat on my face/I pick myself up and get/Back in the race./That's life." To this day I can still recite the words of that song from start to finish.

He had part ownership of a building in downtown Columbus. He and his co-owners eventually sold the property to buyers who planned to build a visitors' center. After a price was agreed upon, Dad and his partners met with the buyers to sign the documents and close the sale. After Dad, who was brilliant at math, looked at the papers, he slid them across the table unsigned. The numbers were wrong, he said; the buyers were about to pay more than they had agreed to. "Go fix it," he told them. And they did. I heard the story years later from a friend of Dad's who was there. He had tears in his eyes when he told me about it.

I was often struck by how respected Dad was. One afternoon when I was out driving along with Dad as he did his daily rounds visiting the gas stations his company supplied, I said, looking out the car window, "Dad, you know, you're really kind of a big deal." He wasn't having it, though. "Michael," he explained, "I just have a lot of friends." Years after he passed, people would come up to me at county fairs, fish fries, and chicken dinners and simply say, "I knew your dad." The emotion in their eyes always told me that Dad had done something for them, had meant something to them, had been a friend.

When it came to his children, he had little use for flattery. If we did well at sports or in school, he offered little praise. At one point I remember asking him why he offered words of encouragement so infrequently but didn't hesitate to criticize. "The whole world is going to tell you how great you are," he said. "My job is to tell you how to do better." And he did. He set a standard and expected his children to meet it. We would keep our word and treat those around us with respect, or we would hear from him.

One day, my brothers and I were playing in the field behind our house, building forts with cornstalks, hurling baseball-sized clogs of dirt pulled from the ground, bouncing on the metal fence that divided the farm from our house, and generally causing chaos. On that particular afternoon there was one bounce too many on that fence. It toppled over, and the hogs on the other side of it escaped, running across our neighborhood. When our father learned of the episode, he forced us to make a large sign that read STOP PLEASE, NEED TO TALK and sent us out to the cornfield, where the farmer was working with his combine. He noticed the band of small boys and their sign and brought the giant machine to a halt. His attention captured, we walked over and each of us apologized for running wild in his cornfield. Dad watched the whole thing from our backyard.

One of my earliest memories is sitting in front of a black-and-white television in the living room of our little house hearing the clip-clop of horses as we watched the caisson bearing the remains of a fallen president to Arlington National Cemetery. On the wall above that television, next to a photo of the pope, hung a portrait of John F. Kennedy.

JFK and Martin Luther King, Jr., were the heroes of my youth.

The two men provided incredible moments of inspiration. They were both gone by my tenth birthday. But the impressions endure. Of course, there was an ethnic affinity for Kennedy, the first Irish Catholic president of the United States and the member of a large family like ours. But both he and Dr. King demonstrated that through words and courageous stands, leaders could encourage Americans to see the best in themselves and strive to achieve great things.

I can still remember hearing Dr. King's "I Have a Dream" speech from the March on Washington in August 1963 replayed in the classrooms of our small Catholic school. And I'll never forget sitting in front of the television in our basement on July 20, 1969, watching grainy black-and-white images from the surface of the moon as President Kennedy's vision to land a man there by the end of the decade and return him safely to the earth became a reality.

The Pences were not a particularly political family. My parents followed the news. Dad, a businessman, was nominally a Republican. Mom, more staunchly, was a Democrat, albeit a conservative one. Truth be told, I probably got my interest in politics from my mom. She had a passion for the United States common to many first-generation Americans. It was contagious. She was patriotic, read voraciously, followed the news, and was always ready to jump into a political debate over dinner. She has an innate curiosity that drove her to enroll in college for the first time at age sixty, where she earned a bachelor of arts in psychology from Saint Mary-of-the-Woods. To this day she follows current events and the events in her public sons' lives with intensity and joy. When something newsworthy or historical was happening in town, she made sure we witnessed it. When Lady Bird Johnson, the first lady, visited Columbus for a tour of the town's architecture in 1967, Mom, my brothers, and I were waiting along her route.

From an early age, like my mom, I identified with the party of the Kennedys—although in 1964, when the Republican presidential candidate, Barry Goldwater, came through Columbus aboard a train on a whistle-stop tour, Mom put us onto the Goldwater float that drove through downtown. Perhaps she could see into my future.

That was a long way off, though. It was the sense of eloquence and tragedy around both Kennedy and Dr. King that placed in my heart, even from an early age on 31st Street in that small Indiana town, the dream of public service. It was on that street that I first felt the call to represent my hometown and the people who lived there in our nation's capital.

Years later, in the mid-1970s, when I wanted to get involved in politics, Dad arranged a meeting with his attorney, John Rumple, a prominent Democrat who would eventually run for statewide office. Mr. Rumple was a kind man who encouraged me to get involved in the local Democratic Party. I soon found myself going door to door on behalf of candidates as the Youth Coordinator for the Democratic Party in Bartholomew County. I enjoyed meeting Hoosiers and handing out literature, and only the occasional door was slammed in my face. My political journey had begun, although back then I didn't always see the sharp lines between the political parties. When I would knock on a door, campaigning for a local Democrat judge, the people inside, not impolitely, would say, "We are Republicans." I was unfazed. "Can I just leave you some literature?" I would ask, not thinking twice. In typical Hoosier fashion they would always say yes. I'm sure the flyer found its way to the circular file pretty quickly after I headed back to the sidewalk. But I learned the value of a pleasant young person handing out literature. When Karen and I ran for office years later, we always took our children along; not even the hardest-bitten Democrat could turn down a flyer from those kids.

What still echoes throughout those early years and will never leave me is Dad's simple charge: "Climb your own mountain." Whatever it was we chose to do with our lives—and he wasn't particular about that—he wanted us to go out and achieve it and strive every day to be the best at whatever we set out to do.

Columbus was an incredible place to begin that journey. By the time the Pence family arrived there, that small town was home to two Fortune 500 companies, Cummins and Arvin Industries—hardly a common feature of small southern Indiana communities.

Those companies attracted young professionals from all across the country. We went to school with kids whose parents were Ivy League–educated executives and kids whose parents were farmers and factory workers. Our next-door neighbor, Julius Perr, was a mechanical engineer who had fled Communist Hungary after playing a part in the 1956 Hungarian Revolution. By the end of his career he held some eighty patents.

Columbus's landscape was profoundly impacted by Cummins and its long-serving CEO, J. Irwin Miller, whose family had founded the company with the engineer and mechanic Clessie Cummins (who for a time had been the Miller family's chauffeur). Miller was a Hoosier Medici. He reasoned that Cummins's efforts to recruit and keep the best and brightest workforce would be greatly aided if Columbus were a city of unique features and amenities. He also happened to be a great lover of art and architecture.

Under his guidance, the Cummins Foundation commissioned innovative architects to design public buildings, turning the town into a mecca of striking midcentury design. So although there was a cornfield behind the Pence house, there was also a futuristic metal steeple on the skyline. It sat atop North Christian Church, designed by Eero Saarinen. The town's panorama of geometric buildings of stainless steel and glass surrounded by farmland as far as the eye can see earned it the nickname "Athens on the Prairie."

Even if there was an element of corporate savvy behind it, Miller's efforts to build and beautify the city echoed another of my dad's most often repeated phrases, "To whom much is given, much will be required." Through Cummins, Miller brought a sense of community and duty to Columbus. He also wasn't afraid to take a public stand; he was heavily engaged in the civil rights movement. As the leader of the National Council of Churches, together with Dr. King, he helped plan the March on Washington and garner support for the Civil Rights Act. He hired minorities and elevated them to leadership roles at Cummins. He closed the company's plant in South Africa to protest apartheid. In 1958, when Benjamin "Mickey" King, an African American, came to Columbus to serve as chief microbiologist for Bartholomew County Hospital, Miller championed his effort to create fair and open housing laws for the city. He made his own company, and Columbus by extension, a more welcoming place by hiring minorities at a time when doing so was the exception rather than the norm.

That likely benefited our family, since of course, technically we were outsiders. The Pences were Irish Catholics in a Protestant community. Columbus was a company town, and Dad didn't work for either company. But we never felt out of place. And the mix helped me learn to get along with and relate to all kinds of people. In our house much was indeed expected as well. Work permits were available in Indiana at sixteen, and sure enough, every Pence boy had one once he reached that age. We like to joke that our two sisters had it a lot easier, but the truth was that at the Pence house, we all worked just as soon as we were old enough and we were all the better for it.

Apart from a newspaper route, my first job was at Ray's Marathon, a full-service gas station supplied by the oil company Dad led, where I would work on and off for five years. On any given day, wearing my short-sleeved Marathon shirt with my first name stitched above the pocket, I would meet Hoosiers from every walk of life from factory workers to CEOs, from farmers to homemakers. I learned to have an easy rapport with just about everybody as I pumped gas—except the rest of the employees at the station.

From my first day on the job, I was met with indifference or scorn from the mechanics who worked the three bays at Ray's. No matter how hard I tried to be friendly or strike up a conversation, my efforts were usually met with a one-word reply or no response at all. I knew what was going on. They saw me as a high school kid who had gotten the job because of who my dad was—which of course was true. One night after I had worked at the station for a few weeks, Dad asked how things were going. I didn't candy coat it. I told him I didn't think the mechanics there liked me and I didn't have the first idea how to get them to respect me. Dad replied, with a mischievous smile, "That's easy, Michael, just out work 'em."

From that time forward, whenever a customer pulled up to the pump, I ran to the car and didn't just fill the tank but also checked the oil and washed the windshield. At the end of the day, I would stay late, scrub the bays, and leave the place spick and span for the morning. Just as Dad had said, in a few short weeks, everything changed, and I count some of those same coworkers as friends to this day.

From first through eighth grades, I attended St. Columba Catholic School. Then, in 1973, I went to Columbus North High School. The schools were a short distance from each other but might as well have been on opposite sides of the earth. The transition was not easy. I had few friends but a desire to be liked.

My older brothers had made the transition before me. But Gregory and Edward were lean and fit, standouts at football and swimming. I was overweight and unhappy about it. And though I gave football and wrestling a shot, I was not much of an athlete. I tried to get people to like me or pay attention to me by goofing off and joking around. It was just a mask. High school was when I had to find my own way, determine what mountain I would climb. And I wasn't sure where to turn or who I was.

Even before high school, I felt comfortable in front of large groups. I had been master of ceremonies at events at St. Columba and regularly took part in public speaking competitions. Since the 1920s, Optimist International, a service club that promotes youth activities, has held its Oratorical Contests. They were especially challenging because participants had little instruction on the content of their remarks other than a few guiding words. We would have to construct a speech around such vague sentiments as "Our Challenge, Involvement." I also joined the Columbus North speech team and participated in National Forensic League speaking tournaments around the state.

Most critically, I participated in the American Legion's Oratorical Contest, a forum designed to promote a better understanding of the Constitution. My immigrant grandfather had instilled in me a love of America; my father's own service in Korea gave me a sense of patriotism and duty. But it was the American Legion contests, which required study and contemplation of the design of the nation's government, that ignited the pilot light of my love of the Constitution.

There I sat, in the Bartholomew County Library, designed (of course) by the famed architect I. M. Pei, poring over books in preparation for the contests. One in particular resonated: *Growth and Development of the American Constitution* by Loren W. Noblitt, who, coincidentally, was from Columbus. I read it over and over again. It's on my bookshelf still. I remember tracking the book down through the Dewey Decimal System, rummaging through those little cards in the catalog drawer, and finding it on the shelf. The cover described the Constitution as "the Foundation for our American Democracy." The pages compared passages from the original document to their modern meaning and explained their historical development, all interspersed with quotes from the Founders. I took special note of the powers delegated to the Congress and president. It was an invaluable tool, as I would soon be speaking extemporaneously about the Constitution. It was my Bible before I had my own Bible.

I wasn't a particularly good student at Columbus North, but I excelled in those speaking contests, winning numerous regional Optimist Club awards. My teachers and the school's speech coach, Debbie Shoultz, provided welcome encouragement. In 1976, during my junior year, I placed second in Indiana's American Legion Oratorical Contest. The following year, I won it. I regularly brought home ribbons, trophies, and scholarships. I was often mentioned in the local paper, the *Republic*.

My father made a habit of not attending his kids' extracurricular activities. He rarely if ever attended my brothers' football games or swimming meets. The same was true for my speaking competitions. It was not that he didn't care. He did. He was proud and encouraging. But he gave us distance; he didn't apply pressure. Those pursuits, he wanted us to see, whether sports or speaking, were ours, not his.

One Saturday evening, I came back from a speech contest with a fistful of blue ribbons. "How did you do?" Dad asked. I threw the ribbons down on the kitchen table where he was sitting. I told him I had cleaned up without even having to put much work into it—which was true. He looked up disappointedly. "All I ever want to know is if you did your best, not if you won or lost," he said. "And you just told me you didn't do your best. I don't have any use for those ribbons." That was Dad: do your best, or don't do at all.

With the attention I was getting from speech competitions, I tried my hand at school elections, running for junior class vice president. The previous summer, I had lost fifty pounds after having been the only member of my family with a weight problem, and I went back to school with a flourish of confidence. I also had a growing interest in public service, so I threw my hat into the ring. I lost, but it whetted my interest in politics. My large and eclectic group of friends voted me class president senior year. During that time, I had lost much of the weight that I was self-conscious about. I had plenty of dates. I had transformed from someone who was unsure of himself to someone who was full of himself.

By the time of high school graduation, I thought I could do it all, I was sure of my own talent. That extended into other parts of my life as well. Religion, so large a part of my upbringing, felt unimportant. I still went to church and said grace before dinner—those were not optional activities—but deep inside I felt I didn't need faith any longer. I was good enough to get by without it.

But for all my supposed eloquence, I knew deep down inside that I actually had very little to say. For all my treasured popularity, something was missing in my heart. I needed to go find it.

I had not even begun to climb my own mountain.

CHAPTER TWO

Bends in the River

Therefore, if anyone is in Christ, the new creation has come:
The old has gone, the new is here!
—2 Corinthians 5:17

In the waning days of the summer of 1977, I packed a suitcase, jumped into the back seat of my parents' station wagon, and headed to Hanover College. Indiana's oldest private school is in a small and intimate spot in Jefferson County, high on a bluff above the Ohio River. Even today the view carries you back to the nineteenth century, people and commerce coming and going along the water.

Standing on the Point, as it's always called, one can see the Ohio bend its way between forests and into the distant horizon. When I first took in the view, it was as an uncertain young man searching for meaning. I still remember, like any other college freshman, the feeling of loneliness as my parents pulled out of the dormitory parking lot and headed back to Columbus. I was away from home for the first time and truly on my own.

In the Pence household, attending college was nonnegotiable. But Dad also had a system. He knew how much, allowing for pizzas and movies, we could save after working forty hours a week earning minimum wage during the summer. Each of us had to write him a check for a portion of our tuition at the end of summer in order to go back to school. Because my parents had achieved a level of economic security, we were not eligible for scholarships or financial aid. But Dad reasoned that we should contribute: You earned the money, and you paid your fair share. "No free rides" wasn't just a slogan in his household. You had to get the grades, too.

I applied to Hanover and Harvard. I was accepted by the first and, although I'd had no expectation of being admitted, saved the rejection letter from the second. No harm trying. When I met Ivy League–educated friends later in life, I would tell them with a wink that Harvard was the Hanover of the Northeast.

The Hanover campus is a small collection of redbrick Georgian buildings with white trim. In my day, there was a common center where all the students dined, a main auditorium, fraternity row, and a series of dorms, in one of which, Crowe Hall, I shared a room with a friend from Columbus. Though I projected a confident front, the truth was that I had very real doubts that I could survive scholastically at college. So I focused on my schoolwork. Just as at Ray's Marathon, my hard work paid off and I had good grades at the end of that first semester. But I was still unsure about my ability.

It was around that time that I was invited to attend a Tuesday night service at Brown Chapel, the unpretentious nondenominational church on campus. It's not much bigger than a room. The service was called Vespers, an old Christian term for evening prayers. I wasn't attending church at the time. I had lost interest in faith and accepted the invitation because I knew there would be pretty girls there.

But I enjoyed the meetings. There was singing, guitar strumming, and always an uplifting message. And I made friends with upperclassmen who also attended, guys such as John Gable and Tom Roberts. At a time when I was haunted by insecurities and put on a front, I was impressed by their genuine ease. They exuded a joy I just did not have. They were members of the Phi Gamma Delta fraternity, or "Fiji," as everyone called it. At the start of my second semester, I pledged and was accepted into the house. Among my class of pledges was a strapping football player from Warsaw, Indiana, named Jay Steger. We became fast friends as we began our respective journeys to a greater understanding of faith and American history.

At the Fiji house, there were many late-night conversations about faith. John and Tom talked often of God, but what they said was new to me, beyond my experience. I had grown up in a liturgical environment. Our family had regularly attended Catholic Mass. But those young men spoke of a personal relationship with God, something I had never experienced but was drawn to.

I noticed that John wore a small cross around his neck. It had an understated elegance about it. It had been bought, I learned, from a mail-order catalogue. Still on my own journey, looking for answers and wanting to emulate friends who clearly had them, I calculated in my mind that wearing a cross would be some sort of solution.

One afternoon I spotted John leaving the cafeteria of our fraternity house. "Hey, John, don't forget to give me that catalogue, I want to order a cross," I said loudly as he walked away.

He stopped and looked at me. "You know, Mike, you've got to wear it in your heart before you wear it around your neck." Then he turned and went up the stairs.

The words hit me like a baseball bat. I realized that John knew I was a phony. Putting a cross around my neck was just the latest pose. I thought that was just what Christian people did. I hadn't gone any deeper. In that moment, my mask fell away.

As my freshman year at Hanover neared its end, I joined some friends on a road trip two hours south to Wilmore, Kentucky, the home of Asbury Theological Seminary. The town was the site of the Ichthus Festival, a weekend-long concert originally conceived as a Christian answer to Woodstock. Contemporary Christian music was in its early days, and I was amazed by the songs of praise by such bands as the Pat Terry Group and Andrus, Blackwood, and Co. More, I was moved by the powerful messages delivered between the sets.

It was April, a wet and muddy season in central Kentucky. On the culminating evening of the festival, preachers presented the gospel. I sat on a campground hillside surrounded by believers while a light rain fell from the night sky. Amid the preaching, the music, and the mist-filled air that night, one journey ended for me and another began. As though for the first time, I truly heard the words of John 3:16: "For God so loved the world that he sent his one and only Son, that whoever believes in him shall not perish but have eternal life."

All the music stopped, and there was an altar call. I stood up and walked down the hill, not just because I was convinced in my mind of the truth of the Gospel but because my heart was broken with gratitude for what had been done for me on the Cross. I found a volunteer counselor and prayed to receive Jesus Christ as my personal Lord and Savior. It was a moment of decision that changed my life forever.

I was Born Again.

The Bible says, "Therefore, if anyone is in Christ, the new creation has come: The old has gone, the new is here!" and that was just how I felt. The old me was gone, and I felt forgiveness and a newness of life that is difficult to put into words. From that day forward I felt that my life was not my own. I had been "bought at a price," and whatever was to come, I would live out my faith in Jesus Christ and follow him wherever He led, no matter the cost.

I returned to college a changed young man. I felt a peace and joy I had never known in my young life. I had a growing desire to understand my newfound Christian faith. I began every day with Bible study and prayer. I devoured books such as John R. W. Stott's *Basic Christianity* and read the works of C. S. Lewis. I also began listening to Christian music. I played Amy Grant's album *Never Alone* in my frat room over and over again. I summarized my new understanding of faith in the margins of the Stott book with the words "Christ in me, enroute to God."

I continued to attend the Catholic church, but I was anxious to share my faith. I founded a youth program at the church and led Bible studies as well. My enthusiasm was admittedly off-putting to some of my friends. Many of them couldn't relate to the new me and moved on. I started to turn away from the party scene on the campus, which further alienated some friends—it was college, after all. I tried to explain to them that my faith had changed me. Some understood; most didn't.

When I returned home after the conclusion of my first year at college, I shared my newfound faith with Mom and Dad. It didn't go well. My parents asked how it had happened, I had been raised in a Catholic home, after all. They had provided that foundation. When I would be on a tear about my new beliefs in the months ahead, I would get a lot of blank stares. Mom would tell me that if I wanted to talk so much about religion, I should go be a priest. But as time went on, seeing the sincerity of my faith, she became my biggest supporter. Dad, too, came to respect my faith; the depth of its conviction mirrored his own. He had deep and abiding beliefs that defined his actions. He didn't talk about God a lot, but his faith was profound. Years later, in a heated discussion about religion he told me, "I believe I have Christ in my heart." And I know he did.

For years my faith would remain a subject of much discussion among my siblings. My oldest brother, Gregory, was the most encouraging. He had given me my first Bible and was studying theology at Loyola University. My other siblings' reactions ranged from curious to skeptical. One of them just thought I was crazy, which was hardly new.

But I finally felt that I had purpose in my life. I wanted to share Christ and live out the Gospel in my daily life. Back at Hanover for my sophomore year, I focused my studies on American history and increased my involvement with campus ministries. But Greek life was still important, and I was elected president of the Fiji house for the next year.

Animal House was in theaters at the time, but we were already living out the movie. Our house was a dump. Our grades were abysmal. The partying was out of control. It was a dry campus, but Fiji keggers were a constant. We had to get our act together, I told my fraternity brothers—to little avail.

One night during a particularly wild blowout, the dean called. The noise was so great that complaints were coming in from the other end of campus. He was on his way over to shut the party down. My fraternity brothers moved with Olympic sprinter–like speed to remove the incriminating evidence before he arrived: kegs were hidden, furniture was righted, music was silenced. When he arrived, the house was quiet and clean. It looked as though a bunch of straitlaced scholars lived there. The dean put the question to me, the president of the fraternity: "Were you having a party here tonight?" I admitted that yes, we'd been having a party. The Fijis were promptly put on probation— "double secret probation," just like Delta in *Animal House*.

Everyone in the fraternity hated me for it. Informed by my faith, I was trying to be a man of integrity. And I truly believed that I was serving the real interests of the fraternity. It was the right thing to do, as painful as it was. When we left to go home for the holidays, my future as house president was in doubt.

During Christmas break, I told Dad the story. For years I had watched him run a company and earn the loyalty of the people around him. He was a leader. I asked for his advice. After some discussion, he observed that a fraternity was really a social club and challenged me to "just make it the best damn social club on campus." I got the point.

Taking his advice, I went back to Hanover after the holidays with a plan to do just that. I proposed a menu full of new sports events, intramural activities, study clubs, and dances. The other members of the fraternity signed on. Our house turned around. In the following year, we had the best GPA and highest recruitment on campus, and we won all the athletic competitions. I was learning that success is often born of failure and that leadership comes from maintaining integrity and putting your foot down.

During my junior year the house wanted me to continue to serve as president, but I declined. I was more focused on running the campus-wide Christian ministry. And I was increasingly captivated by my study of American history. I was enrolled in American Constitutional and Legal History, taught by Professor George M. Curtis III. Dr. Curtis was the great-grandson of an Iowa congressman. He stood six foot one and wore tweed jackets and Brooks Brothers shirts. His hair was jet black; his glasses were horn rimmed. He had impeccable manners and a patrician bearing. He looked like a man who could be elected to the highest offices at any moment. But his calling was teaching.

Dr. Curtis occasionally exhibited a hard midwestern air. One afternoon he strode into the classroom and spotted a book on my desk, a tome on international law. He picked it up, glanced at its cover, then asked the class, "How can there be a book that long about something that doesn't exist?" My fellow students laughed as the professor offered just a hint of a smile.

Later, when I proposed a senior thesis on the religious beliefs of Abraham Lincoln, his eyes widened. "Mr. Pence, you can write your thesis on the religious *expressions* of Abraham Lincoln," he chided. "You cannot, however, speculate about the religious *beliefs* of someone who is not here to defend himself." He was a wise man.

Dr. Curtis sent us back to primary sources. He demanded that we respect the material and one another. But he made us all a promise: If we worked hard, we would never see the world the same way after we left his classroom.

It was through Dr. Curtis that I became acquainted with the Founding Fathers and began to understand the nation they had designed, where government was limited and citizens were free. He encouraged debate and discussion and asked us to take a hard look at what we knew—or thought we knew.

Even as the United States limped through the late 1970s, I remained a proud Democrat. I supported the embattled president, Jimmy Carter, a sincere Born Again Christian with blue-collar roots in Georgia. His opponent in the 1980 election was, I thought, little more than a well-rehearsed B-movie actor. Years later, when I recalled voting for Carter, conservative friends would say sympathetically that everyone had voted for him in 1976. I voted for him in 1980.

I was not unfamiliar with the Constitution before Dr. Curtis's class. I had studied it and given speeches about it during high school in American Legion contests. But I had largely viewed it as the operating manual of the US government. Until then, I had spent less time thinking about the principles underpinning the Constitution and how they allowed Americans to flourish and realize their dreams, as my family had done.

As Dr. Curtis taught the virtues of our constitutional system of limited government, the failings of socialism and the tyranny of Communist governments came into high relief. My political outlook was shifting. But the seeds of that change had been sown even before I had arrived on the Hanover campus.

After graduating from high school, I had flown to Rome to meet up with my brother Gregory, who was studying there. We backpacked north, traveling through France and into West Germany, all the way to the divided capital of Berlin. The streets of West Berlin, with their glittering lights, bustling traffic, and crowded restaurants and shops, led us to Checkpoint Charlie at the intersection of Friedrichstrasse and Zimmerstrasse, the gateway through the Berlin Wall, between West and East, between freedom and tyranny.

Walking past that wooden guard shack and from West to East Berlin was like stepping into a black-and-white movie. The mostly silent streets of the East German capital were lined with drab gray cinderblock structures. The monotony was interrupted by bombed-out buildings, reminders of the relentless Allied aerial assault that had destroyed Berlin in the closing days of World War II some thirty years before. It was also an indication of the stagnant Communist economy that could not rebuild the city. The people were hushed and weary. In my memory, they all wore the same drab overcoat. The cars all dated from the 1950s and seemed perfectly in keeping with their depressing surroundings.

Until then communism, the idea of a state ordered and commanded by its government, had been an abstraction for me. The freedoms and rights such a system took from its citizens—freedoms that I now understood were safeguarded by the US Constitution—had never seemed so real or precious to me.

Dr. Curtis's classroom in Old Classic Hall was full of great truths thanks to the great books he led us to and the conversations he fostered. I could increasingly see them reflected in my own experiences, the impressions of Communist East Berlin, and the commonsense patriotism of my parents.

It wasn't so much that my core beliefs began to change as that my understanding of the values and ideals of the two political parties did. Suddenly what that B-movie actor turned president was saying made sense. Dr. Curtis had promised that we students would leave his classroom changed. The promise was kept.

I graduated from Hanover with a bachelor of arts in history in May 1981. By then I had changed in ways scarcely imaginable when my parents had left me on that campus above the winding Ohio River four years before. I had given my life to Jesus Christ, I had gained early lessons in leadership, and I had begun a conservative political awakening. The young man who left Hanover was far different from the boy who had arrived. But he still had a lot to learn.

CHAPTER THREE

The Beautiful Brunette
with the Guitar

A cord of three strands is not quickly broken.
—Ecclesiastes 4:12

Happiness in life, a saying goes, depends on how well you handle your backup plan.

In fall semester of my senior year at Hanover, I registered to take the LSAT. Law school, I thought, would be the logical pathway to a career in public service. With my dreams on the line, I put incredible pressure on myself to ace the exam. I took multiple practice tests. I studied intensely. I bombed.

Eager to realize my ambition and anxious to succeed, I had wrapped myself around the axle. Trying too hard sank my chances. I entered my first summer as a college graduate with no job and slim prospects. But deep inside, my faith gave me peace that something unexpected was going to happen. Dad insisted that I polish my résumé and start submitting job applications. I told him that God would provide and finding a job could wait until I got back from a much anticipated trip to Ireland. He was not convinced.

I had spent years dreaming about and planning a trip to Ireland. I was to go with Grampa Cawley, who would show me the home he had grown up in. We would travel the highways and byways of the old country while he told me stories. It was, sadly, not to be. Grampa had died after a long bout with colon cancer the previous Christmas Eve. I was devastated. Our bond had been deep. He had often told me that of all the Pence boys, I was the only true Irishman.

Perhaps because of that, I decided to take the trip anyway. In June, I boarded a plane and soon touched down in Galway. From there I connected with my great-aunt and her niece. For nearly two months, I lived above and worked in Pat Morrissey's pub, pulling pints, washing dishes, and spending time with members of my extended family in Doonbeg. The Emerald Isle and her people were warm, familial, and familiar.

During one of my few calls home, Dad, with an air of disbelief, told me that a message had come in from the president's office at Hanover. They wanted to know if I was interested in a job as an admissions officer for the school. I told Dad I would think and pray on it. "Good, do that," he said. I did. And I decided to take the job after I got home.

For most of the next two years, I tossed a bag into my Chevy Malibu on Monday morning and didn't return home to Hanover until Friday evening. I traveled to the four corners of Indiana and everywhere in between, meeting with high schoolers, attending career fairs, talking up my alma mater, and identifying, with the help of Dad's unrivaled knowledge, all the best hole-in-the-wall diners in Indiana. My budget was small, and I often stayed at fleabag motels. But I saw the richness of Indiana driving on two-lane roads, felt the genuine warmth of Hoosiers. I visited every high school in Indiana and learned the state's highways and byways like the back of my hand. Thanks to the job, I got to know and understand my state's regional characteristics and the wide variety of Hoosiers, from the small, largely rural communities in the south to the industrial cities to the north.

The job came with a one-story ranch house on Clemmons Street on the edge of Hanover's campus. I continued to study with Dr. Curtis, though now the "classes" were in his home study, where books were stacked to the ceiling, and longneck bottles of Budweiser were often downed. Away from campus, his opinions on contemporary politics grew more candid, and my own transformation from Kennedy Democrat to Reagan Republican neared its conclusion.

As much as I enjoyed the work at Hanover, I still felt called elsewhere. I looked toward the ministry and even spoke with a local pastor about such a choice. But deep down, I had never abandoned my dream of a public career. It must have been evident to others.

One evening I sat in the backyard of my house on Clemmons Street with Joe Harris. He was a fraternity brother, a good friend, and a strong believer. We grilled burgers and drank beers as the sun went down, talking about the future. "You should try to go to law school, Mike," he said from across the firepit.

"It just didn't work out," I told him, hoping it would end that line of conversation.

Uncharacteristically, he kept pressing me to take the LSAT again.

It got on my nerves, and I lost my cool. "I'm not taking that test again, okay? Get off my back!"

He wanted to know why and kept pressing. So I finally told him, honestly, "I'm scared of failing again."

Joe was silent. After a few minutes, in a near whisper, he asked, "Isn't courage being afraid and going on ahead anyway?"

That one stopped me in my tracks.

The answer was yes. I wanted to pass that exam so badly that I was petrified of taking it again. But Joe made me realize how foolish I was being. From that night I began to gather the courage to try again, to risk failure. But this time I found it in my faith to approach the exam differently. I studied and prepared, yes. But I prayed, too. The Bible says, "Faith is the assurance of things hoped for." Whenever I got anxious, I just thanked God that the test was going to go well. And that calmed my heart. In 1982, with God's grace and a little nudge from a friend, I passed the LSAT—with four times the score I'd gotten the first time I'd taken it.

Several months later, I stood in my driveway holding an acceptance letter to Indiana University School of Law. I began humming the school's famous fight song, "Indiana, Our Indiana."

Though IU's main law campus is with the rest of the university in Bloomington, it also has one in Indianapolis. I chose the latter because a number of clerkships were available in the city and I needed to work my way through school. In the summer of 1983, I arrived in Indianapolis. I took a room in the home of Zelda Metzger, a widow and great-granddaughter of General Lew Wallace, the Hoosier hero who had saved Washington, DC, at the Battle of Monocacy in 1864 and written *Ben-Hur: A Tale of the Christ*. It was a large, old house on

Pennsylvania Street, just north of downtown. The rent was reasonable and included doing a few chores.

There was one thing I had to make official upon arriving in Indianapolis. I scheduled an appointment with John Sweezy, the legendary and long-serving chair of the local Republican Party. I marched into party headquarters, up to his second-floor office, where I declared my intention to join the party. He shot me a look of mild bewilderment from behind his desk. "We're glad to have you," he said. "Though most people don't make an appointment to join the GOP." I had joined the Reagan Revolution, even if I was clearly the only one who thought it a major event.

I began law school with a tremendous amount of enthusiasm. Inspired by my still young Christian faith, I prepared myself mentally, spending time in my morning devotions; physically, too, keeping up a steady exercise regime. I saw the work ahead as an immense challenge and wanted to bring to bear on it everything I had, beginning with my faith.

Maybe I went overboard: I wrote an introductory letter chock full of religious fervor to Larry Grimes, a fellow believer who would be attending IU's law school and with whom I shared a friend. It went strangely unanswered. During the first day of orientation, he sat in the desk next to me and introduced himself. In the years to come we would become dear friends. Larry, who was private about his faith, later admitted that he had expected me to come walking into the room with a twenty-pound Bible, handing out literature.

At that moment, events far beyond Indiana intruded into the lives of all Americans. On October 23, 1983, terrorists drove two trucks loaded with explosives into barracks housing US marines in Beirut. The explosions killed 200 Marines—307 people in total. At the time, my older brother, Gregory, who had joined the Marine Corps after leaving college, was stationed in Beirut. When the news broke, I raced to Columbus to be with my family as we waited for word about him. There were no cell phones to call, no texts to send, not even email. For a day our family waited in limbo, with his devoted young wife, Denise, watching for a vehicle with a military insignia to pull up the driveway and deliver the terrible news. Blessedly, when the call finally came, it was from Gregory himself. He had been transferred aboard a ship shortly before the attack and was safe. But the first shot in the War on Terror had been fired.

Back in Indianapolis, my schoolwork began. There was so much of it that dating or having a relationship wasn't on my mind. I wasn't meeting many people anyway. At the time, I was attending Mass at a Catholic church near Mrs. Metzger's house, St. Thomas Aquinas. It was there on an October Sunday, sitting in the pews, that I first saw her—the beautiful brunette with the guitar.

She was playing in the church band. I had to talk to her. When the service ended, I tried to do so but was interrupted by friends from Columbus who were visiting. I was back at church the following Sunday, but she wasn't there. I put her out of my mind and focused on my studies.

And then one Sunday, as finals approached, there she was again with that Epiphone guitar. After the service, the very same people from Columbus stood between me and her once again. That time I gave them the Heisman and followed her out the door behind the altar.

The first thing I told her was a lie, as she often reminds friends. "I'd like to play in the guitar group," I said. "You need to talk to him," she said, gesturing toward a rather large man with a beard. "He runs it." At that point I dropped the act, extended my hand, and introduced myself: "I'm Mike Pence." She smiled faintly, and we talked briefly. She was holding her guitar case with her left hand. I couldn't tell if there was a ring on it.

She was immediately extraordinary to me: her touching smile, her warm personality. Flustered, I forgot to ask for her number, but I was able to glean some information. Her name was Karen Whitaker. She taught shop, yes, shop, at the Orchard Country Day School on the north side of Indianapolis. She was a Butler University graduate, having earned bachelor's and master's degrees in elementary education, and she could fly a plane. She was full of surprises. Most important, her older sister was a law student at IU.

After we parted, I went straight to the dorm room of my friend and old fraternity brother Jay Steger, who was studying at nearby Butler University. I talked to him about our fifteen-minute conversation for the next four hours. Jay was unfazed. Over the years, we had developed a habit of holding long, detailed discussions on topics ranging from faith to politics to women, usually aided by adult beverages. And this was no different. But as he would tell me years later, from the very start he knew this was different.

The following Monday, I called the school where Karen worked and said I was updating a mailing list at the church and asked if it was Mrs. or Miss Whitaker. Laughing out loud, the woman said, "It's Miss."

That established, I headed to the law school recorder's office, run by Velma Dobbins, a woman who took her job and students' privacy seriously, as members of the national press would discover in a few years when they beat a path to her desk in their unsuccessful search for Senator Dan Quayle's transcripts. I would not be deterred, however.

"I need the contact information for a student—" She interrupted me midsentence and dispassionately explained that the office did not give out personal information of any student under any circumstance. Dejected, I headed toward the door, then spun around and gave it one last try. "Look," I explained, "I just met her sister, and she knocked my socks off. I just want to talk to her." Without moving an eyelash, Velma reached over to the cabinet and asked me to repeat the name. She found it and gave me the phone number; I was at a loss to thank her. "Oh," she said waving her hand, "just invite me to the wedding." We did.

Shortly after, I was standing in a phone booth at 56th and Illinois alongside a friend and workout buddy who had come along for moral support. I dropped a quarter into the slot and dialed the number. The ringtone was interrupted by a sweet voice that told me her sister wasn't home. "Who's this?" I asked. "This is Karen," the voice answered. Startled, I hung up the phone. "It was her!" I yelled to my friend outside the booth. He doubled over laughing.

Humiliated, I put another quarter into the phone and called her back. She answered again, and this time I stayed on; she told me she planned to go ice skating at the Indiana State Fairgrounds with her niece and nephew on Thursday. If I wanted to come, she said, "that would be wonderful." Of course, I said yes. When she opened the door on that night before our first date and I saw that smile again, I knew it was over for me.

During my senior year in college, I had visited my grandfather in the hospital for advice. All my friends were getting engaged; I was dating a girl but was unsure if she was the one. He had been married for fifty years to my grandmother; they held hands until the day she died. So I asked him, standing beside his bed, how I would recognize the right person. "When you don't have to ask anyone's opinion," he answered. The moment I laid eyes on Karen Whitaker, I knew she was different, and from the moment I spoke to her, I knew I didn't need anyone else's opinion.

She was born in Kansas, the third daughter of an air force officer. Her father had left the family when she was a little girl, and her mom had remarried and had two more children. Karen had helped raise them. Her own marriage to a high school sweetheart had ended early. She had then paid her own way through college, graduating early and with high honors. She was strong and kind. She had an astonishingly wide range of interests and abilities, though in her heart she was and still is a teacher. Her faith was deep and settled; we shared the same values. I was completely taken with her.

She eventually took a job teaching second grade at Acton Elementary and, not surprisingly, was one of the most popular teachers in the school. She had a bunny rabbit in the room that would end up spending summers with us during the early years of our marriage. We named another large lop-eared rabbit after the scuba diving instructor on our honeymoon. Tyrone was a big hit with the second-grade class. She took a genuine interest in her kids and made a point to invite them in small groups to her apartment in Indianapolis for dinner once a year. It was a practice we continued well into our married life. Years later, as our political career unfolded, there was hardly a public event where some young family wouldn't walk up, not to meet me but to say hello to their "favorite schoolteacher" ever. I'm so proud of Mrs. Pence.

While dating, we often visited the Broad Ripple Canal, a segment of a never-finished nineteenth-century attempt to connect the Wabash and Erie Canal and Ohio River. We sat on a bench at the edge of the shallow water, feeding the ducks and discussing our aspirations.

One afternoon, nine months after our first date, I sawed off the nose of a loaf of bread and stuffed a ring box inside. The ducks were gathering, anticipating some crumbs. When Karen broke the bread in half, the ring box fell out. I got down on one knee. "Karen, will you marry me?"

"One minute," she responded.

It wasn't the answer I was expecting.

But she reached into her purse and pulled out a little cross with a heart on it. The word "Yes" was inscribed inside.

We paid for our own wedding, booking St. Christopher Catholic Church in the town of Speedway—the home of the Indianapolis 500—on the west side of Indianapolis. Karen and I both love the race; she had saved money from a childhood paper route to buy her first ticket. On June 8, 1985, surrounded by our family and friends, we went down the aisle without any doubts. The reception was at the Midway Motor Lodge, where a DJ played music and little wine carafes sat on the tables. Velma Dobbins couldn't make it, but she sent a gift.

My time in law school seemed almost secondary. God brought me to Indianapolis at the right time to meet the girl of my dreams. Other than the grace I draw from my faith in Jesus Christ, his greatest gift to me is Karen.

But I did graduate from law school in 1986. Dad, who had himself tried a semester of law school, was particularly proud. Work had prevented him from finishing his degree, but he kept his old law books on a shelf in his study at home, and they have been cherished heirlooms of our family all these years.

We rented a bungalow in Broad Ripple, I passed the Indiana bar exam and started my career, working for a well-respected firm that specialized in corporate litigation. I had enjoyed studying law, but practicing was dull. It lacked the pace and action I craved. One afternoon in 1987, I was having lunch with Toby McClamroch, a local Republican activist. I was engaged in GOP politics, volunteering and attending party events. "What do you want to do?" he asked across the table. Shyly, I told him I wanted to someday, presumably after a long career in law and years of political engagement, run for Congress in my hometown of Columbus. "That seat is held by a Democrat, and we don't have a candidate for next year's election," he said. "Why don't you run now?"

I called Karen at her school and told her I was thinking of running for Congress, that the party was asking me to run. I was twenty-eight. It was decades earlier than I had expected. But a door had opened. We talked it over, and we prayed about it. And as she has done innumerable times in the three and a half decades since, Karen said, "Let's go. Let's run until the Lord closes the door."

CHAPTER FOUR

Reaching for Dreams, Enduring Loss

*Those who cling to worthless idols forfeit
the grace that could be theirs.*
—Jonah 2:8

My decision to run for Congress at age twenty-eight was the easy part. My family was surprised but supportive, except for Dad, who was worried that it would delay our having kids. Karen and I had been trying to have children since tying the knot. We were still hopeful. But Dad had doubts; he believed that families and politics didn't mix. Sometimes I think I've spent the last two decades trying to prove him wrong.

Nothing was ever simple with Dad. Despite his doubts, he offered to help—but only on the condition that I first raise on my own what sounded like an enormous amount of money to get the campaign running: $50,000. I accepted the challenge, with no idea how to meet it. I shared with a friend from law school the financial target we had to reach. We had spent time together in Christian Legal Society, so, not surprisingly, he responded with the Bible verse about how God owns "the cattle on a thousand hills" and said, "I think he could spare $50,000 if you needed it!" That perspective put my heart in the right place. Trusting God, we went to work.

College and law school friends, just beginning their careers, stepped up and gave what little they could spare. I had been involved in the local meetings of the Christian Business Men's Committee sharing my faith in Christ at one of their weekly luncheons. When I called several prominent business leaders involved in the group, they enthusiastically stepped forward to help.

The district, Indiana's Second, when viewed on a map, didn't make a great deal of sense. The town of Muncie was its northern border; Columbus, a hundred miles away, its southern one. In between were Richmond, New Castle, and the southern suburbs of Indianapolis. The elementary school where Karen taught was in the district, but our little house in Broad Ripple was not. Selling our first home wasn't easy. We'd had dreams of raising our kids in that little redbrick house, but we knew we had to let it go. We found confidence in a verse from Jonah 2 that reads "Those who cling to worthless idols forfeit the grace that could be theirs." Claiming that promise, we moved from the home we had bought in our second year of marriage to a duplex apartment along a cornfield on the far south side of Indianapolis. It would be the second of eighteen moves.

By the spring of 1988, with the May 2 primary in sight, our campaign was picking up steam. We traveled across the district in our Pontiac Grand Prix day and night, appearing at Lincoln Day dinners, the annual Republican fundraising events hosted by local party organizations. We were warmly received on the rubber-chicken circuit. Our campaign also had a couple of innovations: a fax machine and portable phone carried in a leather bag. It was an exhilarating time.

Though it had initially seemed impossible, we met Dad's fundraising challenge. From that point on, he was all in. He made calls, wrote letters, and even spent a few days on the road taking me to meet friends across the district who were also in the gas station business. I never felt closer to my dad or more hopeful about the future.

Then came April 13, 1988.

I was speaking at a luncheon at a Republican Club in Greenwood when a young campaign volunteer approached me. "Your family is trying to reach you—your dad has been taken to the hospital." I got into the Grand Prix and sped south down I-65. Dad had struggled with high blood pressure since I had been in grade school, but I had never imagined what was to come. On the way I dialed the hospital on the portable phone, hoping for any information. The reception was poor, but I could hear the voice on the other end telling me to get there as soon as possible.

At Bartholomew County Hospital, I parked and rushed through

the doors and toward the emergency room. I could see my brother Edward there with my mom. She met me with her arms open and simply said, "Dad's gone." He had suffered a massive heart attack on the golf course that afternoon. He was just fifty-eight.

It was a time when his children were launching their careers. We were climbing our own mountains, as he had always encouraged us to do. He was transitioning from quarterback to coach. And without warning, with no chance to say goodbye, it was over. It felt as though a meteor had crashed down on me. It was the worst day of my life. At once, the excitement of the last six months was gone. The campaign that had occupied so much of our energy felt meaningless.

Our family was devastated. My brothers and I huddled around our mother and our younger sisters. Annie was in college, but Mary Therese was still living at home and at age fourteen probably took our father's loss the hardest. Our sisters were very close to him. But they both overcame his passing bravely and went on to have beautiful families and great careers. Dad would have been proud.

The funeral at St. Columba Church was standing-room-only. People came to Columbus from all over Indiana to pay their respects to Dad. It was clear to me how many lives he had touched.

In the immediate aftermath, I put the campaign on pause. Karen and I discussed pulling the plug. Well-intentioned friends said that no one would hold it against us if we withdrew. But I knew that ending the campaign was the last thing Dad would have wanted. With only weeks remaining until the primary, we returned to the trail.

I was heartbroken, but it was more than that; I was mad at God. The night before the campaign resumed, I told Karen I needed to take a walk and headed out the door of our duplex on a lonely rural road. Eventually I found myself standing in the middle of a vacant field, not yet tilled for the summer crop of corn. Right there I had it out with the Lord. How could He? Why did He? Why my dad? Why now? I shouted into the strong spring wind blowing across the darkening plain.

When I returned home, I told Karen that I had yelled at God. She was shocked, but I told her I had to be honest with Him. My grief did not lessen, but that night I slowly started to get back on my feet.

A week after losing the best man I would ever know, I walked into a Republican gathering in Johnson County, the same county where I had received that call on April 13. I shifted back to candidate mode as best I could, working the room, shaking hands with strangers. Hoosiers are a caring people, and I was met with kindness and condolences. When I rose to speak, my voice cracked as I announced that our campaign would go on because that was what my dad would have wanted. There wasn't a dry eye in the house.

A few weeks later we won the primary, defeating Raymond Schwab, an accountant who was, like me, a first-time candidate. The numbers were encouraging: previous Republican candidates had been unable to win more than 55 percent of the party's vote in a Second District primary. We had hit 75 percent. A unified GOP was going to be crucial to winning the general election.

The incumbent, Philip Sharp, had been sent to Congress in 1974 in a wave election in which voters, outraged by the Watergate scandal and high inflation, had handed over forty-nine congressional seats to Democrats. Though Sharp was a Democrat in a Republican-leaning district, he was popular. That was in large part because of his office's excellent constituent services. He was a formidable opponent who regularly drew Republican voters. To beat him, we would have to win those voters back.

A busy summer of campaigning began. I went door to door with Indiana's senior senator, Richard Lugar, a global statesman and Hoosier icon. I shared coffee with his junior colleague, Dan Quayle, whose own life was about to change dramatically.

I traveled the district in the Grand Prix with a yard sign taped to the door and campaign flyers strewn across the back seat. It was county fairs, picnics, parades, and grassroots campaigning in our low-budget operation. The campaign garnered some national attention when I declined contributions from political action committees. We were in the middle of a national drought, and it was a long, hot summer. Nonetheless, Karen and I took to bicycling the district with the campaign van and a cooler full of water trailing behind. I stopped in small towns, shook hands at diners, and was often offered a cold glass of lemonade when I stopped at a farmhouse on those blistering Indiana summer days.

I was still a relatively new Republican. I was attracted to Ronald Reagan's optimistic leadership and his connection with everyday Americans. But as a candidate for federal office, I had a lot to learn. During the summer of 1988, I came face-to-face with the leaders who were shaping the movement. They fired my passion for it.

There was a candidate boot camp sponsored by GOPAC, an organization created in the late 1970s to help recruit Republican candidates for office. The drill sergeant was a young congressman from Georgia named Newt Gingrich.

He was not yet a national leader, but he was obviously different from the "go along to get along" GOP leadership in Congress, thirty years in the minority. He was a full-throttle Reagan revolutionary, part college professor and political tactician, historian, and futurist. Newt was fluent in everything from welfare reform to space exploration. And he was fearless and full of conviction: he walked in the door and immediately predicted that Republicans would win in the fall. The first-time candidates gathered at that seminar believed him and went back to their districts ready to fight.

I drove across southern Indiana with Karen at my side, GOPAC tapes playing on the car stereo. They were audio instruction manuals, eloquently narrated by Newt, teaching candidates how to speak as conservatives and to articulate conservative policy positions. I would hit the eject button, and the cassette on balanced budgets would pop out of the tape deck; in would go the one on national defense.

In July, Jack Kemp joined our campaign for an event in Greenwood. The quarterback turned politician had just ended his own run for the presidency. He was a charismatic, larger-than-life figure with a signature vision for the GOP. He spoke of a Republican Party that defied stereotypes; it was the party of blue-collar workers, not big business. It was diverse and inclusive. He believed that an optimistic pro-family, pro-growth agenda appealed to and could win the votes of all Americans, regardless of their color or zip code. And he believed that we should knock on every door in every neighborhood and earn those votes.

Kemp was a grand conservative idealist. His aspirational view of the party of Lincoln would impact my own, pushing me to see conservatism as a means of lifting the downtrodden and providing opportunity where none existed.

And then there was President Reagan.

Shortly before the Republican National Convention in August, along with other GOP congressional candidates, I was invited to Washington for meetings with party leaders, including George H. W. Bush, the party's presidential nominee, and the man he sought to follow. Ronald Reagan was the reason I joined the Republican Party. In the years since joining the GOP, I had come to revere our fortieth president. The rest of the country, seeing an expanding economy, growing national self-confidence, and a weakened Soviet Union, agreed.

Twenty congressional candidates were lined up waiting in the East Room of the White House. One by one we were ushered into the Blue Room, where the president was waiting. My campaign staff had prepared a list of topics I could raise with the president. But I told Karen that that was a moment I knew I would someday share with our grandchildren. She said, "Just speak from your heart, then," and patted my shoulder.

My turn came. I was guided into the Blue Room, where two chairs stood in front of the fireplace. The president sat in the far one, and I awkwardly slid into the other. I was nervous and uncomfortable, sat ramrod straight in my chair, just a few inches from him. A wall of cameras was clicking and flashing in front of us.

"Well, Mike, how's the campaign going?" he began. "Fine, Mr. President," I answered. Then I veered off script. "Mr. President, I have something I'd really like to tell you," I confessed. He urged me to go ahead. "I just want to thank you for everything you've done for this country and everything you've done to inspire my generation of Americans to believe in this country again."

He was genuinely surprised, almost embarrassed. "Well, Mike, that's a very nice thing of you to say," he graciously answered. I will always believe that in that moment the president almost blushed. After some small talk, I was ushered off.

During the same trip Karen visited with Barbara Bush, the then second lady and future first lady, during a reception at the historic US Naval Observatory, which we would call home nearly thirty years later. George Bush's career had carried him from Texas to China to Washington. His family was visibly close and loving, and the children, as the years would show, were all successful. How did the Bushes do it? Karen asked her. "You move with your husband," Mrs. Bush explained. "We have moved twenty-five times over our career." Karen took those words to heart.

In October, Phil Sharp and I squared off in two debates, one on the campus of Ball State University, where he had once been a professor, the other in Columbus. I was happy with my performance. The congressman, probably not expecting much from a challenger half his age, seemed surprised. Newt Gingrich had warned that most incumbents would just ignore their challengers unless they felt threatened. Then they would train their fire. When my opponent's campaign began to throw punches, I knew it was a compliment.

In the end, though, we came up short on November 8. That night George Bush and his running mate, Dan Quayle, won the White House in a landslide. Democrats, meanwhile, held on to both houses of Congress. We had surpassed expectations, losing to Congressman Sharp by 7 percentage points, 53.2 to 46.8 percent, not that I am counting the decimals. He'd won reelection in 1986 by 15 points. The echo of my concession speech had barely faded when talk of a rematch began. Though our path would not take us to our nation's capital for another twelve years, my sister Annie went to work in the White House for Vice President Quayle and to this day reminds our family that she was the first Pence to make it to Washington, DC.

Coming that close in a race against an experienced and popular incumbent was an achievement. I should have savored it and thought hard and prayed harder about the next steps to take. Instead, I jumped right back into the fray. I left the firm I had worked for since graduating from law school, hung out a shingle with a friend, and concentrated on campaigning.

By early 1990, the political landscape was shifting, and not in my favor. President Bush, who had won the White House in part on a promise of no new taxes, cut a deal with Democrats to cut spending and raise personal income taxes, outraging conservatives. Most pundits agreed that the president's party, as it historically had done anyway, was headed for defeat in the midterms. Nothing, though, was going to slow me down.

Over time, I've developed a healthy distrust of my own ambition. But I didn't see its perils thirty years ago. Flush with confidence from a close election and a simmering sense of entitlement, I ignored the caution expressed by many and rushed headlong into a losing battle, outgunned and outmaneuvered by a strong incumbent and a Democratic Party that was determined to hold the seat by whatever means necessary.

Senator Dan Coats, a thoughtful Christian, once told me, "There are two kinds of people in Washington, DC: those who are called and those who are driven." What had begun for Karen and me as a calling, following God's leading with faith and humility, had subtly been overtaken by my drive for success. Though I did not perceive it at the time, it was evident to others.

I continued to pursue support from my late father's peers and business partners. That time, one of them, Dad's closest friend, turned me down. Thomas Vickers was an air force veteran and vice president at Cummins in Columbus. For a time, the Pences and Vickers had been next-door neighbors. Tom Vickers had literally known me since I was a baby and had readily supported my first campaign, despite the company's long-standing support for Phil Sharp. This time, sitting in his well-appointed corporate office, he urged caution and suggested that there might be better opportunities in politics if I was willing to be patient, probably out of genuine concern for my new political career. But I wasn't having it. Certain of victory, I proceeded to explain politics to that lifelong family friend. He saw just how full of myself I had become and didn't hide his disappointment. "Come back when you grow up," he told me. Wish I had listened.

My rematch with Representative Sharp quickly devolved into a race to the bottom, characterized by negative personal attacks with little focus on the issues facing Hoosiers. I spent the summer of 1990 trading punches with the incumbent. The congressman blasted us for using campaign funds to cover some personal expenses as we campaigned full-time. That wasn't illegal, but his commercials characterized it in the worst possible terms. The use of campaign funds to cover personal expenses was considered to be a way to allow challengers to compete with incumbents who had the benefits of staffs and salaries. But it was still a rookie mistake.

"Pence Campaign Pay Legal, but Unusual" read the headline in the *Franklin Daily Journal*. I was angry. I took the accusation personally. "I'm not embarrassed. I need to make a living," I snapped at the reporter. Another rookie mistake.

In response, we quickly adopted a more pugilistic approach. I discovered that nasty advertisements and hard political hits won free media attention—a boon for an underdog campaign. One of my campaign commercials accused Sharp, the chairman of the House Energy and Power Subcommittee, of profiting from turning a family farm in Illinois into a nuclear waste dump. It starred a glowing green cow. Another featured an Arab sheik thanking Sharp for increasing US dependence on foreign oil. It was intended as a humorous *Saturday Night Live*–style skit, but the imagery was offensive to some, and we pulled the ad.

In the end, I paid dearly. In the nasty campaign, I had allowed my ambition to get the better of me. I did myself in. The election night party at Jonathan Byrd's, a spacious cafeteria on the south side of Indianapolis, was brief. The results came in early and painfully: Mike Pence, the Republican candidate for Indiana's Second Congressional District, had been trounced by the Democratic incumbent, Phil Sharp. By 19 points. I delivered a short concession speech to a sparse crowd, many of whom were eyeing the exit. Then Karen and I climbed into a friend's car and drove home.

What had started as a time of great excitement and optimism came to a depressing end. I had run a campaign that betrayed my own values, one that would have disappointed Dad. I hadn't just lost an election, I'd lost my way, lost the dream of public service, and lost my self-respect. And there was another heartbreak: we had still been unable to start a family. There had been so many tests, so many disappointments, and no answers. I was losing hope that we would ever have children.

There's a saying in politics: When you're out, you're out. And I was out. The Lord had closed the door.

CHAPTER FIVE

Done Dreaming

For I have chosen him, so that he will direct his children and his household after him to keep the way of the Lord by doing what is right and just, so that the Lord will bring about for Abraham what he has promised him.

—Genesis 18:19

My political career was over. It was time to move on, but the disappointment lingered. It was a struggle to get off the couch. But for God's grace and Karen's strength, I would have stayed there.

My wife graduated first in her high school class and worked her way through college in three years, and she has little patience for self-pity. The more I indulged in what-ifs, the more impatient she became. Every time I argued that I needed time, she would say in her loving and sensitive way, "Michael, you need to get a job." She was adamant that we put the past behind us and get on with our lives again. She saved me from myself. Karen Pence is tough and loving. Now I knew why my dad liked her so much.

A few weeks after the election, I was approached about a new job, which was good, because as a member of the failed politicians club, I needed one. The position was leading the Indiana Policy Review Foundation (IPR), a think tank that commissioned and shared research, hosted lectures, and published a monthly journal on state policy. I would later call it "news with an attitude." The think tank was modeled after the Heritage Foundation in Washington, DC, which provided intellectual and policy support to conservatives. IPR, which had sister organizations in all the other states, had been designed to serve the same purpose for policy makers away from the nation's capital.

I was still afire with passion for the Reagan Revolution and accepted the offer. But I soon realized that even after running for office twice, there was a gulf between my enthusiasm for conservatism and my understanding of how it translated into governing.

The IPR was based in Fort Wayne in northeast Indiana. I kept my office in Indianapolis and traveled up north regularly. During one of my trips shortly after being named to lead the policy group, I stopped in Richmond, about an hour east of Indianapolis, for coffee with the editor of the local newspaper whom I had met on the campaign trail. He said he had been surprised to learn about my new job. "I just never thought of you as a conservative," he confessed. I was taken aback.

But it was one more reminder of the campaign I had run: bereft of the values that had brought me to conservatism in the first place. Though I had made peace with ending my dream of public service, I still was not at peace with how that dream had ended. It wasn't enough to swear off running again or congratulate Congressman Sharp, both of which I had done; I came to realize that I needed to admit that what I had done was wrong and share what I had learned from it before I could move on. In short, I needed to come clean about how I had failed to live up to what my Christian faith required of me in public life.

So I sat down and wrote "Confessions of a Negative Campaigner" for the *Indiana Policy Review*. I opened the essay with the Bible verse "It is a trustworthy statement, deserving of full acceptance, that Christ Jesus came into the world to save sinners, among whom I am foremost of all." I acknowledged that I had participated in one of the most divisive contests in modern Indiana political history and offered no excuses for my conduct. I wrote that I had come to understand that negative campaigning is wrong for a number of reasons but, first among them is the fact that it deprives voters of the opportunity to deliberate on the issues critical to their daily lives.

Instead of exchanges of personal insults, campaigns, I had learned, should be about three things: They should demonstrate the basic human decency of the candidate. They should advance issues whose success or failure are more important than that candidate. And, very much last, they should be about winning. When office seekers adopt these principles, I wrote, when they run to stand rather than to win, they will occupy as many offices as their party nominates them to fill.

I composed the article mostly to assuage my conscience. To my surprise, though, it was well-received and was carried in a number of newspapers around Indiana, even generating favorable editorials. I felt as though a weight had been lifted off my shoulders. I felt hope for the first time in a long time.

We were moving forward elsewhere as well. After nearly six years of unexplained infertility I had honestly all but given up hope that we would ever have children. But Karen never gave up. She endured multiple IVF and GIFT procedures in an effort to become pregnant with one disappointment after another. And then one afternoon in the spring of 1991 I got some great news at a tiny gas station an hour north of Indianapolis that changed our lives.

I was on my way to meetings in Fort Wayne and had pulled off the highway to call home from a pay phone to learn the results of our latest pregnancy test, certain that I would be consoling my young wife as I had done so many times before. Karen answered the phone with the words "Happy Father's Day!" I cheered so loudly that they must have heard me in the next county. It was a miracle. Months earlier, we had submitted our names to an adoption agency, and shortly after we learned that Karen was expecting, we got the call that a young girl facing an unexpected pregnancy had chosen us. We took the matter to prayer, believing as we still do that God can bring "forever families" through birth or adoption. But when we learned that the family she had listed as her second choice for the adoption was clinically infertile, we withdrew, not wanting to deprive another couple of the joy of parenthood.

In November 1991, Michael Joseph Pence was born. We gave him my father's middle name, and with his arrival, I felt as though I had finally begun to heal from the loss of my father. All my love for Dad could now go to that little boy. There were more miracles ahead. In June 1993, Charlotte Rose arrived. The following year, our youngest, Audrey Ann, came into the world. We were two tired young parents, but our joy and gratitude to God were inexpressible. The thing Karen and I had most wanted, the thing that mattered more to us than our dreams and careers, had come. Our family had arrived, and the years that followed were wondrous and happy, a time of personal and professional growth.

We brought the kids home to a modest two-story house on the south side of Indianapolis with a fenced-in backyard where we poured a concrete basketball court that I dedicated to my dad. His initials are still visible in a corner there. Karen looked after the family all day, taking the kids to Gymboree and Mothers of Preschoolers, which she told me was a great place because the other ladies didn't care if she had Cheerios in her hair or her socks didn't match. When I got home from my office downtown, it was team parenting. First dinner, with high chairs crowded around the small kitchen table. Then I handled bath time. Ever the schoolteacher, Karen let the kids each pick out three books a day for story time—a total of nine. Days ended with nighttime prayers and two tired young parents heading downstairs to collapse for a few quiet moments before calling it a night and starting all over again. It was an exhausting little slice of heaven.

In the wake of our early foray into politics, Karen and I both increasingly felt that it was time to get more serious about living out our Christian life with consistency. Our calling would be defined in those years by a verse from the Book of Genesis in which, speaking of Abraham, God says, "For I have chosen him, so that he will direct his children and his household after him to keep the way of the Lord by doing what is right and just, so that the Lord will bring about for Abraham what he promised him."

From that time on, my calling was my family, and after the kids came, we made the decision to leave the Catholic Church and quietly began attending a small evangelical church on the south side of Indianapolis that focused on Bible teaching and fellowship. We wanted our kids to have the same experience in their Christian faith that we had come to have. I had not mentioned our decision to my mom or extended family, but as evidence of God's sense of humor, at the end of a profile interview for the *Indianapolis Star* around 1995, I was asked where I went to church. I swallowed hard and answered honestly.

The article, entitled "The Kind Conservative," ran a few weeks later on a Sunday morning, and I sort of hoped that Mom might not notice. We were no sooner home from Sunday services with our kids in tow than we saw the light on the answering machine flashing, I pressed the play button and heard the stern voice of Nancy Pence: "Michael! I read the *Star*! Call me!"

In the end, my extended family adjusted to our evangelicalism, and Mom, seeing the way we raised our kids in sincere if imperfect expression of our faith, would become our greatest ally and to this day a source of great encouragement.

It was a time of quiet joy and contentment. We built our dream house, a redbrick three-story in a new development, on Indianapolis's south side. The kids left their handprints and initials in the driveway pavement (they are still there). I built an office upstairs. The neighborhood was full of young families, and there was undeveloped land just beyond the houses for the kids to run wild in and explore. It wasn't unlike my own childhood home in Columbus. There were trips to the Indy 500 and Brickyard 400. I have fond memories of carrying Michael on my shoulders as we walked across the speedway, weaving through the crowds. There were vacations to the space coast, as we packed the minivan and drove south to Cape Canaveral to see the spot where Americans had set off for the stars. If at some point, in the hereafter, I could revisit my happiest days, it would be almost any day walking up the driveway of that redbrick house with those three kids waiting on the steps.

There were calls every two years, asking if I would run for Congress again. At one point, I half jokingly told a reporter that I would be changing the message on the answering machine to "Hello, this is Mike Pence. No, I will not be running for Congress." The truth is, I was done dreaming about all that. My life was centered on Karen and our three kids. I had found my truest calling: to love my wife and raise my children. God's purpose for me was clear. And besides, I was happily engaged in a branch of politics, voicing an aspirational conservatism and playing a part in my community as a private citizen.

My work with IPR also led to a profound deepening of my worldview. The two campaigns for Congress had built my understanding of issues, but I was now learning about an entire intellectual infrastructure supporting the conservative movement, one that predated Ronald Reagan and stretched back centuries.

The IPR regularly brought conservative luminaries to Indiana to lecture, including William F. Buckley and Pat Buchanan. Meeting, listening to, and talking with them was another step in my education, an introduction to brave new ideas and challenging thinkers who were worlds away from the fodder of congressional campaigns, such as the economists Milton Friedman, Friedrich Hayek, and Indiana's Benjamin Rogge.

One of the conservative speakers we brought to Indiana was Russell Kirk, the philosopher and historian whose 1953 book, *The Conservative Mind: From Burke to Eliot*, is widely credited with the rebirth of traditional conservative thought in the United States. Dr. Kirk cordially accepted our invitation and traveled to Indiana from his farmhouse in Mecosta, Michigan, for a series of speeches. During the visit, I shared a quiet breakfast with him on the first floor of a Holiday Inn outside Columbus, just off the interstate. It was June 1993, and Dr. Kirk was seventy-four, nearing the end of a distinguished life and career.

I reviewed the schedule for the day as Dr. Kirk quietly enjoyed a hearty Indiana breakfast. To get the conversation started, I innocently asked, "So what would you consider yourself? Are you a conservative, a neoconservative, a libertarian? Which is it?"

Yes. I asked the intellectual father of modern conservative thought, a man whose work had inspired presidents, publishers, editorial writers, and legions of Americans to reclaim the mantle of our nation's historic commitment to limited government, free-market economics, and traditional values . . . how he would describe himself.

He looked at me with the understanding look that older men sometimes give young ones and replied with a warm and patient smile, saying only "I'm a conservative." Unsatisfied, I actually pressed him further, asking, "But what do you mean by that?" To which he said, "I wrote a whole book answering that question. I'll send you a copy." And that was that.

A few weeks later, I received a signed copy of *The Politics of Prudence* with the inscription "To Mike Pence with thanks for his patronage and hospitality, Russell Kirk." To this day, nearly thirty years later, I have rarely taken a vacation without a copy of that book at my side.

It never fails to encourage and inspire me. Its margins are filled with notes about momentous decisions in my small life that were informed by the wisdom and history captured in those pages.

There is a note I wrote in the margins of that book from later that same year, after I read of how T. S. Eliot, "poor and overworked," had stepped out and founded a magazine. That marked another life change.

As rewarding as the work at IPR was, by 1993 I was ready for a new challenge. I had dabbled a bit in talk radio, hosting a current affairs show between my two congressional campaigns on WRCR-FM in Rushville, the home of Wendell Willkie. But it was during my time with IPR that I began hosting a call-in talk show on WNDE-AM in Indianapolis on Saturday mornings.

Though initially intimidated, I discovered that radio dovetailed nicely with my own growing proficiency in conservative ideas. Campaigning had given me plenty of experience talking in front of audiences. Fortunately, with my Irish gift of the gab, I was rarely at a loss for words, which came in handy, since my call-in show would often go on for long periods of time without people actually calling in. I didn't really notice.

The timing was important. A new voice was thundering across the heartland, that of Rush Limbaugh, who was causing a sensation with his New York–based syndicated three-hour talk show. It was a new era in radio, and political dialogue had been made possible when President Reagan had repealed the Fairness Doctrine, unleashing a wave of talk radio that was introducing audiences to conservative ideas with a healthy dose of entertainment and humor. I felt drawn to the new conservative action on the airwaves and made plans to leave IPR and see if I could make a go of it with a show of my own.

I admired and was influenced by Rush's show, but I had the idea that a lower-key, less caffeinated Indiana-oriented version that aired in the three hours before Rush's show could find a market—and sure enough, it did.

When I stepped down from my position at IPR in 1994, I pitched my idea to Network Indiana, the company that fed news into local radio stations across the state. *The Mike Pence Show*, which first broadcast in April 1994, was conservative in orientation. I opened each pro-gram with a monologue touching on current events, but more than agenda-driven talk radio, it was a forum for dialogue, both with guests and with listeners, who were invited to call in at 1-800-603-MIKE.

As I regularly told my listeners, "I'm a conservative, but I'm not in a bad mood about it"—a line that I would follow long into my career.

The microphone was open to all, no matter what their politics. Some of my favorite guests were Democratic governor Evan Bayh and Harrison Ullmann, the editor of *NUVO Newsweekly*, a liberal India-napolis newspaper. When Governor Bayh dropped by, the first ques-tion I'd ask him was how his family was doing. He'd then ask me the same question, and we would pull out our wallets and share photos of our kids. Ullmann and I agreed on little, but we were always agree-able. "His politics are dead wrong, but he comes by them honestly," he said about me. That was a fine compliment! John Gregg, the Dem-ocratic speaker of the Indiana House of Representatives, would even host the program during my vacations.

We took the show on the road across the state and broadcast from the Indiana State Fair, the Indianapolis Motor Speedway, and the Indiana Republican Party State Convention. We once aired from Vincennes, the state's territorial capital and home of the magnificent George Rogers Clark Memorial, picturesquely placed on the Wabash River. The mosquitos were out in full force that day. When our hosts asked if we needed anything—water, a Coke—we asked for a bottle of bug spray. It was an ongoing adventure.

When callers asked what I was all about or believed in, as I had once asked Russell Kirk, I came to say that I was "a Christian, a con-servative, and a Republican, in that order." My openness about my faith and politics seemed to invite listeners into the conversation de-spite the strong stands I took.

In good Indiana style, we carried on civil conversations, but I didn't hesitate to disagree. I always tried to do so agreeably, however, I was often challenged and regularly learned. But I also defended what I believed in and articulated why I believed in it. There were memo-rable callers, such as Janet from Pendleton, an elderly woman who became a regular caller into the show. She clearly shared my Christian faith, followed the news closely, and always had a word of encouragement. We developed such a familiarity on the airwaves, it was like we were neighbors, and she eventually invited me to come by her farmhouse kitchen for a slice of apple pie. It was the best I've ever had in my life. We had other kinds of callers as well. I remember that early on a man figured out that the program was not on a time delay, and he dialed in and came on the air just in time to deliver an expletive-laced message that aired on family radio stations across the state of Indiana. We installed a broadcast delay the next day.

I approached my new career as a radio host with the attitude that you should take your job seriously but not take yourself in your job too seriously. I treated politics and world events far more seriously than I treated myself. Most of the humorous sound bites that accompanied the bumper music were self-deprecating. When the show came back from a break, a chorus would shout my name; a sound clip, picked by me or my producer, would come before or after to achieve the proper deprecating effect: for example, Franklin D. Roosevelt saying, "The only thing we have to fear is . . . MIKE PENCE!" Or "MIKE PENCE!" followed by Bluto Blutarsky, of *Animal House* fame, saying, "Seven years of college down the drain."

I went to work in a dress shirt and tie. But the tie often featured Looney Tunes characters or the Three Stooges. Amid the news and commentary, we featured humor, some influenced by late-night TV shows, such as "The Top Five Signs Your Child Is About to Become a Republican." Number one was "Asks what his allowance will be after taxes." Karen always listened to the show while driving the kids around in our minivan. When I'd call her to ask how the show had gone, she would invariably say, "It was really good—once you started taking calls."

There was far more than politics on our show. We discussed anything that got Hoosiers fired up: the end of single-class high school basketball in the state, Indiana University's legendary basketball coach Bobby Knight, and the much dreaded Daylight Saving Time, which Indiana, at that time, still resisted. Those were the really hot topics!

The show was eventually broadcast on nineteen stations in Indiana, largely because the tone—civil, informative, and funny—

appealed to a broad range of listeners. But I was also learning about how to run and develop a small business as I traveled across the state selling the program to potential stations and advertisers. Network Indiana was eventually acquired by Emmis Communications, a national radio group.

During my first visit to the downtown studios of WIBC, the company's local talk radio station, I came face-to-face with Greg Garrison, a larger-than-life local attorney who had come to national prominence by successfully prosecuting the boxer Mike Tyson on a rape charge in 1992. Through his numerous television appearances and his own morning talk radio show, he had become a household name in Indianapolis. He had a gruff demeanor and an impatient style on the airwaves, where he fought the conservative fight every day. In a sense, we were competitors, and I didn't think that the "kind conservative" and that bare-knuckled courtroom brawler would have much in common. As it was, we became close friends, and Greg took over my radio show when I left the airwaves just a few years later. Sometimes I think that God used my unlikely friendship with that blunt, irascible street fighter to prepare me for another friendship down the road. Actually, I'm sure of it.

In 1998, I moved my radio show to a downtown studio on Monument Circle in the heart of Indianapolis and began filming a weekend television show. My career in radio and television was taking off. My audience was growing in small towns all across the state. I was big in Bedford. And that was when the future came calling.

In the spring of 1999, we were broadcasting from the White River Canal in downtown Indianapolis, where the state was unveiling a memorial dedicated to Medal of Honor recipients. On the program, I interviewed Jack Lucas, who had thrown himself onto a grenade during the Battle of Iwo Jima, saving the lives of three other marines in their ditch. For that act of incredible sacrifice and valor, Lucas was awarded the Navy Medal of Honor at the age of seventeen; he remains the youngest American ever to receive the honor. When I asked him why he had done it, he answered matter-of-factly, "It was my turn," and explained that the men had had a system for dealing with any ordnance that might make its way into the foxhole. Inspired by his selfless bravery, I asked him innocently on the air whether he was worried about the country when he looked at kids these days, to which he sternly replied, "You don't have the first idea what you're talking about." Taken aback, I asked, "What am I missing?" And that World War II veteran squinted his eyes, looked at me, and said, "When we were growing up, we partied every bit as much as kids do these days, but when the time came, we did what needed to be done, because we're Americans. And when the time comes, these kids will do their duty just like we did, because they're Americans." Just a few years later, I would learn just how right Jack was.

Afterward I lunched with my friend David McIntosh at Acapulco Joe's, a legendary downtown Mexican restaurant. David, a brilliant conservative and talented politician, had defeated Phil Sharp in 1994, the year the Newt Gingrich–led Republican Party had won control of Congress. That development had come as no surprise to me after hearing from Hoosier callers on my radio show who were fed up with the government overreach during the first two years of Bill Clinton's presidency.

David told me that he planned to run for governor in 2000. The party needed to hold on to his seat, which the Democrats were focused on taking back. During our lunch he told me that I was the one best positioned to hold the seat and I was needed.

That was the last thing I wanted to hear. I had moved on, closed that door. And that was a blessing, as evidenced by our young family, our maturing faith, and my own growth as a man. The two campaigns I had run would be something Karen and I would tell our grandchildren about. End of story.

But it wasn't that simple. Rumors started to swirl that I would run a third time. There was interest and encouragement. But I was reluctant. My wounds from the earlier forays into campaigning had healed, but scars remained. I wondered if voters would see my name on a ballot and be unable to look past the unpleasant memories from a decade before.

Deep down, I did want to run for Congress again. But I sincerely wanted it to be because I was not the same person who had run in 1988 or 1990.

In June 1999, I turned forty. My once dark hair was now white. I knew that if (and it was still a rather large if) I ran, I would do so informed by all that had happened in our lives over the past decade, both good and bad. It would be a third attempt at elective office, but it was really more of a second chance. Win or lose, it was an opportunity to do better than those earlier efforts and to conduct a campaign that would honor God and be worthy of the people we wanted to represent.

As I considered leaving my job, selling our dream home, and moving back to my hometown of Columbus with Karen and our three small children, I could almost hear my dad's voice. "Michael, you have a family to support, a mortgage, bills to pay, you have responsibilities and duties. Why would you leave a good job for this?" it said. That made complete sense. But for some reason, even though I accepted all that my dad would have said, I had no peace, I tossed and turned at night. At the time my pastor, Charles Lake, reminded me that God is a God of peace not discontent, so we can follow our peace. And whenever I thought about selling the house, stepping away from the radio, moving back to Columbus, risking it all, I slept like a baby.

It all came to a head during a trip to the Rocky Mountains in the summer, which Karen had planned to celebrate my fortieth birthday. We traveled to a dude ranch near Estes Park, Colorado, nestled in the mountains. We went for long walks, sat by warm campfires in the cool mountain air, and watched gorgeous western sunsets. There were also trails for horseback riding, which is one of our family's favorite pastimes.

One afternoon Karen and I went for a ride on our own in the Theodore Roosevelt National Forest. After leading the horses up a steep trail, we dismounted to take in a vista known as Crow's Nest. We had been back and forth on our decision all week. I knew it was time to make a choice. In that moment, we could see two red-tailed hawks rising from the valley floor on the air current. They pirouetted gracefully, but their outstretched wings never moved.

I turned to Karen and said, "Those two birds are us." With that, she took my hand in hers and gestured toward the sky. "If those two birds are us, then I think we should do it. But we should do it just like the birds . . . spread our wings and let God take us wherever He wants us . . . no flapping." And a family motto was born.

It was settled there and then. It was an opportunity to run a campaign to be proud of, a chance to live up to everything I had been saying since writing "Confessions of a Negative Campaigner." It was a blessing.

Before we left the ranch for home, I made one other decision at the outset of our campaign. Waking up after an evening over a sumptuous western meal and a bottle of red wine, I opened my Bible for morning devotions, and my reading for the day included Proverbs 31. Verses 4–5 admonish those in authority to forsake drinking: "It is not for kings to drink wine, not for rulers to crave beer, lest they drink and forget what has been decreed, and deprive all the oppressed of their rights." The office I sought was far from that of a king or ruler, but it struck me that the principle was the same, that a person in a position of authority should approach the office soberly. Though I drank only in moderation—most always longneck bottles of Budweiser—then and there I decided to quit drinking during our campaign and any public service that would follow. In the years ahead, I never made a big show of it. It was just a promise I had made to the Lord.

I had the support of my wife and felt peace that this time, we were going to do it right. There was one last person I had to convince, though.

My mom was dead set against my making another run for office. Her objections were the same as those expressed by Dad in my imaginary conversations with him. "Why would you do this?" she asked as we talked in the kitchen of her house in Columbus. She thought I was abandoning responsibilities, forgetting about my own family. "This is another ego trip," she said. "That's all this is." As she stormed away, I followed her into the dining room and said just below a shout, "I'm not going to put my little boy on a bus in ten years to go fight a war I could have helped prevent!"

She stopped in her tracks. She knew what I meant. My mother was well read, and like many Americans, she had seen stories of the Chinese government acquiring US military technology through government waivers approved by the Clinton administration. She knew that

China was emerging as a rival to the United States and that another cold war could be on the horizon. In that moment she saw that I was driven by purpose instead of ambition.

She turned to me with a blank look on her face and said, "You have to run."

I was stunned. "Where did that come from?" I asked.

"Michael, that's the first time I've seen any passion from you. If you believe that, you have to run."

And so we did. We sold our dream home on the southside of Indianapolis, packed up our kids and belongings, and moved back to Columbus.

At the outset of the campaign I traveled to Washington, DC, for meetings with Republican Party leaders and had a moment of inspiration that I would recount in the years to come. At the time we decided to run, I had been reading *Flags of Our Fathers* by James Bradley, whose father had been one of the flag raisers at Iwo Jima. I was deeply moved by his account of the lives of the five marines and his navy corpsman father on Mount Suribachi on February 23, 1945. Climbing into the cab the evening of my first arrival in Washington, I asked the driver to stop by the US Marine Corps War Memorial before he took me to my hotel. As we pulled into the parking lot just west of the memorial, the statue was obscured by a long line of trees at the edge of the grounds. When I walked through the trees and my eyes landed on the largest bronze statue in the world, I stopped dead in my tracks. For there were the carved images of the six service members I had come to know in the pages of that book. Just beyond the statue I could see the Lincoln Memorial, the Washington Monument, and the US Capitol lit by the setting sun behind me. Then and there I decided that if I was given the privilege to serve in Congress, the only picture I would ever have of our nation's Capitol in my office would be taken from right here. Every American should have to look past heroes like these before they look at that glistening city, because it wouldn't be there without them.

Karen and I ran a campaign based on three issues: rebuilding the military, reviving the economy, renewing the United States' moral authority. We had promised to keep it positive, and we kept our promise.

In May 2000, we won a five-way primary full of excellent candidates, some of whom had already held office and others who would in the future. The first thing we did after winning the nomination was take the kids to Disney World.

The campaign that followed had its lighter moments. I attended the Republican National Convention held in Philadelphia at the end of July. Along with other congressional candidates, I was given a short speaking slot during an afternoon session. Standing in line nervously with the other candidates backstage, waiting to be introduced over the public address system in the First Union Center, I was hoping to deliver the most memorable three-minute speech ever given at a national convention. The stage manager waved me out to the platform; halfway to the podium I heard the booming voice of the national chairman on the PA system introduce me with the words "From the great state of Minnesota, John Kline!" I stopped and turned to the chairman, who waved me to the podium regardless. Looking out over the crowd with the Minnesota delegation in the cheap seats cheering wildly, the first words I uttered at a Republican National Convention were "I am not John Kline. I am Mike Pence from Indiana, and I will be the next congressman from the Hoosier State." At which point the Indiana delegation, far in the distance, began cheering wildly. It was quite a moment. In the years to come, John Kline and I would become colleagues and friends. He served Minnesota with great distinction and always told me that if I ever wrote an autobiography it should be entitled *I Am Not John Kline*. Sorry to disappoint.

That summer and fall, the campaign was a family affair. Wherever we went—to picnics, county fairs, or parades—Karen made sure that the kids were there with us. Even at their young ages—Michael, seven, Charlotte, six, and Audrey, five—they took great pride in doing their part in the campaign, shaking hands with friendly Hoosiers, thanking people for "supporting our dad," handing out fliers, riding scooters in and throwing candy out at parades. Whatever was to come, we would do it as a family. That has never changed.

Our opponent in the general election was Robert Rock, Jr., whose father had been Indiana's lieutenant governor. He joined us in staging a civil, issues-orientated campaign. On November 7, 2000, I was elected to Congress, winning by 12 points (50.9–38.8). On the night I was elected to Congress, Karen presented me with a framed photograph of our nation's capital taken from the US Marine Corps War Memorial.

Since my childhood in Columbus, I had dreamed of representing my hometown in Washington, DC. But winning that night wasn't just the realization of a dream; I had long since moved beyond that. I approached the assignment with seriousness and purpose, and of course hard-earned humility. The Reagan era was coming to an end. Newt Gingrich and Jack Kemp were no longer in Congress. New leadership was rising, evidenced by a president-elect with a familiar name but a fresh, aspirational form of conservatism. A new century was beginning, and the United States faced significant challenges at home and abroad, seen and unseen. Taking a seat in Congress was a chance to play a small part in the difficult task of meeting them.

We heeded the advice Barbara Bush had given Karen so many years before and moved our family to Washington, DC. That Christmas, Karen gave me a large, framed parchment embossed with a verse from the Book of Jeremiah, " 'For I know the plans I have for you,' says the Lord, '. . . plans to give you a future and a hope.' " I placed it over the mantle of our new home in the nation's capital that morning. It would grace the fireplace of every home from which we would serve in the incredible years to come.

CHAPTER SIX

Time to Serve

*For I know the plans I have for you . . . plans to prosper you
and not to harm you, plans to give you hope and a future.*
—Jeremiah 29:11

We packed up the minivan with kids, suitcases, the dog, and the cat
and headed east on Interstate 70 toward Washington, DC. At the end
of a ten-hour drive we exited the highway and drove into the city. The
kids were only half awake when, as we drove on the George Washington Parkway along the Potomac, we rounded a corner, and there stood
the Washington Monument, brightly lit against the dark night sky. Everyone in the car perked up and cheered. The kids excitedly leaned
forward, peering out the windshield to get a better look. Twelve years
after our first try, we had arrived.

Rather than rent a home or apartment, many congressmen live in
their offices, sleeping on a couch or an inflatable mattress. This is in
part a cost saving, given the high rents in the city, but also a way to
show their constituents that they will not spend more time in DC than
in their district, that they will not "go Washington," a possibly deadly
charge come reelection time.

That was never an option for us. Going to Congress would not disrupt our family life; we would just transport it, for the time, to the DC
area. I've long believed that you never surprise your boss. Or bosses.
Voters had seen all the Pences on the campaign trail, they knew our
commitment to our family, and they wouldn't be surprised or upset
that we had found a house in Washington. Or, more accurately, in
northern Virginia, where we rented and then eventually bought a
small redbrick colonial in Arlington, to go along with the small ranch-

style home we maintained in Columbus. I often told people that we had a small home in Indiana and a smaller home in Washington, DC.

My family was settling into our new life. The kids were enrolled in Immanuel Christian School in Springfield, in kindergarten through second grade, making friends and adjusting. They had the comfort of their mom being just down the hall a few days a week, as Karen landed a part-time teaching job at the school. In the years ahead, I often said what a blessing it was, during my early days living my life-long dream of serving in Congress, that I also got to go home every night to a little house inhabited by four people who had no respect for me whatsoever.

Karen started writing a prayer email recounting our family life and listing specific prayer requests to keep us connected with friends back home. I traveled home to Indiana every ten days and whenever Congress was out of session. And I regularly hosted town halls across my district, open forums for constituents to air their concerns or frustrations. I was, on occasion, their target. Sometimes people would show up with a problem with their Social Security payments, but more often than not they came to talk about the big issues of the day. And they invariably brought strong opinions but always delivered them in a neighborly Hoosier way. In those early days, when I opposed popular-sounding big-government Republican plans, I was always impressed by people's willingness to listen and, even more, by the commonsense conservatism of most of my constituents. They gave me the confidence to take stands against my own party in the months and years ahead.

Not long after arriving in Washington, Karen and I were featured in an article in the *Hill*, a newspaper focused on Congress, about new members and how they and their families were adjusting to the job. Early on it became evident that DC was not exactly a family-friendly environment. And the attention and admiration (much of it super-ficial) given members of Congress and the time the members spent away from their families could be tough on marriages.

I had no illusions about the pitfalls that had claimed the careers and reputations of elected leaders in both parties. I love my wife, and as I prepared for the long days and time away from her and the kids, I gave her my word that I would not dine alone with any other woman. I had been inspired to do so by the example of Reverend Billy Graham, who had also purposed never to be alone with a woman who was not his wife, to protect his testimony for Jesus Christ and the reputation of his global ministry. It had come to be known as the "Billy Graham Rule."

Admitting that "I'm more human than the next guy," I explained that we had taken steps to protect our marriage and the reputation of the people who worked for us. So, we told the reporter, I did not dine alone with any woman other than my wife. And I avoided going to events where alcohol was served without her. In Washington, where perceptions are easily distorted, I wanted to be careful not to send the wrong message or be in the wrong situation. I was there, I said, to do my job by day and be home at night. Over the years, I molded that into a motto: "Vote right and go home for dinner."

The "Pence Rule," as it was later dubbed, was about protecting everyone on our team and encouraging them to put themselves and their families first. Female staffers supported the rule, and it never prevented them from rising to become leaders in our office. Beyond that, the days were busy and the work important, but when the evening arrived, I wanted the members of my team to go home and be with their families. I didn't want to hear from them on the weekend. Occasionally, when, out of habit, I would call my chief of staff, Bill Smith, on a weekend or while he was on vacation, he would hear Karen on the other end asking who I was talking to and then telling me to hang up the phone—which I did.

I took my oath of office on January 3, 2001, with my kids surrounding me on the floor of the House of Representatives and Karen looking on from the gallery. At one point during those heady first few days, I was standing outside the House Chamber, wearing the lapel pin all members are given at the opening of session to distinguish them from tourists and staff. A woman, clearly visiting the Capitol, approached me. "Do you work . . . here?" she asked. "Yes. Yes, I do," I answered with a touch of pride. "Oh, good," she said. "Can you tell me where the ladies' room is?" "Yes. Yes, I can," I answered. Then I walked her down the corridor to the restroom. God has a way of keeping you humble.

My arrival coincided with the certification of the disputed presidential election of 2000. Texas governor George W. Bush beat Vice President Al Gore by only a handful of votes in Florida in one of the closet contests in US history, one that was eventually settled by the Supreme Court.

On January 6, 2001, I drove to the Capitol, walked into the sparsely populated House Chamber, took a seat on the floor, and watched as Vice President Gore certified the results of the election before a joint session of Congress. There was little fanfare or drama; it was simply the business of the republic, part of the peaceful transfer of power. Democratic representatives raised protests about fraudulent votes, but the vice president carried out his ceremonial duty and yielded to the constitutional order. From time to time, from his chair behind the rostrum, he glanced at me, probably wondering who the total stranger was. The fact that the vice president discharged his duty that day despite the fact that many in his party believed he had won the election made an indelible impression on me about the resilience of our institutions when our leaders are willing to keep faith with the Constitution.

My office was on the fourth floor of the Longworth House Office Building. On my desk I placed both a Bible and a copy of the Constitution, a tradition I would carry on through every office in my twenty years of service. We set up a popcorn machine in the lobby, always, of course, popping Indiana corn. Colleagues regularly dropped in to grab a bag of popcorn. Rahm Emanuel, the famously pugnacious Democratic congressman from Chicago, was one of our most frequent customers. Nobody can resist a bag of Indiana popcorn.

Shortly after we arrived in Washington, we lost a beloved member of our family, our little dog, Bud. The first Christmas Eve after we were married, Karen, knowing my fondness for a particular brand of beer, handed me a black lab–cocker spaniel puppy, saying with a smile, "This Bud's for you." Everyone gathered for the holiday laughed and then asked me what I was going to name her. "Budweiser," I told them. We had Bud for fifteen years. She was there when we brought each of our babies home from the hospital; we still have photos of Bud wagging her tail and sniffing at the strollers as we walked in the door. We all loved her. While I was back home during my first year in Congress, Karen looked out the window of our Virginia home and saw Bud collapsed in the snow. She rushed out, picked her up, gathered the kids, and drove to the veterinarian. I was at my mom's house in Columbus in between official meetings when Karen called from the vet's office. We were going to have to put Bud to sleep, she told me. I listened as the kids, one by one, said goodbye. Karen tearfully thanked Bud for all the years of love and told the vet to go ahead. I was sad to lose old Bud. But not being there for Karen and the kids was the greatest heartbreak of all.

While I was in Congress, the kids would spend a part of the summers at our home in Columbus. You could see for six miles and count eighteen barns out our back door. It was just a short walk away from the Flatrock River, which runs through the town. That first summer, the happy memories of splashing in Haw Creek with my brothers on endless summer days on my mind, I told the kids to get their bathing suits on. We hiked down to the Flatrock and stood on its bank. When the kids stared down at the surging dark green water, a look of disbelief came over their faces; it said "You want us to swim in *that*?" They had grown up swimming in chlorinated pools, after all. "You will love it," I assured them. Then they tentatively waded into the water. Soon enough, they were splashing around. It didn't take long before they were hooked. Every summer day after that, we couldn't keep them out of that Indiana river.

The months that followed my swearing in were a blur. I fell in with a troop of fiscally conservative congressmen, including John Shadegg of Arizona and Pat Toomey of Pennsylvania, both truly good men. Shadegg was the feisty chairman of the House Conservative Caucus, and Toomey, a soft-spoken intellectual conservative, had already emerged as one of the leading voices for pro-growth policies in the House. When President Bush proposed a tax cut, we countered with a bigger one. He resisted but was happy that our plan made his cut look modest and made it more likely to get Democratic votes by comparison, a secondary goal of our proposal. When he swaggered into the Republican Congressional Retreat in Williamsburg, Virginia, that February, he pointed his finger at my chest and said amenably, in his characteristic drawl, "Keep on doin' what you're doin', it's really helpin' me!"

For much of the summer of 2001, we were preoccupied with the president's drive to pass the No Child Left Behind Act and an intense debate over research conducted on stem cells derived from human embryos. In August, he announced a compromise on federal funding of research on embryonic stem cell lines, ending future funding but allowing lines existing prior to his decision to be eligible for funding. It was a compromise, and a disappointing one. I was and remain a supporter of research on adult stem cells, but never embryonic ones. I had come to the Republican Party in part because I could no longer be part of the Party of Abortion. I was in Congress to protect life. I believe that human life begins at conception, that it is morally wrong to create human life in order to destroy it for research and use the tax dollars of millions of pro-life Americans to pay for it.

That debate never quite ended, but everything was about to change.

CHAPTER SEVEN

The War on Terror Begins

*You will keep in perfect peace those whose minds are
steadfast, because they trust in you.*
—Isaiah 26:3

On the morning of September 11, 2001, I was leaving a breakfast just off Capitol Hill when I heard news about a plane hitting one of the World Trade Center towers in New York City. It was being reported as an accident, one of my staff members told me. But I immediately thought of the terrorists who had detonated a truck bomb under the north tower in 1993. By the time I returned to my office in the Longworth House Office Building, the word *terrorism* had appeared on the chyrons rolling across the TV screens. "How do they know that it's terrorism?" I asked. "You don't know about the other plane?" an aide responded. I quickly caught up: commercial airplanes had hit both towers. That had hardly sunk in when my assistant Jennifer Pavlik dropped her phone and yelled, "The Pentagon's been hit!"

No official orders were issued, but I knew we had to evacuate the building. Our small staff gathered, briefly, to pray for the families in New York and the Pentagon and then left. My office was across the street from the Capitol. We walked down the stairs and out the exits, and I directed the staff to head away from the Capitol. Then I turned and started walking toward it. The sky was literally cut in half, one part brilliant and blue and the other filled with black and brown billows of smoke rising from the Pentagon.

As I walked forward, the Capitol was hemorrhaging people; they were rushing out of every door. It was pandemonium. A sea of people rolled away from the building, heading in the opposite direction I was walking. What had begun as a beautiful early-autumn morning had turned into chaos.

As I walked against the surging crowd, Capitol Hill police officers saw me and said, "Sir, you need to disperse." But I had not spent twelve years trying to get elected to Congress to disperse.

I just pointed at the badge on my lapel, and they let me through. The Capitol Police had much greater concerns than one errant congressman. In the midst of all the mayhem, I still knew there would be work to be done, actions to be taken by the elected representatives of the American people. I had no clue what I could do, but I knew I had to report for duty, however small that duty might be.

When I reached the grass across from the east steps of the Capitol, I spotted David Bonior, a Democratic congressman from Michigan. He had walked toward the Capitol, too. We stood there together amid the chaos determined but with nowhere to go, unsure what to do. Several police officers had urged us to move off the grounds, but I insisted that as soon as they could tell me where I could report for duty I would leave and not before. Through it all, somehow, I felt peace, remembering the verse "You will keep in perfect peace those whose minds are steadfast, because they trust in you." With that faith, I stood my ground and awaited word. Finally, a young Capitol Hill police officer approached us. "The congressional leadership is meeting in the Capitol Hill police chief's office," he said, trying to lure us away from the domed building. "I could take you there." We followed him away from the Capitol toward the police office, which was half a mile away. As we made our way, walking by the Library of Congress, we passed a group of older veterans. As the sirens blared, the sound of what appeared to be explosions—supersonic military aircraft flying at low altitude—echoed off the buildings. The men were looking knowingly up at the sky. They were calm amid all the terrible chaos. They had heard those sounds before.

When we reached the police station and walked upstairs, we found most of the congressional leaders crammed into a room, organized by party: Republicans Tom DeLay, Trent Lott, and J. C. Watts on one side; Democrats Tom Daschle, Barbara Mikulski, and Dick Gephardt on the other. The chief of the Capitol Police was on the phone. He hung up and announced that another airplane was inbound and headed for the Capitol. "It's twelve minutes out," he said. The room fell silent and still. I glanced out the window and wondered if those were the final moments that historic white dome would grace the Washington skyline. With the television playing images from New York and the Pentagon, we waited anxiously. Fifteen minutes passed. Then the news arrived: a plane, the one likely destined for the Capitol, had crashed in a field in western Pennsylvania, brought down, we would later learn, by the heroism of its passengers.

Once that news settled, everything in the room changed in an instant. As a freshman I stood to the side and watched. The party lines vanished. Chairs were pulled up and jackets thrown over them. Sleeves were rolled up and everyone there got down to work, laying the foundation for the days ahead. There were bills and debates scheduled for the floor of the House and Senate that would have to be sidelined to make room for standing up our national response to what was clearly a terrorist attack on our country. In that moment, there were no Democrats or Republicans in the room—only Americans. It was a moment I will never forget. That spirit animated our nation's capital for months to come. My thoughts turned to my family, and I tried one more time to reach Karen on my cell phone.

That morning she had driven the kids to their school by the north side of the Pentagon. She was teaching when a voice on the school intercom announced, "Bombs are going off in Washington." She raced to the classrooms where our kids and their classmates were sitting in stunned silence and comforted them as best she could. I reached her at 11:00 a.m. "Michael?" was all she said when I got through to her on my BlackBerry. "I'm okay," I said, both of us choking back tears. I told her we would all be okay. Inexplicably, I had peace. And now that the threat had seemingly subsided, it was time to get to work.

A short time later, I joined other members of Congress gathered in the Capitol basement, listening to a briefing including Pennsylvania governor Tom Ridge, the president's new homeland security advisor, who would become the head of the new federal agency in the years ahead. "All we know is they want to hit us again, and hit us worse," he told us. No one doubted the truth of his words.

Later in the afternoon, it was decided, against the advice of the Capitol Police, that members would gather for a press conference on the steps of the East Front of the Capitol. I joined some 149 congressmen and senators to show our resolve to the world before the sun set on that day of days. As the gathered leaders closed together, there was a moment of silence, and then, someone—to this day I don't know who—began singing "God Bless America." We all joined in, not really in song but in prayer—and in showing the American people that even in the darkest hour we would not run, we would not abandon our posts, we would do our jobs.

From there I made my way to my car and drove across the Potomac on empty highways to be with my wife and three small children. As I walked into our rented home, they all rushed up and we just hugged. Karen and I sat the children down around the kitchen table for a family meeting. We talked about what had happened, that bad men had attacked our country. I told them that America was going to have to go to war and Dad would have a lot of work in Congress in the days ahead. We prayed for all the families who lost loved ones that day and for all those who had been injured, including, we would learn, families of children who attended their school in Virginia.

I had to go back to the Capitol after we ended the family talk. I made my way to the door. It was then that little Audrey, our kindergartner, followed me and said, "Daddy, I have a question." I told her that Daddy had to go back to work. She repeated herself in that sweet little voice. When I put her off again, she stomped her feet and said, "Daddy, I have a question!" And when I replied, with some impatience, "What?" she said, "If we have to make a war, do you have to go?"

Looking down into those big brown eyes, my knees buckled, I threw my arms around her and said, "No, Daddy's too old." But there is not a day that has gone by, from that moment to now, that I haven't thought of all the dads and moms, sons and daughters who answered that question differently, not because they had to but because they could.

I thought of that interview with Jack Lucas, the youngest ever Medal of Honor recipient, in downtown Indianapolis only two years prior. He had told me that when the time came, this current generation of Americans would step up and do their duty. He was right. That week lines ringed the block outside armed forces recruiting offices all over the country. God bless them all.

The next day, I visited the site of the attack on the Pentagon, where search-and-rescue efforts were still under way, and a few days later I traveled with other members of Congress to Ground Zero in New York City, where the Twin Towers had stood just days before. Leaving from DC, we arrived in New York and sailed up the Hudson River on a barge. It was a rainy day, the sky was clouded, and visibility was limited. As we headed down the river, looking out the rain-drenched windshield, to our left we could see smoke rising from the remains of the World Trade Center. I turned to the right and caught a glimpse for the first time of the Statue of Liberty across the bay. I had never been to New York, and I had never seen the sight of the great Lady Liberty until that moment.

I immediately thought of my grandfather, who had come through nearby Ellis Island, and realized that that was the same view he might have had when his ship arrived from Ireland in 1923. He had come to America for freedom, the very freedom the terrorists had attacked on 9/11.

We docked near Ground Zero. The buildings still standing were caked with gray soot, and at the site where the towers had once stood, there were twenty stories of smoldering debris, concrete, and steel. Ash and broken glass covered the pavement. A chain-link fence seemed to stretch forever. It was covered with pictures of loved ones who were lost or still missing. I felt as though I had walked up the foothills of Hell.

The authors of this destruction, it soon became clear, were members of Al Qaeda, a radical Islamic group that had savagely appropriated Islam as a banner under which to take innocent lives. Their leader was Osama bin Laden, a scion of a wealthy Saudi family and sworn enemy of America. The organization and its leader had found safe haven in Afghanistan, protected by the sympathetic Taliban government. They killed 2,977 people on September 11, 2001—not just Americans; citizens of 115 nations lost their lives that day. Without warning, war had been declared on freedom and humanity. The United States would lead a coalition in their defense.

I will always admire the leadership that President Bush showed from September 11 forward, the way he returned to the White House that day and addressed the nation and how he traveled to Ground Zero and with an arm draped over a weary firefighter said, "The people who knocked these buildings down will hear from all of us soon." I am certain that some of that strength came from the experience of being raised by a combat veteran turned president and a remarkable mother, but I know to a certainty that it also came from his strong Christian faith. I knew his personal story and how he had come to faith after a long walk with Billy Graham, but I sensed the depth of his conviction the first time I saw him after 9/11. It was at the White House Christmas party in December. I took his hand and said, "Our family is praying for you, Mr. President, every day, by name," and with emotion evident in his eyes, he replied, "Keep it up. It matters."

The first obligation of the federal government is to provide for the common defense, and under our Constitution, Congress has the sole authority to declare war. On September 18, Congress authorized the use of military force against Afghanistan. The case was compelling; the Taliban government had refused to hand over the terrorists who had planned the attacks of 9/11. They had been warned, given time to acquiesce, and still refused. The case for war against the Taliban was clear. But voting to authorize US troops to go into battle was among the weightiest decisions of my life. Casting a vote with the certain knowledge that there would be American soldiers who hugged their families goodbye, never to return home again, weighed heavily on my heart. I could not take lightly the responsibility for taking even a small part in that decision, and years later, spending time with families of the fallen in Indiana and at Dover Air Force Base, I tried to express the profound respect and gratitude that was born from that moment.

In July 1953, a man from Connecticut named William Banning sent President Harry Truman a letter. "As you have been directly responsible for the loss of our son's life in Korea," it began, "you might just as well keep this emblem on display in your trophy room, as a memory of one of your historic deeds." Enclosed was the Purple Heart Banning's son had been posthumously awarded for his valor in Korea—the war Truman had sent him to fight, the same war he had sent my father to fight in. Benning ended the letter with his great regret that Truman's "daughter was not there to receive the same treatment as our son received in Korea." Truman was a combat veteran himself and kept the letter in his desk long after he left the White House, no doubt as a reminder of the heartbreaking losses that had flowed from decisions he had made.

Before casting my vote, I paused on the House floor, bowed my head, and prayed for all those who would answer the call, especially those who would give the "last full measure of devotion," as Abraham Lincoln said at Gettysburg in 1863.

On September 20, President Bush spoke before a joint session of Congress. He delivered a beautiful speech, one that lifted the nation and warned its enemies that we would pursue justice relentlessly. It was the public declaration of the War on Terror. I remember, though, leaving the Capitol that evening, thinking that as soaring as his words were, the president had not asked the American people for anything, had not prepared them for any sacrifices for what would be a long struggle. During World War II, for example, a federal speed limit of thirty-five miles per hour had been imposed to limit the use of rubber and gasoline. Americans had grown victory gardens, held scrap drives, and worked long hours in munitions factories to aid the war effort—all important parts of helping secure victory. Now there was no talk of sacrifices or efforts. Neither was there any discussion of the cost of our national response. The United States had declared war not on a nation but on a murderous ideology that was moving around the globe, hiding in caves and in plain sight. It was unclear what victory would look like. It was an open-ended engagement. The president, understandably, encouraged Americans to get back to normal life as best they could. In hindsight, it was a lost opportunity.

And normal was nowhere in sight; not long after, on an October evening, when Karen and I were hosting some of her distant relatives at our house, I received a phone call from the speaker of the House, Dennis Hastert. Weaponized anthrax spores had been detected in mail sent to my congressional office. The office of Senator Tom Daschle and two other congressmen who also had offices in the Longworth Building had also tested positive for anthrax. At the time, there was no way of knowing with certainty, but it was feared that the anthrax had originated from the same terrorists responsible for 9/11. The federal investigation would eventually focus on a scientist at a government biodefense lab, but in that moment, so close to the terrorist attacks, anything seemed possible. At the speaker's urging, I stayed up all night and reconstructed my schedule. Our entire staff began working from home. Our office was hermetically sealed, and Centers for Disease Control and Prevention (CDC) personnel in hazmat suits collected all our furniture and files. Everything was either destroyed or irradiated.

Among the few items salvaged were the framed pictures of my kids that I kept on my desk. They were Father's Day gifts and bore the name of each of my children, so rather than discarding them, they were decontaminated in an oven and the warped and smudged frames were returned to us. I still have them, and to this day they are reminders of that time in our lives. We were all tested for anthrax; thankfully, the entire staff tested negative. We were promptly put on a regime of ciprofloxacin, a heavy-duty antibiotic. Anyone who had visited our office in the previous weeks was contacted and urged to get tested. That included David Trimble, the first minister of Northern Ireland.

Another difficult vote came in October 2002 when Congress authorized military force against the government of Iraq. Intelligence reports indicated that Saddam Hussein was developing weapons of mass destruction (WMD). There was little doubt that he had been stockpiling chemical weapons; he had used them against his own citizens in Kurdistan in 1988. As a member of the House Foreign Affairs Committee in Congress and a strong supporter of the administration's War on Terror, I was invited to a small meeting in the Roosevelt Room at the White House, where the president's national security team briefed us on the evidence that Iraq was developing WMD.

Saddam was a bloodthirsty dictator who reveled in cruelty and refused to comply with UN requests to relinquish his arsenal or even permit inspections of military facilities. In the aftermath of September 11, there was a very real fear that if Saddam himself didn't launch an attack, he could provide WMD to a would-be terrorist. Congress voted overwhelmingly to authorize force and remove Saddam from power. Again I prayed and voted yes; it was no less gut wrenching than the previous vote—and eventually compounded by the fact that the intelligence that had been so compelling, that had led to the war, was wrong. I don't regret my vote. Based on the threats that our nation faced and the knowledge we had at the time, I believed it was the right thing to do. And I stand by my decision.

When Congress established the Department of Homeland Security and began to carry out the reforms that would protect the United States from another 9/11, I was there. When the congressional leadership asked that I take a seat on the House Judiciary Committee to help shepherd in the legal framework to fight terror, I said yes. But above all, I believed that if you cast a vote to send Americans into war, you ought to be willing to visit with the men and women carrying the burden of the fight. For ten years, I made a point of visiting troops in either Afghanistan or Iraq and would continue to do so as governor and vice president as well. I have always thought that there is no substitute for hearing firsthand from our soldiers their perspective on the progress in the war and assuring them of the prayers and the support of the folks back home. I was there when the remains of those lost in action returned to Indiana, there to pray with their families. I felt so small in their presence but always did whatever I could to assure them that their loved one's service and sacrifice would never be forgotten.

There were trips to Iraq, Afghanistan, and Pakistan, warm welcomes in madrassas, expressions of kindness and common ground found over faith and family. There were the sound of sunrise prayers in the crowded cities, travels across the rugged country where smoke from campfires obscured the landscape. On one trip we shared a meal with grizzled tribal leaders in the region of Waziristan, not far from where Osama bin Laden was rumored to be hiding and would eventually be found. When I asked those tribal leaders, "How is the hunt for Osama bin Laden going?" they became animated and said, "How would we know?" and "If we knew where he was, we would kill him." I never bought it. During most of the dinner, those hardened tribal leaders had repeatedly asked that US aid be sent directly to their region, adding that if that happened, "you never know who might turn up."

On one of my trips to the region in 2004, there was a standoff at the Khyber Pass, where guards refused to admit our motorcade, which included embedded members of the media, despite our having been given express permission by the regional governor. When they ordered us to turn our motorcade around, I told them to contact the governor. The guards said he would not be available for some time. "We'll wait," I said. As we sat waiting, locals gathered and military arrived. Eventually the guards said they would allow us through the checkpoint but the reporters would have to stay behind. We were not going to leave them behind, vulnerable. We would wait to hear from the governor personally. An anxious hour passed before we did. The crowd of locals, all young men, continued to swell with faces that ranged from curious to hostile. When the call came, our entire party was given clearance and passed by a sign reading "Entry of foreigners is not permitted beyond this point." That was one of the few times my Irish stubbornness was a good thing.

And then there were visits with the troops. A thousand Hoosier Army National Guard troops were stationed at Camp Phoenix in Kabul, helping train the Afghan National Army and rebuild the nation. Along with another Indiana congressman, Chris Chocola, I delivered a box of twenty-five thousand greeting cards to the troops signed by Hoosiers back home. When we told them that the people back home were proud, the soldiers were touched. "Really? They really know what we're doing?" I assured them they did, and they were grateful every day.

As the years passed and causalities mounted in Iraq and Afghanistan, the public lost faith—not in our military heroes but in the mission. The initially successful invasion of both Iraq and Afghanistan gave way to deadly insurgencies and faltering attempts at nation-building. Those were laudable ideological goals, but they overlooked the fact that establishing US-style government would be a decades-long project and not one that the American people had agreed to; they wanted to protect the homeland, not build nations far from it. US politics turned on that sentiment. Daily reports of US soldiers dying or being terribly maimed arrived from Iraq. The vacuum left by Saddam's dictatorship was filled by insurgents allied with Al Qaeda terrorists who launched crude but deadly attacks on our soldiers. The public soured on the war, soured on President Bush, soured on the Republican Party. In 2006, they handed Congress over to the Democrats; Bush's approval rating sank to near historic lows. Iraq appeared lost. Demands for a withdrawal grew louder among politicians and gained popularity with voters.

I was part of a small contingent of legislators called to the White House to meet with the president in late 2006. Arizona senator John McCain was there as well. He was launching his own bid for the presidency but had never wavered in his support for the war. The president joined us in the Cabinet Room. "I know the easy thing to do would be to pull out," he told us, "but I've decided not to lose." He told us he had a general to send to Iraq named David Petraeus and a new plan to inject more troops into insurgent-held regions of Iraq, to regain the country and give its fledgling government a chance to succeed. Walking out of the West Wing after the meeting, I was greeted by a wall of cameras and White House reporters wanting to hear about the meeting. All the other attendees had exited from the lower level. I was on my own. Undaunted, I told the press that President Bush had decided to see it through and had my full support.

The plan faced withering attacks from Democrats, many of whom had voted to authorize the war in the first place. More than twenty thousand new soldiers arrived in Iraq in early 2007. The number of casualties initially spiked but then declined. The troop surge was combined with new efforts to build relationships with former US enemies in Iraq, including Sunni tribesmen, who would become a part of what came to be known as the Anbar Awakening.

In April 2007, Senator McCain invited me to travel with him to Iraq as part of a congressional contingent to see the progress firsthand. He was the third generation of a family of extraordinary US military leaders and the first leader in Congress to call for a surge of US forces in Iraq.

At seventy, John McCain was over twenty years my senior, but he had the energy of a man twenty years younger than me. He was inexhaustible. And as I would say at his funeral at the Capitol years later, John was harder on generals and more decent to enlisted men than anyone I ever met. He gave all the senior military men hell, asked them hard questions, and called out their mistakes. He treated every rank-and-file soldier with incredible respect and courtesy. One evening shortly after arriving in Baghdad, jet-lagged, I actually nodded off during a dinner and had to get up and walk outside to collect myself. Afterward John came up to me, patted me on the back, and said, "We're going to go to another meeting, but why don't you get some rest. We won't get started until later tomorrow morning. See you at eight a.m." Thanks, John. The man was a machine.

I had traveled to Iraq on several occasions. This time was different though. We were greeted by General Petraeus at the airport and drove into Baghdad rather than flying by helicopter. There were security stations manned by joint US and Iraqi forces. Citizens had returned to the streets, resumed their lives. John insisted that our delegation go "outside the wire," leaving the base to go to downtown Baghdad, where a local open-air market had resumed weeks earlier. When we exited the armored vehicles, I followed him into the market. He was fearless, throwing himself into the crowd as though he were campaigning in New Hampshire. The Iraqis treated him like the hero he was.

Before I had left, my daughter Charlotte had asked if I could bring a rug back from Iraq. I had made no promises. When I approached a vendor in the market to buy rugs for the kids, he refused to take any money. He kept touching his heart and shaking his head no. It was his way of expressing affection and appreciation for what our soldiers had done. Eventually he relented and took my ten dollars. Later, at a press conference, I tried to convey the optimism and life that we had witnessed on the streets of the war-torn city to a cynical press corps that had long since given up on Iraq. I likened the experience to visiting an outdoor market back home in Indiana in the summertime. It was an indelicate comparison that the press promptly mocked until the *60 Minutes* crew traveling with us broadcast a story about our visit the following week showing footage of busy streets lined with tables and merchandise in the once war-torn center of Baghdad. I took a beating in the press for my optimistic take, but the point remained: the surge was working, it had stabilized the country. By the summer of 2007, violence was waning and casualty levels had fallen significantly.

Years later, during the Green Revolution, the democratic uprising against the Iranian government, I filed a resolution supporting the protestors. Shortly after, McCain phoned me in the House Republican Cloakroom, a narrow room filled with phones and chairs that serves as a lounge of sorts off the House floor. He was putting his and Connecticut senator Joe Lieberman's names onto the resolution and was going to file it in the Senate. I thanked him, but he wasn't interested. "Just mention that I filed this someday when you write a book." Promise kept, John.

There were visits during that trip with cabinet ministers and government officials. But what moved me most, what always moved me most on trips to Iraq and Afghanistan, was the time I spent with our troops. At Ramadi and Tikrit, I dined with groups of Hoosier soldiers. They told me about missing their children's birthdays, about caring for the victims of car bombs and other terrorist attacks, often just infants. They told me of the progress being made in Iraq and how little of it was being reported in the United States. And they asked me when they could go home. "When will it be enough?" "When will we be done?"

Back home, Americans were asking the same thing. In the 2008 presidential election a Democratic senator from Illinois, Barack Obama, emerged as the candidate for Americans who were tired of war. He alone among the major contenders that year had opposed the war in Iraq, having spoken out against it as a state senator from Chicago. When he was elected president in November 2008 over John McCain, his victorious coalition included Republicans who were disillusioned by the war. Some commentators even predicted that the decision to go to war in Iraq would lead to the GOP's demise. The party was indeed in trouble. But not just because of the war.

CHAPTER EIGHT

Defending Limited Government

*Be sure you know the condition of your flocks, give careful
attention to your herds; for riches do not endure forever.*
—Proverbs 27:23–24

On a January evening in 2001, I stood cheering in the House chamber. President Bush had just concluded his first State of the Union address, laying out an agenda for the coming year. I joined my colleagues in politely applauding. Amid the noise, I turned to Jeff Flake, a close friend and congressman from Arizona, and whispered, "Just because I'm clapping for it doesn't mean I'm voting for it." It was a regular occurrence.

I supported President Bush and the Republican leadership in the War on Terror unwaveringly, right to the end. But I increasingly found myself at odds with the GOP when it came to domestic policies. I often felt like a Republican Rip Van Winkle who had first run for Congress before the Republican Revolution had started and had been elected after it was over. I had landed in Washington just when the party of Ronald Reagan was turning to big-government conservatism. There I could not follow the president or the party. A decade had passed between my second unsuccessful campaign in 1990 and my winning a seat in 2000. During that time I had determined not just the right way to run for office but the right way to govern once in office. Countless times over the coming years, when asked by the leaders of my party to vote on legislation that ran counter to my beliefs, that were the opposite of the promises I had run upon and that disregarded the limited-government principles enshrined in the Constitution, I would turn to Karen and say, "I didn't come here to do this."

Early in my time on the Hill, I fell in with a group of like-minded conservatives—committed to limited government, offering free-market, fiscally responsible alternatives to President Bush's "compassionate conservative" agenda. The group included Flake, Shadegg, and Toomey, as well as Jim DeMint of South Carolina and eventually Jeb Hensarling of Texas, who became my closest friend in Congress.

Flake and I had a great deal in common. We both had led state-based conservative think tanks—he had been the executive director of the Phoenix-based Goldwater Institute before his election to Congress in 2000. We were close in age, had neighboring offices, and made a habit of sitting next to each other during the State of the Union addresses. Along with the rest of the conservative rebels, we found common cause—or distress—over our party's drift into big-government Republicanism.

Jeff is a son of the West. He is the descendant of pioneers; his great-great-great-grandfather founded the Arizona town Snowflake, where he was born. I love horseback riding and once asked Jeff, knowing his western background, if he was interested as well. No, he told me plainly. He said he had spent countless hours of his childhood in a saddle and not one hour for pleasure. I thought that was a really cool answer, but afterward I understood the difference: I liked riding horses; he was a cowboy.

Regardless of our difference of opinion on horses, we were close allies every time a fight over big government came to the House floor. Not that we won too many. Our friendship made me think of Butch Cassidy and the Sundance Kid—not the actual historical figures, but Paul Newman's and Robert Redford's interpretations of them in the 1969 film, with me, as I often said, "the less physically attractive but more cunning of the two." When we found ourselves defying our party's leaders, it often felt as though we were playing out the end of that movie, where the two outlaws, surrounded by the entire Bolivian army, make a last-ditch run for their horses. On the eve of tough votes, we would look each other in the eyes and ask, "What do you think?" The answer was usually "Looks like we are going to Bolivia." Two cheerful warriors, going out in a blaze of glory. Those were the days.

Before his presidency was consumed with the War on Terror,

President Bush pushed for and won a giant expansion of the federal government's role in education with the No Child Left Behind Act. It was designated H.R. 1, signifying its priority to both the president and the congressional leadership. Believing that education is a state and local function, I voted against it (one of thirty-four Republicans), not that my vote was needed: the bill passed easily with majority Republican support. Not long after, a quaint little red schoolhouse facade was placed in front of the colossal Lyndon Baines Johnson Department of Education Building on Maryland Avenue. It was fitting symbolism: big government masquerading as a local school.

I was a backbencher in the No Child Left Behind debate. But when the president and congressional leadership pushed for a prescription drug benefit for seniors in the summer of 2003, I took on a larger role in opposing it. Medicare, as originally created in 1965, did not cover prescription drugs. Bush had campaigned in 2000 on a promise to provide it. It was a promise he wanted fulfilled before he went up for reelection in 2004. From the get-go, I was against the bill. I had not come to Washington to create new entitlements, and the president's prescription drug plan was a giant new entitlement.

Conservatives in Congress were not unwilling to compromise. I made it clear that I would vote for some form of a prescription drug benefit if it was based on need—specifically, a plan that would provide prescription assistance to those making up to 200 percent of the poverty line. But the bill that my own party put before us was another expansion of the welfare state policies Democrats had been advancing for decades. I was not joining in.

In the heat of the process, the White House launched a full-court press against the wavering and opposed GOP members of Congress. In June, along with Jim DeMint, I was summoned to the White House for a face-to-face with the president. We were ushered into the cabinet room, seated across from Bush and his team, including Vice President Dick Cheney and the president's chief political advisor, Karl Rove.

Bush was always charming and always prepared. It was my daughter Charlotte's tenth birthday, and I was hosting a backyard full of little girls later that afternoon. Showing evidence of great staff work, the president asked, "Isn't it your daughter's birthday?" and slid an auto-graphed birthday card down the table for her.

President Bush is a truly good man. His devotion to his faith, family, and country was evident every time we met. The president always took time for the kids at events. At a Republican retreat early in his presidency, my kids met him for the first time. Always prepared, our son, then all of nine years old, had brought along a three-by-five card for an autograph. When the president asked if the girls had brought cards for him to sign, starstruck, they silently shook their heads no. So the president promptly signed the card two more times for Charlotte and Audrey and said, "I better not see that on eBay." We still have the card.

Charlotte was going to love that birthday card, but I wasn't going to budge. "What's your problem with this bill, Pence?" the president asked. I told him respectfully that I hadn't run for Congress to create new entitlements. I didn't have any objection at all to helping people who couldn't afford medicine, but I couldn't vote for a bill to give free health care to my mom, who buys a new car every year just because she can, and then pass the bill along to my kids and their kids. There was nothing else to say; the meeting ended. I went home for Charlotte's birthday party and held a piñata up in our little backyard as a gaggle of schoolgirls whacked it to get the candy. Standing your ground against the president—especially a president of your own party whom you like and admire—isn't easy, but there are greater loyalties, and I was determined to keep faith with the people of Indiana and do what I'd said I would do if they sent me to Congress: stand up for fiscal responsibility and a limited federal government.

When the vote was called after midnight in late November, House conservatives stood firm even as party leaders chose to leave the vote, which usually lasts for only fifteen minutes, open for nearly three hours. Conservatives were treated to arm-twisting, threats, incentives, offers, cornering, and phone calls from the president. I remember a courageous freshman congressman from Florida named Tom Feeney, surrounded by Republican leaders and White House staffers who were explaining the limits a no vote would supposedly place on his future in the House, as he recited, "This isn't about my future; this is about my country" over and over again. He never broke.

That was one of the times I was reminded how important it is to surround yourself with men and women of integrity. I had known my chief of staff, Bill Smith, for more than fifteen years. Prior to working with me, at the age of twenty-two years, he had been named to lead the office of another Indiana congressman, making him the youngest chief of staff on Capitol Hill, maybe ever. That night, when many other staffers were being lobbied and no doubt lobbying their bosses to cave in to the pressure, Bill's only texts to me were "Praying for you" and "Stand firm." I will always be grateful for his years of service, especially that night.

Late in the vote, I was in the middle aisle on the House floor when Speaker Hastert approached me with one final plea. "We are going to need your vote on this one, Mike." I told him, "Mr. Speaker, you put a means test in the bill, and I'll change my vote." And one last time I was told that that was impossible: In order to secure the support of Senator Ted Kennedy and other Democrats, who wanted an expansive new entitlement, a means test was impossible. The pressure worked in the end, with the GOP leadership getting three House members to flip their votes. When the gavel fell, it was recorded as the longest vote in the history of the House, ending at 5:53 a.m. on November 22, 2003. The vote occurred on my son, Michael's, twelfth birthday. So after two hours' sleep, I took his friends to a paintball park the next morning. It felt like I was back on the House floor.

Having my family with me in Washington, DC, was an indescribable source of strength. But being away from our extended family in Indiana presented challenges and heartache as well. That December, we lost my sister-in-law Judy to cancer, after the courageous mother of three and my brother had bravely faced her diagnosis for several years. Judy had met my brother Thomas at Indiana University, and the two of them couldn't have been more different. She was an elegant, sophisticated young woman from a prominent Jewish family in Milwaukee. He was a pickup-driving, dirt bike–riding, banjo-playing country boy from southern Indiana. But the love they shared was undeniable. She made him a better man. I was the best man at their wedding in 1986 and credit her family with helping me translate my youthful admiration for Israel into an appreciation of the unique challenges facing the Jewish state since her birth in 1948.

Judy's family's influence was amplified by my long friendship with Tom Rose, a Jewish Hoosier who was the publisher of the *Jerusalem Post* from 1997 to 2004. I met Tom, a fellow conservative, shortly after my failed campaign when he was working as a policy director for Indianapolis mayor Stephen Goldsmith. Tom's influence and that of a legendary Indiana banker named Hart Hasten were instrumental in my understanding of the vital importance of the United States' alliance with Israel. And I will always be grateful.

There was a snowstorm blasting across Pennsylvania when we received word that Judy had taken a turn for the worse. We loaded up the minivan with kids and pets and fought our way through the sleet and dark trying to get home in time. In the end, we pulled the car over at some darkened exit and I stood outside in the driving wind and learned that Judy was gone. I got back into the car and told Karen and the kids. We cried. We prayed. We drove home to our heartbroken family, wishing then and every day since that we had been able to be there with my brother.

At the start of 2004, I was invited to give the keynote address at the Conservative Political Action Conference (CPAC) (where I would eventually exceed the record set by Ronald Reagan for most frequent appearances). After the battles within my own party over fiscal responsibility, I told the thousands of activists that I saw "the conservative movement today like a tall ship, with a proud captain: strong, accomplished crew," but I warned that the ship was "veering off course into the dangerous and uncharted waters of big-government Republicanism" and that we would pay a price if we became what we had been elected to replace.

Ronald Reagan died that summer. I attended the state funeral and, surrounded by my family, watched the riderless horse pace up Pennsylvania Avenue. Reagan, who had suffered from Alzheimer's disease, had long been out of public life and view. But his passing was a symbolic moment, a time of renewed resolve for conservatives.

In 2005, I was named the head of the hundred-member Republi-

can Study Committee, a caucus within the GOP conference responsible for creating and pushing for conservative legislation. The group
had been founded by a handful of conservatives in 1973 and over
the years had become the "keeper of the conservative flame" in the
House. Since I had made fiscal responsibility, often neglected during
the Bush years, a priority, the founders of the group approached me
about leading the caucus, and, after prayer and discussion with Karen,
I readily accepted. It wouldn't be too long before my new responsibilities would again put me onto a collision course with House Republican leaders.

In August 2005, Hurricane Katrina made landfall on America's
Gulf Coast. It left behind incredible damage to New Orleans, killed
nearly two thousand people, and submerged much of the city under
water for weeks. It was heartbreaking. It was a low point for the Bush
presidency as delays in aid and services played out on cable television hour by hour. Everyone in Congress knew we had to do whatever
was necessary to help New Orleans recover and rebuild. But I also
believed that we had to have a plan to pay for it all. I do not believe
that the proper response to a national emergency is to create a fiscal
emergency. Back in Indiana, when a tree falls on your house, you tend
to the hurt, clean up the mess, rebuild, and then figure out how you're
going to pay for it.

So when Congress put together a Katrina rescue package costing
tens of billions of dollars to help rebuild the city and other damaged
areas, House conservatives balked because there were no corresponding budget cuts, also known as offsets, to cover the cost. Congressman
Tom DeLay, the fiery Texan serving as House majority whip, lashed
out at the Republican Study Committee, saying, "Show me the offsets!" So we did. With the capable work of Jeb Hensarling, who would
chair the House Budget Committee in the years ahead, we took to the
House floor and to the airwaves to make our case, which included a
hundred specific offsets equaling $500 billion, such as reductions in
pork-barrel spending, cuts in subsidies and federal aid to the pet projects of legislators, such as Amtrak, and lower federal baseline spending by $102 billion in 2006.

Once again, we irritated the leaders of the party. Once again we were summoned to the White House. This time, though, we won the day. Our plan, dubbed "Operation Offset," won favor with the president. Federal spending had increased by 33 percent the four years prior, and he was aware of the restlessness among Republican voters. When the Deficit Reduction Act was signed into law in the East Room of the White House in February 2006, I stood at the back of the crowd with other junior members of Congress. As the cameras clicked and President Bush started to sign the bill, Speaker Dennis Hastert asked him to wait and looked around the room. Spotting me, he hollered, "Pence, get up here! We wouldn't be here without you!" I was at center stage, right behind the president, when the largest real cut in federal spending since 1997 was signed into law.

CHAPTER NINE

Life and Liberty

Choose life, so that you and your children may live.
—Deuteronomy 30:19

My time in Congress involved much more than opposing my own party or voting no. In 2003, I authored a bill that brought me into contact with a rising US attorney from New York named James Comey. At the dawn of the internet age, pornographers were using misleading domain names to trick unsuspecting internet surfers, including children, to their websites, which had names such as Dinseyland.com. In response, I introduced the Truth in Domain Names Act, which made doing so a crime. An early use of it was the arrest of the internet pornographer John Zuccarini, the man responsible for many of those websites. Comey had led the investigation. And when he appeared on the evening news soon after the arrest, complimenting the new law and commending me by name, my son, Michael, happened to be watching. "Dad, you got the bad guy!" he told me when I walked in the door that evening.

In Washington I made many great friends and found common cause with colleagues from all walks of life. After I arrived in Congress, I developed a treasured relationship with Illinois congressman Henry Hyde, the lion of the Right to Life movement. The Hyde Amendment is the federal provision outlawing tax dollars from funding abortion. He did more than anyone else to make it law.

I believe that life begins at conception and have long believed that taking an innocent unborn human life is morally wrong. I equally believe that it is morally wrong to take the taxpayer dollars of millions of pro-life Americans and use them to pay for abortions.

I became an advocate for life five years after the Supreme Court's fateful 1973 decision in *Roe v. Wade*, when I made a personal decision to put my faith in Jesus Christ. When I opened his Word, I read, "Before I formed you in the womb I knew you, before you were born I set you apart." And "I have set before you life and death, blessings and curses. Now choose life, so that you and your children may live." I knew that His cause must become my cause. And ever since that day, I have stood without apology for the sanctity of human life.

When Karen and I reentered politics in the summer of 1999, we explained our decision to run for Congress to our three small children by saying that it was "for the babies," and all three remember those words to this day.

One afternoon late in 2006, near the end of his distinguished time in Congress, Henry Hyde waved me over on the House floor and requested I sit down with him. He was frail and wheelchair bound, and I asked him how he was feeling. In response, he elegantly recited the ending of Alfred, Lord Tennyson's "Ulysses," and it has since become one of my favorites:

> ... and tho'
> We are not now that strength which in old days
> Moved earth and heaven; that which we are, we are;
> One equal temper of heroic hearts,
> Made weak by time and fate, but strong in will
> To strive, to seek, to find, and not to yield.

When he was finished, he lowered his voice and asked for my help. "Everyone knows what a fiscal conservative you are," he said. "But I know what a strong pro-life conservative you are. I want to challenge you to be more active in the Right to Life cause after I'm gone. We need you." I was incredibly moved by the charge and determined to keep it.

Inspired by his example, the next year I authored the first legislation to deny federal funding to Planned Parenthood. I continued the fight until I left Congress and actually cast the tiebreaking vote as vice president, enabling states to defund Planned Parenthood in 2017. I couldn't help but think that the late congressman Hyde was smiling at his understudy that day.

I will also always count it a privilege to have known and worked with a close confidant and colleague of one of the heroes of my youth. John Lewis was not simply a congressman from Georgia but a giant of the civil rights movement. He was also a man of sincere Christian faith, and while our politics may have differed, we had a connection. John knew I had been inspired to pursue a life in public service because of Dr. King and he knew I saw the civil rights movement as a great and courageous moment in American history—and one deeply connected to the Founders' vision enshrined in our Declaration of Independence that "all men are created equal."

In 2010, John asked me to lead a congressional delegation with him traveling to Selma, Alabama, on March 7 to mark the anniversary of Bloody Sunday, the day in 1965 when he had led a six-hundred-person march from Brown Chapel A.M.E. Church through downtown Selma to the Edmund Pettus Bridge, where state troopers wielding billy clubs, sent by Governor George Wallace, were waiting on the other side. When the marchers refused to disperse, they were savagely beaten and tear-gassed. The images horrified the nation, shone a spotlight on the horrors of segregation, and lifted the "great revolution" that Dr. Martin Luther King, Jr., Lewis, and so many other Americans of all races and faiths were waging. It led to more marches and the passage of the Voting Rights Act of 1965.

I was touched by the invitation and of course accepted it. Our entire family traveled to Alabama. We wanted our kids to see the site, to hear the sonorous voice of John Lewis tell the story of that day forty-five years before. The congregation of dignitaries and congressmen began the morning with a rousing service at Brown Chapel and then began our walk toward the bridge. Along the way I came side by side with Dr. F. D. Reese, the ninety-year-old pastor of Ebenezer Baptist Church in Selma and one of the early leaders of the civil rights movement. As we walked, he told me how the marchers couldn't see the other side of the bridge until they reached the peak of the overpass. That was when the mounted police and flashing lights had come into view. I asked if he had ever thought of turning back after they had reached the bridge's crest and the state troopers had come into sight. "No," he answered with a smile. "We had prayed at Brown Chapel and decided we would go on regardless."

When our group arrived at the entrance to the bridge, we took our place alongside John Lewis and started the walk with all those around us singing hymns and cheering at the progress won that day in 1965. Walking across the Edmund Pettus Bridge at John Lewis's side was one of the greatest honors of my life. Later that day, I searched out Dr. Reese in the crowd and thanked him for what he and John and the other foot soldiers of the civil rights movement had done for all Americans that day. He put his hand on my shoulder and said, "God did something here." I felt a warm glow as he spoke those words; I feel it still. I nodded slowly and knew he was right. I know it still.

My strong support for Israel won me an unlikely friendship with Congressman Tom Lantos, a liberal Democrat from California. Tom was the only Holocaust survivor ever to serve in Congress and had twice escaped from concentration camps in Hungary; he had provided food and medicine to other Jews in hiding. He had immigrated to the United States in the 1940s to attend college and settled in California. He and I almost always disagreed on politics, but I was always inspired by his moral clarity and courage. Late in my career in Congress, Tom came to my office with his wife, Annette, to ask if I would cofound a Bipartisan Task Force for Combating Antisemitism with him. They both told me how much they admired my support for Israel and with the rising tide of anti-Semitism across the Western world thought it was important that Republicans and Democrats stand together to confront it. I accepted on the spot and will always be grateful for the impact Lantos had on my understanding of the dangers of anti-Semitism and the righteousness and importance of the state of Israel.

Beyond the walls of Congress, I had the privilege to come to know Chuck Colson, an incredibly consequential American whom I counted as a friend and a mentor. He had risen to the heights of political power during the Richard Nixon administration—and then had fallen to the depths of disgrace through his involvement in the Watergate scandal, for which he had spent time in prison. In his fall, though, he found his faith in Jesus Christ, and inspired by his own time in prison, he carried the Christian message of second chances to prisoners for the rest of his life. He was a great advocate for prison reform and reconsideration of the US judicial system.

In 2005, he joined a Republican Study Committee retreat at a hotel on the Maryland coast. He offered to conduct a devotional for members of Congress but, as it turned out, had forgotten to bring a Bible. So I lent him mine, which, like the pages of all the Bibles I own, was embellished with marginal notes and observations. He approvingly took note of my annotations before he returned my Bible and added a cherished inscription inside the cover: "Mike—you are the real deal." I kept that Bible and eventually took my oath of office as vice president on it. The lesson he taught us at the retreat was on the topic of Psalm 15, about one "who keeps an oath even when it hurts," a verse that served as an anchor for me during tumultuous times in the years ahead.

Chuck provided tremendous support for the Second Chance Act, a bill I cosponsored in 2007 to help former inmates successfully return to freedom by providing mentoring, substance abuse treatment options, and reentry programs. Its other sponsor was a fellow member of Indiana's congressional delegation and another unlikely friend, Representative Julia Carson, a Democrat from Indianapolis. She was a larger-than-life figure, always dressed to the nines, and a devout Christian. When I would see her on the House floor or in the halls of the Capitol and ask her how she was doing, "Blessed by the best," she would answer with a wide smile.

Julia, Chuck Colson, and I worked together on the passage of the United States President's Emergency Plan for AIDS Relief (PEPFAR) to fight the spread of HIV/AIDS in Africa. The United States has a moral calling to help humanity and to lead the world by example. PEPFAR was a demonstration to the world of our compassion, and it is one of the great legacies of the presidency of George W. Bush. It saved millions of lives. But that initiative, which provided medicine to fight the terrible virus and prevent infection, was initially opposed by conservatives, who didn't want foreign aid going to groups that also provided or promoted abortions.

Working with members of both parties, we fashioned a carefully crafted bipartisan compromise, one that was accompanied by pro-life guidelines that prohibited any of the money included in the program from funding abortion, making it possible for Republicans to support the bill. It was a victory for compassion and a victory for life.

Not every moment was quite as epic; some were just downright fun. Having authored bills codifying the Fairness Doctrine, the Reagan administration policy that had launched the talk radio revolution, I was invited to accompany President Bush on Air Force One to the National Religious Broadcasters Convention in the summer of 2008. It was my first ride on the presidential aircraft since three previous invitations by the White House had been rescinded given my resistance to some of its key initiatives. I often joked that I had much in common with a soap opera actress who had been nominated for more Daytime Emmys than any other actress but had never received one: I told people I was the "Susan Lucci of Air Force One." When I finally made it aboard, after snapping lots of pictures, the flight staff explained that the aircraft's operator could connect me to anyone in the world if I just picked up the phone on my armrest and gave them a name and city. Though it didn't win me any points with Karen, I decided to call my mom, not knowing that the comms officer on the aircraft begins all calls with "Can you hold for a call from Air Force One?" When the light started flashing, I picked up the phone and said, "Hi, Mom!" after which I heard a long pause and the startled voice of my seventy-two-year-old mother saying, "Michael, what is going on?" After she settled down, we shared a laugh. Next time, I promised, I would give her a heads-up beforehand.

It was my mother's heritage that led me into another unlikely battle on the Hill. I am the grandson and the namesake of an immigrant. During my time in Congress, we endlessly debated the nation's broken immigration system. It wasn't a new problem; attempts to secure the US border and fights over how to treat those who had crossed it illegally had raged for decades with no operable solutions.

The Reagan administration's Immigration Reform and Control Act of 1986 had granted amnesty to 3 million illegal immigrants with a promise from Congress to secure the border—a promise it did not keep and that would not be kept until a brash New York real estate tycoon arrived in our nation's capital thirty years later. The reform temporarily slowed illegal immigration, but it picked up again in the 1990s. For years on the radio, I heard a growing chorus of concern from grassroots Americans about border security and the impact that illegal immigration was having on jobs and wages. If there had been rumblings about illegal immigration in the 1990s, by the time I arrived in Congress in the 2000s, the rumbling had become an earthquake. Congressmen such as Tom Tancredo and J. D. Hayworth gave voice to the rising tide of concern among the American people. There was a general perception that we had two signs at our southern border; one said "Keep out," the other "Help wanted." It seemed as though there was an unspoken rule in big business and big government: if you can get here and get a job, we are not going to worry too much about you.

Against that backdrop, in 2006, President Bush put forward his own set of reforms. One of the features of the president's bill was blanket amnesty for workers who had entered the United States illegally, and although it garnered some support from Democrats and a handful of Republicans, I could not support it. The president had said there must be "a rational middle ground between granting an automatic path to citizenship for every illegal immigrant and a program of mass deportation." I set out to find it.

During the ongoing debate I met a rancher from Colorado named Helen Krieble. She told me about the importance of guest workers to US industries, especially agriculture. I had heard the same thing often back home as someone who represented a part of the country largely supported by agriculture. But she also understood the injustice of a system in which workers could cross the border, flouting US laws without consequences, while others waited their turn to enter legally. There was a moral element as well: How could we humanely treat those who had come here illegally, settled, and started new lives? What Helen proposed was a new system, one that would use the private sector to solve the US immigration problem. First we would secure the US border. And then, only then, would private placement companies set up centers for workers to apply for legal status in the United States, but from their country of origin. I had the idea of calling them Ellis Island Centers. The federal government would issue biometric visas to those who applied outside the country and were accepted. It was a free-market solution, a middle-ground approach that respected our laws and sovereignty but also our tradition of humanity and the need for labor in the growing economy. Working with the formidable Texas senator Kay Bailey Hutchison, we wrote a short bill proposing those fixes. KBH, as her staff fondly referred to her, was a tough, experienced legislator from a border state, and she was determined to fix our broken immigration system.

Almost immediately, we came under fire from both ends of the political spectrum. One side said the reforms were too harsh, requiring people to apply outside the country for the right to live and work here; and the other said that a guest worker program amounted to amnesty. Some online conservatives even labeled me "Amnesty Mike." As the national columnist Ruben Navarrette wrote, "When you're being equally attacked by the hard left and the hard right, you might just be on to something." And we were.

Teddy Kennedy, the liberal icon from Massachusetts, gave me a meeting to pitch the proposal in his spacious office in the Russell Senate Office Building, where his two Portuguese water dogs had free rein. He was standoffish until I said, "Senator, it may come as a surprise to you that the chairman of the House Conservative Caucus has a bust of your brother in his office." He was genuinely surprised at my youthful admiration for President Kennedy. That comment, and talk of our shared Irish heritage, set him at ease. During the meeting he questioned me about our proposal and pledged to talk it over with his colleagues and staff. Despite his courteous tone, I left his office with little hope that he would see his way clear to helping fix a system he and his party had left in such disrepair.

Predictably, there was another White House meeting, which afforded me my first visit to the Oval Office. My mom purchased me a nice new suit for the occasion. I arrived and sat down on one of the big yellow couches that flank the fireplace with President Bush, Vice President Cheney, and the White House team gathered around. We talked at length about the Pence-Hutchison proposal. The president was well versed in the details and peppered me with questions for the better part of an hour. At the end, he asked, "You mind if I ask you a personal question?"

When I said, "It's your office, Mr. President, you can ask me whatever you want," he chuckled.

"I notice Indiana is not exactly a border state," he joked, adding "You want to tell me why you got into this?"

"April 11, 1923, has a lot to do with it," I said.

There was a long pause. "Okay, I'll bite."

"That was the day that Richard Michael Cawley stepped off a boat from Ireland onto Ellis Island," I explained. "That's how Michael Richard Pence ended up here in the Oval Office meeting with the president of the United States. That man was my grandfather. I was named after him."

"You get it, don't you," he responded. "This is a nation of immigrants."

"I don't get it, I've lived it," I replied, adding "that Irishman's brogue still rings in my ears."

Though Speaker Hastert said on Fox News that Sunday that our bill was within the scope of what he could support, in the end, it never came to the floor. It was opposed by too many Democrats *and* Republicans. It is said that Congress does two things well: nothing and overreaction. In the case of immigration reform, we did nothing. And I will always believe that that failure to lead, combined with the war in Iraq and the drift toward big-government Republicanism, set the stage for the political defeat that was to come.

On election night 2006, Republicans lost the majority of seats in the House for the first time since 1994. With the strong urging of many of my conservative colleagues on the Republican Study Committee, I threw my hat into the ring and announced plans to run for House minority leader. Roy Blunt of Missouri and John Boehner of Ohio were the front-runners, but I felt called to provide the Republican Conference with a conservative alternative. When the votes were cast in a closed meeting of the Republican Conference, John Boehner was elected minority leader by a wide margin. When a reporter asked me after the meeting what the final vote had been, I simply replied, "I'm not asking for a recount."

In the summer of 2008, gas prices in the United States hit four dollars a gallon. When House Republicans, in an effort to bring prices down, introduced legislation allowing drilling for oil off US shores, Democrats opposed it. Echoing radical environmentalists' claims that it would harm the environment, they had long supported a federal ban on offshore drilling, dating back to the early 1980s. Speaker Nancy Pelosi would not even allow the bill to come to the floor for a vote. When she adjourned the House for the five-week August recess, some Republicans—including myself, John Shadegg, and Tom Price from Georgia—stuck around and staged a protest.

For the entire month of August, we delivered speeches in favor of US-produced energy on the House floor, with the microphones silent and the lights off, while tourists watched from the galleries. When the speaker ordered the Capitol Police to close the galleries, we invited the tourists to watch from the House floor. Our goal was to draw national attention to the Democrats' refusal to allow more domestic oil production. It worked: when the House reconvened in the fall, with an election nearing, Pelosi and the Democrats had a convenient change of heart and negotiated a compromise bill that allowed drilling fifty miles offshore.

But it was a charade. The bill didn't allow drilling in Alaska or off the eastern Gulf of Mexico. And Democrats filled it with taxes on oil companies. It passed in the House but failed in the Senate. President Bush opposed the bill. Still, it was great that our protest had forced the Democrats to take a vote on offshore oil exploration; but it was a missed opportunity to expand domestic oil production. Boehner commended my effort as one of the leaders of the band of House Republicans that had held the floor that summer and cited it when he called to encourage me to seek the position of House Republican Conference chair a year later. Dozens of Republicans joined in. But I will always remember Congressman John Culberson telling me in his Texas accent, as he held his phone up on the darkened House floor, that he was "tweeting" about the protest. It was the first time I heard about tweeting or Twitter. I would become very familiar with the platform in the years ahead.

As the Bush presidency was coming to a close, another catastrophe struck: the housing market crashed, the result of banks' having played fast and loose with mortgage granting for years. The administration's response was to bail them out. Treasury secretary Henry Paulson came up Pennsylvania Avenue to Congress to speak to members just days after the crash. The administration wanted billions of dollars to rescue Wall Street banks and secure all those bad mortgages. The White House and congressional leaders pushed hard, taking to television talk shows to claim that both political parties were united behind the plan.

It looked as though nothing could stop the massive federal giveaway, but once again I had to just say no. Driving on a Saturday across my eastern Indiana district, I dictated a short statement that I would be opposing the Wall Street bailout. I had not come to Washington to nationalize every bad mortgage in America, and I said so.

The next day, Democratic and Republican leaders in Congress appeared on the Sunday shows to make their case that Congress was united behind the bailout. On ABC's *This Week*, George Stephanopoulos pulled out the press release from my office and read it on air. Watching at home after church, I nearly fell out of my chair. When I got back to DC that night, members began approaching me, saying in hushed tones, "You're against this? I'm against it, too!" A small cadre of conservatives was again rebelling against the administration, and there I was, leading the pack. The administration got its way, and the $700 billion Emergency Economic Stabilization Act—a giant Wall Street bailout—passed the House in October with a vote of 263–171 and the Senate with a vote of 74–25. Not long after, the administration dropped all pretense of sorting out bad debt and just started buying banks. Afterward, William Kristol, the editor of the *Weekly Standard*, approached me at a conference in Florida. He had supported the bailout and criticized me harshly for not doing the same. But now he struck a contrite note. "The government is nationalizing banks!" he said. "I would have never supported this bailout if I knew this was going to happen." "Well, Bill," I replied, "what did you expect? The bill was a page and a half long; they can do whatever they want with it."

The American public was outraged. They gave the presidency— and Democratic majorities in both houses of Congress—to Barack

Obama in the fall of 2008. At the luncheon inside the Capitol following his inauguration, the new president approached my table and told me that he was familiar with my record and hoped we could work together. Any cooperation would be short lived, however. Where fiscal irresponsibility was a bug of the Bush administration, it was a feature of the Obama administration.

In 2009, I joined the House Republican leadership, having been unanimously elected to the third-ranking position in the House Republican Conference. John Boehner and I had a good rapport. I believe he knew that if we were to defeat Speaker Nancy Pelosi's majority in 2010, we would need to steer back onto the conservative agenda I had been championing throughout my years in Congress. Early on in his administration, while the Democratic leadership was preparing to ram a $787 billion stimulus bill into law without a single Republican vote, President Obama attended a meeting of the House Republican Conference. We met in a large room in the basement of the Capitol: every Republican in the House, the president, and his senior White House staff.

During the meeting President Obama spoke repeatedly of "the bill negotiated in the House" leading up to the vote on his stimulus bill. After he finished, I stepped up to the podium to share two things with him. First, I told him, everyone in that room would be praying for him, the first lady, and their two daughters just about every day for the next four years. The attendees applauded gently, and the president, clearly moved, mouthed the words "Thank you." Then I told him that although he kept referring to "the bill negotiated in the House," there had in fact been no negotiations in the House. The Republicans had had zero input on the stimulus bill that was going to be brought to the floor the next day. We had been shut out of the process. And that, I told him, would be reflected in the vote. He shot his senior staff an unhappy look.

In quick succession, the president and Congress passed the massive stimulus full of supposedly "shovel-ready" jobs that were not ready at all and included a bailout of the auto industry. And then, even after the citizens of deep-blue Massachusetts rebelled against it by sending a Republican to fill the seat of the late Ted Kennedy, they fought to pass the Affordable Care Act, a colossal reordering of America's health care system, without a single Republican vote and against a rising tide of public opposition. The administration and congressional Democrats were facing real political headwinds.

In a last-ditch effort to drum up public support for the health care bill, President Obama, at the urging of Rahm Emanuel, now White House chief of staff, hosted a televised meeting with the Republican leadership in Blair House, a historic building just across Pennsylvania Avenue from the White House. The meeting gave Republican leaders and House reformers such as Congressman Paul Ryan a televised platform to make their case for alternative health care reform ideas to a national audience. When I heard about the invitation, I informed John Boehner that I would not be going. We had Obamacare on the run. Millions of Americans knew that it was a government takeover of health care cooked up by lobbyists behind closed doors, and I thought the forum would give the legislation an entirely false veneer of bipartisanship. I knew it was a stunt and a trap. And it was. In the end, the Affordable Care Act passed on a party-line vote, and we Republicans would spend much of the next ten years trying to repeal and replace it without success.

Back home at town halls, although some of my constituents were unhappy with my opposition to the Obama agenda, the stimulus package, the health care bill, and the auto industry bailout, most Hoosiers saw through it. Increasingly I talked to constituents who had voted for Obama but were growing angry, anxious, and disappointed about runaway federal spending and a big government that was working for Wall Street but not for Main Street.

In the midst of it all, a new movement emerged, one that had actually predated Obama, originating as a reaction to Bush's Wall Street bailout. When I received an invitation to address a rally in Washington on September 12, 2009, the Tea Party was just getting started. As I prepared to travel down to the National Mall on a Saturday morning, I was expecting to deliver a speech to a small but passionate crowd of maybe ten thousand faithful patriots. Instead, when I rounded the south side of the Capitol, my knees nearly buckled. There at the west front of the Capitol was a crowd estimated at six hundred thousand.

Seeing my reaction, Karen reached over, touched my elbow, and gave me a reassuring smile, and we made our way to the small podium in the middle of the crowd. The passion and patriotism of those gathered were evident. I told them it was time to win back Congress by reaffirming the principles of the American founding—fiscal discipline, freedom, and limited government. The response was thunderous, as was their evident respect for the Capitol they had come to visit. After the rally concluded, DC garbage trucks showed up to clean up the grounds, but, as the local media reported, they didn't see a single scrap of trash or an empty Coke can on the ground; the Tea Partiers had said what they'd come to say, packed up, and gone home, leaving the Capitol grounds as they had found them.

The Tea Party movement was full of concerned patriots, but it was also an early indicator of something leaders across the political spectrum were missing: there was discontent across the land, outrage at ineffective and wasteful government, and a loss of faith in institutions. Americans distrusted both parties and were angry about—and in many cases had carried the burdens of—the wars in Iraq and Afghanistan. They were people who had not benefited from globalism and saw the Communist Chinese government as a competitor, not a partner. Their discontent was leading not just somewhere but to someone—someone who could see and give voice to the growing sense of alienation and frustration across America.

The following year, in large part thanks to the Tea Party's energy and work, Republicans took back the House and leveled the Democratic majority in the Senate. That year I was elected to my sixth term in Congress. Despite often bucking my own party and even taking fire from the Right, I had been regularly reelected since 2000. If the party leaders in DC didn't always understand my votes and principles, the folks back home did. But entering that sixth term, I had a growing sense that my time in Congress was coming to an end, that my work was done. Dating back to my time at the *Indiana Policy Review*, I had supported term limits; six terms in the House, twelve years, seemed about right.

CHAPTER TEN

Closer to Home

*Those who work their land will have abundant food, but those
who chase fantasies will have their fill of poverty.*
—Proverbs 28:19

On a Saturday afternoon in September 2010, I was at Ross-Ade Stadium on the campus of Purdue University, where our son, Michael, was studying. Just after the football game ended, my phone pinged. It was an email from a staffer with the unexpected news that I had won a straw poll of most preferred presidential candidate among a gathering of conservative activists in Washington. I had also topped a companion poll for vice president.

Earlier that year, I had been the subject of flattering articles by respected commentators, such as George Will. There had been honors, such as the Conservative Man of the Year award, from the storied conservative publication *Human Events*. Terms like "star of the Right" and even "potential president" were being bandied around. I had never been shy about communicating my ideas and beliefs and often prayed to be a voice for conservative values nationally. And now others, outside Indiana, were taking note of what we had done during the past decade. Increasingly, improbably, I was being encouraged to run for president in 2012. And, if I was being honest with myself and my family, I was interested.

The following Wednesday, I stood on a podium at Hillsdale College in Michigan delivering an address on, of all things, the presidency, which I described as "the most visible thread that runs through the tapestry of the American government. More often than not, for good or for ill, it sets the tone for the other branches and spurs the expectations of the people.

"Its powers," I acknowledged, "are vast and consequential, its requirements"—from the outset and by definition—"impossible for mortals to fulfill without humility and insistent attention to its purpose as set forth in the Constitution of the United States.

"Isn't it amazing," I asked, "given the great and momentous nature of the office, that those who seek it seldom pause to consider what they are seeking?" I was determined not to make that mistake.

The next day the networks carried word of the poll, my potential candidacy, and the swell of support among conservative activists and Tea Party members. It was overwhelming. I had worked on that speech at Hillsdale, a meditation on the chief executive and the Constitution, for months. It was a direct rebuke of what I saw as the ever-expanding presidency of Barack Obama, but it also served as part of my own deliberations. Friends and supporters continued to encourage me to run. Political action committees were proposed. I traveled to the early and important states in the primary process: picnics in Iowa and luncheons in New Hampshire. It was encouraging, but deep down, I felt swept along by a current. Through it all I never fooled myself: running for president is an enormous undertaking, one that would expose our entire family to incredible stress and scrutiny. And that was only a small part of it.

Seeking the office was one thing; holding it was another. A potential candidate should be sobered by the prospect. I was. Any public-spirited person who claims to be unexcited by seeing their name associated with the highest office in the land isn't being honest with you. And if they tell you the prospect doesn't fill them with some fear or stir self-doubts, then they are not being honest with themselves. The early runs for Congress came back to me, when I had been driven, not called, to seek office. I had harbored a healthy distrust of my own ambition ever since. I had seen so many good Americans and talented politicians reach for the brass ring of the presidency only to fall—and fall hard—never to be heard from again. I was often astounded at how few people who rush into a run for the presidency seem to have given real thought to what's actually required: the knowledge, the experience one must bring to the office to execute its responsibilities effectively. When I looked in the mirror, I had to ask myself: Do I have the background, the training to do this? Am I ready to step into the role upon which the prosperity and security of the American people greatly relies? If the answer was not a certain yes, I risked wrecking my career again on the reef of my own ambition.

Matters back home in Indiana complicated my decision. The Republican governor, Mitch Daniels—just "Mitch" to all Hoosiers—had created a bit of national speculation himself. Over seven years in office he had modernized the state's government and strengthened its economy during a national downturn. He had created innovative health care and education programs, but always with an eye to protecting taxpayers and trusting citizens to make the best decisions to guide their lives. He was a visionary and reformer. He had won the state its first-ever AAA bond rating and done the unthinkable by making the Indiana Bureau of Motor Vehicles run efficiently. There was chatter among Republican activists and national media that he was considering a presidential run. He remained popular with Hoosiers, who had rewarded him for his boldness with reelection in 2008 while voting for Barack Obama for president. Daniels was term limited by the Indiana Constitution, and Democrats were eager to reclaim the governorship and turn back much of his progress. Becky Skillman, his lieutenant governor and heir apparent, had declined to run. Now, on the heels of the presidential chatter, I was encouraged to fill the void; to return home and run for governor.

I prayed and reflected on the decision. The Bible says that in multiple counselors there's wisdom. So in November 2010 I began a process of talking with family, colleagues, and longtime supporters, soliciting their advice: senior members of my team, such as Marc Short; colleagues such as Jeb Hensarling and Joe Pitts; Ed Feulner of the Heritage Foundation; Chuck Colson; and the most recent Republican presidential ticket, John McCain and Sarah Palin. Many encouraged me to move forward with a presidential campaign. Others were more cautious. Van Smith, one of my oldest and strongest supporters in Indiana, urged me to remember the Peter Principle (that people in a hierarchy tend to rise to a level of respective incompetence), saying, "The presidency is a big job." Dr. George M. Curtis, my old college professor who had helped mint my Republican philosophy, also had great enthusiasm for me coming home to lead our state.

I read a verse on a plane coming back from a picnic in Iowa in the fall of 2010 and found a stone on which to stand. It was Proverbs 28:19: "Those who work their land will have abundant food, but those who chase fantasies will have their fill of poverty." Increasingly, it felt that my calling was to return home and "work the land," rather than chase a fantasy elsewhere. It was also about listening to my family. One night Michael confided in me about the presidency. "Dad," he began, "I think Mom could do it, but I don't think she feels ready to do it now." Neither did I. I was touched by how well my college-age son knew his mother; he felt, as we all did, that our calling was closer to home. When I approached my decision, several people pointed me to a sermon of Oswald Chambers in his classic devotional, *My Utmost for His Highest*. It includes the lines "We are uncertain of the next step, but we are certain of God. Immediately we abandon to God, and do the duty that lies nearest." With that I concluded that we would choose the duty nearest.

In January 2011, I announced that I would not be running for president. I spent the following weeks traveling throughout Indiana, hearing from Hoosiers. I had to listen before I could lead. I declared my candidacy for governor in May, the same month as the Indy 500. Big races in Indiana always start in May. A formal kickoff took place before an overflow crowd at the Commons Mall in downtown Columbus. There I promised, if elected, to govern Indiana as a constructive, commonsense conservative.

We made the decision to sell the small house on North 28th Street in Arlington, Virginia, that we had called home near the nation's capital for more than ten years. It was the house where our kids had grown up. Michael had already begun his college career, and Charlotte would be heading to college in the fall. Audrey was entering her senior year of high school in Virginia when we announced for governor. We rented a home in Indianapolis near the public high school she had chosen to attend. She would go on to a spectacular academic career, graduating from Yale Law School, but it was a hard transition for her and our family.

I will never forget the night we moved out of the Arlington house. The furniture was gone, and Audrey and I were doing one final walk-through, as much to say goodbye as anything else. I left the house first and took a seat on the front porch. My mind was flooded with memories of the kids: on Halloween nights, playing basketball in our hoop on the street, raking leaves, and on the many first days of school that had begun on those steps. When Audrey came out, seeing the emotion in my face, she sat down, put her arm around her dad, and asked if I was okay. So here was this kid, whom we had asked to leave all her friends and nearly the only home she had ever known to follow my dreams, and she was worried about me. When I nodded, she said, "You know, some of the best things in life are the things worth crying about." What a kid.

In the summer of 2012, we were home again in Indiana, and the campaign was on. My Democratic opponent was John Gregg, a mustachioed former speaker of the Indiana House of Representatives; his campaign logo even featured his facial hair. I was also facing Rupert Boneham, a Hoosier star from the popular TV program *Survivor*, who was running on the Libertarian ticket. I didn't know Rupert, but I went way back with John; he had occasionally hosted my radio show in my absence and was fun and smart. He was from southern Indiana and a Blue Dog Democrat, an increasingly rare breed: pro–Second Amendment, pro-life, and the type of politician Hoosiers had a history of electing. I knew it was going to be a close contest. And it was.

We kept it clean and civil. My campaign was led by Bill Smith, who left my congressional office to lead the Pence for Indiana team, and we relied on the expert counsel of a conservative pollster and long-time friend, Kellyanne Conway. We built a "Roadmap for Indiana," a governing plan focused on jobs, the economy, and education. We had nearly three hundred volunteers organized into ten committees working on fleshing out the plan. We called it the Idea Factory. Traveling to all of Indiana's ninety-two counties, often in my red Chevy Silverado truck, I came up with ideas myself. In Attica, I sat down with the town's mayor and school superintendent and the CEO of the western Indiana town's largest employer, the Harrison Steel Castings Company. During our conversation, I learned that there was no program in the local high school to prepare students for careers at the foundry, the town's top employer. That didn't make sense. Where had all the vocational programs for students gone? I had heard laments from the heads of companies in Indiana about a lack of technically trained workers. The light bulb went on over my head: we needed to make technical and vocational education a priority in every high school in Indiana.

Election night 2012 wasn't a great one for Republicans: President Obama was reelected easily, and his party picked up seats in the Senate, including one in Indiana held for decades by Richard Lugar. Despite a little nail-biting early on, as the evening went on, it became clear I would be elected governor. I gave a speech in the end zone of Lucas Oil Stadium, the home of the Indianapolis Colts, and then went to bed. The next morning I took my mom to breakfast at Shapiro's Delicatessen and then headed to the governor's office on the second floor of the Indiana Statehouse. Mitch was waiting for me with congratulations and a gift: a tape measure. "Now you can measure the drapes," he deadpanned.

Though I still had duties on Capitol Hill, the work on a transition began almost immediately. I had learned long before that personnel is policy, and we went right to work assembling an administration. Karen planned our move into the Governor's Residence. But before the year was out, I found myself back in Washington, DC, sleeping in a spare bedroom in Jeb Hensarling's apartment, casting a vote on New Year's Eve to extend Bush-era tax cuts that were slated to expire. I lost count of the number of colleagues who asked, "What are *you* doing here?" I replied, "I'm doing the job I was elected to do!"

CHAPTER ELEVEN

Take It Around the Block and See What It Can Do

Anyone who wants to be first must be the very last,
and the servant of all.
—Mark 9:35

Inauguration Day was January 14, 2013. I took the oath of office, swearing to uphold the Indiana Constitution, on a cold morning, just beyond the west doors of the state capitol; thanked my predecessor; paid tribute to his predecessors; and told Hoosiers that the time had come for Indiana to shine. Then I walked inside, through the large wooden doors, under the stained-glass rotunda, and across the hall to the expansive governor's office. The family posed for a photo leaning against my new desk surrounded by packing boxes. We joined hands in prayer in the middle of the office. Then I kicked them out and got to work.

I took my seat behind the desk in my new office. Its top is made of teakwood from the battleship USS *Indiana*. The room is ringed by portraits of notable Hoosiers. Each governor selects his or her favorites. My additions to the walls were portraits of Indiana's lone president, Benjamin Harrison; Civil War general Lew Wallace, whose great-granddaughter had been my landlady when I had first lived in Indianapolis; and Madam C. J. Walker, a daughter of slaves whose hair care and cosmetics company had employed thousands of Hoosiers. She was the first self-made female millionaire in our nation's history. I couldn't think of a more perfect example of Hoosier courage and ingenuity.

I was a world away from my office on Capitol Hill. The gulf be-tween the two jobs was just as distinct. In my twelve years as a con-gressman, I had always said I just had to get up every morning and be right about my own opinion, to do what I'd said I would do if I got there. Now I had to get up every morning and figure out what the most right thing we could get done was. A congressman has a staff of about thirty. The Indiana governor leads a workforce of more than a hundred thousand. He is the head of an administration and has a cab-inet. And, importantly, he shares the task of governing with a legisla-ture that can override his veto with a simple majority. State senators and representatives are not term limited; they remain in office as long as voters wish. From their perspective, it's governors and their grand plans who come and go. I could relate to that as a former legislator, and I approached the role of governor as a coequal in Indiana's gov-ernment, just as the job had been designed to be by the state's consti-tution. At the onset of my term, I met with all the state legislators in small groups in my office and made it clear that I was open to their ideas. When I had been in Congress, I had not worked for the pres-ident, no matter what his party; I had worked for the people of my congressional district. And I knew that Indiana's lawmakers had the same loyalty to their constituents.

There were other stark differences: There is a community in Con-gress; you are one of 535. There is only one governor. It's a lonely job. You can keep the wisest counsel, have the most talented staff, but at the end of the day, the decisions are yours alone. Because of that, I de-veloped and valued relationships with other governors: Scott Walker of Wisconsin, Chris Christie of New Jersey, Bill Haslam of Tennessee, Nikki Haley of South Carolina. All of them had a strong record leading their states and the beginnings of a national profile themselves, but to a person, they were quick to return a call and offer wisdom and sup-port. I am grateful for their friendship to this day.

Following a successful governor is never easy. But I had run on a platform to build on Mitch's successes, not to be a caretaker for them. He had rebuilt Indiana's engine. I wanted to take it around the block and see what it could do. How far could we responsibly cut taxes? How economically competitive could we be? How many more Hoosiers could find jobs? I wanted the state to go from good to great. In fact, during our first cabinet meeting, I handed out Jim Collins's book of the same title, which described, in a series of examples, private-sector companies that had gone from successful to phenomenal. Then I challenged each member to draft a plan to take his or her agency to the next level through fiscal responsibility and reform.

Karen took an active role, too. As first lady of Indiana, she set up an office at the statehouse with a small staff. Before the end of my first year in office, she had created the Indiana First Lady's Charitable Foundation, a 501(c)(3) nonprofit organization, whose mission was to encourage and support the youths and families of Indiana. The beneficiaries would include individuals, schools, communities, and families, along with arts organizations. The initial First Lady's Luncheon took place in April 2014, and two former first ladies of Indiana joined more than six hundred attendees at the inaugural fundraising event to support the foundation. The luncheon featured unique gift bags made by Indiana's Vera Bradley; Karen's watercolor of the peony, Indiana's state flower; and a performance by the Christian music singer Sandi Patty. At the luncheon, the foundation presented a check for $100,000 to the art therapy initiative at Riley Hospital for Children. Over the next four years, the foundation awarded more than $600,000 in grants to charities serving Hoosiers in all ninety-two counties.

When I arrived in office, Indiana's Senate and House were controlled by supermajorities of Republicans. But that was no guarantee of success for my agenda. The centerpiece of my economic program, the one I had campaigned on, was a 10 percent tax cut. Indiana ranked twenty-fifth out of the fifty states in the tax burden shouldered by its citizens. But Mitch had balanced budgets, improved the state's credit rating, and built sizable reserves, and I did not want to put any of that at risk. I knew, though, that the state had enough in savings to deliver the tax cut. When I had unveiled the proposal during the campaign, it was in a detailed presentation explaining that the cuts were affordable and would make the state even more competitive.

The speaker of the House, Brian Bosma, was an old friend—we had gone to law school together—and I also had a good relationship with the head of the Senate Committee on Appropriations, Luke

Kenley. But both men were skeptical of my tax cut and worried about its negative impact on the surplus. At the same time, their proposed budget spent more than I wanted. I let them know that; fighting with friends is never fun, but I had plenty of practice from my years in Congress. During the entire session, from January until April, we debated with no results or compromise. As the legislative season neared its end, the drama escalated.

On one of the last days before legislators returned home, I met with all of the House and Senate leadership to continue negotiations in my office, papers spread everywhere. Bosma, Senate majority leader David Long, and all their key committee members were there. And so were all our staffs, crowding around a large wooden table inlaid with a map of the state of Indiana that had been created by prisoners in the Department of Correction.

We worked through every section of the state budget and a proposed tax cut and got nowhere. Tensions rose. I asked the legislators plainly if their budget was going to include a tax cut or not. Silence. At that point, I asked all the staffers to leave the room. Surprised, they nervously gathered their papers and binders and left. "But you want me to stay, right?" my own budget chief, Chris Atkins, asked. "No," I told him. "You leave, too."

I wanted to have a heart-to-heart with the other elected officials. Often in meetings when office holders or politicians are surrounded by staff members, they are preoccupied with leading them as much as they are focused on engaging with the other principals in the room. With the staff gone, the posturing ended. I asked how we could get this done for the people who had elected us. I told them that if I was successful, they would be, too. And they would have to face the voters the following year. The negotiations were straightforward. There were no threats, there was no cajoling. We regrouped, restarted the negotiations, and thirty-six hours later found our way to a compromise: we would reduce the state income tax by 5 percent, creating around $300 million in tax relief, and pair it with an accelerated phaseout of the state's inheritance tax. Altogether it was a bigger tax cut than the one I had originally proposed. We were able to cut another $300 million in taxes the following year. Today Indiana has the lowest taxes in the Midwest and the twelfth lowest in the country. And the state has maintained its AAA bond rating and its strong reserves and at this writing is advancing another round of tax relief for Hoosiers. That's what we call a state that works.

A few weeks after the session was over, a fire alarm went off at the Governor's Residence, and personnel from Indianapolis Fire Department Station 31 were on the scene in no time. It turned out to be a false alarm, but as the firefighters packed up their gear in the night, one tall, rough-looking man said, "Oh, and thanks for my tax cut, governor." That was all the thanks I needed.

When the legislative session ended in the summer of 2013, Karen and I fulfilled a goal by going with all three kids to visit my grandparents' homes in Ireland. We visited the major sites in Dublin and kissed the Blarney Stone at Blarney Castle. But the high point was visiting my grandparents' hometown of Doonbeg, where I'd tended bar all those years ago.

What I'll never forget, though, is our family's relentless search for the now-vacant plot where once had stood the two-room thatched home my grandfather had grown up in. I had visited the exact spot during my stay in Ireland in 1981 and taken a photograph that had become a family icon. After driving back and forth across the countryside outside the small hamlet of Tubbercurry, I was ready to give up looking when Charlotte scolded me from the back seat, "Dad, we have to go back. When are we ever going to all be here again? We have to find Grandpa's house." With that I turned the car around and drove back into the countryside. And as we drove up an unexplored hill, sure and begorrah, there I spotted the empty field where Grandpa's house had once stood. We pulled the car over and took pictures of the remnants of the home Grampa Cawley had left when he had emigrated to America.

Only a few years later, in a different role, Karen and I would host the prime minister of Ireland, known as the taoiseach, at the vice president's residence in Washington, DC, on St. Patrick's Day. During our visit, the taoiseach, Enda Kenny, presented us with a copy of a page from the Irish census of 1911. Written in his own hand, a particular name on it touched my heart: Richard Cawley, my grandfather. That Irishman had to have been grinning from ear to ear.

Having passed historic tax relief during our first year, we turned our administration's attention to ensuring that taxpayer dollars were being spent in an efficient and transparent way. Indiana had an Office of Management and Budget. I understood what the *O* and *B* represented, of course; the agency's staff direct the state resources. But, I asked Chris Atkins, where was the *M*? How were we managing those funds and keeping tabs on how efficiently we managed state operations? Taxpayers deserved a robust management program, one that would help the state allocate funds most efficiently and enable the citizens who provided those funds see to where the money was going.

One of the earliest initiatives on that front was the establishment of the nation's first state government–based big-data center to better guide the spending of Indiana's resources and make government functions more visible to the public. In Indiana funds are distributed evenly to counties. Like so many things in government, this may have been the way things had always been done, but it certainly wasn't the best way of doing things. Why not, I wondered, figure out where the need was greatest and concentrate resources and help there? For example, traffic accidents and fires and, in a growing trend, opioid overdoses and infant deaths were concentrated in greater numbers in specific parts of the state. If we could track those trends, we would have a better chance of reversing them and better managing state funds. To do so, we refurbished a space in the basement of the statehouse in an area largely untouched since the 1980s where there was an office for reporters and a little concession stand that sold popcorn and soda. The symbolism was notable; in that space we created a state-of-the-art data hub with wall-to-wall touch screens. The Management Performance Hub (MPH), as it was called, resembled the bridge of a starship. But it was more than just a futuristic assortment of computers; it pulled in data reports from numerous state agencies in real time, enabling us to comb through and identify problem areas. We also created a website so Hoosiers could track how their tax dollars were being spent.

The data showed us the drivers of infant mortality rates in our population, including the lack of access to prenatal care. That allowed us to pinpoint those most at risk, to develop a tool that could actually predict birth-outcome risk and enable the state to direct resources toward encouraging doctor visits, and even help with transportation to doctors' offices.

The MPH also gave us better insights into the day-to-day operations of the state. At first, I received piles of reports, printed out on paper or attached to emails. But the data were usually out of date before they reached me. We replaced this system with a dashboard that monitored the number of state employees and health care trends across the state and even predicted crashes on state-owned roads. It put the *M* into OMB. And it won several awards. We allocated resources to the most urgent needs, a practice I would carry out years later in the midst of the worst pandemic in a hundred years.

The new hub was paid for by a private grant and by canceling a state lease. The taxpayers weren't on the hook for it. One reporter called it the "Moneyball approach" to governing, a reference to the analytics-driven style of making small-market sports teams competitive. I called it the future of state government, and I still believe that technology and transparency hold great promise to rein in waste, fraud, and abuse at the federal level.

We looked out for taxpayers in other ways as well. Most Hoosier families don't live beyond their means; neither should their government. We balanced the budget, spending less than we took in, and looked for places where we could save taxpayer dollars. The state had an airplane it didn't need. I figured that if I needed to fly, we could rent a plane or fly commercial. So if anyone out there was looking for a great deal on a Beechcraft King Air 200, I said to give me a call. A company in Florida was and did. We sold it the aircraft for $2.5 million. Most of that money went to the state police. To ensure Indiana's long-term fiscal health, we introduced a Balanced Budget Amendment to the state constitution, which was adopted four years later with more than 70 percent support of Hoosiers. The state also passed nearly zero new substantive regulations during my term. My message was clear: Don't come to me with new intrusions into the lives of Hoosiers. After my first two years as governor, Indiana had a billion dollars in reserves.

But we had to do more than just cut; Indiana had to continue growing.

At that point in our state's history, we had only one city, Indianapolis, that was regularly featured on lists of the best places to work and live in the United States. I wanted more than that. Cities regularly competed in regions to attract workers or businesses. My administration proposed a different approach: cities within regions of the state could collaborate rather than compete. We created a contest, the Regional Cities Initiative, that encouraged parts of Indiana to create and present long-term plans to attract talent, develop industry, and turn themselves into national destinations. The prize was millions of dollars in grant money, part of it from the state but matched by private and philanthropic donations. In its initial iteration—the program lives on today—southwest, southeast, and north-central Indiana were the winners. The city of South Bend, in that last area, had struggled with stubbornly high unemployment and crime rates under the leadership of a young Democratic mayor named Pete Buttigieg. Despite our political differences, we developed a good working relationship that resulted in funds from the Regional Cities Initiative helping to rebuild the old Studebaker plant in the heart of the city, transforming the decrepit six-story factory into a tech center. Pete called the project one of his top accomplishments during his time in office.

During his tenure, we spoke often, and I made a point to call him as he was leaving for naval reserve duty in Afghanistan to offer my support for the city and assure him of our prayers. In 2015, in the middle of his reelection campaign, Pete published an essay informing the public that he was gay. Following a tumultuous spring in Indiana, a breathless press corps raced for my reaction during a visit at the RV/ MH Hall of Fame in Elkhart, Indiana. I replied, "My reaction? I think Pete is a good public servant, a patriot, and I look forward to continuing to work with him." They dropped their cameras and walked away. Pete and I maintained our good relationship all the way through my governorship. But Mayor Pete's attitude changed dramatically after he announced his campaign for president in January 2019; he suddenly adopted the caricature of me and of Indiana held by many of his West Coast donors. Politics can do that to you.

The project in South Bend and the rest of the regional city awards were made possible only because we cut taxes and went out and sold

Indiana's success story. Five years later, seventeen regions including all of Indiana's ninety-two counties vie for the grants, which have led to $13 billion in investments. But for Indiana to continue to lead and grow, I was determined to bring innovative solutions, grounded in conservative principles, to bear on two paramount areas of state responsibility: education and health care.

Mr. Ed and Mrs. Nancy Pence after tying the knot, January 14, 1956.

My dad, Second Lieutenant Edward J. Pence, US Army, receiving his Bronze Star on April 15, 1953. The medal stayed in a drawer; he talked little of his time in Korea.

Me in my mom's arms, outside our small apartment in Columbus, Indiana, October 1959. She was an avid reader and follower of the news, and I owe my interest in politics, among many things, to her.

Celebrating my second birthday, June 7, 1961. I asked for horses on my birthday cake, beginning a lifelong love of horseback riding.

Ed Pence and his boys at Kiel Brothers Oil Company, circa 1970. He always told us: "Climb your own mountain."

Pence family portrait in our home on Hunter Place in Columbus, Indiana, 1977. While posing for the picture, we knocked Mom's modern art off the wall, so we put our hands behind our backs to hold it up for the photo.

Family reunion with my siblings *(from left to right)*, Mary, Gregory, Edward, Thomas, and Annie, at the Republican National Convention in Cleveland, July 2016. The support and love of my family has been a hallmark of my public career.

Onstage with my mom, Nancy Pence Fritsch. In the background *(from left to right)*, Michael's fiancée, Sarah, Michael, and Charlotte after my acceptance speech at the 2016 Republican National Convention. She says I'm her claim to fame.

Karen and me on one of our very first dates in downtown Indianapolis, 1983. When I saw that smile, I knew she was the one.

Our wedding day at St. Christopher Catholic Church in Speedway, Indiana, June 8, 1985. The happiest day of my life.

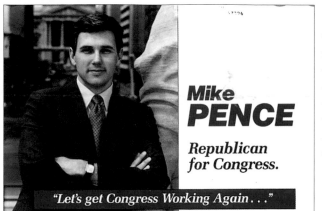

Campaign flyer from my first run for Congress, with a photo taken in May 1988 at Monument Circle in Indianapolis, with the Indiana Statehouse in the background. It would take me twelve years to get to Congress, but this is where it all began.

Meeting with President Ronald Reagan in the Blue Room at the White House, August 1988. He's the reason I became a Republican; I was so nervous to meet him I felt like I was talking to Mount Rushmore. He inspires me still.

Karen with Barbara Bush at the vice president's residence during the 1988 campaign—the same house we would move into nearly thirty years later. She told Karen, "You move with your husband."

Meeting with Vice President George H. W. Bush in the Indian Treaty Room at the White House, August 1988. There was a kindness about him that was evident from the first time we met. In many ways, I modeled my vice presidency after his.

Election night November 2000 in Anderson, Indiana, with Karen, Audrey, Michael, and Charlotte. This time we ran the right way and won.

At the White House Congressional Picnic with Michael, Karen, Audrey, and Charlotte in the summer of 2001, keeping our family close and giving the kids memories for a lifetime. The girls always liked the face painting.

Taking the kids to the Reagan Ranch in the summer of 2005, the year after President Reagan passed. We wanted them to see the home of a president who had meant so much to me and to millions of Americans.

Visiting troops in Ramadi, Iraq, and chatting with Ty Cotton from Anderson, Indiana, in 2005. I visited our troops each year I was in Congress and while governor and vice president. There is no substitute for hearing firsthand from our soldiers and assuring them of the prayers and the support of the folks back home.

Republican Study Committee press conference opposing the Wall Street bailout, September 23, 2008. I didn't go to Washington to nationalize every bad mortgage in America.

Joining President George W. Bush and congressional leaders for the signing of the Deficit Reduction Act at the White House on February 8, 2006.

Meeting with President George W. Bush in the Oval Office to discuss my immigration reform proposal. He said there had to be a rational middle ground between mass deportation and amnesty. And I set out to find it.

Crossing the Edmund Pettus Bridge with Congressman John Lewis in Selma, Alabama, marking the forty-fifth anniversary of Bloody Sunday, March 7, 2010. Also pictured with Dr. F. D. Reese, who told me "God did something here."

Inaugurated as the fiftieth governor of Indiana at the Indiana Statehouse on January 14, 2013. I took the oath of office and promised to be "governor of all the people of Indiana."

Posing for a family photo in the governor's office at the Indiana Statehouse on Inauguration Day 2013. We said a prayer, then I kicked everyone out and got right down to work.

2015 State of the State address at the Indiana Statehouse. During my term we cut taxes, modernized state government, and expanded school choice. More Hoosiers were working than ever before.

Meeting with President Barack Obama on the tarmac in Evansville, Indiana, on October 3, 2014, and pitching my Healthy Indiana Plan 2.0 that would provide consumer-directed health care to 350,000 low-income Hoosiers.

My official portrait as governor, honoring faith, family, and the first lady, who put that smile on my face.

Karen, Charlotte, and me before our first dinner meeting with the Trumps at Bedminster, July 2, 2016. A copy of this photo hung just outside the Oval Office during all four years of our administration.

Praying with Donald Trump on Trump Force One before hitting the campaign trail in 2016. When he asked me how we were going to win, I told him that we were going to "outwork 'em." And we did.

Working with my daughter Charlotte on campaign remarks on Trump Force Two in the fall of 2016. She was with me for 105 of 107 days during the campaign and regularly helped draft my speeches and statements for the press.

Playing a pickup football game before boarding Trump Force Two in Iowa during the campaign, October 28, 2016.

Election night 2016 with Michael's fiancée, Sarah, Michael, Karen, and Charlotte, with Audrey on the phone from Tanzania. There were lots of high fives, hugs, and prayers of thanks.

With my son, Michael, on election night 2016 as I introduced the president-elect of the United States, Donald Trump, for the first time.

Taking the oath of office as the forty-eighth vice president of the United States with my wife and children at my side, January 20, 2017. Justice Clarence Thomas did me the honor of administering my oath, which ended with a prayer: "So help me God."

Inaugural Parade with Audrey, Charlotte, Karen, Michael's wife, Sarah, and Michael, with the Capitol behind us and the White House ahead.

Participating in the presidential daily brief, or PDB, in 2018. I made a point to receive my PDB every morning at the vice president's residence and frequently joined the president for his PDB in the Oval Office.

With President Trump at Camp David, speaking with French president Emmanuel Macron on January 6, 2018. The presidential retreat was a welcome respite from 1600 Pennsylvania Avenue, but we were always working.

Celebrating the passage of the Tax Cut and Jobs Act at the White House on December 20, 2017. It was one of our administration's signature achievements, which set the stage for the creation of seven million jobs and record employment.

Karen and me arriving at the Salute to America celebration at the Lincoln Memorial on July 4, 2019.

Speaking to US and Georgian forces at the Noble Partner military training exercise in Tbilisi, Georgia, July 31, 2017. We stood strong to counter Russian aggression.

On the tarmac with my daughter Audrey at Joint Base Andrews in 2017. Having my kids join me on this journey was a continuing source of joy and strength.

CHAPTER TWELVE

Doing the Right Thing the Right Way

To act justly and to love mercy and to walk humbly with your God.
—Micah 6:8

Success in life is dependent on education, but in the latter half of the twentieth century, it became clear that not all Americans have equal access to good schools and many inner-city families were relegated to some of the nation's worst and most dangerous ones. That was when the idea of allowing parents to choose the school their child would attend was born. As my friend Alveda King, the niece of Martin Luther King, Jr., said memorably, school choice is the civil rights issue of the twenty-first century. And in that spirit, in many ways, Indiana became the birthplace of school choice.

In the 1990s, an Indianapolis insurance executive named J. Patrick Rooney created the first private educational choice trust in America, investing $1 million in scholarships for inner-city kids to go to the school of their choice. It inspired a generation of private scholarship programs across the United States. As the husband of a public school teacher, I have always taken a great interest in education reform. I championed the cause of school choice and spoke often with Mr. Rooney and a local business leader working with him on the program. Not surprisingly, when Mitch Daniels was elected governor, he worked tirelessly to expand school choice and in 2011 created the state's first voucher program, giving low-income families the means to pay for tuition at the school that best fit their kids' needs. The program originally enrolled four thousand students.

As I had argued in Congress, I believe that under the Constitution, education is the responsibility of state governments. As governor, I was determined to build on Indiana's reforms of the recent past. I expanded the school voucher program to thirty-three thousand students, allowing middle-income families to participate as well. We also gave charter schools an extra $50 million in funding. Before I left office, Indiana was the home of the largest school choice program in America.

In an effort to revive vocational education in Indiana, we created state and regional work councils to better prepare and track students for employment in local industries. A year into my term, participation in the program had hit two thousand students statewide. Most of them moved from school to college or into the workforce.

We also expanded educational opportunities for early childhood education for underprivileged kids. It was no easy task. I will always believe that the best preschool is a prosperous two-parent home, but as I could see firsthand in my travels across the state, the reality is that not every child has that, and Indiana was one of only ten states in the union that did not fund any form of preschool. I believe that a great weapon against poverty is to prepare children for school. But here, too, access was unequal, with many kids from families of lower means beginning their education without any preparation and often falling behind through no fault of their own. As soon as I took office, I began to try to change that, offering a bill to create state-funded pre-kindergarten and even testifying personally before Indiana's Senate Education and Career Development Committee, something newly elected governors don't often do. Many of my Republican colleagues were skeptical and resisted paying for a state-run preschool or believed that early education belonged at home. My first efforts went nowhere. I kept at it, though. I visited preschools around the state, sitting on floors with students in disadvantaged parts of Indiana. And though it often felt like pulling teeth, I worked with legislators and in 2014 signed into law a program that provided preschool tuition for low-income students in five counties, expanding school choice for disadvantaged families and reviving vocational education in four short years. All told, during my term, Indiana had the single largest budget increase in K–12 education in its history.

Then we focused on health care. During my term Indiana faced the choice confronting all fifty governors: Obamacare sought to expand Medicaid, the state and federally funded health care program for low-income Americans, and the federal government was offering states the money to do the expanding. A number of my fellow Republican governors were not having it. Sure, for a Republican governor, saying no to the money was an easy political decision. Medicaid, as noble as its intentions were, doesn't produce better health outcomes or reduce the cost of care; it has no incentives for healthy choices or cost transparency. But I had campaigned on seeking thoughtful solutions to difficult problems. Too many Hoosiers were uninsured. I saw a chance for Indiana to lead. I proposed that we accept the federal Medicaid money, but only if we could then use it to fashion our own program that would promote personal responsibility and reduce costs. The catch was that the Obama administration had to sign off on that alternative use of the money with what is called a federal waiver.

Here, as in many areas, the building blocks had been laid before my arrival. Among Mitch Daniels's many innovations was a health care program called the Healthy Indiana Plan, or, as it was better known, HIP. Under the plan, uninsured Hoosiers were eligible for coverage that combined a traditional high-deductible plan with state-funded Health Savings Accounts, personal savings accounts dedicated to health care costs and funded by both the government and the enrollees' own contributions. They were first conceived of by a Hoosier (of course!), in fact the same one who had created the first privately run school choice program in Indiana: J. Patrick Rooney. HIP was popular. And it worked: encouraging Hoosiers to manage their health care reduced emergency room visits and encouraged preventive care, two drivers of costs. HIP provided coverage to forty thousand low-income Hoosiers, and I proposed using the federal Medicaid dollars to greatly expand the program.

President Obama's team was not enthusiastic—to put it mildly—about the idea. Consumer-driven care was a far cry from the centralized system preferred by his administration. There was a time crunch, too: HIP would expire at the end of 2014, giving them considerable negotiating leverage. Early phone conversations with Kathleen Sebelius, the secretary of Health and Human Services, were not encouraging. "Mr. Governor," she stated bluntly, "we are not in the waiver business." "Well, Madame Secretary, we are not in the expanding Medicaid business," I answered. End of conversation. She left office in the summer of 2014. A little daylight emerged in my negotiations with her replacement, Sylvia Mathews Burwell. In a face-to-face meeting in Washington in the giant Hubert H. Humphrey Building, the HHS headquarters, she was receptive to the idea—or at least not hostile to it. But the deputy director of the Centers for Medicare & Medicaid Services, Cindy Mann, remained steadfastly against it. There were many, many follow-up phone calls. Our team was led by a brilliant health policy advisor named Seema Verma. She was relentless. But as the year wound down, the administration had yet to make a decision. There was a sense that its members were dragging their feet, running out the clock.

While all those negotiations were going on, our family was undergoing great changes. Audrey was studying in Boston at Northeastern University and just starting to sort out her life and career. Charlotte was studying at Oxford University in England, and Michael had graduated from Purdue University with the hope of gaining admission to the Marine Corps Officer Candidates School. I will never forget the day we were waiting to hear from Michael whether he would be given the opportunity to serve our country. Among my duties that day was posing for the official photograph that would appear on Indiana maps and in rest stops across the state. When my assistant said that my son was on the phone, I was all ready for a pep talk about how proud I was that he had tried and how I was sure God had a better plan even though this hadn't worked out. When he said, "Dad, I got in," I was speechless. Suffice it to say that the official photos I sat for later were a piece of cake. I couldn't stop smiling all day.

My requests for meetings with President Obama about HIP were always turned down. So when he announced a visit to Evansville in southwest Indiana, I sent him a letter asking for a meeting to discuss approval of the HIP expansion, which we now called HIP 2.0. I explained that absent that, Hoosiers currently on HIP would lose their health care. Obama's trusted advisor Valerie Jarrett took my call, and we had a productive conversation on the eve of his visit. During the call I asked again for a meeting. His schedule was too full, she told me. But if I happened to be there when his plane landed, she said, I could talk to him on the tarmac. That was all I needed to hear.

When Air Force One landed at Evansville Regional Airport and Obama jogged down the stairs, I was there waiting to welcome him to Indiana. "Hey, Mike, tell me what you're working on," he said after we shook hands. Then, as the media snapped photos, I made my pitch. In detail. For every point I made, he had a question. I would explain one part of the proposal; he would ask how it would work and point out his concerns. He was well versed on our plan. I knew that my time with him was limited, my window of opportunity was closing. I had known him for some time; we had served in Congress together. He is as liberal as I am conservative, but I always felt I could level with him.

"Look," I told the president, "this is something I really want to do. It isn't about politics, it's something I want to do for my state, and I think it could really work." He understood. And he knew that the easy thing for Indiana to do would be to just say no to the Medicaid money. I knew that the easy thing for him to do would be to give us a hard no. But by saying yes, Indiana would be able to build its own health care plan designed by Hoosiers with free-market ideas, and the Obama administration would have a version of Medicaid expansion in one more state. It was a genuinely respectful conversation. "Mike, I am not philosophically opposed to the idea," he said as the conversation came to an end. It was the turning point.

Negotiations went on till the end of the year, but our persistence paid off. In January 2015, Indiana and the Obama administration reached a deal to allow 350,000 Hoosiers access to their own health insurance plan. Some conservatives called it a sellout, but I am certain that we did the right thing and did it the right way. In 2020, HIP 2.0 provided innovative health care coverage to 550,000 low-income Hoosiers and was extended for another decade. It became a model for consumer-directed health care in states across the country. Cindy Mann, the progressive who had been so opposed to HIP 2.0, resigned from her post at CMS the day after we got our waiver.

On a personal level, March 2015 featured one of the proudest moments of my life, when Karen and I traveled to Quantico in Virginia to watch our son, Michael, graduate from Officer Candidates School and be commissioned as a second lieutenant in the Marine Corps. When we arrived on a rainy morning, the base commander invited us to his office for coffee, informing us with some admiration that he had learned only a few days earlier that our son was a member of Indiana's first family. When Michael had filled out his entry documents, in what I understood was an effort to "climb his own mountain," he had listed his father's occupation as "former talk radio show host," which I informed his commanding officer had the benefit of being true. We made our way to the VIP section of the grandstands and saw the graduating class of new officers standing at attention in the rain. We strained our eyes to see if we could pick Michael out of the crowd of hundreds of new marines. When the commanding officer announced that the governor of Indiana and first lady were in attendance, he also memorably simply added the name of Michael's girlfriend with the words "and Sarah" echoing across the parade ground.

It was altogether fitting, as Michael would be the first to say he never would have made it through Officer Candidates School without the support of that remarkable girl from Knightstown, Indiana. The two of them were engaged a year later. "And Sarah" has been a blessing to our family ever since.

Governing a state is so much more than finding efficiencies, cutting taxes, or creating new laws. A governor's work often takes place far away from his desk or the statehouse. There are late-night and early-morning phone calls with news of approaching storms and tornado touchdowns, quick efforts to warn those in their paths, such as the day in November 2013 when north-central Indiana was struck by the second largest tornado outbreak in history. I have always believed in leading from the front and was on the ground the very next day, not just to survey the damage but, I hoped, to be a comfort to Hoosiers who had seen their homes, schools, and businesses destroyed by the storm. In the aftermath of such events there are visits to towns, places to stand and embrace survivors amid the wreckage, the upturned trees, overturned trucks, and leveled homes. The work to help those communities rebuild begins by being there.

No state is immune to events occurring oceans away. In 2013, the Indianapolis-born Peter Kassig, a former Army Ranger, was abducted in Syria while delivering humanitarian aid to refugees during that nation's civil war. Kassig, who converted to Islam while in captivity and changed his name to Abdul-Rahman Kassig, was a hero and a humanitarian. Staying in close contact with his parents, we worked with the Obama administration and federal intelligence agencies attempting to secure his release. During a trip to Washington, DC, I requested a meeting with the director of the FBI, James Comey. From my years in Congress, I knew that the agency leads in international hostage situations, and although I was in the nation's capital for other business, I was not going to leave without talking to Comey.

After we had waited for more than an hour in a small conference room, the lanky director arrived. He told me they were working around the clock, but against the odds. Heartbreakingly, not long after, in late 2014, Kassig was barbarically murdered by his radical Islamic captors, who recorded the terrible act in a video. Sitting with his grieving parents at his funeral at Butler University is seared into my memory. It minted my resolve that the United States must take the fight to ISIS, on our terms, on their soil, and protect the people of this country from the terrorists who had claimed the life of a selfless Hoosier.

In late 2015, three teams of terrorists carried out attacks across Paris, killing 127 people and wounding hundreds more. ISIS took credit for the horror. According to the French government, one of the jihadists had entered Europe, arriving in Greece in a wave of refugees escaping Syria's civil war. He had carried a forged Syrian passport and even passed through a refugee camp in Croatia. European intelligence officials suspected a new strategy: ISIS murderers would slip into countries undetected along with Syrian refugees. The US government had begun resettling thousands of Syrian refugees starting in 2014. Indiana is a welcoming state, but as governor I had to balance that with the very real concern that we could not guarantee people arriving from Syria had been properly vetted. All it would take to bring violence to Indiana was one terrorist slipping in among the families escaping war. I ordered the state to suspend funding the resettlement of Syrian refugees until we had total confidence in the federal government's vetting procedures. It was meant as a deterrent. We were not closing our borders or discriminating against anyone based on nationality; we were erring on the side of caution. Twenty-five other governors also acted to temporarily stop resettlement of Syrian refugees in their states.

After I announced that decision, I received a phone call from my daughter Audrey. She wasn't happy about it. Karen and I had raised our kids to think for themselves, meaning that they don't agree with us on everything. When I was inaugurated as Indiana's governor in 2013, Audrey, who was eighteen and a senior in high school, told an Indianapolis TV station that she was "politically independent and socially liberal" but said she still supported her dad. Over the years we had had political disagreements. But the matter of the Syrian refugees was different.

In the summer of 2014, as a college student, Audrey had visited refugee camps in Jordan. The following year she had interned in Istanbul, Turkey. She had seen firsthand the desperate plight of the men and women fleeing the violence in Syria. And she knew how important it was that resources be made available to help them adjust to their new countries. She had felt incredibly frustrated when she'd heard about my decision to pause funding to resettlement agencies. "This is so important, why would you do that?" she asked me. I appreciated her perspective and experiences; I valued them truly. But we disagreed. I told her that I'd had to make my decision for the safety of our state. I had made a decision based on my charge as governor of Indiana. And she had her deeply held views born out of her real-life experiences. The discussion got heated, and the call ended.

After a couple of hours passed and we had both cooled down, I called her back. I knew we were not going to see eye to eye on the issue, but we needed to hear each other out and find boundaries so we could have respectful conversations for the sake of preserving our family. She agreed. We had a long and productive talk, and we resolved to be respectful of each other's views. And we have done that ever since.

In 2015, the first reported US case of Middle East respiratory syndrome (MERS) was identified in Indiana. Health officials believed that the virus, which attacks the respiratory system, had the potential to cause a severe outbreak, with a 30 percent mortality rate. A health care worker had traveled from Saudi Arabia to Chicago by plane and then to northwest Indiana by bus. When symptoms developed, he had checked into a hospital in Hammond. We swung all of Indiana's health resources into action, working day and night with federal agencies to ensure that the patient had appropriate care and that his family's travels were tracked. Though it would become a household term in the years ahead, I had never heard of "contact tracing," but our team at the state and local level went to work. People who had come into contact with the patient were notified. Health care workers who had been in his presence were quarantined and monitored. The public was notified, and information about the risk of contracting MERS was widely distributed. Thankfully, the man recovered and was released. The risk of an outbreak was eliminated. It was difficult to say if our response was textbook because there was no textbook. We responded in real time. It was an invaluable experience in managing a health care crisis, as I learned about the importance of collaboration among health officials, federal agencies, and local health care providers.

The MERS threat emerged suddenly. But another public health challenge in Indiana had been spreading for months. In February 2015, our state's health officials received word of a spike in HIV/AIDS infections in Austin, a small town in Scott County, a rural area in the southeastern part of Indiana. Between 2004 and 2013, there had been five reported cases of infection; by the end of March 2015, there were seventy-two publicly reported cases in Scott County.

The vast majority of the cases were due to intravenous drug abuse involving sharing needles during the injection of a crushed opioid, Opana. Interstate 65, which runs from Chicago to Mobile, passes through Scott County, making the area especially vulnerable as the truck stops along the way are opportunities for drug sales and prostitution. We surged state police into the area to combat the illegal activity.

The outbreak due to drug abuse was not unique to Scott County. For decades, across the United States, highly addictive opium-derived pills, whose danger was downplayed by the pharmaceutical industry, were overprescribed, easily obtained, and flooding economically struggling regions. Austin, with a population of 4,200, had been hit hard by the loss of manufacturing jobs over a generation, culminating with the closure of an American Steel plant during the Great Recession.

A month after the initial report of a rise in HIV/AIDS infections in Scott County, the number of infections doubled. Sitting at the large conference table in the governor's office with officials from the Centers for Disease Control and Prevention (CDC), I was informed that, despite the relatively small numbers involved, the outbreak could be characterized as an epidemic. We immediately swung into action.

In March, I declared a public health emergency. We provided testing, treatment, and access to health care to the infected in the area. There were also calls in the community for a needle exchange program. CDC officials who were on the ground working with us to stop the outbreak were in favor. Indiana state law prohibited needle exchanges, and I was opposed to them as well. I don't believe in needle exchanges as a means of fighting drug abuse because my experience of public policy has been that whatever you subsidize, you will get more of. I will never believe that it's in the public interest to subsidize drug abuse. But this was an emergency, and I believe in letting the people on the front lines play a large part in determining how to act. Along with the state health commissioner, Dr. Jerome Adams, I traveled to Scott County for a roundtable discussion with the sheriff, Austin's mayor, health care providers, local citizens, and those suffering from the virus.

It was a vigorous discussion, and I was deeply impressed by the participants' resolve and compassion. Some desperately wanted the needle exchange; others were equally opposed. On March 24, I had a late-night talk on the phone with the local sheriff, Dan McClain. He had originally objected to the idea of a needle exchange but told me, "Mike, we have tried to arrest our way out of this. I believe the only thing we can do to stop or slow this thing is to get clean needles out there." I told Sheriff McClain that I appreciated his counsel: I would pray on it and make a decision.

I listened to national health experts as well. Almost 100 percent of the HIV/AIDS transmissions in Scott County were through shared needles. The quickest way to stanch the spread of HIV was to temporarily provide needles to drug users so they wouldn't be borrowing needles from other addicts. I did not make the decision lightly. The Bible counsels us to "act justly and to love mercy and to walk humbly," and I was torn between a strong stand for justice under the law and the kindness of attending to the advice of health officials. Two days later, I issued an emergency order, suspending state law and allowing a temporary needle exchange program in Scott County.

In the days ahead, we worked closely with both the CDC and local officials in Scott County to design the program. There was to be a one-stop shop, providing not only needles but testing. There was another crucial component: many of those with HIV/AIDS in Scott County, the great majority of whom had also contracted hepatitis C, were eligible for the newly created HIP 2.0. The program immediately demonstrated its value, as the state enrolled them and gave them access to anti-retroviral treatments that transformed the virus from lethal to manageable. No other state facing the opioid crisis in our part of the country had a program like that, one that quickly provided that type of emergency care. By the summer, the rate of new infections was down sharply. I will always believe that we did the right thing, but it wasn't easy. I came to public service with a set of principles, and they have guided my career. But governing, doing the right thing, means finding realistic solutions within the framework of your principles, and that was just what we did to end the HIV epidemic in that small Indiana town. In 2020, there was only one reported new case of HIV in Scott County.

In the middle of Indiana's HIV/AIDS crisis, I stopped to speak with a group of reporters. Expecting questions about our work with the CDC and the latest numbers, I walked over to the microphones and cameras. Instead my remarks about our work in Scott County were ignored and I was peppered with questions about a bill working its way through the Indiana Statehouse called the Religious Freedom Restoration Act (RFRA).

CHAPTER THIRTEEN

Lessons Learned Defending Religious Freedom

Everyone will sit under their own vine and under their own fig tree, and no one will make them afraid.
—Micah 4:4

In 1993, President Bill Clinton signed a federal Religious Freedom Restoration Act into law. The legislation aimed to restore the First Amendment of the Constitution by requiring that laws be narrowly tailored to meet a compelling government interest when the free exercise of religion is affected. The law was intended to ensure that Americans' exercise of religion would not be restricted except in very narrowly defined situations.

Connecticut and Rhode Island had passed their own religious freedom laws even before the federal government did. By 2015, nineteen states had passed religious freedom laws and eleven state courts had interpreted them as providing a heightened standard for reviewing government action. In 1998, when Barack Obama was a state senator, he supported Illinois's version of the law. Historically, such laws had always received wide bipartisan support.

In the spring of 2015, *Obergefell v. Hodges*, the Supreme Court decision that would legalize same-sex marriage, was just a few months away, and many states around the country had taken up religious freedom laws to safeguard the religious beliefs of citizens who hold a traditional view of marriage. Indiana was attempting to join them.

Indiana's Religious Freedom Restoration Act was not part of my administration's legislative agenda, but I had certainly defended the traditional definition of marriage throughout my career in Congress. My faith informs me that marriage is between one man and one woman. I believe that marriage wasn't our idea, that it was ordained by God, was instituted in law, and is the center of our civilization. I had also sworn an oath to uphold the freedom of religion enshrined in the Indiana Constitution and the Constitution of the United States.

When I expressed support for the bill in a weekly press briefing early in the year, it generated little commentary or controversy. My position was hardly out of the mainstream. Bill Clinton, George W. Bush, and Barack Obama had all run for election and then reelection upholding the view that marriage was between one man and one woman. Every major party presidential nominee until 2016 had held that position throughout our nation's history.

But although my view remained the same, the nation's was changing and the legal definition of marriage was becoming part of a broader culture war. Indiana legislators wanted to ensure that Hoosiers who believe in traditional marriage would have the full protection of the law should the Supreme Court rule in favor of same-sex marriage, as was looking increasingly likely. The Indiana General Assembly passed the Religious Freedom Restoration Act by overwhelming majorities: 63–31 in the House and 40–10 in the Senate.

There were few warning signs that the bill would be controversial as it moved through the legislature, where it was the subject of hours of testimony and debate before arriving for my signature. Editorials condemning RFRA were few and far between in Indiana. Letters of warning from business leaders in the state garnered little attention. When the bill reached my desk on March 26, 2015, I signed it without hesitation. Then all hell broke loose.

The ink had hardly dried on the bill when boycotts were announced. Angry statements were issued by corporations. The woke brigades of politicians, media, and corporate America mobilized before wokeism was even a thing.

The progressive Left and its allies in the media began by grossly mischaracterizing the bill as a "license to discriminate." Nothing could be further from the truth. Indiana's religious freedom law did not legalize discrimination. RFRA ensured that Indiana law would respect religious freedom and apply the highest level of scrutiny to any state or local governmental action that infringes on people's religious liberty. The most often cited practical use of the law was to protect a baker or florist who, believing that marriage was between a man and a woman, declined to use his or her artistic skill to bake a cake or construct a bouquet for a same-sex marriage. Under RFRA they could not refuse other services, but they could decline to provide those particular services, according to their beliefs, without punishment of the law. A few short years later, the Supreme Court would uphold that exact position in a unanimous decision in *Fulton v. City of Philadelphia*.

There were other applications as well that had nothing to do with same-sex marriage: prohibiting zoning laws that barred religious organizations from renting space in downtown districts, for example, and giving employees the right to wear a beard because their faith mandated it.

Several states were working to pass RFRA laws, but Indiana was the first that year, and the overwhelming opposition we faced from the Left, the media, and corporate boardrooms had all the markings of a coordinated effort designed to make an example of any state that led on traditional marriage in the run-up to the Supreme Court's decision on same-sex marriage. We were blindsided.

Companies such as Angie's List threatened to cancel promised economic expansions in Indiana. Connecticut forbade state employees from traveling to Indiana; so did Seattle and San Francisco. RFRA was instantly a national headline, and Indiana was in jeopardy of becoming a national punch line. It was catnip to the media, portraying a flyover state as an outpost of middle American intolerance. There were potential negative economic consequences for Indiana and the possibility of negative political ones for me.

And there were unforced errors from the outset. Instead of signing the bill in public, I had held a private signing ceremony in my office with legislators, religious leaders, and activists who had worked to move the bill through the General Assembly. Our office tweeted a photograph with a few of the bill's sponsors and the religious leaders who had been in attendance. Twitter users quickly attacked the pastors, priests, nuns, and rabbis for supporting the bill, suggesting that the legislation had been the work of religious zealots rather than a monthslong legislative process. These faith leaders were all good Hoosiers, who deserved better. I should have signed the bill in public.

But what pained me most was to see and hear the attacks on Indiana and the inaccurate portrayal of our great state. Hoosier hospitality is not a slogan, it is a way of life. The hospitality and character of Hoosiers are synonymous with everything good about America. Six and a half million of the best people in the world were being unfairly maligned.

I wanted to explain the bill and why I had signed it to the entire country. There was debate among my staff as to what the proper venue should be. Some suggested that I appear on a conservative network such as Fox News with a more receptive host and audience. I thought, though, that going before a broader audience, with a host who wasn't necessarily sympathetic, would be a better option. I was wrong.

On Sunday, March 29, I appeared on ABC's *This Week* with George Stephanopoulos to try to set the record straight. I made my case that the law was not about discrimination; it was about fighting government overreach. I said that Hoosiers had come under an avalanche of intolerance and reckless media coverage. When Stephanopoulos repeatedly asked me if the law would allow businesses to discriminate against gay couples, I was so offended by the question that I just insisted that that wasn't the issue and moved on. So much for all my eloquence.

The truth was that I didn't think the question warranted an answer: Hoosiers don't believe in discrimination against anyone. We are welcoming, neighborly, tolerant people. Perhaps today it sounds old-fashioned, but like most Hoosiers, I was raised to treat others the way I would want to be treated. I should never have assumed that our critics knew that about me or Indiana. Indiana speaker Brian Bosma called me personally after the interview with some none-too-kind feedback. I probably deserved it.

The interview only intensified the hysteria. Indiana's nine largest companies, including Eli Lilly, Anthem BlueCross BlueShield, and Cummins, joined the chorus of those criticizing our state. The NCAA, headquartered in downtown Indianapolis, was threatening to relocate. It was, in retrospect, the first battle between woke corporate America and the American people.

The *Indianapolis Star*, the state's largest newspaper, once a bastion of midwest conservatism that had been purchased by the East Coast liberals at Gannett, was now run from afar. It demanded that the legislature address the crisis regardless of the impact on Hoosiers' religious beliefs. The *Star* pushed beyond advocacy to activism, organizing meetings of the companies and parties that opposed the bill.

That Tuesday, I took another shot at making our case to a national audience in an essay for the *Wall Street Journal*. I wrote that "I abhor discrimination" and "I believe in the Golden Rule that you should 'do unto others as you would have them do unto you.'" I added that "anyone who knows me or my family knows that's how we live."

I pointed out that "Indiana's new law contains no reference to sexual orientation" and said that as governor of Indiana, if I were presented a bill that legalized discrimination against any person or group, I would veto it. I also added, "If I saw a restaurant owner refuse to serve a gay couple, I wouldn't eat there anymore."

I quoted Professor Daniel O. Conkle of Indiana University's Maurer School of Law, a supporter of gay rights, including same-sex marriage, who had written in the *Indianapolis Star*, "The proposed Indiana RFRA . . . is anything but a 'license to discriminate,' and it should not be mischaracterized or dismissed on that basis."

Later that day I held a two-hour press conference, fielding and answering every question imaginable about the bill. It was carried live on all the cable TV news channels across the country and, as I would later learn, on the twenty-sixth floor of Trump Tower in New York. I was encouraged by some allies to dig in and fight.

But daily the state's reputation was being dragged through the mud; the progress made by our administration, and the previous one as well, was clearly at risk.

In my inaugural address, I had told the people of my state that I was "eager to be the governor of all the people of Indiana—young and old, city and country, rich and poor." I had taken an oath to support the Indiana Constitution, and that I would do, but it saddened me to think that any Hoosier had felt put upon.

At this time Karen and Charlotte were in Turkey visiting Audrey, who was studying there. I was alone, and thankfully, my brothers came over to the Governor's Residence with pizza to buck me up. But it was a solitary time. I was constantly praying, seeking God's wisdom and finding great comfort in the verse "The Lord is my refuge." And so He was. In the end, I knew that my job as governor was always to put the best interests of our state first; always to ask, What is best for Indiana and its people?

So I called on the General Assembly to reaffirm that nothing in RFRA authorized unlawful discrimination of Hoosiers. I also insisted that the amendment include language expressly reaffirming the religious freedom enshrined in the Indiana Constitution. It wasn't legally necessary, but I was persuaded that it would move our state and all its people past the harsh criticism of the previous week. After the bill cleared the General Assembly, I signed it, disappointing some conservatives who wanted the fight to go on, despite the fact that the amended bill still enhanced protections for every church, nonprofit religious organization, religious school, rabbi, priest, preacher, or pastor facing government action and left Hoosiers' constitutional liberties unchanged.

The threats of sanctions and boycotts ended. The waters calmed overnight.

The controversy was quelled, but the amendment to RFRA did little to end the debate in Indiana, and soon the same media and woke corporate cabal began a full-court press to expand our state's civil rights statute and reignite the controversy we had just brought to a close.

For all our state had endured, the corporate and media elites who railed against RFRA were intent on pressing during the next session of the Indiana General Assembly for full civil rights protections based on gender identity and sexual orientation regardless of the impact on Hoosiers' religious freedom. In that moment I learned a painful lesson that for many on the American left, the most sincere efforts to allay concerns are never enough. There is no satisfying the woke Left.

With the prospect of additional legislation on the horizon, I was determined to chart a course based on the Constitution from the outset. In the summer and fall of 2015 I met with religious and civic leaders, academics, corporate executives, and members of the LGBT community. If additional action was to be taken, this time we would get it right with buy-in from all of Indiana.

The meetings took place in my office in the statehouse, with attendees seated on the couches and chairs surrounding the historic fireplace featuring a portrait of Governor Oliver P. Morton, Abraham Lincoln's favorite governor and champion of Indiana's historic role in the Civil War. The meetings were often lengthy and emotional. I heard religious leaders' alarm about a growing intolerance of Judeo-Christian values. I talked with corporate leaders about their concerns about attracting talent. Academics weighed in on the legality of changing the civil rights statute. And I met with members of the LGBT community regarding their concerns about discrimination.

During a meeting with LGBT Hoosiers, one attendee confided his personal story and I could tell how nervous he was. After all that had been said about me, I knew it must have been incredibly difficult for him to attend the meeting. So I paused, looked him in the eye, and said I thought it had taken a lot of courage to come to my office. I assured him that he was safe. And I told him and everyone else in that room that even if we might not ultimately agree on the proposed changes to Indiana law, it was a privilege to be their governor and how moved I was that they had taken the time to meet with me. Whatever the state decided to do next, I would often tell my children that I was determined to lead in the spirit of Micah 4:4, which reads, "Everyone will sit under their own vine and under their own fig tree, and no one will make them afraid." That was my prayer.

Six months later, in January 2016, I chose my annual State of the State address to outline my position. I had worked and reworked the speech over and over, editing and writing in the small wood panel–walled study in the Governor's Residence. I paid particular attention to the close. I wanted the General Assembly and Hoosiers to know exactly where I stood should they decide to revisit RFRA: changing the state's civil rights laws would carry implications for every citizen, especially people of faith.

In a lesson that would serve me well in another January, I turned my attention to the Indiana Constitution. Our state charter is a remarkable document. It was the first state constitution to ban slavery, to establish a system of free public education, and to expressly protect freedom of religion *and* conscience.

Before leaving to deliver the speech at the statehouse, I made last-minute edits, prayed with Karen, and donned the blue-and-gold Indiana tie she had designed for our administration. I was ready. Arriving at the House Chamber, I took to the podium with the great seal of the state behind me, the legislature in front of me, and opened my speech.

It was our state's bicentennial, so I first reflected on how forty-three founders had gathered under an elm tree in Corydon, the original capital, to craft a constitution for the place they would call the state of Indiana. Before a statewide television audience, I was proud to report to my fellow Hoosiers that it had been not just a remarkable year but three remarkable years. Indiana was strong. The state's economy was roaring; more of its people were working than ever before in our history. We had emblazed "Indiana: A State that Works" on the side of one of our government office buildings. And it did.

We had balanced the budget, doubled the number of students in the state's school choice program, and passed the largest increase in K–12 funding in Indiana history. We had worked with Washington to create our own health care program. We were revitalizing struggling regions of the state and had faced down health emergencies. But under the continuing pressure from woke media and corporate boardrooms, there was much anticipation of what I might say on the subject of expanding full civil rights protections to LGBT Hoosiers.

I began by reminding Hoosiers that our two-hundred-year-old state constitution declares that "all people are created equal," and I told that statewide audience that "no one should be harassed or mistreated because of who they are, who they love, or what they believe." I said that Indiana was a welcoming state that respects everyone and that anybody who doesn't know that doesn't know Indiana.

In almost the same breath, I also said that Hoosiers cherish faith and the freedom to live out their faith in their daily lives and that "no one should ever fear persecution because of their deeply held religious beliefs."

I reminded them all that we are a state with a constitution that not only protects the right "to worship Almighty God, according to the dictates of [our] own consciences" but also provides that "No law shall, in any case whatever, control the free exercise and enjoyment of religious opinions, nor interfere with the rights of conscience."

If legislators wished to revisit the issue and attempt to reconcile those two values in the law, I told them, they should do so without compromising the freedoms Hoosiers hold dear.

And though I assured them that I would give careful consideration to any bill they sent me, I stated emphatically, "I will not support any bill that diminishes the religious freedom of Hoosiers or that interferes with the Constitutional rights of our citizens to live out their beliefs in worship, service or work," adding that "Our freedoms are too precious to our people . . . and have been bought at too high a price to do any less."

With that, I paused, ready to conclude the speech. Republican legislators interrupted with applause. A few even stood at their desks. More joined them, and then spectators in the gallery joined the standing ovation. Many Democrats stood and clapped, too. When the cheering faded, I moved through the remainder of the speech, racing to beat the end of the allotted time on the television broadcast just seconds before the satellite feed would black out at the bottom of the hour.

What had begun the prior April ended that January night. In the time between—ever since taking office, really—I had listened, I had learned, and I had led. By God's grace, I had staked my ground firmly on the freedoms and values enshrined in the Indiana Constitution, and the impending controversy never came to pass. It was a lesson of keeping faith with the Constitution that I would carry with me in service to all the American people in the years ahead.

CHAPTER FOURTEEN

Changing Direction

There is a time for everything . . . a time to plant and a time to uproot.
—Ecclesiastes 3:1–2

It was early 2016. I was running for reelection, and I was going to win. There was no denying that my popularity and approval ratings, which had been encouraging coming into 2015, had taken a hit during the controversy over RFRA. But as the election approached, I had no challenger for the Republican nomination, had plenty of fundraising support, and was leading my Democrat opponent in the last public poll, and with the eventual Republican ticket poised to carry Indiana by nineteen points, my reelection was all but assured.

I went into the legislative session determined to build on my success. I had campaigned on bread-and-butter issues—job creation, tax cuts, education—because I believed that those were areas where I had the greatest ability to make progress. But I never hesitated to take a stand on other issues.

A society can be judged by how it deals with its most vulnerable, the aged, the infirm, the disabled, and the unborn. In the spring of 2016, in the midst of my campaign for reelection, I signed a law making abortions based on race, gender, or disability illegal. Its prohibition of abortions based on disability made Indiana only the second state in the country with such a law. In the United States and around the world, the vast majority of babies diagnosed with Down syndrome are aborted. Some studies show that the number is as high as 90 percent. Karen and I had spent time with families with Down syndrome children at charity walks and picnics during our tenure in the statehouse and had always been moved by the parents' devotion to the child and the boundless joy of those special-needs kids. I signed the bill without hesitation. The majority of Hoosiers are pro-life, and we took an important stand in restoring the sanctity of life. After I left office, parts of the law were overturned by the Supreme Court, but the case gave rise to a historic dissenting opinion authored by Justice Clarence Thomas, who described the role of eugenics in the history of abortion, laying a historical and moral foundation to restore the sanctity of life to the center of American law.

In Congress I had also always stood with and defended Israel, which I describe as the United States' most cherished ally, for so long a solitary outpost of liberty in the Middle East. By 2016, a movement known as Boycott, Divestment, Sanctions, or BDS, which aimed to eliminate the Jewish state, was advancing around the globe. It sought to leverage economic pressure against states, businesses, and institutions that had transactions with Israel. But Indiana turned the tables. In 2016, with bipartisan support, the General Assembly passed a bill forbidding the state to conduct business with organizations aligned with the BDS movement. The Israeli ambassador, Ron Dermer, flew to Indianapolis for the bill signing and called it the strongest anti-BDS bill in the nation. We made it clear: In the heart of the heartland, America stands with Israel.

When the legislative session ended and legislators headed home in the spring, I hit the campaign trail seeking a second term based on the accomplishments of my first. I had arrived at the statehouse back in 2013 eager to see how fast and far we could take Indiana's engine. And now, in 2016, it was roaring.

My old friend John Gregg was back. He wasn't just ready for a rematch; he'd had a makeover, going from Blue Dog Democrat to progressive policy wonk. He even trimmed his mustache and donned a suit and tie, hoping to take advantage of the controversy over RFRA. He never once led in the polls. Our rematch collided with another election: the Republican presidential primary. It was an election like no other. Donald Trump, the New York billionaire, was upending the GOP and looked to be headed for the nomination. By the time of Indiana's May primary, Trump had already amassed a large haul of delegates; the once crowded field of rivals had been reduced to two:

Texas senator Ted Cruz and Ohio governor John Kasich. If there was to be any chance of denying Trump the prize, it would have to be in the Indiana primary, as the Hoosier delegate haul would secure the nomination for Trump.

All three candidates solicited my endorsement, Kasich in his own unique way. When he campaigned in Indianapolis, the Ohio governor granted me an audience and acknowledged that he wasn't expecting my support. His bluntness was refreshing if nothing else.

New Jersey governor Chris Christie was an old friend who had made an early endorsement of Donald Trump after ending his own presidential campaign. Chris called to ask if I would meet with the front-runner. I was intrigued by Trump's candidacy and welcomed the meeting. But it was still a little surprising.

In December, in the aftermath of a mass shooting in San Bernardino, California, by a Muslim couple that had claimed the lives of fourteen at an office Christmas party, Trump called for "a total and complete shutdown of Muslims entering the United States until our country's representatives can figure out what the hell is going on." I shared the outrage that every American felt about that terrorist attack but called Trump's proposal "offensive and unconstitutional."

It was not that the idea of suspending immigration from countries on the terrorist watch list was without merit. In fact, the Supreme Court would uphold our administration's measure, barring nearly all citizens of Iran, Libya, North Korea, Somalia, Syria, Yemen, and Venezuela in the interest of national security in 2018. But Trump's call to temporarily suspend all immigration based upon religion was inconsistent with our nation's highest traditions of religious freedom, and I said so.

Despite that disagreement, on April 19, a few weeks before the primary, Trump and Christie visited the Indiana Governor's Residence. As we sat on couches in the living room, I suggested that we begin the meeting with a brief word of prayer. In the years ahead, Trump would recount our first meeting and jokingly refer to my prayer, saying, "That's not exactly how we start real estate meetings in New York." But we were all immediately at ease and discussed our families, the current campaign, and Hoosiers, too. Trump was a fan of Indiana. He admired the way we had balanced budgets and cut taxes and was curious about how we had done both. He was gracious and respectful and said he would be honored to have my support.

I had a similarly good meeting with Ted Cruz. I had known him in Congress. We had common ideological ground. He is a conservative; we had the same mooring, had read the same books. Cruz's vision of our party hewed the closest to mine. He had a record of deferring to the Constitution, defending taxpayers, and standing for life. He had demonstrated a willingness to take on Republican leaders in Congress, just as I had done during my years in Washington, DC.

Marty Obst, my campaign manager, had been fielding calls from supporters all across the state, urging me to either stay out of the primary and not endorse any candidate or to support Trump. He wholeheartedly agreed with those sentiments. When I endorsed Ted Cruz, I thought Marty was going to have a heart attack. And his willingness to stay with the campaign remains one of the greatest acts of loyalty I've ever known.

There was no slight intended toward the other two men. Nor was it an attempt to be clever and thread the needle. After a year of tacking my sails through difficult political headwinds, I just decided to follow my heart. I wrote myself a note that I still have to this day. It reads, "I'm tired of politics, I just want me back." So I endorsed the candidate who was most closely aligned with my conservative philosophy, regardless of the odds.

When I announced the endorsement in April, I also praised Donald Trump, saying that he had "given voice to the frustration of millions of working Americans." Years later he would kid me about that fabulous nonendorsement, saying it was nicer than most of the endorsements he had been getting at the time. That's not what it was, though; it was a recognition of a movement under way that rejected politics as usual, that was ready for the United States to move in a different direction at home and abroad.

I had seen it across Indiana during my own campaign. Perhaps it was not as visible from other vantage points, but the country's political foundations were shifting right under the feet of its political class. They were oblivious, as usual. Trump's instincts and imagination were a part of that shift, yes. But the change coming was never exclusively about him.

I had met many Hoosiers who were frustrated and fed up. They were tired of being looked down on by Washington elites who didn't understand their values and knew nothing about the places they called home. They felt firsthand what the US leadership elite barely realized: wages weren't keeping up with inflation, entire communities were being hollowed out as factories closed and moved to Mexico or Asia, an opioid epidemic was destroying families and communities, and many ways of earning a living were simply vanishing without replacement. What they saw from Washington was contempt and constant reminders that their country was just one of many, no better than any other and probably worse. And they had lived with the fallout from a long series of policy choices—from trade pacts to unending foreign wars, from starry-eyed attempts at nation-building to big-government programs to be paid for by future generations. During my years in Congress and as governor I had supported free trade and the wars in Afghanistan and Iraq. But with the rise of China, the struggles I had seen firsthand in manufacturing, and the War on Terror nearing twenty years, my outlook was changing as well.

Donald Trump was giving voice to the desperation and frustration caused by decades of government mismanagement and neglect. He articulated, in his own blunt way, the economic and social anxieties felt by Americans in a changing world—anxieties that the leaders in both parties ignored.

It was hardly a shock then that on May 3, Trump easily won Indiana's primary, beating Cruz by nearly 20 percentage points. In my defense the Texan did win every county I had campaigned with him in—all three of them.

The movement to deny Donald Trump the Republican nomination was over. The nomination was his. And I had pledged, before the votes were cast and counted, to support and work for the Republican candidate, whomever he ended up being. I endorsed Donald Trump for president before the week was out.

That settled, I focused on my own campaign for reelection. But I could not entirely avoid presidential politics. In early June, Trump stated that Judge Gonzalo Curiel, a Hoosier with a civil lawsuit against Trump before his court, was incapable of giving him a fair trial because of his Mexican heritage and Trump's pledge to build a wall between the United States and Mexico. When asked about it by the Indiana press, I answered forthrightly. I called the candidate's statement "inappropriate" and said it was never right to question a judge's impartiality based on his ethnicity. I also reminded the press that I was running for governor and that if I had wanted to weigh in on every comment made by the candidates for president, I would have run for president. Not long after, Kellyanne Conway, my pollster and a friend of the Republican nominee, told me that Trump had said, "How come everyone can't criticize me the way Governor Pence does?"

CHAPTER FIFTEEN

"Mike, It's Gonna Be Great!"

Should you then seek great things for yourself? Do not seek them.
—Jeremiah 45:5

My summer was county fairs, campaign stops at diners, and quiet days in the statehouse, which is delightfully casual when the legislature is out of session.

On June 10, at the end of one of the quiet days, I was in the back of the state-owned black Chevy Suburban, heading home. We passed through downtown Indianapolis, then north up Meridian Street, where that warm light particular to midwestern summer afternoons was shining on the historic homes. My cell phone rang, and it was the last call I ever expected.

At the other end was Steve Hilbert, an old acquaintance, an insurance industry executive and confidant of Donald J. Trump. He opened with some friendly banter but then got to the point: he said a friend of his wanted to know if I would be interested in being considered as his running mate, even if that meant I would have to give up running for reelection as governor. Indiana law forbids running for state and federal office at the same time, and it would obviously be impossible, given the demands of a presidential campaign.

It was a quick conversation; he asked me to get back to him, I said I would pray about it and talk to my family and left it at that. The word "Trump" was never mentioned. I spotted Karen in the driveway, talking with a friend who was visiting from out of town. Shaken, I stepped out of the Suburban and interrupted. "Karen, we need to talk."

Other than during the days leading up to the Indiana primary, I had met Donald J. Trump only twice before. They had both been instructive meetings. The first was during a small fundraiser at his Mar-a-Lago resort in Palm Beach in 2010. He didn't attend the event but stopped by the lobby where I was standing and introduced himself. It was a brief but warm conversation. "I've seen you on TV," he told me, "and I like your style." I was actually kind of shocked that Donald Trump had any idea who I was. The second time, in November 2011, was at his office in Trump Tower. I was beginning my campaign for governor and stopped in New York to share our plans to build on Indiana's recent string of successes and see if he might chip in financially. The meeting was once again short and positive: He offered his fundraising support, and I went on my way, down to the lobby to the golden escalator and out the door. By the time I reached the sidewalk, members of my staff were receiving calls from Indiana media outlets asking about my meeting with Trump. Annoyed, I asked, "Who told the press what we were doing today?" No one, a staffer told me; Trump had tweeted about our visit and endorsed me for governor before I got to the car. It was my first experience with the man and his medium, one that would dominate American politics for the next five years.

I reflected with Karen and prayed about how to respond. The first part of the deliberation was easy. I was basically being asked if I would be willing to give up my job if I thought I could help the country. I thought of Dad. He had risked his life for his country in Korea. He had raised me to believe that you ought to be willing to give up your life for your country, that sacrifice and duty are part of what it means to be an American. After all, as he said, to whom much is given, much is expected.

Giving up my job as governor of Indiana, honor and privilege as it was, was a rather small sacrifice compared to what a soldier risked—but one that carried with it a chance to do some good for our entire country. But that was the question. In fact, the day Steve called, I wrote and then circled a note in my day planner: "If I could help the country." But to know whether I could help, I needed to know what the job description was. What role would the vice president play in a Trump administration? John Nance Garner, one of Franklin Roosevelt's three vice presidents, had described the job as "not worth a bucket of warm spit." I kind of doubt he actually said "spit." But in any event, I wasn't interested in holding that bucket, whatever was in it. But if Trump wanted a vice president who would play a part in helping him lead, that was another matter.

I decided not to call Steve back. If the interest was real, he would call again. We placed the outcome in God's hands, took a deep breath, and headed off for the weekend to Aynes House, the Indiana governor's retreat in Brown County State Park, to celebrate Charlotte's twenty-third birthday. The Hoosier Camp David is a cabin built in the late 1920s. The surrounding park, with its rolling hills, steep valleys, and breathtaking vistas, is Indiana's largest and often claimed to be its most beautiful. It was always a place of comfort and peace for our family. We were sitting on the screened-in porch, staring down the slope of green leading away from the cabin toward one of the most gorgeous expanses of southern Indiana's rolling hills, when I told Charlotte about the call. She turned to me and said, "We all saw this coming. We all knew you were going to get this call. And he would be smart to pick you." Things only a daughter would say. During that weekend, as we talked as a family of that possibility, it became clear to me that the only way it would work, the only way I could be a partner of Donald Trump, whom I did not know beyond the two brief meetings, would be if our family was able to meet and get to know him, find out who he really was and what his family was like. And since the Republican National Convention was just a few weeks away, it seemed fairly obvious that there wasn't enough time for that.

Steve called again on June 16. I was transparent: I told him I was certain that there were better choices than me, candidates who knew Trump better, but I wanted to help. At the end of eight years of Barack Obama as president and with the possibility of another eight with Hillary Clinton, the Democratic candidate, who was already hugely favored, I thought the country was in trouble. It could not endure even another four years of leaders who believed that there was no problem facing America that couldn't be solved with more government, more spending, and less freedom.

Responding to his first question, I told Steve that I had no problem leaving my current job if I thought I could help the country. But in the event that I was asked to join the ticket, I told him I wouldn't be able to provide a yes or no answer unless my family and I had time to get to know Trump and his family. I needed to see if we could work together, and I needed to know what the job description was, which is defined every four years by the president. I told him very respectfully that I needed to know those things before we went any further. Steve said he would relay the message.

The phone rang again the next day. "He loved your answer," Steve said. "He wants you and your family to come to Bedminster." While we waited to hear from the Trump team when that would be, I focused on work at the statehouse and my campaign for reelection. On July 1, I was in Newburgh playing golf with some supporters at Victoria National Golf Club when a member of my team interrupted. Trump's team had called and wanted us to fly to Bedminster for Independence Day. I walked off the course, leaving the game with eight holes still to play. I did promise my companions, who knew where I was heading and why, that if it all worked out I would come back someday and finish the game. I kept that promise five summers later with the same golfers on the same course. My game hadn't improved.

Karen, Charlotte, and I flew to New Jersey that night, a Friday. We arrived at the golf club before the Trumps did and settled at a tall table on the balcony overlooking the golf course to order dinner. The club manager stopped by to let us know that Donald and his wife, Melania, were on their way. He asked if we were okay. I told him we were. And we were not expecting to see them until the morning. He replied, "You know how he is!" "I have no idea how he is," I responded. "Well, he just wants things to be right," the manager said, adding "Mr. Trump has called three times to make sure everything is okay." It was my first glimpse of the insistent and personal attention that I would see him give to important matters for the next four years.

We didn't see them that night, but we spent much of the following day together. Donald wanted time to talk with Charlotte, so we added a breakfast to the schedule. First thing, Karen, Charlotte, and I headed to a sunny room in the clubhouse for a light brunch and were joined by Donald, dressed for the round of golf we had scheduled for a late-morning tee time. From the outset, he peppered my daughter with questions about her time in college, her generation, and, of course, her dad. He engaged her without a hint of condescension, and she responded with her characteristic candor, not the least bit intimidated by his celebrity status. The four of us had a great conversation.

At one point, I said that his message to working people reminded me of a book by the historian Amity Shlaes: *The Forgotten Man: A New History of the Great Depression*. The book chronicled Franklin Roosevelt's distortion of the term "forgotten man" to advance his welfare state agenda, when the forgotten man of that time was actually the workingman who wasn't looking for a handout but just wanted a job. No sooner had I used the term than Trump reached for a napkin to write down the title, saying, "The forgotten man, that's good. We could use that," to which my daughter offered, "Well, it would be the forgotten man and woman." At that, Donald stared at her briefly, nodded approvingly, and wrote the addition on the napkin.

Since we were at Bedminster, Trump invited me to play a round of golf at the Trump National Golf Club. I love golf but am not much of a player. Donald, on the other hand, is a 7 handicap. We took on a team of two scratch players and began the match with a minor miracle. Given my level of play, it was agreed that I would have two strokes a hole to reduce my score and keep things competitive. On the first hole, I managed to finish with one stroke over the par scores of the other three and won the hole, eliciting some skeptical looks from the other team. On hole two, I was able to drive the green on the par three and one-putt for a net score of 0. Donald was ecstatic and proceeded to announce at that moment and in recounting the story in the years ahead that I was the only man ever to shoot a zero on the second hole at Trump National. The other players thought they had been had. I would often say it was proof of the existence of God.

Though I enjoyed my brief flourish of golf magic, right on cue, my normal game showed up. It was a close match. While we were golfing, I asked what he had in mind for his potential vice president. He repeated the word "active." He mentioned my experience as a congressional leader, on the House Foreign Affairs Committee, and as governor. He asked about Indiana's string of successes. How had we managed to balance budgets? How had we cut taxes? He wanted a partner who would be a presence on the Hill, around the country, and around the globe, playing a part in foreign policy.

Toward the end of the game, we were alone in the golf cart, traveling along the immaculate greens, when he put the question to me. "What do you think will happen?" he asked. "We can take these guys," I answered. "I don't mean the golf game!" he shot back. "You're going to be the president of the United States of America," I told him. Donald tapped the brake. The cart came to a halt, and he looked right at me. "Well, that's pretty definitive," he said. Then I told him, "And that's irrespective of who you choose to be your running mate."

When he asked why I could be so sure, I told him what I had seen back in Indiana. As a candidate, Donald Trump was reaching, connecting with, and inspiring people who had been left out in the cold by both Democrats and Republicans. He was offering not just an agenda that put American jobs and American workers first but also a style of leadership that was distinctly American. His message was delivered with a brashness that sometimes—well, often—shocked. That was nothing new in the history of US politics, though. Earlier that year, I had read a book by Jon Meacham entitled *American Lion: Andrew Jackson in the White House.* It was no real surprise to me that President Trump had a portrait and statue of Old Hickory in the Oval Office all four years of his administration. Like Jackson, Trump was a counterpuncher; if attacked—and he was constantly—he didn't turn the other cheek. The political class feigned outrage at his combativeness, but the voters appreciated it; they saw him as not just fighting to win but fighting for them. Beyond that, though, was a sense of optimism and confidence in what the United States was capable of. I knew he was going to prevail in the fall.

Our day at Bedminster provided a clue as to why. He spent most of his time talking to the men and women working on the grounds and in the club—the people who made the place run with their hands. It was clear that he motivated them and made them feel seen and respected. That was the secret of his success, first as a businessman and now as a politician: he didn't talk to the contractors, he talked to the subcontractors. I understood it. I had seen it before. My dad had had the same quality. He was just as comfortable talking to the mechanic working at one of his gas stations as he was with the CEO of Marathon. With that background, I could see that Trump understood voters in a way that more conventional politicians couldn't.

During the discussion in the golf cart, he asked why I was interested in being vice president. On top of telling him that I believed he could do a great deal of good for the country and I believed I could help him, there were two other matters. I had run for Congress in 2000 because I was alarmed by the way Bill and Hillary Clinton had diminished the presidency with a lurid scandal and the fundraising tied to China by the Democratic Party in the 1990s. Sixteen years later, the Clintons had their bags packed, ready to return to the White House, and China was now the United States' chief geopolitical foe. I told Trump that the Clintons could never be in power again. Aware of my history opposing the Clintons on the radio and in my first election, he said, "Well, this has really come full circle for you, hasn't it?"

Our visit ended with dinner on the patio overlooking the beautiful grounds as the sun went down. There we sat, just the four of us, at a table in the middle of the restaurant talking like old friends for hours as club members dining nearby tried not to stare. On paper it seemed a strange gathering: the billionaire mogul and his supermodel wife breaking bread with the small-town lawyer and his schoolteacher wife. We probably looked like the odd couple of couples. Everyone was comfortable, though; the rapport was natural.

They spoke to us with gentleness about our faith; Trump told me he was a believer, too. They asked us if we prayed often, and we told them we had just done so. We had prayed for them just before we had come to dinner. The Trumps were surprised and caught a little off guard, but they were touched. We talked about our lives, not just politics or the election. The Trumps seemed fascinated by the fact that we had followed a calling into public service, forgoing the opportunity to build financial security. Despite our differences—and our different bottom lines—we had plenty in common. He had spent a decade on television hosting a reality show; I had spent years on radio and TV as well. The audience sizes were, of course, just a little different, but it was common ground. He spoke about Queens, New York, where he had grown up. As far as it seemed from Indiana, Trump explained that it really wasn't. He didn't deny his own family's wealth but explained that Queens is a working-class borough and not that different from say, Terre Haute, a city in southwest Indiana he was familiar with.

As we were preparing to call it an evening, he gave me some parting words. "Whatever happens, this has been good for you," he reassured me. I had a bright future, he said, and if nothing else, he would find a place in his cabinet for me. "That's fine, it's been an honor," I responded. On the flight back to Indiana, the three of us reflected on the visit. Charlotte remarked, "He was Trump, but he was nice." She said he was the same person she had seen on TV. It was not an act. He had shown real kindness to her and our family in the time we had spent together. She was impressed. Karen said, " I really liked them," but in a moment of wifely candor said, "but there is no way he's picking you." That hurt. She interpreted his parting words at dinner as a soft letdown. When I thought about it, her words made sense, as they usually do. Either way, it was out of our hands. We resolved to put it to prayer and trust the Lord for the outcome. There would be no lobbying. I actually forbade my staff and political team to pursue the vice presidential slot on my behalf. If we were called, we would serve, but I was determined to put it all in God's hands. As the prophet Jeremiah wrote, "Should you then seek great things for yourself? Do not seek them."

A few weeks later, on July 12, the Trump campaign stopped in Westfield, a town just north of Indianapolis, for a rally. I was asked to speak and cheerfully obliged. There were few updates on the selection process, which involved submitting materials to the campaign for vetting, but the Trumps had asked that Karen and I fly to New York the next day to meet the rest of the Trump family. The candidate was still deliberating, and we were in the mix.

That night in Indiana, the explosive impact he had on voters was on full display. The crowds were only growing. Afterward Karen and I joined Trump and his middle son, Eric, for dinner at the Capital Grille in downtown Indianapolis. The Trumps had rooms upstairs in the Conrad Hotel, just a few blocks from the statehouse. Donald had not yet appeared, so I had some alone time with Eric. I asked a personal question, in a fairly direct manner: "What's the deal with you kids?" He understood what I meant.

He told me, "We worked." He said that he and his siblings had worked at construction sites from an early age. As a family, they believed that all work was valuable. Their income was not blue collar, but their work ethic certainly was. Again, it explained his dad's connection with voters. I connected with it as well. At my parents' urging, as a teenager I had washed dishes at Gene's Cafeteria, the home of Columbus's finest fried chicken and pies, and pumped gas at one of my dad's gas stations. It had taught me the importance of work— that all honest work is honorable—and given me the ability to relate with people, no matter their background. The Trump kids had had the same experience.

Karen and I had not yet met any of Eric's brothers or sisters, hence the planned trip the next day. There was a hitch, though. That night, Trump Force One, the candidate's Boeing 757, had a flat tire at Indianapolis International Airport. For the record, I had nothing to do with that.

An alternate plan was quickly hatched: the Trump kids and their spouses would come to Indianapolis the next day. We suggested a brunch, which the Trumps agreed to, but we needed a venue. Without thinking, I suggested the Governor's Residence.

It may be the second smallest governor's residence in the country, but it is a beautiful and accommodating house. The state, quite rightly, doesn't provide its chief executive with a chef or any culinary service, though. So after the dinner with Donald and Eric at the Capital Grille concluded at 11:00 p.m., Karen and I went home and sprang into action. We asked our residence manager to get a hold of the Illinois Street Food Emporium and ordered a breakfast quiche. We brought down our own coffeepot from the private quarters of the house. We set the table, but it needed some flowers. So at midnight, by the light of our cell phones, we picked flowers from the gardens. In the morning we got up early and put it all together, just in the nick of time.

Donald, along with Don Jr., Ivanka, and Ivanka's husband, Jared Kushner, arrived a little after 9:00 a.m. Karen and I served breakfast and poured the coffee. It apparently made an impression. They seemed to appreciate the personal attention and down-home feel of the morning. We sat together at a long table in the residence's dining room for a couple of hours talking. The Trump kids were disarming, easy to talk to. It was evident how much they cared about their dad and that they were a real family. There was no faking it. It was also very clear to me as the prospective running mate how important their approval would be. As we sat sipping coffee after breakfast, it was the younger Trumps who asked most of the questions; Donald himself did relatively little talking, interjecting only to push his kids to get the answers they were looking for from us. After a serious question from Ivanka he would follow up with "What do you mean by that?" Trump was listening carefully.

The week prior I had bought and read a copy of *The Art of the Deal*, Trump's first book, from 1987. It didn't seem a bad idea to give it a read. As he was leaving, we wandered into the small, paneled study on the first floor of the Governor's Residence and the candidate spotted the book on my typically cluttered desk. "What did you think?" he inquired. I told him I had enjoyed it, and then I grabbed a pen and asked him to autograph it. I thought I wasn't going to see him for a while and I'd better take the chance to get it signed while I had it. He quickly dashed off "Best Wishes, Donald Trump" on the inside cover page, and that book was displayed in my West Wing office during all four years of his presidency.

By 10:30 a.m., he and his family were gone, out the door past the crowd of reporters waiting for some word on the vice presidential sweepstakes. The fact that he had brought his children to Indiana, that he valued their counsel, had been reassuring to me. It's how the Pence family operates as well. I wasn't going to make a monumental decision unless my wife and kids felt good about it, and neither was he. He'd told me he would make a decision that day. I had no expectations. There were other contenders, men such as Newt Gingrich and Chris Christie, who had known him better and for much longer.

The rest of the day disappeared. Then at 7:00 p.m., Nick Ayers, our lead advisor during the selection process, received a call: I would be getting a phone call from Trump, who was in California, late that night. In advance of that, Karen and I gathered on the couches in the private quarters on the second floor of the Governor's Residence with Charlotte, Audrey, Michael's fiancée, Sarah, and Michael on the phone at his Marine Corps base in Mississippi. We told the kids that if we were asked to join the ticket, we would say yes. We prayed; we took it to the Lord and asked him to bless the decision. We felt peace, and we waited for the call.

At 10:00 p.m., I was in the study, a small wood-paneled room full of books, sitting in a brown leather chair, when my phone rang. I picked up the phone and heard a now-familiar voice. "Mike, it's gonna be great!" he boomed and then plowed ahead. "But we are going to have to work," he continued without pause. "I'll go north, you go south, we can turn this country around!" It was more than five minutes before he took a breath and I interjected, "Donald, if there is a question in there, the answer is yes." He stopped for a moment. "Oh. Yes, of course I want you to do it!" Then he went right back to rallying his newly selected running mate for the relentless campaign we would wage for the next 118 days.

CHAPTER SIXTEEN

Hoosier, Hummingbird, and Harmony

Who am I, Sovereign Lord, and what is my family,
that you have brought me this far?
—2 Samuel 7:18

The next morning, July 14, we were off to New York, but under a cloak of secrecy; Trump wanted to make the announcement himself. Three separate cars were dispatched from the residence, and three separate flight plans were booked in order to elude the press. Karen, Charlotte, and I crouched in the back of a staff member's car, escaping to the airport without detection. We landed at Teterboro Airport in New Jersey and then headed to Manhattan. Helicopters were circling in the sky overhead. I had made a mistake and not worn a hat when we disembarked the plane, and reporters had spotted a middle-aged man with white hair.

While I was headed into the city, news broke of a terrorist attack in France. An Islamic extremist, the world learned, had driven a truck full of explosives into a crowd celebrating Bastille Day in the city of Nice, killing more than eighty people and injuring hundreds more. Once we reached our hotel in New York, I talked with Trump on the phone. He felt that the announcement introducing me as his running mate should be delayed; it was inappropriate in light of the news from France. I agreed. But with no announcement imminent, rumors began to swirl in the press and among staff, perhaps coming from other candidates, that Trump was having second thoughts.

As I had agreed to run as Trump's vice president, I had also made plans to withdraw from Indiana's governor's race. I had already filed the appropriate paperwork to run. Now, in order to withdraw, I had to submit additional paperwork. And I had to have it done by noon the next day, July 15. And once the paperwork was filed, I was out. No turning back. I had also informed my lieutenant governor, Eric Holcomb, that I would not be running for a second term. That had opened the door for the tall, cowboy boot–wearing Hoosier to seek his own term as governor. He intended to run and had to file the paperwork by the same deadline.

I didn't doubt Trump's word, but I explained to him the delicate matter of timing of my statutory commitment to get off the ballot by noon the next day; once I was off, I was off. No problem, he said, I'll just tweet an announcement. "I am pleased to announce that I have chosen Governor Mike Pence as my Vice Presidential running mate. News conference tomorrow at 11:00 A.M.," he tweeted Friday morning. "Honored to join @realDonaldTrump and work to make America great again," I tweeted back. And with that, on July 15, 2016, I became the first vice presidential nominee ever announced on Twitter. Back in Indiana, the paperwork was filed within minutes of the deadline.

That afternoon, we were whisked across Manhattan in a small motorcade from our hotel to Trump Tower for an afternoon visit with Donald and Melania. Arriving at the building's entrance on Fifth Avenue, Karen, Charlotte, and I were taken aback by a wall of cameras and reporters shouting questions as we walked into the building. I had seen crowds of press before in my career, but nothing like this. It was pretty overwhelming. We rode the elevator to the top floor of Trump Tower, and the Trumps greeted us warmly as we entered their penthouse apartment. They invited us to make ourselves comfortable in the ornate living room with antique furniture and gold-colored trim, which was easier said than done for this modest Hoosier family, but they set us at ease quickly. Sitting in the living room of their spacious penthouse, Trump laughed about the speculation over his having second thoughts, even joking with Charlotte, "Your dad told me that God wanted him to do this if I asked him. I am not going against *that*!"

The next morning, we gathered in the ballroom of the Hilton Midtown for the formal announcement. Trump took the stage alone, ten

American flags behind him and five rows of reporters in front, cameras recording and clicking. He called it "a wonderful day" and explained that he was there to introduce the man who "will be *my partner on this campaign and in the White House*." Then he took a detour. He spoke about the Islamic terror attack in France; he blasted the foreign policy blunders of Hillary Clinton as Obama's secretary of state. Among the improvised material he interjected praise for my record in Indiana. He also spoke of unfair trade deals and open borders and promised to cut taxes and reduce regulations. He mentioned his overwhelming support among evangelical Christians and finally mused about Lyndon Johnson. "Okay, back to Mike Pence," he continued, returning to the business of the day. Then he hit NAFTA and talked about bringing jobs back to the United States and fighting for veterans. Twenty-eight minutes into the announcement, he called me to the stage.

I thanked Trump and Melania and accepted the invitation to be his partner, expressing my gratitude to God for his amazing grace and to Karen for her unending support and promising to do my part to make Trump's campaign promise to make America great again a reality. Then I got out of there. Backstage, Trump pulled me aside. "Was I okay?" he asked. "You know what I was doing, right?" I did. The press had arrived expecting to cover a quick introduction of a vice presidential candidate and had been treated to an almost thirty-minute-long campaign speech. They couldn't cut away; he could have introduced me at any minute, and they would have missed it. It was another example of how savvy Trump was about the political press, despite never having run for office before. He saw the opportunity for free national coverage of a campaign speech, and he took it.

Shortly after I officially joined the ticket, I received a phone call from Paul Ryan, the speaker of the House and the previous Republican vice presidential candidate. Paul and I had been close friends during my years in Congress. We had attended a Bible study together and had both been members of the conservative Republican Study Committee, and even though we had differed on some of the big fights over Medicare and the Wall Street bailout, those fights had never undercut a friendship that continues to this day. On the call, Paul was characteristically gracious and congratulatory, offering simple advice. Don't stress the day-to-day of the campaign, he said. A vice presidential candidate has only three big things to focus on: the introduction, the convention speech, and the debate. I had made it through the first one unscathed. But the second one, the biggest speech of my life, loomed ahead. It was, in fact, four days away. The sheer enormity of it was like nothing I had experienced before. If not for my faith and my wife, it would have been overwhelming.

When we arrived at the Republican National Convention in Cleveland, Ohio, I felt like Alice in Wonderland, but it was our new reality. The Secret Service had told us we would have more security than we had been used to in the governor's office, but it didn't really hit us until the next day. Traveling to a lunch during the convention, we walked into an alley and saw what seemed like twenty SUVs surrounded by police officers. I turned to the agent escorting us and asked, "Are all those cars for us?" He smiled and said, "Yes, sir, those are your cars," and told us we'd better get used to it. It was unreal. We also were told that we would have to pick out code names for the Secret Service to use on radio transmissions, but they would all have to begin with the same letter. Karen asked if she could be "Hummingbird." So of course, I asked them to refer to me as "Hoosier." Later that day we learned that the Secret Service had given Charlotte the code name "Harmony," which we thought perfectly described the role she would play in the campaign.

With just days remaining until I accepted the nomination, I got to work on my acceptance speech. I was offered and accepted the help of two talented speechwriters who had drafted major convention speeches before. As we wrote and rehearsed in two hotel rooms, something was missing. As good as the writers were, we were just not hitting the mark, not capturing my voice or the energy or urgency I had seen in the crowds who came out to cheer on Trump. At some point Jared, whom I quickly developed a good working relationship with, came by to see how the speech was coming along. It wasn't quite there yet, I told him. He had heard the speech I had given at the rally in Indiana a day before the Trump family had flown out to meet us. "Just do that one, it was great," he suggested. Taking his advice, I used that speech as a road map to draft an almost entirely different set of remarks. I put on my headphones, listening to music from the soundtrack of *Rudy*, one of my favorite movies, based on the story of Daniel "Rudy" Ruettiger, an underdog walk-on member of the Notre Dame football team, and started writing. With Charlotte's help we finished the new draft that night.

I knew, remembering Paul Ryan's advice, that it was the moment to introduce myself to Americans, to let them know who I was: a Christian, a conservative, and a Republican, in that order. I was going to let them know my big family had lived the American Dream, to tell them about that cornfield in the backyard, to let them know about my heroes JFK, MLK, and EJP—Edward J. Pence, my father. I wanted them to meet Karen and our kids, and my mom, too. And to tell those gathered at Quicken Loans Arena and watching at home that Donald Trump needed backup in his race with Hillary Clinton and I was there to provide it.

I didn't have to create eloquent passages; I just had to report what I had seen: that Americans were tired, tired of being told that this is as good as it gets, tired of being told, as Ronald Reagan said, "that a little intellectual elite in a far-distant capital can plan our lives for us better than we can plan them ourselves"; that we had to resolve right then and there that Hillary Clinton would never be president of the United States; that whether it came to America's economy, its foreign policy, or leaving mountains of debt for future generations, we could do better.

I told folks that we had done better in Indiana; that Donald Trump would do better for all Americans, not just the ones who stereotypically voted Republican but also union members, African Americans, Hispanic Americans—all Americans. I shared with them what I had seen up close with the Trump family and that I had recently heard a farmer back in Bartholomew County say he didn't know what to think about Trump, but added, "You can't fake good kids." I was going to tell them that at that moment, the only way to end the failed status quo was to turn to an independent spirit, a man who never turned his back on the men and women who make America grow and who said out loud what most Americans were thinking.

When Wednesday, July 20, arrived, I was happy with the draft.

Writing a speech and delivering it were separate matters, however. I had given many, many speeches over the course of my life, from the Optimist Club events in the backroom of Gene's Cafeteria in Columbus to the House floor in Congress to the Indiana Statehouse. But never one of this magnitude. I was anxious, nervous as a cat in a room full of rocking chairs. There was no margin for error, no chance for a do-over. Backstage, as the hour neared, I prayed—only to be interrupted. Two hours before I was set to speak, my team conveyed the news that Ted Cruz, who was set to speak that evening at the invitation of Donald Trump, might not endorse the candidate—the very thing he had been invited to do. There was talk that Cruz's speech could be canceled or rescheduled, but I felt he had earned the right to speak and I believed he would do the right thing. I was wrong. When he took to the stage, Cruz gave a fiery conservative speech and did not formally endorse Trump, encouraging delegates only to "vote your conscience." It was a pointed jab at the nominee, and the slight was not lost on the convention delegates. Boos rang out across the hall. Tempers flared backstage. Newt Gingrich, who was scheduled to speak after Cruz, wasn't moved. "I've got this," he said. Then the old master reworked his speech on the fly, hit the stage, and told voters, to roaring applause, that if they were to vote their conscience, the only possible choice was the Trump-Pence ticket. It was brilliant. There is nobody like Newt Gingrich.

There was still teeth gnashing and anger over Cruz's remarks, in the arena and backstage. Months later Ted would apologize to me, insisting that he hadn't intended the slight, but the damage was done. At that moment, I didn't have the time to think about it—since his refusal to endorse Trump had brought a sense of angst to the crowd, only adding more pressure to my task. The crowd was fired up when Paul Ryan, following Newt, walked onstage and introduced me. I came out from behind the curtain, shook Paul's hand, then walked to the right and went with my eyes to where I always do, to Indiana. I searched the crowd for my state's delegation, made eye contact with them, pointed right at them. They went wild. It softened my heart. Then I walked to my left and located my family in the crowd, looking on with love and support. A peace settled into my heart. I was home, among family and friends. I walked back to the podium and began my speech with humility and gratitude, saying, "On behalf of my family, here and gone, I accept your nomination to run and serve as vice president of the United States of America." The cheering in the hall was as loud as I have ever heard.

The Republican convention wrapped on the night of July 21. Then we hit the trail, spending three days campaigning together as a ticket before parting ways and traveling across the country separately. Riding in the car to the Cleveland airport, Donald tapped me on the shoulder. "That speech you just gave, I need you giving it all over the country!" he said. "So I'm giving you the big plane. I could have given you the small or midsized plane, but no, I'm giving you the big one." He was half joking, half serious. Our "big plane" was a Boeing 737-700 with sixty-four seats and the Trump-Pence campaign logo wrapped on its side; we called it Trump Force Two, a reference to the candidate's plane, Trump Force One.

As the car drew near to the airport, Trump grew reflective about the campaign ahead. "We are really going to have to work," he admitted in a departure from his usual exuberance. "This is my last chance. You will have other chances, you're young, but this is my last chance." I knew he meant something much bigger than his chance at the presidency. "Can I tell you two things and you will just agree to believe that I mean both, because we don't know each other well?" I asked. He agreed. "I think this is my last chance, too," I said. "That's a good attitude!" he interjected. "It's not my attitude," I went on. "I honestly believe this is my last chance, and, secondly, I think this might be the country's last chance. Eight more years of the direction we've been headed in under Obama, and this won't be the country I grew up in anymore." Trump's eyes lit up. He slapped me on the knee and said, "That's why I'm running!"

We both headed back home for the weekend and met up on Monday for joint campaign appearances in Virginia, North Carolina, and Florida. After three days on the road, we gathered a final time on his plane, where Karen suggested that we say a prayer before going our separate ways. Trump readily stretched out his arms and said, "C'mon!" and we huddled together in the main cabin of his airplane.

Karen offered a prayer for safe travels, good health, and victory. Some-one standing nearby captured the scene in a photograph that went viral on the internet, followed by the usual cynical skepticism that it had been staged to make a political point. But that wasn't so; the photo captured a spontaneous moment of the three of us appealing to God for his grace and protection, and it remains one of my favorite images of the campaign. The convention was over. The campaign was on, and we were off.

Often a vice presidential campaign is an extension of the larger presidential campaign and runs on staffers and managers assigned by the top-billed candidate. That doesn't always work, as the staffers or advisors don't understand and don't have the time to get to know the second-tier candidate. Sarah Palin's campaign in 2008, when she was saddled with staffers from John McCain's campaign, led to chaos and backbiting that were a great disservice to her family and proven rec-ord as the Alaska governor. Dan Quayle's campaign in 1988 was filled with Bush people, who didn't understand the young Hoosier's genu-ine talent for campaigning. But 2016 was different.

As a candidate with no prior experience running a political race, Trump wasn't beholden to any traditions. There was a freewheeling, entrepreneurial approach to the campaign, one that reflected his background in business rather than politics. In early discussions about campaign staff, I asked if I could bring a few members of my own team on board. Trump said sure and that I could have a few members of his team, but that was it. "Don't take this the wrong way. One of the reasons we picked you was because we liked your people," he said. So uncharacteristically, I was able to assemble a vice presidential team from my gubernatorial campaign staff. Nick Ayers, a young political phenom who had been the head of the Republican Governors Asso-ciation, took a lead role. Marc Short, a gifted strategist, veteran of the conservative movement, and my former chief of staff in the House Republican Conference, joined the team as well. Josh Pitcock, a tal-ented administrator from my days on Capitol Hill, took a hiatus from running Indiana's Washington, DC, office to keep the trains running on time in the campaign. Our pollster, Kellyanne Conway, and our campaign manager, Marty Obst, rounded out Team Pence. It was like old home week from day one. Kellyanne would eventually take the helm of the Trump campaign and become the first woman to manage a winning presidential campaign in American history.

In addition to trusted staff, our daughter Charlotte also joined us on the campaign trail. She had just graduated from DePaul University and was taking a year off before beginning her graduate studies. As she explained it, she had discussed it with Michael and Audrey and they had concluded that "somebody needs to be there to watch Mom and Dad." And she was.

Charlotte (or Harmony) traveled with us for 105 of the 107 days of the campaign and regularly helped me draft speeches and statements for the press. She was a constant presence on Trump Force Two and a favorite of the staff, the flight crew, and even the press. She even helped my staff keep me on schedule. Anytime I saw Charlotte approach me to tell me it was time to move on to the next meeting, I knew she had been sent by the numerous staffers I had ignored as I was engrossed in a conversation, interview, or handshaking after a rally. What a trooper. She would go on to write a book chronicling her life growing up in a family in politics and on the 2016 campaign trail entitled *Where You Go: Life Lessons from My Father*, and she is a much better writer than her dad.

There was very little shared staff between the presidential and vice presidential operations. Though there was not much in the way of directives from the top, our staffs were in continuous communication, prioritizing our travel, and we would often look at where Trump was, find a state where the campaign needed to be where he did not have any events on that day, and point the plane in that direction. In the days after the convention, I would campaign with Trump once every ten days, as we were still getting to know each another. We would never be on television or onstage when he was; if Trump was doing an event at noon, we would plan one in another state for 2:00 p.m. Initially I was hesitant to call him regularly, not wanting to be presumptuous, but I quickly learned that with Trump, more is more. Early on, he and I developed the habit of talking by phone every day. Either he would call me or I would call him. It was a practice we would continue on the days either one of us was traveling through all four years in the

White House, and I believe it contributed mightily to the close working relationship we forged. Every time I answered his call, I would hear "Mistah Vice President" coming from the other end. Not playing along, I always called him "Donald."

Despite our different personalities and backgrounds, we became friends. I was always struck during long plane flights by his attentiveness and considerate demeanor toward me and my family. Walking through the cabin of the airplane, he would invariably stop to ask me, Karen, and Charlotte if we were comfortable, if we had everything we needed—food, drink, or a blanket—reflecting a penchant for hospitality that probably came from a lifetime in the hotel business. It was refreshing and unexpected.

During one of our early travels together, Trump was sitting in his usual spot, facing backward at a small table in the middle of the plane, while Karen and I were on a couch across the way. Fox News was on the big-screen television to the rear of the main cabin and was playing a documentary about Harry Truman. Trump, busy working through a tall stack of newspapers and memos, popped his head up. "Mike, do you ever think they will be running footage of us like this in a hundred years?" he asked. "Yes, very humbling," I answered. The images on the screen were of Truman's whistle-stop campaign in 1948 against Thomas Dewey, the highly accomplished and highly favored governor of New York. Nobody thought that Truman could win the election; the media had decided that Dewey was going to be president. Trump snapped his fingers and asked, "So how did he do it?" already knowing the answer. "He outworked 'em," I said. "That's right!" Trump shouted. He looked around at the campaign staff also on the plane. "Did you hear what he said? That's what we're gonna do, we are gonna outwork 'em!" In the back of my mind, I could still hear my dad's advice about making my way at Ray's Marathon: *Outwork 'em*. That was our only option.

CHAPTER SEVENTEEN

"Knock the Cover off the Ball"

A gentle answer turns away wrath.
—Proverbs 15:1

From the convention to the election, a constant of the Trump-Pence campaign was a sense in the media and from virtually every political pundit that we were doomed to defeat. Polls, both nationally and in swing states, predicted that Hillary Clinton would be the forty-fifth president of the United States. Some even suggested that she would be elected by a wide margin. I never bought it. The pathway to our victory, though, went through several industrial midwestern states, ones that no Republican had won in recent elections or even decades; ones where Trump's message of American renewal resonated. My first solo campaign stop was in Waukesha, Wisconsin, on July 27. For the next three months, I traveled across not just Wisconsin but also Michigan, Pennsylvania, Ohio, and Iowa, not only firing up the conservative parts of those states but also winning the votes of midwesterners who had voted for Barack Obama in the last two elections.

In August, Karen and I visited the Iowa State Fair, accompanied by Governor Terry Branstad, the longest-serving governor in US history. We were no stranger to state fairs; Indiana's is a beloved summer tradition. But Iowa's was a spectacle, even to the seasoned state fair goer. The highlight, at the end of a Disney World–like line, was the butter cow, a life-size sculpture of a cow made of, yes, butter. Terry, Karen, and I walked along the line of those eagerly awaiting a glimpse of the butter cow, shaking hands and introducing ourselves. "It's nice to meet you, but I hope you lose," one Iowan politely told me. "Well, it's a free country," I replied, adding "Thanks for not being unpleasant."

Then he looked at Terry and told him the same thing as nicely as possible: "I hope you lose, too." The governor was unfazed and replied, "I never lose." The man's eyebrows went up as the governor went on, saying, "No, seriously, I've run twenty times, and I have never lost an election. You will be disappointed." The man was not angry or offended, and neither were we. I'd seen it before, and I've seen it since: America's political debates may be loud and rancorous, but away from the internet and television, they are most often respectful and good natured.

My primary task during those travels was to carry and deliver Trump's message that the status quo, whether it came to jobs and trade, the United States' relationship with China, its immigration policies, its foreign policy, or the way it treated its veterans, just wasn't working for everyday Americans. Sending Donald Trump to the White House, I promised, would be a way to grab Washington by its lapels and demand that the government be as good as its people; that it put America first. Of course, that was delivered in my slightly more mellow, less flashy midwestern manner. I shared Donald's passion and conviction for the stakes in the election, but we didn't always agree on tactics.

Hillary Clinton accepted her party's presidential nomination during the Democratic National Convention in late July. On the last day of the convention, a couple named Khizr and Ghazala Khan gave a speech critical of Trump. Their son, Humayun, was an army officer who had been killed in action in Iraq in 2004. The Khans are a Gold Star family, a distinction dating to World War I given to families who have lost loved ones on active service. Donald Trump, as his opponents and voters had already discovered, always punches back. And during an interview with George Stephanopoulos, he attacked the Khans in a way that many thought had crossed over a third rail of US politics. To Trump, the Khans had stepped into the arena, they had criticized him, they were fair game. But they weren't. No Gold Star family will ever be.

In the short time we had worked together, I had already learned how deeply Trump cared for our military and their families. He was outraged by years of scandal in the Department of Veterans Affairs that had seen veterans die while waiting for access to care. Our first joint appearance was at the Veterans of Foreign Wars convention in Charlotte, North Carolina, where he committed our administration to reform. Before we left office, the president had signed historic legislation and the Department of Veterans Affairs was enjoying a 90 percent approval rating. Backstage I also saw the way he made time for veterans, how he showed them warmth and was genuinely humbled in their presence. It was what I would observe in private moments with the president and American veterans for the next four years.

When it came to the Khans, I told him that Gold Star families have a special place in the hearts of the American people. I conveyed my own experiences with them. As governor of Indiana, I had hosted a private ceremony for Gold Star families every Friday before Memorial Day, the weekend the Indy 500 takes place. I had stood at grave sites with those families, I had handed the folded flag to those mothers and fathers. Time may pass, but for those families, their grief and sense of loss never will. That was our first disagreement since I had joined the ticket. Donald listened to me respectfully and took it in with little comment. I don't think I changed his mind about the Khans, but in the years that followed, seeing the way he cherished Gold Star families, I think he got the message.

No matter how hard we worked, how much ground we covered, poll after poll showed our opponents with a lead. To the press, we were going down and going down hard. We were told that even Indiana was in play, which I never believed. Our opponents believed it, though.

On September 9, Hillary Clinton, speaking at a fundraiser in New York City, said that half of our supporters belonged in a "basket of deplorables." She called them "racist, sexist, homophobic, xenophobic, Islamophobic—you name it." She said they were "irredeemable." She also claimed, wrongly, that I had signed a law legalizing discrimination in Indiana. That was the same woman who had once described Indianapolis as "Indianoplace," so it was no surprise that she would be quick to distort our laws or my record. But the most shocking part of her message was that she, a candidate for national office, would write off tens of millions of Americans as "irredeemable," a judgment that contradicted our nation's history and our Judeo-Christian heritage. It's one that nobody had given her or any politician the right to make.

Such disdain for voters, delivered in a prepared speech, not improvised remarks, revealed an incredible confidence in the certainty of her victory. The following morning, speaking at a Values Voter Summit—an audience of those so-called deplorables—in Washington, DC, I vented my anger and threw out my scripted remarks. Our supporters were not deplorables, I said, and directly addressing the Democratic nominee, I said, "Hillary, they are not a basket of anything, they are Americans, and they deserve your respect!" The crowd roared, and the media ran the sound bite coast to coast.

I was genuinely offended by what she had said about the millions of people rallying behind Donald Trump. I was with them every day; I had known them from Indiana long before I had accepted Donald's charge. They were farmers, police officers, steel workers, and mechanics. Many were veterans. They were not racists or homophobes. They were fellow citizens who simply disagreed with Hillary Clinton. But it wasn't even the "deplorables" insult that was most offensive or that truly got my Irish up. It was that Clinton had dared to claim that some Americans were beyond redemption. That in itself was un-American. This is a nation of second chances, of fresh starts. That moment of honesty from the Democratic campaign was a fulcrum moment in the election and US history.

After the election, bewildered commentators attempted to figure out how they had been so wrong in declaring Clinton's victory inevitable by latching on to fake stories about Russian collusion. They should have contemplated Hillary Clinton's insulting half the country. It fired up our already energetic crowds, full of Americans who had not voted for Republicans ever before or in a very long time. If they were deplorable, I was proud to be among them.

My days in the summer and fall were beyond full. Not only was I campaigning for vice president and being a surrogate for Donald Trump, I was still governor of Indiana, still taking briefings every morning, heading back to the Indiana Statehouse every Monday, then hitting the road for the rest of the week before returning home on Sunday; I had a long-standing rule of never campaigning on Sunday.

Those were fifteen-hour days that usually ended at a different hotel than where they had begun. There were two to three events a day, meetings with supporters and the press. Then I was up the next morning to do local live television. It was up early, out late. And though the race preoccupied so much of my time and energy, there were priorities higher than the presidential campaign. When a tornado devastated the town of Kokomo in August, I left the campaign trail and headed home to be with the Hoosiers whose lives had been upturned, who had lost their homes. And as we crisscrossed the country on the campaign trail, Karen was traveling the state as Indiana's official bicentennial ambassador and played a key role in celebrating Indiana's two hundredth birthday in 2016. It was a busy time for both of us.

The days flew by, and the vice presidential debate came into view. I was scheduled to meet Tim Kaine on October 4 on the campus of Longwood University in Farmville, Virginia.

Our campaign schedule was relentless, but Nick Ayers, as chair of the vice presidential campaign, insisted that I begin prepping for the debate. I said, sure, we can do one fewer rally a week and use that time for some informal prep sessions. But that wasn't what Nick had in mind. Instead, he had a makeshift studio built with a debate stage, complete with cameras. Josh Pitcock assembled stacks and stacks of thick policy books, detailing every proposal Tim Kaine would champion, and asked me to read them. Every page.

I was hesitant, almost resentful; I needed to be out on the campaign trail. But they were right: if I flopped in the debate in October, none of the rallies would matter. To really prepare, I would have to find a sparring partner who could challenge me the way I knew the senator from Virginia would in the real debate. My mind immediately went to Wisconsin governor Scott Walker. He had a spectacular record as governor of the Badger State and had run a strong campaign for president before dropping out. When I called, I must say I was moved by how quickly he agreed to play the part of Tim Kaine in mock debates. I had no idea what I was in for.

Scott and I had always been friends, but he took up his antagonistic role with zeal. Our team would not even allow us to talk beforehand or during breaks, creating the tense atmosphere of an actual debate.

Scott did his homework. He memorized almost everything Kaine said on the campaign trail, practiced all his tics and mannerisms, and prepared attacks not just on my record but on Trump, too, trying to trip me up defending him. Despite our friendship, Scott tried to rip my heart out during the practice sessions, which ran ninety minutes. And if that wasn't rough enough, I would have to watch him ripping my heart out on tape afterward to see what I had done wrong and could do better at. Scott, you're the best.

I arrived in Farmville incredibly well prepared and incredibly nervous. I had been in many debates, dating all the way back to high school, but never one in front of an audience of millions, never one with so much at stake. There was an outdoor track on the campus near our hotel rooms, and to cool down and clear my head, I went for a jog with my Marine Corps son.

I was pretty sure he could keep up the pace I set. Characteristically, Michael didn't say much, but his presence and steadiness have always been a source of great comfort for me. We talked as we went around the track, but seeing how anxious I was, he eventually encouraged me to put on my headphones and listen to some music. He just jogged along beside me as I listened to the soundtrack of *The Natural*, the Robert Redford film chronicling the redemptive career of Roy Hobbs, the oldest player in the major leagues. The music by Randy Newman is always stirring. The movie culminates with Hobbs hitting a game-winning home run so powerful it smashes the stadium lights out, sending sparks across the stands and field, while a dramatic score plays. But my favorite scene is his first major-league at bat, when he "knocks the cover off the ball" while a dramatic score with the same title plays in the background. Listening to the music fired me up for the debate.

Shortly after the jog, as Michael and I made our way back to our hotel, I ran into Nick. His insistence on such intense debate preparation had created tension in our otherwise terrific relationship. But all that dissipated by the time of the debate. "I know you are going to knock the cover off the ball," he told me—a reference that came out of nowhere; he had no idea I'd been listening to the film's soundtrack. I had chills. I told him I felt his words were of the Lord, an affirmation that gave me confidence that God was going with me that night.

With hugs from Charlotte and a word from my son, saying, "You got this, Dad," we asked the kids to go take their seats so Karen and I could have a moment alone backstage. As always, she was reassuring and confident. She told me to trust the Lord and we would be fine either way. Then she leaned over and whispered "Knock 'em" in my ear. That is something she has said to me before every big moment in my political career since our very first campaign. We hugged. It was time.

When I sat down across from Tim Kaine, I was clearly anxious, and it showed: in my opening remarks, responding to a question about presidential leadership, I thanked the people of "Norwood University." But I settled in quickly and made my case, not just for Donald Trump's presidency but for my own role to be a heartbeat away from it. I was so well prepared that I often anticipated Kaine's answers and attacks, even word for word. At one point, when he took a line of attack that ended with a reference to what kids in grade school knew, I said without thinking, "Oh, this is the grade school thing again." Senator Kaine seemed momentarily taken aback that I knew his rhetorical moves before he made them.

Tim Kaine is a good, public-spirited man, a man of faith who has a reputation for bipartisanship. But the Clinton campaign had sent him out to attack and insult, to reiterate slogans I saw coming a mile away. They included "Hillary is a hire-you president; Trump is a fire-you president" and the point, hammered over and over again, that Trump had not released his income tax returns. That gave me an opportunity to explain how a President Trump would revive a struggling economy at home and show strength abroad. I wasn't in a hurry; I kept my composure and my smile. But I also made my case. I didn't hesitate to mention the taxes Hillary Clinton would raise, the regulations she would sign off on, her role in the Obama-era withdrawal from Iraq that had enabled the rise of ISIS, and her belittling millions of Americans as deplorables. I was kind but firm.

After an hour and a half passed, Kaine and I stood and shook hands and Karen came onstage for a hug. I thought the debate had gone well, that I had given as good as I got. After taking a congratulatory call while I was still onstage from our daughter Audrey, who was on an internship in Tanzania, I headed back to our dressing room and got a call from Trump, campaigning in Las Vegas. He was overjoyed by my performance. He called again shortly after to tell me to get a copy of the debate and put it into a safety-deposit box so someday my grandchildren could watch it. He said, "You will never do better than you did tonight!"

When I got up the next morning and resumed campaigning in Harrisonburg, Virginia, the world had changed; the crowd at my first rally was energized by the night before and roared when I said, "We had a little debate last night, and some people thought we won." Walking down the street on our way to another campaign stop, there were thumbs-up, waves, and fist pumps from people seated in diners and stepping out of storefronts. We headed off to Pennsylvania by bus. There was a new wave of enthusiasm and energy everywhere we went, a feeling that I had really helped the campaign out. Then, three days later, on October 7, the campaign crashed.

CHAPTER EIGHTEEN

"That Doesn't Look like Second Place to Me"

He changes times and seasons; he deposes
kings and raises up others.
—Daniel 2:21

I was in Toledo, part of a swing through northwest Ohio, visiting with a local reporter at Tony Packo's, a fabled Hungarian restaurant, when a member of my team rushed to my side and told me I had to leave. At once. I made my way back to the campaign bus through a rear exit of the restaurant. The press stampeded after us. I knew that something big had happened and whatever it was, it wasn't good. Back on the bus I heard the news: the *Washington Post* was about to release a 2005 video from a television show called *Access Hollywood* featuring Donald. It was just a snippet but a lewd and offensive one, in which he boasted in terrible terms about his sexual conquests.

It was all over the TV screens on the bus and across the country. The press wanted my reaction. We needed time to absorb the news, but there wasn't much time: left and right, major Republicans were withdrawing their endorsement of Trump, calling for him to get off the ticket, and asking what I was going to do. What were we going to do? I took a call from Donald on the bus. Huddled in the privacy of the motor coach's bathroom, I listened as he apologized for what had happened and specifically asked me to tell Karen he was sorry. I heard him out and said I would consider what he had told me. Then I called Karen, who was seeing the same news on the television back at the Indiana Governor's Residence. It was a long trip home. I thought of our decision to join the ticket, the opportunity we had to serve the country, and knew that was all at risk. But I also knew the release of that eleven-year-old video just weeks before the election was a late political hit designed to upend the campaign. It was a moment that called for wisdom.

After I arrived back in Indianapolis, Karen and I talked, prayed, and sought some sort of clarity. We wanted to see how Trump would make it right. That night, he released a video on national television. He was candid; he said he had never pretended to be a "perfect person" and took responsibility, saying, "I said it, I was wrong, and I apologize." It was a good start.

Rumors abounded that Karen was so upset that she urged me to abandon the ticket. Nothing could be further from the truth. We were both offended by the tape, but it was Karen who was the more forgiving and sympathetic. She had always liked him personally and appreciated how considerate he was about our family. But it was my wife's deep faith and belief in forgiveness that guided our response. We had never seen or heard that type of behavior from Donald, and after his apology, she reminded me that grace is the centerpiece of our faith.

The following day, Saturday, we put together a plan: we would cancel a scheduled campaign stop in Wisconsin and issue a statement. I wanted to make it clear that as a husband and father, I was offended by the words and actions described in the video. I wrote, "I do not condone his remarks and cannot defend them," but added that I was grateful that Trump had expressed remorse and apologized to the American people, concluding that we would "pray for his family and look forward to the opportunity he has to show what is in his heart when he goes before the nation tomorrow." His second debate with Hillary Clinton was just a day away.

He called me shortly after the statement was released. "Mike, that was pretty tough," he bristled. He was not pleased. I told him, "You gotta be you. I gotta be me." I said we would be praying for him to show his heart to the American people on Sunday night. Back at Trump Tower, I learned, close advisors were warning Trump that he had two choices: to get off the ticket or lose in a landslide. Very prominent and early supporters of Trump were calling me, telling me to be ready in case Trump stepped away from the race and I was moved to the top of the ticket. I rebuffed them all, saying let's give him a chance to make this right with the country.

Back in Indiana on Sunday, we planned to watch the debate at the Governor's Residence. I was encouraged by Trump's forthrightness with the country, but I wouldn't be honest if I didn't say it was an incredibly trying time. The stakes were high for both our country and our family. Donald had apologized. We had stated our position. He had one shot to turn things around. Everything was riding on his debate Sunday night. There was nothing left to do but put it into the Lord's hands.

As I sat in the residence that Sunday night, not long before the debate began, Nick Ayers, the head of our campaign, came into my study and asked if I was okay. And he didn't mean politically; he really wanted to know how I was feeling. I didn't offer an immediate answer. I had to be clear with him because the rest of our team would look to him to determine where we were going. "It's not whether I'm okay," I told him. "I've never been clearer about the fight on our hands for the future of this country." I pointed to my dad's Bronze Star, sitting in its old frame and hanging on the wall. "He was willing to give his life for this country. If he could do that, I'm okay. We have to keep fighting. And you make darn sure everyone knows how I feel." When the cameras rolled and Trump took the stage that night, he squared his shoulders, apologized to the American people, and then took it to Hillary Clinton. The smoke cleared, and he was still standing. I issued a tweet right after the debate ended, saying, "Congrats to my running mate @realDonaldTrump on a big debate win! Proud to stand with you as we #MAGA." The country had heard from Trump. The party knew where I stood. We were back on track.

The next day, at a rally in North Carolina, people were hanging from the rafters. I stood up and said that my faith teaches me to give second chances. There was too much at stake not to. I said I was impressed with Trump's resilience. He hadn't flinched or run. He'd never tried to obscure the offensiveness of what he had said, but he had apologized and demonstrated a toughness essential to the presidency. The audience roared.

We returned to the campaign trail and headed for the finish line with less than a month to go before election day. The news coverage focused less on who was going to win and more on how many points Clinton would win by. Even some members of my campaign team began to think about making contingency plans. If we lost the election, I would be out of a job. But when several of my campaign staff came to me in the front row of the campaign plane and said they wanted to talk about what would happen if we lost, I shut them down. The plan was that we were going to win the election.

I truly believed that. I could see it along the roads we traveled, where Trump signs, often constructed with cardboard and a Sharpie, were fiercely on display for miles and miles. I could see it the night I spoke to a crowd in the middle of a driving rainstorm in Williamsburg, Virginia. Nearly seven hundred people stood in the rain just to hear Mike Pence give a speech. We were going to win. My staff dried out the note cards I used to deliver the speech on our plane when it was over.

The final days of the race were frenetic, and they weren't always smooth. We flew into and out of smaller regional airports in our 727 and got used to what I called "long days and short runways," but nothing prepared us for the evening of October 27. With severe thunderstorms in the northeast, our campaign plane was grounded on the runway of a small airport in Iowa. As we waited for the ground stop to be cleared, I told the pilots to radio for a staircase so we could exit the plane and enjoy a sunny day in the Hawkeye State on a lush grassy field next to the runway. With our weary press corps enjoying a moment of respite nearby, my longtime assistant Zach Bauer organized a touch football game, where I showed my team that I could throw a perfect spiral. Maybe I missed my calling.

The storm had hardly abated when Trump Force Two finally touched down at LaGuardia Airport in a driving rain, with little visibility. The plane braked unusually hard after landing, then shook violently for ten seconds as we rolled to a stop. I watched as mud splattered onto the plane's windows. I got out of my chair and walked to the cockpit. "What's going on?" I inquired. "Sir, we are off the runway." I peered out the windshield and saw that the plane had come to a stop just about a hundred yards from a fence and a busy New York highway. I told the pilots I was grateful that they had gotten us down safely, and I breathed a prayer of thanks to God.

Walking to the back of the plane, I made sure that everybody on the campaign was okay and then went back to where the press sat. They were almost all young reporters, in their early or midtwenties. I went into Dad mode, checking to see if they were okay and telling them that all was just fine. The fire engines arrived, and we were escorted off the plane as TV cameras broadcast the whole scene on cable television nationwide. After taking time to thank the police, firefighters, and Port Authority ground staff on the tarmac for their swift response, I made my way to our waiting cars to make the drive downtown. It was then that I got my first introduction to my running mate's dark sense of humor. My cell phone lit up with the name Donald Trump on the screen. When I answered, Donald said he had heard about what happened, had been watching it all on TV, and asked earnestly if we were all okay. When I assured him that we were fine, he said in a wry tone, "Well, that's good, Mike, because it would really be a hassle to have to get a new running mate this late in the campaign!" "Thanks for your concern," I said, and we both laughed.

There was no quit in either one of us. On Halloween, I was speaking at an event in an airplane hangar in Clearwater, Florida, when the power failed and the lights went out. I grabbed a megaphone, and the crowd pulled out their cell phones and lit up the room. We kept going until the power was restored. I finished the speech, and Karen and I passed out candy to families with kids who had showed up in Halloween costumes. Going trick-or-treating was always one of my favorite nights of the year. Okay, it still is.

The final stop, in the wee hours of November 8, was at DeVos Place in Grand Rapids, Michigan. As I took the stage at midnight, Trump was in the air and on his way to join me after his fourth rally of the day. Walking to the podium to thunderous applause, I looked at my watch as it ticked one minute past midnight and told the thousands gathered there that election day had arrived, that this was the day Donald J. Trump would be elected president of the United States. The roar from the standing-room-only crowd was deafening. I delivered my final speech of the 2016 campaign, ending by saying that the election was not a choice between two people; it was a choice between two futures. In my introduction, I said, "Donald Trump literally embodies the spirit of America—strong, freedom-loving, optimistic, willing to fight every single day for what he believes in," and with that he took the podium at nearly 1:00 a.m. and spoke for an hour before it was over.

As Trump stepped down from the stage, he looked at me, gestured over his shoulder with his thumb toward the cheering crowd, and said, "I don't know about you, Mike, but that doesn't look like second place to me." Before leaving the arena, Jared Kushner approached me. "I don't know what's going to happen later today," he said, "but I want to thank you and Karen. You have exceeded every expectation of our family. We couldn't have asked for more." I was touched. I had never met Jared before joining the ticket, but we had developed an easy rapport. I respected his faith, his devotion to his family, and his steady presence on the campaign. For him to take that moment to express those sentiments is something I will always cherish.

Karen, Charlotte, and I were back in New York by the time the sun was up on Tuesday morning. The election-night party was to be at the Hilton Midtown, where I had been introduced as Trump's running mate in July. I went to my room to take a nap, knowing it would be a long night. When the exit polls rolled in, they looked terrible for our ticket. Marc Short was texting me the discouraging results. Lying in bed, I looked them over on my cell phone and responded to him only by sending the famous photo of Harry Truman holding a copy of the *Chicago Daily Tribune* with the headline "Dewey Defeats Truman." Then I went to sleep.

We left our hotel in the early evening and made our way to Trump Tower to watch the results come in with Donald and Melania. The campaign headquarters was a large room with wide-screen televisions on its yellow walls. Staffers were still working the phones, making final calls as the early returns came in. Standing in the middle of the room, Karen and I were joined by Charlotte, our son, Michael, and his fiancée, Sarah. Audrey was still in Tanzania, and one or another of us kept calling her. Donald, Melania, and eventually the entire

Trump family joined us. I was proud that Indiana was one of the first states called for Trump. No surprise there. But soon states we were supposed to lose started to fall our way. Florida. Ohio. North Carolina. Then Michigan, Wisconsin, Pennsylvania. Every time we won a big state, Trump punched me on the shoulder, pointed at the screen, and asked, "Did you see that?" As the evening wore on, my shoulder got pretty sore, and the Electoral College tally got bigger and bigger. At 10:26, CNN projected that Donald would win the presidency. The campaign headquarters erupted in applause. Karen and I embraced. We hugged and high-fived the kids. As I turned to shake hands with my running mate, he was embracing Melania and his kids. It was the first time he cracked a smile all night.

We went upstairs to their penthouse apartment to prepare for the victory party. No acceptance speech had been prepared beforehand, so it was written there and then by the ever-capable Stephen Miller at the dining room table in Trump's ornate apartment. An initial draft was presented to Donald, reiterating many of the themes of the campaign, but Donald thought it was too divisive. I agreed. He challenged the staff to recast it as a pledge to unify the nation after such a difficult election.

Soon we returned to the Hilton, and, surrounded by campaign staff, the Trump and Pence families awaited official word that Hillary Clinton had conceded the election. As he looked over his remarks, Donald told me, "You should say something, too, more than an introduction. Say whatever you want." I borrowed a scrap of paper and huddled with my family to write a few words for a national television audience in the middle of the night. I would say that this was a historic night. That America had elected a new champion. I would thank God, my wonderful wife, Karen; Michael; his fiancée, Sarah; Charlotte; and Audrey—after all, I would not be there without them. I would thank my running mate and the American people. And then, for the first time, I would introduce the president-elect of the United States, Donald Trump.

As I scribbled, I was informed that Hillary Clinton was calling to concede the election. The crowd made way as I walked to stand with my running mate during that historic moment, as my family waited back in the wings. He was soft-spoken and gracious, even gentle, ending with "please give my best to Bill." Then he hung up. I stuck out my hand. "Congratulations, Mr. President." It was the first time I had called him that. He looked up at me, and the gravity of the moment was clear.

"Thanks, Mike."

CHAPTER NINETEEN

Dead Sprint

Give your servant a discerning heart to govern your people . . .
For who is able to govern this great people of yours?
—1 Kings 3:9

Three days had passed since Donald and I had been elected to the nation's highest offices, an eternity. So much had already happened.

The stock market soared in defiance of the predictions that Trump's election would tank the economy. We also heard political commentators, many of whom had been certain of our defeat, strain to make sense of the American people taking Donald Trump up on his promises. But we wasted no time in keeping them. Before returning to Indiana, I traveled to Washington and met with congressional leaders. The president-elect, Melania, and I had lunch with Speaker of the House Paul Ryan at his office and afterward walked out on the balcony, looking down on the space where platforms were already being built for the place where we would take our oaths of office. We also met with Senate majority leader Mitch McConnell. Republicans had retained control of both chambers of Congress in the election. There was a tremendous opportunity to change the country's course for the better. I knew, though, as a former legislator and governor, that even with Republican majorities, it wouldn't be easy.

The most immediate task was forming a government, filling the thousands of posts that begin and end with each president's term. The most urgent of those were cabinet secretaries, the heads of the federal agencies responsible for carrying out the president's plans.

"You did a transition before as governor, right?" Trump asked the day after the election from across his cluttered desk, the fall colors of Central Park visible in the windows behind him. Yes, I had done that as governor of Indiana, I told him. When I had been elected in 2012, I had selected a cabinet and built a team across state government. Indiana's government is, of course, a bit smaller than the federal equivalent. Trump didn't hesitate with his next question. "Great. Do you want to lead our transition?" My answer was the one that I would repeat over the next four years: "I'm here to serve." And that was that. I was running the transition for the Trump administration.

Donald Trump was an outsider. He had never held office in his life. In the days following the election, when he flew to Washington, DC, to meet with Barack Obama, he called me from the car as his motorcade wound its way through our nation's capital. He spoke excitedly, talking admiringly about the beauty of the city's buildings and monuments. It was clear that he hadn't spent much time there. I couldn't help but think of the scene in Frank Capra's classic movie *Mr. Smith Goes to Washington* where Jimmy Stewart goes breathlessly on a sightseeing tour from monument to monument before taking his seat in the Senate. It was Mr. Trump Goes to Washington.

I gathered my staff, and we shifted from campaigning to conducting a talent search for the new administration. But it was not entirely a startup; New Jersey governor Chris Christie had laid the foundations for the transition during the campaign. We could build out from the operation he had created. We compiled lists, often off the top of our heads, of men and women who could be candidates for a Trump cabinet. I knew and had worked with many of them during my time in Congress and as governor of Indiana. Phone numbers were located, calls were made. I approached the recruiting for the administration in much the same way I had been recruited to join the ticket in the spring. Without making any promises, I would ask, "Is working for President Trump something you would be interested in?" and my phone rang constantly with recommendations from governors, senators, and congressmen eager to help us build a winning team—and in some cases join it themselves.

Back in Indianapolis, I had to help with a transition going in the other direction. My lieutenant governor, Eric Holcomb, won the election handily, another result the pundits hadn't seen coming. The governor-elect and I had known each other since our college days (we had both attended Hanover College, if a few years apart). Eric is a Hoosier through and through: modest and approachable. Apart from his being almost a head taller than me, there wasn't anything I didn't like about him.

As Indiana's next governor began to assemble his cabinet, my administration had to take a bow. There were personal matters back in Indiana to take care of as well. The Governor's Residence, our home for four years, was getting a new occupant. Karen broke out the packing boxes once again. I was rarely in the same place for long, working variously in Trump Tower, Bedminster, and temporary offices in Washington, flying back home at the end of the week. As she had done every time our family had moved throughout our political career, Karen took the reins and made it look easy. That woman could move an army.

The Trump administration formed quickly. A number of administration posts were filled by Trump's own associates and colleagues. Wilbur Ross, a global financier and storied businessman who was a legendary figure for his work rebuilding the Japanese economy during the 1990s, was designated secretary of commerce. The banker Steven Mnuchin, an early and often lonely Trump supporter—most of his Wall Street colleagues had backed Hillary—was nominated to lead the Treasury. Linda McMahon was slotted for the Small Business Administration. Along with her husband, she had turned a family wrestling company into a global sports entertainment brand.

Calls came in on my phone with advice and suggestions from the likes of Dick Cheney, Bob Dole, and Jeb Bush. Jeb and I had been friends for many years, and I had great respect for him. Given the bad blood between him and Trump, I was pleasantly surprised that he called with one of our very best recommendations. Betsy DeVos and Jeb had worked on education reform for years, including in Indiana when I had been governor, and when he told me she would be willing to serve in the administration, I put her at the top of the list. She came to Bedminster to meet with the president-elect, and the search for a new secretary of education was over.

I'll never forget the congratulatory call I took from former president George H. W. Bush. I was in Trump Tower in New York when the call came in. During the campaign, a reporter had asked which vice president I might most identify with, assuming that my lifelong friendship with former vice president Dan Quayle would provide the likely answer. Instead I had chosen Bush. As vice president, Bush had served another outsider president and brought a lifetime of experience that I was certain had contributed to the extraordinary success of the Reagan administration at home and abroad. When I recounted that opinion to the former president, he seemed genuinely moved, saying, "That's nice, Mike, but I just called to say congratulations to you both and to let you know we will all be pulling for you."

In Washington I met with Henry Kissinger, who applauded Trump's hard-line stance on China. I reached out to candidates around the clock. Pools were formed and narrowed, names were shared with Trump. I cold called General John Kelly and floated the idea of his taking the reins of the Department of Homeland Security. I didn't know him, but I knew of his illustrious military career and that he was the highest-ranking military officer to lose a son in combat since the Civil War. He met with Trump and was hired. I phoned South Carolina governor Nikki Haley, an old friend, to see if she'd be interested in serving as ambassador to the United Nations. If it meant being part of the cabinet—each president decides if that particular appointment is cabinet level—she was. I carried the message to Trump. He wanted her in his cabinet. She wanted to serve. The job was hers.

I looked for men and women whose experience and accomplishments dovetailed with our goals. I had served in Congress with Tom Price, a congressman from Georgia and orthopedic surgeon. He had succeeded me as leader of the Republican Study Committee in 2008. During the campaign, we had pledged to reform US health care and create a market-based alternative to Obamacare. He was the conservative health care policy expert in Congress and the perfect man to lead that charge at the Department of Health and Human Services. He was offered the job and accepted it. I brought Seema Verma, the gifted Hoosier who had helped design the Healthy Indiana Plan, in for a meeting with the president-elect in Trump Tower. Before the meeting was over, she was tapped to lead the Centers for Medicare & Medicaid Services. Two years earlier, Seema had been at my side as we had battled to reform Medicaid with the bureaucrats of the very same agency she would now lead. Is this a great country or what?

Trump had promised to rebuild the US military and was looking for a strong partner to lead the Department of Defense. We assembled the entire transition staff to review names with the president-elect in a sunny conference room in Trump Tower looking out at the New York skyline. There were many names on the list, but one stood out to me: the retired marine general James Mattis. He was a legendary figure among marines. My own marine son admired him greatly and had talked about him reverentially for years. He is an intellectual, a warrior, and a relentless advocate for American strength. He famously coined mottos for marines, including "Be polite, be professional, but have a plan to kill everyone you meet."

When I pointed out that his name was on the list, Donald asked, "Do you mean 'Mad Dog' Mattis?" He told me to find him immediately and see if he was interested. When I reached him by phone the next day, he answered from a soup kitchen where he was volunteering. He stepped into an alley to hear me out. Would he be interested in leading the Department of Defense? I asked. "Sir, you don't understand," he answered. "If the president of the United States of America asks me to serve, I'm going to serve." "I ride for the brand," he added, using an old cowboy saying. Mattis is from Washington State. He came to Bedminster and met with the president-elect. To little surprise—both men have a tendency toward bluntness—they hit it off. After the meeting Trump told me, "I shook his hand." During the transition I quickly learned that that meant a deal was done.

During the transition, I saw that though Trump hit back hard when he was hit, he could also be incredibly magnanimous. One of our campaign pledges was to make America energy independent. Texas governor Rick Perry had overseen a natural oil and gas boom in the Lone Star State. He was a good fit for the Department of Energy. But he had delivered a speech searingly critical of Trump in 2015. He interviewed and was given the job anyway. Same with former governor

Nikki Haley who, like me, had opposed Trump early in the Republican primaries and with Ben Carson, the brilliant neurosurgeon who was invited to helm the Department of Housing and Urban Development. The president-elect, a former Democrat himself, even met with Democrats such as senators Joe Manchin from West Virginia and Heidi Heitkamp from North Dakota about joining the administration.

When it came to secretary of state, former Massachusetts governor and 2012 Republican presidential candidate Mitt Romney's name kept coming up. Late in 2016, during a campaign swing through Utah, I had taken a private meeting with Mitt and had a sense that he would be willing to serve in some capacity if we prevailed. A good, public-spirited man with a servant's heart, Romney had strongly criticized President Obama's lead-from-behind foreign policy during his presidential campaign. But he had also been a vocal critic of Trump, delivering a major address attacking his candidacy early in 2016.

Nevertheless, Trump was intrigued by the idea of working with Romney. He had me call Mitt to ask if he would be willing to discuss the secretary of state position. He was. He and Trump had a productive meeting at Bedminster. But another name, that of recently retired ExxonMobil chief executive officer Rex Tillerson, emerged at the suggestion of Condoleezza Rice. Condi and I had gotten to know each other when she had been George W. Bush's national security advisor. The former secretary of state suggested that we needed to "think outside the box" about who should lead State. She said that Trump was unconventional on foreign policy—which she thought was good—and he ought to look outside traditional foreign policy circles.

Tillerson was a businessman with no political experience but a global presence and existing relationships with world leaders. He appealed to Trump because he was an unconventional pick. But Trump took Romney's candidacy seriously and, despite what some pundits assume, never dangled the job in front of him out of spite.

William Bennett, Reagan's education secretary, would later commend the conservative bent of Trump's team. "I was on Ronald Reagan's cabinet," he told me, "and this one is way more conservative." The fact that Trump had asked me to oversee the transition was a sign of the growing trust between us. The process of finding and review-

ing candidates with him also strengthened our relationship as we prepared to take office.

As we worked on filling spots in the administration, numerous
visitors and well-wishers made their way to Trump Tower for an audience with the president-elect. The media camped out like paparazzi
in the building's lobby, watching a long line of politicians and celebrities make the trek upstairs. It was a separate process from the transition and one that garnered much more attention as Kanye West, Al
Gore, Leonardo DiCaprio, Bill Gates, and many, many others took the
gilded elevator to Trump's office. Even the filmmaker Michael Moore
and the Naked Cowboy appeared in the lobby. They were not, however, granted an audience.

Not only was there a presidential administration to staff, but Karen
and I had to move into a new home. Since Walter Mondale held the office, vice presidents have lived in a beautiful Queen Anne–style house
on the grounds of the US Naval Observatory in Northwest Washington.
On November 16, Vice President Joe Biden and his wife, Jill, welcomed
Karen and me to the residence for a lunch in the sunroom. During the
transition, Biden was always courteous and helpful. He gave Karen and
me a personal tour of the house, a very thorough one. He took us all
over, opening what seemed like every door to its thirty-three rooms.
"They don't need to see every single closet, Joe," the second lady eventually interjected. There was so little time to think of my surroundings,
but we were immediately struck by the home's beauty, particularly its
wraparound front porch. The Bidens showed us the Family Heritage
Garden they had created near the front lawn, a series of stones bearing
the name of each vice president who had lived in the house and their
family members' and pets' names, too.

Standing on the front porch of the residence with our spouses at
our sides, the outgoing vice president was magnanimous, telling the
assembled press, "Everything is going to be okay," adding that he
was "confident on day one everything will be in good hands." I was
genuinely moved by the generosity of his comments and the couple's
hospitality. Joe Biden and I had always had a cordial working relationship during his years in the Senate and the vice presidency. All of that
would change in just a few short years.

These were long days with little rest and no recreation. Toward the end of one of these weeks in mid-November, I suggested to Charlotte, who was working on the transition, that we ought to take a Friday night off and do something fun. Since we were in New York City, I thought maybe we could even take in a show. I suggested *Hamilton*, the wildly popular musical about the Founding Fathers. But the wait list was a year long, so the kids just laughed at me. Undeterred, I wondered aloud whether the president-elect of the United States, who was a lifelong New Yorker, might be able to help us out. After a quick call to Trump's longtime secretary Rhona, we had five tickets to *Hamilton*. Glad we asked.

With three of her cousins in tow, Charlotte and I piled into the Suburban and headed to the Richard Rodgers Theatre on West 46th Street. Going to a show—or anywhere else—now meant being part of a long motorcade of black SUVs. It was not a subtle entrance. Though our request for tickets had tipped off the musical's cast and crew to our attendance, the crowd was unaware of it. When we walked into the theater toward our seats in the orchestra section, some fellow theatergoers spotted us. Some boos rang out. Some cheers, too. At that point in my career, I was not unaccustomed to the occasional mixed reception. But Charlotte and her cousins were wide-eyed. So as we took our seats amid the chorus of opponents and supporters, I leaned over to them and whispered, "That's what freedom sounds like." They all nodded and smiled.

When the musical came to a close and the Secret Service began to usher us out, one of the stars of the show, Brandon Victor Dixon, came to the front of the stage and addressed me directly. "We hope you will hear us out," he said. I stopped in the hallway leading out of the theater and listened. He thanked us for coming and explained that he and his fellow cast members were anxious about our incoming administration. He hoped we would uphold American values and work for all Americans. I wasn't offended by anything he said. Then we stepped out into the street to get back into the SUV and saw hundreds of protestors in both directions who had gotten wind that we were there. Some were yelling vulgarities. Some were holding signs with vulgarities. Some were yelling *and* holding signs. As we climbed into the Suburban and drove off, I glanced out the window and took stock. "I am going to put them down as undecideds," I said to Charlotte. *Hamilton*, by the way, is a great show.

When Trump caught wind of our theater experience, he was outraged—mostly as a New Yorker. "Broadway is almost like going to church," he told me. It wasn't really a church, he qualified, fearing that the comparison might offend me. But to him it was almost a sacred space. "Anyone from anywhere in the world ought to be able to go to a show and be treated with respect," he went on. "For them to do that to you, that crossed a line." He promptly tweeted his disapproval. But when I went on *Fox News Sunday* with Chris Wallace the next morning, I said I wasn't offended and had enjoyed the show. "You took the high road," Trump good-naturedly grumbled later. "I never take the high road."

On December 2, back at my desk in the Indiana Statehouse, I signed the document certifying that Indiana's eleven electors would soon cast their votes for Trump and myself and shortly thereafter mailed a copy of the certificate to the Senate. Under our Constitution, states conduct our elections and certify the results for president and vice president. In January, the electoral votes would be opened with Vice President Biden presiding. Little did I imagine how significant carrying out that routine exercise as a governor would inform decisions I would make in the years ahead.

While finishing up the transition, completing my duties as governor, and moving from Indianapolis to Washington, Indiana's bicentennial arrived. As first lady, Karen had served as the ambassador of the Bicentennial Commission, attending events around the state celebrating our two hundredth anniversary of statehood. A replica of the torch on the Indiana flag was carried through all ninety-two counties, and Karen was on hand at the Old State Capitol in Corydon for the kickoff. She also headlined numerous events throughout the year, culminating with a gala we hosted in Indianapolis celebrating the anniversary on December 11.

There was a small respite in late December, when Trump suggested I take a break for the holidays and gather my breath for the big push ahead toward the inauguration. "Save your energy for the big stuff," he encouraged. Back home kept a Christmas tradition: shopping for gifts for Karen with my daughter Audrey and twenty-five Secret Service agents. I'm not sure Target and the Fashion Mall will ever be the same.

In the midst of everything, we also had a son to marry off. Michael, a second lieutenant in the Marine Corps, had gotten engaged to Sarah Whiteside, the remarkable young woman he had met while they had both attended Purdue University and he was in the middle of flight school at Naval Air Station Meridian in Mississippi. There had been little time for him and Sarah to plan a large wedding. So on December 28 they were married in a small family ceremony in the living room of the Indiana Governor's Residence. Seeing our son marry the girl of his dreams surrounded by family was easily the high point of our year. A year that had changed our lives ended on an incredibly happy note.

CHAPTER TWENTY

With My Right Hand Raised

Those who humble themselves will be exalted.
—Matthew 23:12

On January 6, 2017, joined by Reince Priebus, the designated White House chief of staff, Trump and I met in a conference room in Trump Tower with the heads of all the intelligence agencies: James Comey, the FBI director; John Brennan, the CIA director; James Clapper, the director of national intelligence; and Michael Rogers, the director of the National Security Agency. They had come to New York to give us our first national security briefing, a sobering event. I had worked with Comey as congressman and governor, but judging from the blank look on his face when I greeted him on a first-name basis, he had completely forgotten. After the men outlined the pressing national and international challenges, the meeting was about to break, when Comey lingered. "There's just one last thing, Mr. President," he said to Trump, adding "Your vice president can stay for this if you want." Trump looked at me and shrugged. "You don't have to stay, Mike," he said, adding "I'll fill you in later." Folding my briefing book and walking out, I thanked Brennan, soon to retire after a long career, for his service to the country. He seemed surprised and moved by my words. It wouldn't take too long for me to understand why he was surprised; after witnessing his harsh and reckless partisanship all over cable news, I realized that he was not a man much acquainted with kindness or truth.

That same day, as Biden opened the electoral votes to certify the 2016 election, Democratic members of Congress repeatedly rose to voice their objections. The electors were not lawfully certified, one representative claimed, because of Russia's supposed meddling in the election. Another stood and claimed that the election had been stolen because of voter suppression. One more waved a letter objecting to the results. Just four years later, some of those same Democrats would accuse Republicans of attempting to overturn the election simply for raising objections as they had done. How soon, and how conveniently, they forgot.

I headed back to Indiana for my last few days as governor. I swung by the statehouse for a final visit. Governor-elect Holcomb was set to take the oath of office on Monday. The desk I had worked from for four years had been cleared of my clutter. My staff, who had been responsible for so many of our successes, gathered around for a melancholy farewell. I went to the residence, where boxes, filled with our belongings, lined the hallways. I sat in the small study and worked on a farewell address to the state. When there was a moment of quiet and solitude, away from the constant work and travel, I could see clearly that I would soon be parting from the people to whom I owed the most, and the place that had made me who I am, where I had lived most of my life, where my children had been born. I was saying goodbye to them to assume an office I was humbled to hold but would not take without a profound sense of inadequacy. I knew it was only because of the grace of God, the love of my family, and the support of the people of Indiana that I had come this far. I couldn't help but think of the Bible verse I had recited at the Republican National Convention: "Who am I and who is my family that you have brought me this far?" The responsibilities were great, and the future was uncertain. Now, as it was time to move forward, I knew I needed my fellow Hoosiers' support and prayers more than ever. I let them know that.

On Monday, January 9, joined by my predecessors Evan Bayh and Mitch Daniels, I watched Eric Holcomb take the oath of office as the fifty-first governor of Indiana. At noon my term concluded. Karen, Charlotte, and I traveled to the airport to board Air Force Two, bound for Washington, DC. The Pences have always been a pet family, and although our beagle, Maverick, had passed away during the campaign, we boarded the plane with our two cats, Pickle and Oreo, and a new family member, a little black-and-white rabbit we had inherited from our daughter named Marlon Bundo. As the story goes, Charlotte needed a rabbit for a college film project, and when she asked the seller on Craigslist how much he wanted for the bunny, he replied, "Make me an offer," a reference to the famous line in *The Godfather* in which Marlon Brando says he'll "make him an offer he can't refuse." That gave her a name for the rabbit on the spot. A star was born. He was a historical figure in his own right, the first rabbit to ride on Air Force Two.

For the last two weeks before the inauguration, we lived in a rented home northwest of Washington. A few rainbow flags were unfurled in front of neighborhood homes when we arrived. We didn't mind at all. But when protestors threw a dance party at the end of our block and CNN put it on national television, we started to get the impression that Chevy Chase, Maryland, might not be Republican territory.

I got my first real taste of postelection social media one night when I was commuting from our transition office in downtown Washington to our rental. Karen had asked me to pick up some ice cream on the way home, so I asked the Secret Service to pull over to a grocery store. Walking into a neighborhood Safeway, I grabbed a few cartons of our favorites, paid up, and left. A few patrons greeted me kindly, but it wasn't until I got home and learned that my ice cream stop had gone viral on the internet and was being reported on cable television across the country that I began to realize that we weren't "in Kansas anymore."

I was in New York on January 10 when the online news outlet BuzzFeed grabbed the world's attention, publishing a dossier full of salacious claims about Trump and purporting to document a plot between Trump and the Russian government to win the 2016 election. It was that dossier, gathered by a former British intelligence officer turned gun-for-hire named Christopher Steele, that Comey had told Trump about at the end of our national security briefing after I'd left. Years later we would learn that the dossier had been bought and paid for by the Clinton campaign.

"Can you believe this bulls—?" Trump furiously asked me when I walked into his office in Trump Tower shortly after the dossier was made public. None of it was true, he told me; and he didn't have to. It was another sign that there were some people—in the Democratic

Party, in the media, and in the national intelligence community—who would never accept the result of the 2016 election and, before Donald and I had even taken office, were working to overturn that result. They were soon calling themselves "the resistance."

Soon enough, the press and Democrats were baselessly alleging that Russian interference had tipped the balance in the election and that there had supposedly been direct contact between the Trump campaign and the Kremlin. On January 13, the *Washington Post* reported that retired lieutenant general Michael Flynn, tapped to be Trump's national security advisor, had communicated several times with Sergey Kislyak, the Russian ambassador to the United States, in late December. The conversation coincided with the outgoing Obama administration censuring Russia and expelling its diplomats for attempting to interfere with the election. The press speculated that Flynn and Kislyak had discussed sanctions recently imposed on Russia by the Obama administration as a response to election interference, allegedly in violation of the Logan Act of 1799, which prohibits private citizens from engaging in diplomacy. It's only actually ever been invoked twice, both times in the nineteenth century. But the speculation that Flynn had discussed peeling back the Obama administration's sanctions fed into the growing narrative that Russia had worked with our campaign to win the White House. In the resistance's telling, Flynn was paying back a favor to the Russians.

Two days later, I was scheduled to appear on *Face the Nation* and other Sunday news shows. As the inauguration approached, my appearances were billed as upbeat previews of the new administration. On Saturday night, my team huddled at the transition office in downtown Washington to prepare for the interviews. Anticipating questions about the calls with Kislyak, though, I called Flynn from the car as my motorcade wheeled past the White House on my way home. I wanted to hear straight from Flynn that he had not discussed the sanctions with Kislyak. There had been no talk of sanctions, he assured me. It had been only a courtesy call to convey Christmas wishes and condolences for those lost in a recent plane crash in Russia. I asked him three times if he was absolutely sure about any sanctions talk, and he was adamant. Trusting Flynn, the next morning I denied that there had been anything improper about the calls and said that the two men had not discussed sanctions. I left it at that.

Preparations for the inauguration were under way; the giant platform in front of the west front of the Capitol was taking shape. During the planning I learned that though the chief justice of the US Supreme Court has administered the oath of office to every president since John Adams, the vice president can select any justice on the Supreme Court to administer his oath. I didn't have to think twice about my first choice. During a trip to New York, I was driving across the Triborough Bridge to Manhattan when I called Justice Clarence Thomas to ask if he would do me the honor. I had met Thomas during my time in Congress at a lunch arranged by a mutual friend, Mark Paoletta— who would go on to serve as my general counsel when I was vice president. Thomas is the embodiment of the American Dream: a Black American born into poverty in the segregated South who had risen to the highest court in the land despite a withering assault by liberal Democrats. When I asked if he would swear me in, he replied, in his booming voice, "Mike, I cannot express what this honor means to me. The grandson of a sharecropper from Georgia and a small-town guy from Indiana standing on that stage together as a Supreme Court justice and vice president of the United States. Think about what that says about this country." I thanked him and told him that the honor was all mine.

When January 20 arrived, it was cold, thirty degrees and rainy. Somehow during our move from the Governor's Residence to our rental home, I had misplaced my overcoat. At the last moment a friend of Charlotte's who was joining us for the inauguration offered to let me borrow his. It was at least one size too small and a touch snug but good enough.

The day began with a service at St. John's Episcopal Church, the church of the presidents across Lafayette Square from the White House. It was closed to the press, but it shouldn't have been. The prayers and preaching were inspiring. I will never forget the sermon by Pastor Robert Jeffress of First Baptist Church Dallas. In the aftermath of a campaign that had pledged to build a wall on our southern border, Pastor Jeffress reminded those assembled that morning that Nehemiah had rebuilt the wall around Jerusalem, concluding, "God likes walls."

After the service, Donald and I met with Obama and Biden at the White House for tea before leaving in separate limousines for the Capitol. I have no memory of the conversation with Biden during the short drive. That is a reflection not on its worth but on my nerves in the moment. During his own ride to the Capitol, I would later learn from Trump, Obama had offered the incoming president some advice about the vice presidency: "I hope you have the same relationship with your vice president that I had with Joe." There is incredible value, he told Trump, in having someone who knows everything you know and whom you can trust. When he told me about it later, I could tell it had made an impression on our new president.

Two Bibles were brought onstage for my oath. A former aide of the fortieth president had brought Ronald Reagan's family Bible from California. It had belonged to his mother, and he had twice taken the oath of office on it. Though I had met him only once, and briefly, without Reagan I would never have been a Republican; I would not have been standing on the platform in front of the Capitol. The Bible was opened to Jeremiah 29:11, the passage that has hung above the mantle in every one of our homes since our first election in 2000. Along with Reagan's Bible was the leather-bound edition I had carried with me through much of my time in Congress, the governorship, and the campaign. The kids had insisted I also take the oath on one of my own.

I stepped forward to take the oath of office with Karen at my side holding both Bibles and our kids standing shoulder to shoulder to her left. I looked Justice Thomas in the eye and with my right hand raised repeated after him as he read the oath of office. But as we reached the final line, I turned the promise into a prayer. I promised to preserve, protect, and defend the Constitution of the United States. And I ended with a prayer: "So help me God." Shortly after noon on January 20, 2017, I became the forty-eighth vice president of the United States. I stepped back and embraced Karen and the kids. And looking on from a few rows back, I saw Mom. I knew Dad was there, too, looking down, maybe a little bit surprised but still telling me to climb my own mountain and reminding me to do the right thing.

After I took the oath of office, Karen and I stepped to the railing and waved to the large and enthusiastic crowd. As I looked to the west past the leafless trees and the massive government buildings, over even the Washington Monument and the Lincoln Memorial, my thoughts carried me eastward, across the Atlantic, to Tubbercurry, Ireland, the birthplace of my grandfather. He had taught our family to believe in America and believe that in America anyone can live their dreams. On this day, as the grandson of that Irish immigrant who had stepped off a boat at Ellis Island with next to nothing was entering the second highest office in the land, there was no doubt that my Grampa had been right.

Afterward, following Trump's oath of office and inaugural address, as tradition dictates, Karen and I walked the Bidens to their car. A parade on foot up Pennsylvania Avenue followed. I learned later that the resistance was staging protests, some violent, across Washington. The protestors, dressed in black and wearing masks, clashed with law enforcement, injuring several police officers. Almost by magic, all of our belongings had been moved into the vice president's residence. And not just left in boxes on the floor. Every item was stored away in a closet or cupboard; even our paintings and pictures were hung precisely. Karen had worked out and planned every little detail with the government's movers. When we returned to the Naval Observatory after the inauguration, it was home.

In the evening there were inaugural balls at the Walter E. Washington Convention Center. The Trumps had the first dance of the night to, appropriately, "My Way," sung by Frank Sinatra. Two minutes into the song, Trump, who it is fair to say is not an enthusiastic dancer, waved for Karen and me to join him and Melania at center stage. Before we moved on to the next ball, he told me to join them on the dance stage just a little bit quicker. We were happy to comply.

Before the festivities, as the ladies were getting dressed for the evening, Michael and I had accompanied President Trump as he went to the Oval Office for the very first time. We had watched as Trump had sat down behind the president's desk, the Resolute, looking as though he had worked there all his life. The White House legal team had prepared a series of executive orders that were piled on the desk, and he began to sign them one by one. But when he came to a hiring freeze on federal employees, he put his pen down. "Does this exclude the military?" he asked. When the attorneys said that it technically did not but assured him that it could be interpreted that way, he replied, "I'm not signing it, then. Fix that and bring it back." He had run on a pledge to rebuild the military. Afterward Michael, my marine son, said to me, "That was awesome, Dad. I was so glad to see it." But it wasn't because the president was shielding the military that my son was impressed; he was impressed by his attention to detail. I have often told our kids that the little things are the big things. That was what he saw and what would characterize the president's style in that office for the next four years.

Sometime later, President Trump and I walked out of the Oval Office, along the Rose Garden with its colonnaded walls. The White House was fully illuminated as night began to fall. It was beautiful and imposing.

"Mike," Trump began, "this is . . . " His voice trailed off in a cloud of cold air.

"Humbling," I said, finishing his sentence.

"Yes!" he exclaimed. "That's it. It's humbling!"

It was a moment of optimism and boundless possibilities for both of us. Just outside the Oval Office, now dark, sat a pile of newspapers placed on a small desk for the president, an avid consumer of news. In the stack was a copy of the *Washington Post*. Its headline read, "The Campaign to Impeach President Trump Has Begun."

CHAPTER TWENTY-ONE

Be Informed. Be Prepared.
Be of Service.

Anyone who wants to be first must be the
very last, and the servant of all.
—Mark 9:35

Moving into the Naval Observatory, the official residence of the vice president of the United States, was a privilege. For the better part of our country's history, the living arrangements of vice presidents said something about their status: they rented homes or lived in hotels. The office was not important enough for the federal government to spring for a permanent residence. Eventually, though, as the safety needs of the chief executive and the second-in-command increased, securing private residences or hotels grew costly and logistically complicated. So in 1974, Congress at last gave the vice president a home at Number One Observatory Circle.

The three-story Queen Anne–style cottage was built in 1893 as a home for superintendents of the Naval Observatory. In 1923, the chief of naval operations took over the house, and it's easy to see why with its columned entrance, sunny solarium, and accommodating wrap-around porch—the very same porch where Barbara Bush chatted with Karen in 1988. The home, though not huge, is warm and comfortable. Joe Biden told me that Barack Obama, tired of the fishbowl of the White House, had once jokingly asked him if they could trade houses. In our four years working together, the forty-fifth president never proposed a trade.

We learned after settling in that each vice president since Walter

Mondale, the first to live there, had left their mark not only on the office but on the house as well. George H. W. Bush had built a horseshoe pit. Dan Quayle had installed a pool. Joe Biden had created a heritage garden in the backyard. Karen and I added a guesthouse, a beehive, and, of course, a basketball court with the word "Hoosiers" printed on the pavement.

I made one little temporary addition that no guest ever saw. On the mirror of my bathroom in the residence, I wrote in black marker a reminder for the next four years: *Be informed. Be prepared. Be of service.*

At Number One Observatory Circle I found a clue to the evolution of the vice presidency: Gerald Ford, who was vice president when the residence was established, became president before he could move in. His vice president, Nelson Rockefeller, lived in his own, bigger house in the city and used the Naval Observatory house only for entertaining. It wasn't until 1977 that a vice president, Walter Mondale, settled in, and that was fitting; he was the first modern vice president.

Mondale was a two-term senator from Minnesota who ran with Jimmy Carter, a one-term governor from Georgia, in 1976. As Carter's vice president, he was given important domestic and international assignments. As the administration's agenda faltered, he traveled the country rallying Democrats and helping with Carter's attempt to reorganize the executive branch. He also met with both Israeli prime minister Menachem Begin and Egyptian president Anwar Sadat in 1978, paving the way for the Camp David Accords. Mondale was never an afterthought in the Carter administration but a member of the cabinet who even had an office in the West Wing.

A quote from Mondale resonated with me. A vice president's job, he said, is to give the president his honest opinion, in private and only once. The American people do not elect two presidents or copresidents. Whatever his ambitions, a vice president should remember that. Carter was an unpopular president. But Mondale stayed loyal, never fled from his side. To a man with higher ambitions, such loyalty is not an easy task. But that is the vice president's duty; the only greater one is to God and the Constitution.

During my vice presidency, I was often asked how two such seemingly different men could work so well together and even become friends. Some couldn't see how a person who had aspired to put a premium on civility in public office could work with someone who had a confrontational approach to politics. But that's because they didn't understand my calling or my respect for the president and the will of the American people.

I knew from the outset that no other Republican could have defeated Hillary Clinton. No other Republican was capable of bringing about the level of change on taxes, regulation, energy, trade, judges, and foreign policy that Trump proposed. What his critics failed to understand was that his agenda and his approach were part of what the American people voted for.

I believe in the collective wisdom of the American people. I believe that Providence put President Trump behind that desk, and I was elected to serve as his vice president. My job, my calling, was to help him be successful in the presidency he had been elected to advance. It was that simple.

Be informed.

So I set out to know what the president knew, to be informed, if only to serve as a sounding board or, when asked, to offer my best advice. I built my daily routines and interaction with the president and his cabinet around that approach. Every piece of information the president was presented, I made sure to see as well.

Early on after taking office, I placed a call to the president on the White House switchboard. The phone rang, and Reince Priebus, the chief of staff, answered. We were both confused. Why was I calling him? he asked, and why had my call to the president been directed to him? I wondered. We quickly surmised that previous administrations had set up a system of phone rules: if the vice president wanted to talk to the president, he had to first go through the president's chief of staff. But that wasn't how Trump and I worked. Dating back to the earliest days of the campaign, we had talked on the phone several times a day, almost every day. Again, it was informal: he would call me from the road to hear what I was seeing on the campaign trail. We carried that over to the White House. So, with the president's blessing, we changed the rules: from that point forward, if I wanted to talk to the president, the White House operator would connect me directly.

As vice president, I received the presidential daily brief, or PDB, the high-level overview of national security threats put together by cabinet members and national security officers. Dick Cheney told me that he had read his PDB in the morning before going to his office in the West Wing, so that he was already aware of what the president was going to hear in his briefing. I followed his example and was briefed every morning at the Naval Observatory before joining the president for his briefing. I would rise early and, after some private devotional time, read four newspapers: the *New York Times*, the *Washington Post*, the *Washington Times*, and the *Wall Street Journal*. Those were the four papers Trump read. Like him, I read them only in hard copies; it's important to know what's above the fold. Then I would check the internet and take a look at his Twitter feed before heading to the White House.

The president made a habit of rising early and sending out tweets on a range of topics drawing from headlines or upcoming events. He told me many times, "I probably wouldn't have gotten elected without Twitter." I had my doubts about that, but it was his direct line to the American people. He often laughed at how with the press of a button headlines broke all over television. Though some tweets were clearly for his own amusement, I came to believe that there was a method to them. With the click of a button of his phone, he would send the media in one direction and we would spend the rest of the day working our agenda. When I walked into the Oval Office on most days, the president would almost invariably first ask, "Did you see my tweet?" with a wry smile on his face. When I would acknowledge that I had with a nod, a smile, or a wince, he would seem pleased and quickly move on to the topic of the meeting.

Be of service.

Usually I met with the president in the late morning, when I would join him for his PDB on the days he had one. The briefings were conducted by experienced CIA personnel, and we were often joined by the director of the CIA and the president's national security advisor.

Knowing the president's priorities, I was often able to highlight matters that I thought would be of particular interest to him. I would periodically interject, "Excuse me, but for the president's benefit, could you explain," at which point he would almost invariably nod appreciatively in my direction.

Early on, I asked President Trump about whether I should attend some particular meetings on his schedule. "Yes, everything," he responded. It was always clear that whenever I could, he wanted me to be there for meetings and briefings. And I made sure I was.

In the days ahead, I would often receive a phone call from the president's assistant, Madeleine Westerhout: "He's looking for you." It often meant that a meeting was under way and the president wanted me there, even if it wasn't on my schedule. I would make my way to the Oval Office, but when I arrived at the door, I never just walked in.

The Bible is filled with admonitions of waiting to be invited. In Luke 14:10–11, Jesus tells a parable, admonishing, "When you are invited, take the lowest place, so that when your host comes, he will say to you, 'Friend, move up to a better place,'" adding "For all those who exalt themselves will be humbled, and those who humble themselves will be exalted."

So when I arrived at the door of the Oval Office, I always waited for the president to invite me in with a wave or a nod, whether he was alone or with others. The Oval Office was not my office. I was not the president of the United States. I never strode in as though I owned the place or was entitled to be there. The American people had not elected me president; they had elected me to support the president. I never forgot that. And Trump understood and appreciated that. Never once during our four years of working together did he tell me to just come into his office. My waiting at the door was a token of respect that helped build trust in our relationship.

On a typical day, we would go from one meeting to the next, often with Reince Priebus, Jared Kushner, and the cabinet members, working on everything from tax cuts and trade to building a wall on the southern border. If the president and I were both at the White House, I generally spent three to four hours of the day in the Oval Office attending meetings. They were informal, almost like jam sessions. Chairs would be set up around the Resolute Desk, while cabinet secretaries and staffers hovered behind on the nearby couches.

We had inherited protocols for Oval Office meetings: First, deputies would meet to hash out policy recommendations. Then their principals would meet to formalize the proposals. Then they would meet with the president in the Oval Office. Trump blew that system up. He wanted principals and deputies in his meetings; he wanted a wide range of perspectives and views. An informal, freewheeling way of conducting business and running his office was something he carried over from his companies. He would solicit opinions and encourage energetic debate between cabinet members, even if it got heated. He would listen intently. His countenance would range from amused to serious as he took it all in. If things got too tense, he would interrupt with a funny comment to lighten the mood.

Sometimes, when the president grew frustrated with the lack of progress on the administration's priorities, he would end meetings with a high-decibel charge to members of the cabinet and a bit of drama to go get it done. The cabinet officials would sheepishly pack up their binders and head out of the Oval Office. Once they were gone and only the president and I remained, he would often turn to me and ask, "How was that?"

It always reminded me of a scene in the movie *Patton* starring George C. Scott. During the Battle of the Bulge, the general grows impatient with his troops' inability to advance because of bad weather and lack of air support. "There are brave men dying up there. I'm not going to wait. Not an hour. Not a minute," he tells his subordinates. "We're going to keep moving, is that clear? We are going to attack all night, we're going to attack tomorrow morning! If we are not victorious . . . let no one come back alive!" His orders delivered, an aide-de-camp tells Patton, "You know, General, sometimes the men can't tell when you're acting and when you're not." With a wry smile, Patton replies, "It's not important for them to know. It's only important for me to know." I felt as though I lived that scene a hundred times in our four years together.

During meetings, I always sat in a chair to the right of the president, listening but seldom speaking. If I interjected, it was usually to ask a question, again preceded by "for the president's benefit." Occasionally Trump would interrupt the debate to ask for my thoughts. But I almost always said, "Let me talk to you about that later," at which point the president would invariably nod and move on. Yes, I always had my own opinions, and, no, they were not always the same as the president's. But I delivered them to him in private, one on one. Barring an issue of principle or morality, the vice president is there to support the president, not to present a divided front to the cabinet or Congress.

Be prepared.

There was something important beyond offering the president advice. For there is always the possibility of the unthinkable happening. Nearly five years before accepting the vice presidency, I had wrestled with pursuing the presidency but had reasoned that I wasn't ready, that I could be of better service to Indiana. In the years that had passed, serving as governor and as vice president, my aim was to be prepared for every exigency; that is the job. I never woke up in the morning with it on my mind, but by staying informed, always trying to be of service, and being present, I knew that if history called, I would be ready.

I was inspired by the example of our forty-third vice president. In March 1981, Vice President George H. W. Bush was on his way back to Washington from Texas when he learned of the attempted assassination of President Ronald Reagan. In time, aboard Air Force Two, Bush received word that Reagan, though wounded, would survive. As the plane approached the capital, the Secret Service suggested that Bush land at Joint Base Andrews and then fly by helicopter to the White House, landing on the South Lawn. History records that Bush refused. A Secret Service agent who was actually on the helicopter told me that Bush said, "Only the president lands on the South Lawn." He knew that the image—a hospitalized president, and his second-in-command arriving at the White House in dramatic fashion—would send the wrong signal to the nation watching on television. It would depict chaos and uncertainty and also demonstrate disrespect toward the president and first lady. Bush stayed cool in a time of terrible anxiety. He was aware of the importance of symbolism. And though the Secret Service protested about the inconvenience, Bush flew by helicopter to the Naval Observatory and then traveled by car to the White House—business as usual.

Just as I was settling into my new duties, Karen was assuming her role as second lady of the United States. She had recruited an experienced staff and chosen to focus on an art therapy initiative, Healing with the HeART. Karen had become an advocate for art therapy during my time in Congress and helped establish the art therapy program at Riley Hospital for Children in Indianapolis when she was first lady of Indiana. Art therapy is not arts and crafts; it is a method of enabling patients with serious illness to express themselves through art to a trained therapist, and it beautifully combines Karen's gifts as a painter with her deep and abiding empathy. As second lady she could educate people about the benefits of art therapy and encourage more young people to go into the profession.

As her term progressed, with two military wives in our immediate family, she also immersed herself in issues relating to military spouses, working to enable them to transport their professional licenses between states. Later she would devote endless hours to encouraging our veterans to seek help as the ambassador for PREVENTS, the President's Roadmap to Empower Veterans and End a National Tragedy of Suicide. And she became a national voice for mental health during the depths of the covid pandemic in 2020. She also led two official delegations to the Special Olympics, in Austria and Abu Dhabi. Everywhere she went, she also met with beekeepers.

Given the importance of the bee population to agriculture, Karen had installed a beehive at the governor's residence in Indiana and visited beekeepers during her travels around the country on a regular basis. When she hosted the media at the unveiling of a beehive at the Naval Observatory, I was skeptical that there would be much interest in the press. But honestly, the event created quite a buzz.

The president once said, "People have no idea the incredible job

Karen Pence does representing this nation," adding "Everybody loves her, she's special in every way." Fact check: true.

As we settled into our new home, I studied the history of the vice presidency and the examples of the men who had held it, and every day for the next four years I was determined to be informed, be prepared, be of service.

CHAPTER TWENTY-TWO

And So It Begins

Forgetting what is behind and straining toward
what is ahead, I press on.
—Philippians 3:13

My new job often took me back to my old stomping grounds, the US Capitol. I made a point, following another bit of advice from Dick Cheney, of attending the weekly lunch of Republican senators. It helped me serve as a line of communication between congressional leadership and the president. It was an opportunity to maintain old friendships and cultivate new ones while waiting in the food line or over lunch. At the outset of the meetings, Majority Leader Mitch McConnell would ask if I wanted to say a few words. On most occasions, I declined. Unless I had been asked by the president to offer direction, I was there to listen.

Most days, though, began in my office in the West Wing. It's not particularly large. When I first saw it after the election, portraits of John Adams and Thomas Jefferson, the first and second vice presidents, adorned the walls. I kept them, of course. But I added paintings of two other former vice presidents. On one side of my desk was Theodore Roosevelt, the father of the modern presidency, a larger-than-life, bustling, outspoken New Yorker. During his lifetime, a contemporary referred to TR as "pure energy." I always said, "That must come out of New York City about every hundred years."

On the other side was Calvin Coolidge, a taciturn, soft-spoken, penny-pinching Vermonter with a far more minimalist attitude toward public service. I had read Amity Shlaes's epic biography of Coolidge and been inspired by "Silent Cal's" humility, devotion to the Constitution, and principled conservative leadership. I would never compare myself to TR or Silent Cal, but they had both been vice presidents and, I would often note with a smile, they had both had one other job, too.

Of course, over the fireplace I displayed a portrait of one of Indiana's favorite sons, Abraham Lincoln. Lincoln grew up on a farm in southern Indiana, moving there when he was seven years old and leaving for Illinois after turning twenty-one. Otis Bowen, one of my predecessors in the governor's office, said, "Lincoln made Illinois, but Indiana made Lincoln." I secured a historic portrait of the sixteenth president from the Union League of Philadelphia if only to repeat that line to virtually every visitor. Joe Biden had hung a Delaware seascape on the wall. It was a fine painting, but it didn't suit me. I wanted something that would remind me of home. So Karen and I hung a rolling southern Indiana landscape called *Blue Hills in the Distance* by T. C. Steele, the dean of Hoosier painters, the man who had brought impressionism to the Midwest. The Indiana State Museum loaned us that painting and another one, *Road Through the Woods*, which we placed in the vice president's ceremonial office in the Capitol.

On January 26, I was with the president and Reince Priebus as they went over the president's schedule for the week when they came to an invitation to attend the annual March for Life. The march—it's a solemn protest, really—falls on the anniversary of the Supreme Court's decision in *Roe v. Wade* that legalized abortion in the United States. Tens of thousands of Americans, particularly college age and younger, gather and walk on the National Mall. In doing so, they are following one of this country's great traditions: seeking redress of what they consider a terrible grievance at the heart of the nation's capital. Priebus, himself an ardent pro-lifer, explained to Trump that Republican presidents, rather than attending, usually address the march by phone. Ronald Reagan and George W. Bush had done that. But Trump was scheduled to meet with British prime minister Theresa May at that time, his first bilateral meeting with another head of state. Perhaps he could tape a greeting, Priebus suggested.

"I wish I could go," Trump mused aloud.

"Well," I interjected shyly, "they invited me, too."

Trump turned suddenly to me. "They invited you to speak?"
They had, I told him.
"Well, is that something you would want to do?"

I told him that Karen and I had attended and spoken at the March for Life many times while serving in Congress. I couldn't have been more proud that Trump had made it one of his first acts in office to restore the so-called Mexico City Policy, banning taxpayer dollars from going to any organization around the world that promoted abortion. Our administration had already given hope to millions of Americans who cherished the Right to Life, and I said I would be honored to present the face of our new pro-life administration to the movement. "Well, you gotta go!" Trump nearly shouted.

The next day, and it was a beautiful one, we made history as the first vice president and second lady ever to address the March for Life. There were a hundred thousand people there, and when Karen took the podium, she said, "This is not our first March for Life, but it is the warmest," to laughter and applause. When I addressed the crowd, I told them what I had seen since that first march so many years ago. I spoke of the progress we had made since that fateful decision in 1973. That science was illuminating when life begins. That millions of adoptive families were opening their hearts to children in need. That compassion was overcoming convenience at crisis pregnancy centers. That the truth about abortion was being told through quiet counsels between mothers and daughters, grandmothers and granddaughters, between friends over coffee at college campuses. And I announced, "Life is winning in America," and it was.

In the next four years, ours would become the most pro-life administration in history. We restored the Mexico City Policy, ensuring that no taxpayer dollars could be used to promote or provide abortion around the world, we strengthened conscience protections for pro-life doctors and nurses, and we made it possible for states to deny taxpayer funding to Planned Parenthood. And five years hence, when three Supreme Court justices appointed during our administration joined a majority in the historic opinion overturning *Roe v. Wade*, life won and a new era where the question of abortion would be resolved by the states and the American people dawned. But it all began with the new president's choice to fill a vacancy of the court left by the late (and great) Justice Antonin Scalia.

In the second week of January, during the transition, Trump requested that I meet with candidates for the vacant seat on the Supreme Court created by the death of Justice Antonin Scalia. We interviewed a pool of nine candidates, all drawn from the list of judges Trump had shared during the campaign. I never once asked the candidates how they would rule on any issue. The president would choose from among them according to their judicial philosophy and fidelity to the Constitution, so I focused my inquiries there. At the end of each meeting, I asked the same question: "If the president does not choose to nominate you, who would you suggest he nominate?" Five out of the nine said Neil Gorsuch, the judge on the US Court of Appeals for the Tenth Circuit. When I asked Gorsuch that question, he gave it considerable thought. "You could throw a dart at this list. Any of these judges would be a great pick," he answered. Yes, I said, but if you had to pick one. "In that case, I would need to read their opinions." You have to love Neil Gorsuch.

After weeks of deliberations, President Trump nominated Gorsuch to the vacant Supreme Court seat. The announcement was made on January 31 in the East Room of the White House. I personally called to invite Maureen Scalia, the widow of Antonin, to join. She attended along with one of her sons, Father Paul Scalia. He said a short prayer with Karen and me, the Trumps, and the Gorsuches in the Green Room before the announcement. The Republican leadership in the Senate set a goal of confirming Gorsuch by April. In the intervening months, the nominee spent time visiting with the senators who would vote to confirm his nomination. At the urging of White House counsel Don McGahn, a brilliant conservative lawyer, I regularly met with the judge, not to offer advice but to serve as a sounding board, to listen to his concerns about the process, to help interpret questions and comments made during his interviews with senators. When Gorsuch had been confirmed to the US Court of Appeals for the Tenth Circuit in 2006, it had been without opposition. Immediately after his nomination to the high court, though, Democratic senators expressed their hostility toward Gorsuch and spoke of blocking the nomination.

The ever-partisan Connecticut senator Richard Blumenthal raised the temperature at both ends of Pennsylvania Avenue in early February when he told the press that Judge Gorsuch had found Trump's public criticism of judges to be "demoralizing" and "disheartening." His remarks followed a private meeting with Gorsuch as the judge was making the rounds meeting senators before his confirmation hearing. The judge assured me that he had been speaking in general terms only, and when I informed the none-too-happy president, he promptly took to Twitter and blasted Blumenthal for mischaracterizing the judge's remarks and, while he was at it, reminded millions of Twitter followers that Blumenthal had been found to have lied about serving in Vietnam a few years back.

I had a sense that Gorsuch was growing frustrated with the back-and-forth between the Democrats and the president, so I invited him to my West Wing office. When we met, he vented a bit about the process and the politics until I gently reminded him that it was the president's nomination, not his, and told him I was certain that President Trump would continue to make the case in the best way he saw fit. I tried to say without saying it that the president had nominated him and the president could withdraw his nomination. Things settled down very quickly after that. Sometimes it helps to remember who is in charge. In the end, Judge Gorsuch sailed through the process and actually carried three Democratic votes, being confirmed 54–45 on April 7, 2017. The country is fortunate to have a man of his caliber on the highest court in the land and to have had a president willing to fight to get him there.

The administration wasn't facing opposition just in Congress; the press and Democratic politicians talked incessantly about so-called collusion with Russia, saying that Trump and those around him had somehow worked with Russian president Vladimir Putin to alter the outcome of the election. A congressman from California named Adam Schiff, the ranking member of the House Permanent Select Committee on Intelligence, began to speak with certainty of collusion, even suggesting that he had seen evidence of it. The evidence would never materialize. I had been elected to Congress the same year as Adam and early on had considered him to be a friend. We had even founded the Freedom of the Press Caucus together. But judging from his partisan and reckless disregard for the truth during our administration, it was clear he had changed. Cable news personalities such as Rachel Maddow filled their shows with talk of Russia and watched their ratings rise. The resistance was well under way; its foot soldiers were in Congress, the media, and elsewhere. I was always convinced that there was nothing to it. Trump had assured me from the outset that it was absurd, and for my part, I had never heard even a whisper about Russians during the campaign.

But in early February, Don McGahn pulled me aside on the portico outside the West Wing as I walked to a meeting in the White House and said, "There may be a problem." I had appeared the previous month on national television and said that Michael Flynn, the president's national security advisor, had not discussed sanctions during his phone call with the Russian ambassador. Flynn had assured me of that. Three times. Now Flynn's story was evolving. Or devolving. A *Washington Post* reporter had asked him if he was still so sure that sanctions hadn't been discussed. Now he had "no recollection." The following day, the newspaper published a report that Flynn had indeed discussed sanctions with the ambassador, as confirmed by anonymous sources. That led to speculation that I had intentionally misled the public. I immediately demanded that the transcript of the call be brought to the White House by an FBI official. There had been numerous calls between Flynn and Kislyak, and in one of them, they had indeed discussed sanctions. I was furious.

The next day, as the story broke in the press, Flynn pulled me aside in the cabinet room just outside the Oval Office and apologized. I told him that I believed in grace but that he hadn't told the truth—to me, to the president, to the American people. And that fact needed to be addressed. The president was traveling, but during a call on Saturday he assured me that he would "take care of it" when he got back. It wasn't an easy decision for him; Flynn had been a lonely voice of support for Trump in the early days of his candidacy, and they were friends. But when Trump met with Flynn on February 13, he told him that because he had lied to the vice president, he could not remain national security advisor. He asked for his resignation. An indication of how difficult a moment it was for Trump, a man who was not prone to hugging, is that he stood up and embraced Flynn. The episode added fuel to the growing Russia collusion myth. But the decision to dismiss Flynn also signaled to me the growing bond between the president and myself. His willingness to dismiss a loyal ally to protect my reputation meant a great deal to me.

Flynn eventually pled guilty to lying to the FBI, but years later, documents surfaced that revealed that when FBI agents had interviewed Flynn in late January about the calls, they had not shown him the traditional courtesy of showing him actual transcripts to refresh his memory—a curious deviation from normal FBI procedure. Jim Comey would later publicly boast about how the FBI had taken advantage of the early days of our administration to circumvent the practice of alerting White House counsel when Justice Department officials were approaching a senior administration official. In May 2020, Attorney General William Barr would dismiss the case because of prosecutorial abuses, but it was a mess at the time. Most presidencies begin with a protracted honeymoon. Only a month in, we were already in a dogfight.

CHAPTER TWENTY-THREE

America First, Not America Alone

*Also, seek the peace and prosperity of the city
to which I have carried you . . .*
—Jeremiah 29:7

Across the Atlantic, America's allies were warily sizing up the new administration. One of the central promises of Trump's candidacy was a clear-eyed reevaluation of US foreign policy. He was rightly skeptical of nation-building in the Middle East and articulated what many Americans felt but their leaders wouldn't say: that other nations should have more skin in the game when it came to global defense. It was a blueprint for a policy that put US citizens and their interests first but did not abandon our commitments around the world or desert our partners.

In the early months of our administration, I met frequently with my counterparts from other nations or with heads of state before they met with Trump himself. King Abdullah II of Jordan, for example, came to the vice president's residence for breakfast. I developed relationships with foreign leaders, telling them what the president's position was and conveying their messages to the president. I think many of them saw me as someone who had risen through the ranks, who was a more traditional figure within the political establishment than an outsider like Trump.

In late February, foreign and defense leaders from around the globe gathered in Germany for the Munich Security Conference, a forum originating during the Cold War for the discussion of transatlantic security challenges. The US congressional delegation had long been led by Senator John McCain, but US presidents do not often attend. Vice presidents, however, do. Biden had joined the conference during the Obama presidency, so I was asked to represent the administration.

It was to be not only my first major foreign policy address but also the new administration's first foray abroad, where a skeptical audience awaited. "The unthinkable has come to pass," the German newspaper *Die Welt* had declared when Trump had won the Republican nomination. Now he was president, and his vice president was coming to town. The European foreign policy establishment was anxious.

My speechwriters worked on drafting my remarks together with the president's National Security Council and the State Department before they reached my desk. I redrafted the speech before flying to Germany. The night before I delivered it, Trump and I went over it line by line on the phone. He did not usually review or work with me on my addresses. But for that audience and that occasion—the global debut of the Trump foreign policy—we wanted to get it just right. When I took the podium, German chancellor Angela Merkel was in the front row, just a few feet away, surrounded by European technocrats. I had been in warmer refrigerators. But I was prepared to deliver a firm message in my low-key manner. The president had reminded me, "Sometimes it's just better when you are friendly." It was Trump's job to bring the thunder; I could best be of service as the gentler voice of the administration.

I reassured our allies that America First did not mean America Alone; that the talk of isolation was just talk. The United States' commitment to NATO and the transatlantic alliance were as firm as ever. But the new president was challenging everyone gathered at that conference, both our allies and our friends, to meet their commitments as well—and to contribute their share to the common defense that for many years the United States had shouldered largely alone. The twenty-eight member states of NATO had pledged to contribute up to 2 percent of their gross domestic product to national security and had repeatedly failed to meet that mark. Now Russia was growing increasingly belligerent, and China was eyeing a century of its own. Radical Islamic terrorism continued to spread across the Middle East. To meet those challenges, a common effort would be necessary; we were asking our allies to play their part. By the end, I noticed that the writhing in the audience had subsided for the moment, or at least until President Trump arrived at NATO headquarters in May.

I had a last stop before heading back to Washington. On the eighteenth, a Sunday, we landed in Belgium. The following day I was scheduled to meet with NATO officials while Karen and Charlotte made an official visit to the Flanders Field American Cemetery and Memorial in Waregem. That evening I had dinner with Charles Michel, the prime minister of Belgium, at the Château de Val-Duchesse, an opulent palace just outside Brussels.

The setting was perfect. Michel, the son of a Belgian politician, was younger than me by twenty years. When we greeted each other in front of the ornate marble fireplace on the castle's first floor, he announced to the assembled press that he wanted to discuss "important changes." And sure enough, the minute we sat down to a lavish multicourse dinner, he started in. He kept pressing the point, over and over again, that the United States must remain the "leader of the free world." I listened respectfully and smiled.

When he finished his lecture, I thanked him for his hospitality but then responded, "Mr. Prime Minister, the American people have no problem paying for seventy-five percent of your national defense." His eyebrows arched. "But let me say with no great disrespect, when you hear President Trump say that nations like yours need to live up to your commitments for our common defense, that's what we call being 'leader of the free world.'" At that, Michel cracked a smile. When he spoke to the press afterward, he said that I was "exceptionally" well informed. It had evidently come as a surprise.

Back in Washington, the president delivered his first address to a joint session of Congress on February 28. I had been in the audience for these spectacles as a congressman, but now I was part of the choreography, making my way down the center aisle, shaking hands with old colleagues before stepping up to a seat on the dais, behind and to the president's right and next to Paul Ryan. It had a surreal quality: two old friends, who had spent years as rank-and-file conservatives in Congress, now on the dais as vice president and speaker of the House. Beyond those sublime thoughts, a moment of humor broke the tension. Beforehand, my staff had cautioned that for the sake of television appearances I should wear a different-colored tie from the speaker of the House. Somewhere along the way, the colors were confused. When I reached the dais where Paul was waiting, we realized we were wearing identical outfits: navy suit, white shirt, blue tie. It made for a good laugh. Despite the sartorial faux pas of the men standing behind him, Trump's speech was a resounding hit, different from his inaugural address, which had spoken of "American carnage" and the challenges facing the nation; this night he spoke with optimism about a "new chapter of American greatness." In thoughtful tones, he called on Congress to put "trivial fights" behind us and pass an infrastructure bill, and he made a strong case to repeal and replace Obamacare. Even the national media offered praise in the aftermath, though it was quickly muted.

From the time the Affordable Care Act had been passed into law in 2010, opposition to Obamacare had been a driving force in Republican politics. The law was instantly unpopular. Its promises—if you like your doctor, you can keep your doctor; if you like your insurance, you can keep your insurance—were quickly broken. The outrage about the act helped Republicans win the House in 2010 and then the Senate in 2014. After taking control of Congress, Republicans tried several times to introduce bills that would repeal it. Replacing Obamacare with a market-driven alternative was among Trump's campaign promises. It was not, though, his top priority.

During the transition, Paul Ryan and Mitch McConnell had visited Trump Tower to map out a legislative agenda for 2017 with the president-elect. Though building a wall on the southern border was paramount from the start, Trump's first choice was getting the economy moving and delivering the tax cut he had campaigned on. Congressional leaders preferred tackling health care reform first. Ryan had explained that repealing and replacing Obamacare would open up revenue to then cut taxes. Tom Price, the administration's designated Health and Human Services secretary, had written the conservative alternative to Obamacare in Congress. The pieces fit. Against his instincts, Trump agreed to do health care first.

During my years in Congress, I had helped lead the fight against

Obamacare. I saw the Affordable Care Act as a government takeover of health care and believed that ordering Americans to buy medical insurance was unconstitutional. When it passed in the dead of night on a March Sunday in 2010, I said we had broken with history and turned our back on the country's finest traditions of limited government. I pledged that Republicans would work every day to repeal the law and start over. This was our chance.

Republicans in the House of Representatives started working on the repeal early in 2017. I traveled to the Hill frequently, sitting in on policy meetings, digging into the details of the bills they were writing, explaining to them what the president's goals were. Back at the White House, we would discuss the process and the peculiarities of Congress. The House introduced its health care bill on March 6, but it was pulled from the floor two weeks later. We didn't have the votes. There was consensus among Republicans that Obamacare, as is, could not stand. But there was little agreement beyond that. Should it be fully repealed and replaced with a totally different plan? Or should components of the bill be left in place and corrective elements added? A huge stumbling block was the ideological division among House Republicans: the split between the Freedom Caucus and more mainstream Republicans. It was nearly impossible to get them to sing from the same page. When negotiations faltered, the Freedom Caucus pointed a finger at the White House. Trump was furious. But he had no intention of abandoning his pledge. Sitting in the Oval Office after the House bill crashed, he vowed to veto every single bill Congress sent to him until Republicans found a solution to health care.

The morning after the House Republicans pulled the bill repealing and replacing Obamacare, I had my own controversy, this one very personal. On the front page of the *Washington Post,* under the headline "Beside the Vice President Stands a 'Prayer Warrior,' Gut Check and Shield," was a flattering profile of my wife, Karen. The newspaper reported her active role as second lady and described her as a godly mother and wife. The article also revealed what came to be known as the Pence Rule, that I never dine alone with a woman other than my wife.

It was a revelation to that generation of reporters, but my rule had been widely known for years. The reporter who "broke the story" got it from an interview I had done with the *Hill* when I had first arrived in Congress sixteen years earlier. Everyone who had worked with me over the years knew about it. Of course, after the national media reported it, it was treated with sensation and scorn. The *Washington Post* itself spent months engaging in chin-stroking analysis of why a man would avoid dining alone with a woman other than his wife. Absent in all the editorializing about how my official policy was sexist and a symptom of attitudes that were holding women back was the fact that women had always been high-ranking members of my teams.

My first lieutenant governor, Sue Ellspermann, was, of course, a woman, and an exceptional leader who would go on to serve as president of Ivy Tech, the largest statewide community college system in the country. My first national security advisor, Colonel Andrea Thompson, was a career army intelligence officer with a distinguished record in uniform. And my deputy chief of staff at the White House was Jennifer Pavlik, a gifted administrator who had joined our staff fresh out of college during my days in Congress and would bring her great administrative talents to my office as governor and later to the vice president's office. I am also the husband of a woman who graduated first in her class and paid her own way through college, and I am the father of daughters who attended Yale Law School and graduate school at Harvard. I have always been surrounded by strong, accomplished women. The Pence Rule wasn't holding anyone back.

Still, I was self-conscious about the press coverage, never wanting to create controversy for the administration. I didn't know how he would react, but the morning the story broke, I walked into the Oval Office to join the president for his intelligence briefing and was greeted with laughter. "Can you believe it? After all they've said about me, now they are attacking Mike for being faithful to his wife!" the president howled from across the Oval Office. Having fielded so many accusations of impropriety during the campaign and now all sorts of salacious allegations in the Steele Dossier, he saw the irony in the fact that the press and our political opposition were seizing on the Pence

Rule to denigrate me. It made for a good laugh and reminded me of the president's ability to take almost anything in stride.

Eventually, the controversy subsided. In July, the *New York Times* published a front-page story about a nationwide poll showing that a majority of women thought it was inappropriate to have dinner alone with a man who was not their spouse. Later that year, the #MeToo movement took off, and disclosures emerged of serial sexual harassment by Hollywood executives and media figures. That led to some serious rethinking of corporate culture. And President Trump often quipped, "Mike was way ahead of his time!"

I was in my office on April 4 when news broke that Syrian president Bashar al-Assad had launched a sarin gas attack in Khan Sheikhun in northwest Syria, killing nearly ninety people, including children. Photos of the dead bodies and injured babies provoked international outrage. But the outrage wasn't new. In 2013, Assad had killed 1,400 people with chemical weapons. Such was Syria's civil war. President Obama had promised that if the Syrian dictator used chemical weapons, he would be crossing a "red line" that would trigger US military intervention. That was just talk, though. The US government had not responded. Instead, Obama and his secretary of state, John Kerry, had negotiated an agreement with Russia, Syria's ally, that promised that Assad would destroy all his chemical weapons. He didn't.

Trump called Assad's use of sarin an "affront to humanity." Those weren't just words. He was deeply outraged by the images arriving from Syria. This time the US response to Assad's butchery would be different. Surrounded by Secretary of State Rex Tillerson, the new national security advisor, H. R. McMaster, and other members of the staff and cabinet, the president was briefed by military officials in a secure room at his Mar-a-Lago resort in Palm Beach. I joined the briefing from the Situation Room at the White House. The president had been clear: if international leaders use chemical weapons, there would be consequences. He was presented with a slate of options, and, just before a formal dinner with Chinese president Xi Jinping, President Trump made the decision to fire fifty-nine Tomahawk missiles into the air bases from which the chemical attack had originated.

He did not agonize over the decision. He asked for options, he asked for opinions, and then he led.

Roughly fifteen minutes before the missiles struck but after the birds were in the air, I was tasked with personally calling the "big four" congressional leaders from the Situation Room. I reached Mitch McConnell, New York senator Chuck Schumer, Nancy Pelosi, and Paul Ryan before the missiles landed and informed them of the strike. I remember being moved by their expressions of support. As the president told me later over the phone, as timing would have it, when the military aide approached him with an initial report that the missiles had reached their targets, he was seated next to the Chinese president. The two were just finishing a meal at Mar-a-Lago, and Trump informed his counterpart about the strikes. Later the president told me he thought it made quite an impression on Xi. With extraordinary precision, our armed forces had devastated the facility Assad had used to kill his own people. We signaled to the world that the United States meant business.

The next morning I picked up the phone at the Naval Observatory. "Good morning, Mr. Vice President," the operator said warmly. Amazingly, the White House operators were able to connect me to anyone, seemingly, around the world. They are among the true unsung heroes who make the US government run. That morning I asked to please be patched in to the secretary of state. After a short pause, I heard a voice on the other end say hello. "Mr. Secretary," I began, "I just wanted to check in and see what you're hearing about the strike from abroad." There was a short pause. "Mike, this is John Kerry." Wrong secretary of state. The switchboard must have had an outdated number, I explained apologetically. Kerry was happy to have me on the line, though. "I want to tell you I fully support the action the president just took," he said. "Our administration should have done that." I thanked him and asked if he would say that publicly. Not long afterward, a source close to Kerry was quoted as saying we had his support.

A few days later, Karen, the kids, and I gathered on Sanibel Island for spring break. We had first gone to the island, just off Fort Myers, Florida, the year after Dad had died and had returned many times as the kids had grown up. We loved the long sandy beaches and being among all the fellow Hoosiers who vacation there. Michael and his wife, Sarah, who were stationed in Meridian, Mississippi, met us there. It wasn't much of a break: on April 7, I dashed back to DC to preside over Neil Gorsuch's confirmation vote and then later to attend his swearing in. I wasn't going to miss that. Then it was back to Florida. While the rest of the family were at the beach, I sat under a palm tree with a phone and lists of names and numbers as long as my arm to call. True to his word, Trump refused to give up on health care reform. In the spring we stepped up our efforts, working with members of Congress; I was making dozens of calls a day, no matter where I was.

Less than two weeks later, I was aboard Air Force Two, destined for the Korean Peninsula, when my military aide informed me that North Korea, which had been in pursuit of nuclear weapons since the 1990s, had test fired a missile in an apparent message to the United States as we approached. It was my first trip to Asia as vice president, kicking off with a visit to Seoul to affirm the administration's solidarity with South Korea in the face of the North Koreans' increasing aggression. But as we flew west and I prepared myself for the meetings ahead, I realized how much more meaningful this assignment was to me.

CHAPTER TWENTY-FOUR

The Hermit Kingdom

*The light shines in the darkness, and the
darkness has not overcome it.*
—John 1:5

Reading my briefing book as we approached Seoul in Air Force Two, I realized that my first visit to the Korean peninsula fell sixty-four years almost to the day from when Dad had been awarded the Bronze Star for his service during the Korean War: an incredible, perhaps Providential coincidence. A black-and-white photo of that day featuring a skinny kid in uniform standing at attention while his commanding officer pinned the medal on his chest stood behind the desk in my office. When we touched down, got into the motorcade, and headed to our hotel, I looked out the window and was heartened to see posters outside bus stops and on buildings declaring "Welcome Vice President Pence." But looking closer, I saw that the posters bore another message, and I had to fight back tears. "Thank you Lt. Ed Pence for your service." South Koreans, I knew, revered the American GIs who had fought alongside the South Korean Army, but nothing could have prepared me for that. The US vice president was in town, but the second lieutenant from the 45th Infantry Division had equal billing.

The following day, we headed to the Korean Demilitarized Zone (DMZ), the 150-mile border between North and South Korea, the Frontier of Freedom, two and a half miles wide and lined with barbed wire, mines, and soldiers. We walked into Freedom House, the four-story building on the southern side of the DMZ in the Joint Security Area used for diplomatic meetings and visits. The original plan, approved by my Secret Service detail, had been for me to remain in the building and be briefed from behind the safety of bulletproof glass. I told my staff that I wanted to go outside to see the border for myself. At first the Secret Service strenuously objected. There were, after all, heavily armed North Korean guards within eyeshot, and there was no guarantee of safety. But I knew that doing so was important. President Trump had struck a defiant tone with Kim Jong-un. We wanted him to know that things weren't going to be as they had been in the past. I was there to send a message. I wanted the North Koreans to see my face.

Joined by General Vincent K. Brooks, who commanded the US troops in Korea and several highly annoyed Secret Service agents, Karen, Charlotte, Audrey, and I made our way onto the steps overlooking the border with North Korea. I could see the robin's-egg blue huts in front of us where South and North Koreans meet. The North Korean soldiers were about a hundred yards away, staring and clicking photos. I made the decision to go outside, to carry the message that after decades of "strategic patience" with North Korea, its brutal treatment of its citizens, its nuclear aspiration and provocations, time was up. When I spoke to the president later, he had seen us on television outside at the DMZ and said he approved. He told me the message on my face had been "No games."

Traveling farther down the border, we hiked up to an observation post overlooking the DMZ. It was raining with fog in every direction, and visibility was limited. As we looked out onto those North Korean hills and into the distance, though it was spring, the trees were mostly colorless, like a photo from days gone by. That was when General Brooks pointed and told me that those were the same hills—Pork Chop Hill, Old Baldy—where my dad had fought. He said that if it were a clear day, we would've been able to see the hallowed ground where his friends had died. My dad had refused to call himself a hero. The real heroes, he always insisted, were the ones who had never come home.

After South Korea, we traveled across Asia and then to Hawaii. When we arrived at the airport for our flight back to Washington, Audrey received a phone call while Karen and I were shaking hands before boarding Air Force Two. After we were on the plane, we walked into the cabin and saw Audrey sitting on the couch with Charlotte. I immediately knew that something was wrong. Audrey's boyfriend, Dan, had been in a plane crash in Connecticut. There were no other details other than that he was in the hospital. Dan had been found outside the wreckage, though it wasn't known if he had been thrown out, had crawled away, or had been pulled from the crash. She also learned that Dan's father, Joseph Tomanelli, a distinguished doctor in Connecticut, who had been piloting the single-engine aircraft, had died in the crash. With thousands of miles to go in the sky, headed back to DC, there wasn't anything else we could do but pray.

When we landed in Washington, Karen took Audrey straight to Reagan National Airport, where she caught a flight to be by Dan's side in the hospital. They had met while studying at Northeastern University and had grown close since. She stayed with him at the hospital for six weeks and was with him when he went home. He endured burns and a broken femur, and his hip was shattered. During his recovery, they both missed college graduation, but Charlotte went to Boston and picked up their caps and gowns. We were thankful that Dan had been spared, though I regret never having met his dad. It was a critical moment for our family, proof that even the highest public offices are no shield from personal tragedy. Karen and I wanted to visit Dan while he was still in the hospital, but the security necessary would have been too disruptive. Instead, we went up to Connecticut and visited him after he got home. Dan went through months of rehabilitation; today he's training for a marathon.

In Washington, House Republicans had gotten off the mat and back to work on health care reform. During my whole time on the road, I had been on the phone, shuttling between calls with the president and leaders in Congress.

Our efforts seemed to be paying off; the theme from *Rocky* was even played during a meeting of the House Republican Conference in the Capitol. The president worked the phones day and night. During my twelve years in Congress, I had received only one call from a president. During that and other legislative pushes, I watched President Trump call dozens of congressmen and even the same member several times in one week.

Congressman Mark Meadows of North Carolina, the chairman of the Freedom Caucus, committed to the president that he would find a way forward, and, working with Congressman Tom MacArthur, a moderate Republican from New Jersey, he did just that. Both men played a critical role in the negotiations, writing an amendment giving states waivers from federal coverage standards to lower their health care costs while protecting people with preexisting conditions. The bill also cut taxes and repealed the individual coverage mandate at the heart of Obamacare. It was a plan designed to win the support of both House conservatives and moderate Republicans, and it worked. After weeks of furious negotiations, the American Health Care Act passed the House. The vote was 217–213 to repeal and replace Obamacare. It was a remarkable comeback.

The repeal of Obamacare had taken its first steps, and Republican members of the House of Representatives made their way to the White House for a celebration in the Rose Garden. The president felt that the legislators deserved a victory lap, even if more work remained to be done. In typical Trump fashion—always remember his background in hospitality—he opened the doors of the White House, letting members of Congress, many of whom had never been there, take a tour of the mansion and the West Wing. They all loved it. Introducing the president, I tried to capture the historic nature of the moment, saying, "This is the beginning of the end of Obamacare." Clearly, I don't own a crystal ball.

CHAPTER TWENTY-FIVE

The Summer of Russia

Save me, Lord, from lying lips and from deceitful tongues.
—Psalm 120:2

Just as the health care bill was reaching the finish line in Congress, I met with Trump to discuss the legislation's prospects. I walked into the Oval Office and headed into the small dining room, where the president was waiting. I saw the television on the wall broadcasting the May 3 congressional testimony of Jim Comey, the director of the Federal Bureau of Investigation. Trump asked, with some irritation, if I had seen the footage. With a roll of the eyes, I said yes, I had seen some of it.

During his testimony before the Senate Judiciary Committee, Comey said that he was "mildly nauseous" that he had possibly impacted the outcome of the 2016 presidential election. It was a little late for that. On July 5, 2016, he had held a press conference at the conclusion of the FBI investigation of Hillary Clinton's use of a private email account as secretary of state, recommending that she not be charged for any wrongdoing. It was a showy political exoneration of the candidate, a major departure from standard FBI procedure. Then, in an abrupt about-face, on October 28, he had reopened the investigation into Clinton's emails less than two weeks before the election. He then, on November 6, had written to Congress stating that the FBI's original recommendation not to press charges against Clinton stood, and the investigation was once again closed. In the weeks after her defeat, Clinton counted Comey's reopening of the email investigation as being among the reasons she had lost the election to Trump. Collusion with Russia was also on her list. Neglecting to campaign in Wisconsin was not.

The charitable interpretation of Comey's "mildly nauseous" re-
mark was that he was sick to his stomach that he had impacted a US
election with his public pronouncements, regardless of the outcome.
The less charitable version was that it was Trump's victory that made
him feel queasy. Trump squinted at the television. Why was the director of the FBI making this type of comment? he asked. What type
of judgment did that display? he mused out loud. What type of judgment had his handling of the Clinton email issue demonstrated? At
that moment he clearly had doubts that Comey could lead the FBI.
Trump hadn't begun his presidency feeling that way. Like me, he had
respected Comey and been impressed by his career in law enforcement. We had been briefed by him after the election and after being
inaugurated, including a productive session on domestic threats in the
Oval Office on February 14.

At the time, the FBI was conducting an investigation into Russian
interference in the 2016 election. Evidence suggested that the Russian government had attempted to meddle, to drive divisions among
Americans by using propaganda on social media. It was absolutely
right that the FBI investigate it. But the resistance claimed that the
investigation was into the Trump campaign's alleged collusion with
Russia and into Trump himself. I would later learn that Comey had
assured Trump in personal conversations numerous times that he was
not under investigation.

But whatever Comey was really up to when it came to the president, that was not the reason Trump wanted to replace Comey as
the head of the FBI. On Monday, May 8, I joined the president in the
Oval Office, where he kept returning to the problem of Comey's "poor
judgment." Trump and I met later that day with Attorney General Sessions and Deputy Attorney General Rosenstein. Both men agreed that
Comey should go. They subsequently penned a letter recommending
Comey's termination that Trump then wrote a cover letter for. Before settling on his decision, though, Trump was warned by one of
the White House attorneys: if you fire Comey, it will likely trigger the
appointment of a special counsel. Trump understood. "I don't care,"
he said. "It's the right thing to do for the country." So not only did
he not fire Comey to prevent the investigation, he was told that it

would likely accelerate the inquiry and did it anyway because it was the right thing to do. The firing was made official and public on May 9. In Trump's cover letter he mentioned Comey's telling him on several occasions that he was not under investigation for collusion with Russia. The media immediately assumed that the president's decision had been related to the Russia investigation.

The following day, Wednesday, I was at the Capitol, visiting with legislators beginning work on the Senate's health care reform bill. I stopped to speak with reporters. Kristen Welker, a reporter from NBC News, asked if the decision to fire Comey had been related to Russia. "That's not what this is about," I told her. I explained that Comey had lost the country's confidence and the president had done the right thing.

On Thursday, the president sat for an interview with Lester Holt, an *NBC Nightly News* anchor, and he mentioned that he had specifically asked Comey if he was under investigation and Comey had said no. "When I decided to just do it, I said to myself, I said, 'You know, this Russia thing with Trump and Russia is a made-up story.'" During the interview Trump also said that he had no problem with the FBI investigation into Russian interference and expected it to go on. But the lasting impression from the interview was that Trump was frustrated that Comey had told him he was not under investigation but would not say so publicly. The press and Democrats went wild. Trump, they wrote, had fired Comey because of Russia.

By that point, Attorney General Sessions had recused himself from the Russia investigation, which was a great source of irritation to the president. Jeff, whom I knew from my time in Congress, had been an early Trump supporter and an original immigration hawk. The two had formed a strong alliance early in Trump's candidacy. Sessions had been an enthusiastic surrogate on the campaign trail. But eventually the relationship had become strained. After Jeff was confirmed as attorney general, news broke that he had met with Russian ambassador Sergey Kislyak in 2016.

During his confirmation hearings Jeff was asked if he knew of any meetings between Trump campaign officials and the Russian government. He said no. When news of the meetings leaked, Democrats quickly jumped to the conclusion that not only had Jeff lied, but he, too, must have been conspiring with the Russians to throw the election. Jeff had been a senator at the time of the meetings and a member of the Armed Services Committee, so it had not been irregular for him to meet with the Russian ambassador in that context. And he insisted that that had been the context of the meeting.

The fact is that the Russia narrative had already taken flight long before Jeff's confirmation in February. My view was that he should have disclosed that the meeting with Kislyak would require him to recuse himself before Trump picked him to run the Justice Department. The entire episode could have been avoided, and the president could have picked another attorney general. And with an investigation into his campaign under way, the president needed someone at the Department of Justice who would make sure that everything was handled above reproach by an attorney general who could oversee the investigation without fear or favor, especially since the involvement of FBI agents with political agendas was eventually brought to light.

In the wake of Comey's firing—as the president had been warned—on May 17, Rod Rosenstein, the deputy attorney general who had taken over responsibility for the Russia investigation after Jeff Sessions had recused himself, appointed former FBI director Robert Mueller as special counsel. I had nothing but esteem for Mueller, a marine veteran with a long and distinguished career. But I was surprised at his selection, since the day before, Mueller had met with Trump in the Oval Office to talk about returning to his old job as FBI director. Mueller subsequently denied that he had interviewed for the position, insisting that he had met with the president to offer advice. But I know it was an interview and that Mueller did express interest in the job. I was there. In any case, the special counsel's investigation only intensified the insanity over Russian collusion.

Near the end of that tumultuous month, Trump was openly talking about firing the attorney general. He was angry about the Russia investigation and was disappointed that Sessions had not disclosed that he would have to recuse himself before Trump had picked him to run the Justice Department. Despite all the difficulty, I thought firing him was a bad idea. I knew that in the end Mueller's investigation would come up empty-handed. Firing Sessions while it was under way would be interpreted by Democrats and the press as an attempt to thwart the Russia investigation and an implicit admission of some sort of guilt.

Returning from an event at the Capitol in late May, I told the president, "You know, I believe God put me next to you to help you be successful." "Yeah," he said, probably sensing what was coming next. "Well, I'm telling you, you should not fire the attorney general. That would be a mistake. Let this play out." I could give him my candid opinion because we were friends. In the end he would not dismiss the attorney general until a few days after the midterm elections and there was very little criticism of his move, given that the Mueller investigation was seen as approaching its completion.

There were multiple Russian collusion investigations under way, including not just Mueller's Special Counsel, but a House Intelligence Committee probe. The ranking Democrat on that committee, California's Adam Schiff, was regularly filling the airwaves with lies about the Trump campaign's ties to Russia. None of it was true. But the constant stream of misinformation began to shape public perception. Presidents always have to take on multiple tasks at once. It's part of the job. But simultaneously fending off a false narrative that the president had won the White House by conspiring with a hostile nation was, to put it mildly, an unwelcome daily distraction. Some days, the Russia frenzy was so intense, I didn't know how the president put up with it. Then I remembered that he had spent a lifetime making a living in New York City, one of the toughest media markets in the world. From time to time, after a particularly harsh attack in the press, the president would pause, look up at me from his desk, and say, "You know, Mike, it's been like this my whole life." That really said it all.

For my part, I instructed my staff to cooperate fully with the investigation and enlisted the services of Richard Cullen, a former attorney general of Virginia and US attorney who was recognized across Washington for his integrity and sound legal counsel. We continued to push back hard on the whole Russia narrative every time we were asked the question—and we were asked it a lot.

The story never added up, though—not just because our campaign hadn't collaborated with Russia but because the Trump administration, in both deed and action, was far tougher on Russia than almost any of our predecessors had been. George W. Bush had looked into Putin's eyes and been able "to get a sense of his soul," describing him as "trustworthy." Barack Obama had reassured Russian president Dmitry Medvedev that he would have "more flexibility" with Vladimir Putin after the 2012 election. And when Mitt Romney had described Russia as America's "number one geopolitical foe" during a 2012 presidential debate, Obama had mocked him, saying that the 1980s were "calling to ask for their foreign policy back." It was Obama who had refused to send weapons to Ukraine when Russia armed separatists in the Donbas region and even after Russia seized Crimea. The years following our administration showed just how wrong Obama had been in underestimating the threat that Putin and Russia posed to the West.

True, Trump made it a practice to at least attempt to be on welcoming terms with all world leaders. He had run for president in some sense as an anti-war candidate, arguing that the United States had spent too much treasure and wasted too many lives in the War on Terror. If it meant ensuring peace, building stable relations, he was willing to give other heads of state, even those leading hostile countries, a chance to find common ground. As a result, he did not loudly criticize Vladimir Putin. That didn't mean he admired him or was in some way in debt to him. It was a strategy. "I don't love, I don't hate. . . . We'll see," he said about Putin in 2016.

But I knew what Putin was. I didn't need to look into his eyes or see his soul. During my years on the House Foreign Affairs Committee, I had become convinced that Putin was, as I had said during my debate with Tim Kaine, "the small and bullying leader of Russia." Trump didn't agree with the tone, but his policies took a similar one: he pulled the United States out of the Intermediate-Range Nuclear Forces Treaty, which Russia had continually violated. He imposed sanctions on Nord Stream 2, Russia's pipeline project for exporting gas to Germany, and our administration approved the sale of lethal arms to Ukraine. And Trump attempted to fortify NATO, none of which could possibly have been welcome news to Putin or the Kremlin.

In a speech at NATO headquarters on May 24, the president called on our allies to live up to their commitment to our common defense by spending at least 2 percent of their GDP on defense. In the speech, which provoked outrage and derision and sent American journalists into fits of hysterics, Trump made no mention of America's commitment to NATO's Article 5, a pledge of mutual defense among member nations. Instead, he chided NATO members for failing to meet the agreed-upon percentage of GDP to be dedicated to defense spending. At the time, only three countries other than the United States were meeting the requirement. And Trump said that that was "not fair to the people and taxpayers of the United States." He had encouraged me to be cool when I had delivered the same message during my trip to the Munich Security Conference. Now he brought the thunder.

Trump was channeling the men and women who had made him president: we expect our friends to kick in, too. Trump delivered his message like a landlord speaking to deadbeat tenants—not a totally appropriate metaphor, but it was how he viewed it. NATO secretary general Jens Stoltenberg was a fan of the message. Vladimir Putin was not. NATO had been created to forge a transatlantic alliance against the Soviet Union. In the post-Soviet, post–Cold War world, its membership had expanded into Eastern Europe, pulling nations away from Russia's orbit. By encouraging other nations to meet their defense spending commitment, we wanted NATO to be stronger than ever—not a goal shared by Putin.

We were also advancing Americans' interests against Putin elsewhere. Later that year, in a conversation with John Kelly, the subject of the upcoming Russian military operation known as ZAPAD 2017 arose. That Russian military exercise, the country's largest since the end of the Cold War, was scheduled for September. Lasting six days, military maneuvers were planned that, at the time, were predicted to involve more than 100,000 soldiers staged across Russia, Belarus, and Kaliningrad. It was an anti-NATO exercise, and it greatly alarmed Ukraine, whose leaders feared that it would be a pretext for an invasion. "We need you over there," Kelly told me, meaning checking in with the United States' allies in Eastern Europe.

On July 30, I was wheels up for Estonia, touching down in the capital city of Tallinn. I spoke at the Estonian Defense Headquarters in front of soldiers from the United States, Estonia, the United Kingdom, and France under a blazing sun, while the temperature hit over 90 degrees. The troops were in formation and in full gear. I later learned that a few had passed out—from the heat, not my speech. After spending time with the troops, we met with the heads of state of Estonia, Lithuania, and Latvia, all nations that had been locked behind the Iron Curtain during the Cold War and all NATO nations now.

The following day, July 31, Karen and I arrived in Georgia's capital, Tbilisi. I spoke on the tarmac of Tbilisi International Airport, again in the scorching heat, in front of a jumbo jet fighter with airmen on its wings, surrounded by hundreds of US and Georgian soldiers cooperating in Noble Partner, a multinational training exercise for Georgia's army. After my speech, Lieutenant Colonel Adam Lackey, the commander of the 1st Squadron, 2nd Cavalry Regiment, presented me with a gift: a black Stetson hat, the ceremonial headgear of US cavalry. The last stop on the trip was Montenegro, the newest member of NATO and a nation that Russian-backed agents had attempted to overthrow and whose previous prime minister, Milo Đjukanović, they had tried to kill.

In those three free nations I delivered the same message: that the United States had no small allies, only strong allies. We stood committed to NATO and ready to honor Article 5; my presence there was proof of it. I delivered a message to Putin as well: we hoped for better relations with Russia. Those would come only, though, when Russia curbed its aggressions toward the democracies on its border and stopped its attempts to destabilize them.

I had no illusions about that happening, however. The true nature of Putin's Russia had never been clearer to me than when we arrived in Georgia, a nation Russia had invaded almost a decade before. Standing high on a balcony with Karen just before a dinner sponsored by Prime Minister Giorgi Kvirikashvili, we looked out over Tbilisi, the beautiful ancient city with its chaotic mix of Eastern and Western architectural styles, the Kura River winding its way through the crowded streets, and out into the distance toward the Trialeti mountain range. It was a stunning view. As we took it in, Kvirikashvili pointed out into the far distance. He told me that Russian tanks, the ones that had rolled into his country and torched its villages in 2008, were still standing there, even if we couldn't see them. That was why I was there: to stand with the United States' allies and to make sure Putin saw it. During the trip I even backed Georgia's potential membership in NATO, infuriating Russia. Days later, on August 3, despite his reservations that relations with Russia were at "an all-time and dangerous low," Trump went ahead and signed a bill passed by Congress sanctioning Russia for interference in the 2016 election as well as human rights abuses and the annexation of Crimea. Putin, in retaliation, sent home 755 staffers from the US Embassy in Moscow. All while the press and Democrats spoke endlessly about collusion with Russia, Russia, Russia.

CHAPTER TWENTY-SIX

New Frontiers

If I go up to the heavens, you are there.
—Psalm 139:8

Since the dawn of the Space Age, the United States had led human space exploration, firing the imagination of the American people and inspiring the world. Over the past ten years, since the last space shuttle flight, we had all but ceded human space exploration to Russia. Trump wanted to change that, and, boy, did we.

Back in 2016, I was scheduled to deliver a speech on Florida's Space Coast in the closing months of the campaign when Trump called me. He was kicking around the idea of reviving the National Space Council, an executive-level office established by President George H. W. Bush in 1989 to develop space policy. It had been disbanded in 1993, a casualty of the United States' diminishing space exploration ambitions. Trump wanted to revive the council, however, as a launching pad for a revival of America's space program. Since Lyndon Johnson had overseen the Mercury program, vice presidents had played a central role in NASA, and Vice President Dan Quayle had led the council when it was created.

Trump wanted to know if I would lead it if we won. What he didn't know was that some of my favorite memories as a kid were sitting in front of the Pence family's black-and-white television cheering on the Apollo astronauts. He didn't know that the House Committee on Science, Space, and Technology was the only congressional committee I had requested a seat on; that Karen and I had taken our kids to shuttle launches during my days in Congress; that Charlotte and I had even watched one at the side of Neil Armstrong. Would I, Mike Pence, be interested in leading the National Space Council? Would I! I was tempted to give him the Vulcan hand salute: "Live long and prosper."

But sci-fi and *Star Trek* aside, even as a budget hawk, I believe firmly in the US space program. It is an incredible source of pride and progress, a launching pad for industries that have powered America's economy and improved life the world over. And it is a frontier that someday may be settled. If and when that happens, it should be settled by free men and women carrying the American flag. The answer was yes.

In the summer of 2017, I traveled often to NASA sites. On June 7, I visited with Astronaut Group 22 at the Johnson Space Center in Houston. To the twelve new astronauts who were about to begin their training, I emphasized the importance of the families and friends who had helped them come this far. I told them that back in Indiana we have a saying, "When you see a box turtle on a fence post, one thing you know for sure, he had help getting there." The class liked it so much that they adopted "turtles" as their nickname. Once they graduated and began missions, I was told that several of the astronauts had taken toy turtles up to the International Space Station.

In July, during a trip to Kennedy Space Center at Cape Canaveral, I was joined by Senator Marco Rubio for a tour of the NASA facility and we passed by the spot where the *Orion* capsule, a spacecraft being built for deep-space exploration, was under assembly. While the senator and I learned about the project from NASA acting administrator Robert Lightfoot, Jr., caught up in the excitement, I put my hand on one of *Orion*'s forward bay covers—right below a sign reading DO NOT TOUCH. A reporter helpfully snapped a photo of the moment that quickly went viral and produced many memes at my expense. I played along happily over Twitter, saying that Senator Rubio had dared me to do it. "In fairness, I warned @VP that 'you break it, you own it,'" he tweeted back. NASA later explained that the sign was there just to reduce human contact with the equipment. No harm done—to *Orion*, at least.

In the fall of 2017, the National Space Council held its first meeting since 1992. Providing the US space program with a new, ambitious mission and clarity of purpose was another Trump administration goal. No American astronaut had gone beyond low Earth orbit in forty-five years. The space shuttle program had been mothballed in 2011. The country had ceded space to its rivals at a cost: the US government was paying Russia for rides up to the International Space Station at $76 million a seat. Even more concerning, both Russia and China had made great advances in anti-satellite technology, which was jeopardizing our own military's effectiveness. The United States' economy and national security are highly dependent on satellite-based systems, and with the development of offensive satellite technology by Russia and China, our defense assets in space could be at risk.

The original plan was to bring the members of the council together at a government building in DC. But I thought we needed a venue to match the occasion and the mission. Just outside Washington, near Dulles International Airport, is the Steven F. Udvar-Hazy Center in Chantilly, Virginia, an annex of the Smithsonian's National Air and Space Museum. In that hangar and among its galleries the United States' greatest aerospace innovations had come to rest: the SR-71 Blackbird, the plane that had flown faster than three times the speed of sound; the P-38 Lightning, the single-seated fighter that had helped win World War II; and space shuttle *Discovery*, which had flown more flights than any other shuttle—and provided the backdrop for the day, a far better one than a government conference room. The Space Council included members of the cabinet James Mattis, Rex Tillerson, H. R. McMaster, Wilbur Ross, and National Security Director and former Indiana senator Dan Coats. Executives from Lockheed Martin, Boeing, SpaceX, and Blue Origin joined the meeting as well. It sent the message that government and private industry were ready to partner in ushering in a new Space Age and return Americans to the moon—and send them to Mars after that.

It was an auspicious start to achieving that goal.

CHAPTER TWENTY-SEVEN

Repeal and Replace

All you need to say is simply "Yes" or "No."
—Matthew 5:37

Summertime came, and though our schedule never slowed down, it did allow us to fly home to Indiana on some weekends, which was a blessing for me, Karen, and the kids. Governor Holcomb and his wife, Janet, were always willing to make the governor's cabin in Brown County available any time we were home. Karen had raised private money to completely refurbish a cabin that sits in Brown County State Park, overlooking a vista of rolling southern Indiana hills. We spent many happy days and holidays at the cabin and were grateful to return during my service as vice president.

On one occasion during the transition, I took a call from the president-elect and mentioned that we were at the governor's cabin for the weekend. In a friendly tone he said, "Well, you know you have that Camp David, too." To which I responded, "Well, Mr. President, *you* have that Camp David," and he said, "Oh, no, that's more your speed—I don't really get into that out-in-the-woods stuff." Once we took office, he would ask if I had gone to visit the historic presidential retreat, but I was steadfast. I told him, "As soon as you go, Mr. President, Karen and I would love to go," but I wasn't going to go before he did. By June that first summer, he and Melania finally put it onto the calendar after he was persuaded by his national security advisor, General H. R. McMaster, how much it would mean to the navy personnel who man it twelve months a year. The morning after they arrived, I got a call from the president: "Mike, you gotta see this place, it's amazing!" It is. Camp David is a woodland compound with cabins, pool, movie theater, shooting range, golf course, and chapel. From then on, the president and first lady frequented the retreat and were generous in permitting Karen and me to spend time there when they were elsewhere. Turned out he was an "out-in-the-woods" guy after all!

That summer the Pences also welcomed a new family member. When Karen and the kids asked me what I wanted for Father's Day, I didn't have to think long. I had ridden motorcycles as a kid and given them up when I got married. But as governor I had gotten back in the saddle and even led an annual veterans' ride through the state each year. There's almost no better way to take in the beautiful highways, byways, and countryside of Indiana than in the saddle of a Harley-Davidson Road King. So what did I want for Father's Day? A motorcycle, of course. But when Karen and the kids presented me with my gift, it was a black-and-white Australian shepherd puppy. I named him Harley.

On Wednesday June 14, I was scheduled to make a morning speech for the National Association of Home Builders when we received word of the horrific shooting that had taken place at a baseball practice for the Republican congressional team on an Alexandria field. A lone gunman said to be angry over Trump's election opened fire at the GOP team and struck four people, including Majority Whip Steve Scalise. Two members of his Capitol Police security team were injured as they exchanged fire with the gunman, who was killed. After Steve was evacuated out, I called several members of Congress who had been there, including Arizona senator Jeff Flake, to see if they were okay.

Steve was struck once in the left hip and grievously injured. I had served with him for many years in Congress and counted him a close personal friend. The president and Melania visited him in the hospital on Wednesday night, and Karen and I visited on Thursday morning. Steve had just regained consciousness shortly before we arrived. We were standing with his wife, Jennifer, who was bearing up bravely. We assured them of our prayers and our support and the universal concern and admiration for him that spanned Congress and the country. Ultimately, Steve would show his personal toughness and faith when he returned to the Congressional Baseball Game a year later at Nationals Park. From his position at second base, he fielded the first hit, a ground ball, and threw the batter out at first base. There wasn't a dry eye in the house.

As the summer of 2017 passed, it became obvious that getting health care reform through the Senate would be no easier than it had been in the House. Whereas all Democrats in the chamber were opposed to replacing Obamacare, gaining consensus among the Republicans on how and what to replace it with was elusive. The original Senate bill, the Better Care Reconciliation Act, was introduced on June 22 and quickly took heat from the right. Senator Rand Paul of Kentucky felt it didn't go far enough, that it left too much of Obamacare standing. He threatened to kill the bill. Votes were postponed. I worked the phones, talking to senators, and made regular trips to the Capitol to meet with legislators. A revised plan was introduced in July. The wrangling went on until late July, when a stripped-down proposal emerged.

At the most heated moment of the debate, John McCain announced that he had been diagnosed with a malignant brain tumor. John was as tough as they come, but that was an incredibly aggressive form of cancer, and all that was left for us to do was pray. His absence from the Senate for surgery delayed votes on the bill. Not surprisingly, he was back at work on July 25, when his vote moved forward the debate over the "skinny repeal." That bill was a stripped-down version of the original, but it ended the mandate that all Americans have health insurance, and it gave states the power to create their own health care programs, as Indiana had done with the Healthy Indiana Plan.

Shortly before the vote, McCain stood on the floor, a surgery scar visible over his right eye, and admitted to looking "worse for wear." He addressed me as Mr. President, the honorific title given to whoever is presiding over the Senate. Before he began his prepared remarks, he smiled and said, "I've been so addressed when I sat in that chair, and that's as close as I will ever be to a presidency."

What followed was an impassioned speech in defense of the Senate's history of incremental progress, forging consensus and civility, and it was a statesmanlike speech, high-minded and noble. It was also a warning against the health care reform bill now passing through the crucible, one that would pass on a party-line vote if successful. It wasn't perfect, as its primary author, South Carolina senator Lindsey Graham, admitted, but it was a vehicle that, if passed, could be improved in conference committee with the House. Lindsey and John were the closest of friends, and I believed that if anyone could get John to move the bill forward, it would be Lindsey. I just couldn't imagine John embarrassing someone who had been there with him through thick and thin, through presidential campaigns, and through countless overseas trips supporting our war effort and our troops. I had a lot to learn.

When the vote began on the night of the twenty-eighth, it was clear that two Republican senators, Lisa Murkowski of Alaska and Susan Collins of Maine, would vote no. The other outstanding vote was McCain's. As the evening went on, it was still unclear how he would vote. At 10:00 p.m., I took a call from Arizona governor Doug Ducey. We had become friends when I had been governor. He's an entrepreneur who built an ice cream business and a tremendous leader whom I respect to this day. "You can't tell anyone, but McCain is good," he said, delivering the news we had been hoping for. I breathed a giant sigh of relief. "You mean he's a yes?" I responded. "Yes!" said Ducey. I called Trump. "Put your phone down, no tweeting, McCain is good," I said. Shortly after our call he did send out a tweet, an encouraging one, though. It said, "Go Republicans Go!"

As the evening went on and votes were cast, rumors started to swirl that McCain's yes vote was actually far from certain. I spoke to John on the Senate floor and still felt good about what he was going to do. At 12:45, I talked to Trump again. Things still looked okay. Then I received a second call from Doug. Now something was wrong; McCain was wavering. I talked to Trump again. He wanted to speak with McCain. I walked up to the Senate Cloakroom, where McCain was. If you have a few minutes, I told him, the president would like to talk to you. He said sure. He followed me down the aisle to my office. I picked up the phone. "Mr. President, you still there?" He was. I handed the phone to McCain and left the office to let the two men speak in private.

The two had a rocky relationship, often taking shots at each other in the media. They were both sharp-elbowed men who punched back hard when attacked. But I always believed that had McCain lived, they would eventually have become friends. As I would learn later, during their conversation, McCain told Trump that he was honored by the call. He was respectful, told Trump that he appreciated the time on the phone, and gave no indication that he would vote against the bill. Then he walked out of the office, onto the Senate floor, caught the eye of the Senate clerk, gave a thumbs-down, walked over to his desk, and sat down. There was an audible gasp. The effort to repeal and replace Obamacare was dead. The Trump administration had just been knocked back on its heels. Trump was irate. I was, too. He hadn't wanted to do health care first. Our early defeat in the House had actually been at the hands of House conservatives. And Reince Priebus's relationship with Speaker Paul Ryan, both of whom are from Wisconsin, had failed to deliver a win. But he leveled his harshest criticism at John McCain.

The truth is that John McCain had been one of Obamacare's most vocal critics. He had run for reelection, fending off a Republican challenger in 2016, by running against Obamacare and promising to end and replace it. And now he had rescued it.

In a fitting twist, immediately after McCain voted down Obamacare repeal, Rand Paul blocked consideration of the fiscal-year spending for the Departments of Defense, Energy, and State, which was nicknamed the John S. McCain National Defense Authorization Act. Trump was delighted. McCain was incensed. He actually said, "It is unfortunate that one senator chose to block consideration of a bill our nation needs right now." Takes one to know one. Washington is a tough town.

The other, perhaps more poignant, part of the story, was that the Obamacare repeal that McCain had rejected had been authored by Lindsey Graham, his best friend in the Senate. Graham is smart, principled, and courageous. Like McCain, he is a maverick, but on the big issues, the ones conservatives care most about, he has always been there. He deserved better. The media, which had forcefully opposed McCain's presidential run in 2008, loved it, of course. It was the maverick at his most mavericky. The lone, principled statesman standing against his party is always a hero in Washington, as long as it's the right party he's standing against.

Morale, already under siege by the steady stream of Russia, Russia, Russia, took a hit with McCain's thumbs-down.

After a tumultuous six months, my office had its first major turnover. My chief of staff, Josh Pitcock, who had been with me in one role or another for years, left to pursue opportunities outside government. Josh had always served me well. He had been my last chief of staff in the House and had been Indiana's man in Washington during my governorship. He had been a key advisor on the vice presidential campaign. And, above all else, he was a man of integrity. He would be missed. He departed at the end of July. I replaced him with Nick Ayers, the former executive director of the Republican Governors Association, who had also played a key role in the 2016 campaign and was a gifted political tactician.

August also saw the departure of Reince Priebus and the president's "chief strategist," Steve Bannon.

Reince had done an admirable job in the early days of our administration, but the job hadn't been easy. Trump was really his own chief of staff, running a freewheeling, entrepreneurial operation in the West Wing. Reince had done his best to bring order to the personalities that the president had brought to the White House, but in the end even he said that it was "a good time for a reset." He is a good man and will always have my respect.

Bannon had been a ubiquitous presence in the Oval Office during the early days of the administration. I hadn't interacted with him much during the 2016 campaign, and although his office was just a few doors down from mine in the West Wing, I hadn't had many dealings with him. There was a moment though in early February 2017, when I'd realized that he would not be a long-term player in the administration.

A few weeks after our inauguration, Bannon was featured in a cover story in *Time* magazine under the headline "The Great Manipulator." The article called Bannon "the architect" of Trump's victory. I remember the day I walked into the small dining room off the Oval Office, and the president, with a look of irritation, held up the issue of

Time, asking, "Did you see this?" There had been only one architect of the Trump campaign. Bannon lasted six months.

John Kelly, the secretary of homeland security, replaced Reince. Kelly was a four-star marine general and the highest-ranking military official to lose a child in combat since the Civil War. His son Robert had been killed in action on November 9, 2010, while leading a platoon of marines in Sangin, Afghanistan. John had done a remarkable job at Homeland Security and had won the president's confidence. As chief of staff, he quickly brought order and routine to the White House. With momentous events just around the corner, we needed it.

CHAPTER TWENTY-EIGHT

Fire and Unexpected Fury

Why do the nations conspire and the peoples plot in vain?
—Psalm 2:1

Whereas the focus of the summer of 2017 had been on domestic policy, during a series of meetings in Bedminster in early August, Trump's new approach to dealing with foreign adversaries was on full display.

When it came to North Korea, numerous administrations had played a game of wait and hope with the Kim dictatorship, hoping it could manage the regime's ambitions to develop nuclear weapons. Sanctions had been imposed, diplomatic meetings staged, frameworks agreed on, but the promises had never been honored. And the Hermit Kingdom was inching closer to producing an atomic bomb.

When Trump took office, North Korea had attempted five nuclear tests dating back to 2006. Reports indicated that the nation had as many as sixty nuclear weapons, some capable of hitting the US East Coast. North Korean leader Kim Jong-un blamed the United States for the sanctions.* His government called them a "felonious crime" and promised "ultimate measures" in retaliation. Kim probably wasn't expecting the response he got.

On August 8, during a roundtable discussion with members of the administration at Bedminster on the opioid epidemic, a reporter asked the president about North Korea's nuclear weapons program. After months of menacing rhetoric from Pyongyang and warnings

---

* Council on Foreign Relations, "North Korea's Military Capabilities," June 28, 2022, https://www.cfr.org/backgrounder/north-korea-nuclear-weapons-missile-tests-military-capabilities.

about strikes on the continental United States, Trump had clearly had enough. "North Korea best not make any more threats to the United States," he said, folding his arms. "They will be met with fire and fury like the world has never seen."

Sometimes the most reasonable thing is to be unreasonable. When President Trump spoke to our global adversaries, he wasn't afraid to talk trash or make threats, but I always had the impression that it was because he understood who he was dealing with. I think he intuitively knew how to make his point in a way they would understand. The press and the foreign policy establishment—most of the world really—immediately went apoplectic. But the American people had elected Trump because they wanted to go in a different direction at home and abroad. Previous presidents had taken the same approach to North Korea time and again. The United Nations had imposed sanction after sanction on the country. Nothing had stopped the Kim family from developing nuclear weapons and threatening the United States with them. Trump understood that his unpredictability gave the United States an advantage against regimes that had played previous administrations like a fiddle. It was a new approach to US foreign policy. It was the reason I went to Munich in February and Eastern Europe during the summer; it was a coordinated strategy: our tones were starkly different, but the message was the same. That was by design. And it wasn't only directed to the Far East.

At another meeting at Bedminster with Rex Tillerson and ambassador to the United Nations Nikki Haley, the topic of Venezuela and its dictator, Nicolás Maduro, was front and center. Maduro and his predecessor, Hugo Chávez, had driven the prosperous country of Venezuela into dictatorship, socialism, and poverty. Their policies had starved children, demolished an economy, created 100 percent inflation, and forced millions of citizens to flee to other countries. It was a failed state and had become a haven for drug traffickers. Whereas previous administrations used sanctions and diplomatic pressure, Trump said that all options were on the table with regard to Venezuela, including military action. Venezuela's defense minister called the comment a "crazy act." The United States' allies in Latin America were rattled as well. I was scheduled to visit Latin America three days later to reassure our allies in the region and show the face of the new administration. I was going to deliver a message to Venezuela's dictator and rally America's friends on his borders.

On August 11, before leaving for Colombia, Karen and I visited Indiana. The trip was important to me: each Indiana governor, right before or after leaving office, sits for a portrait that is then hung in the governor's office at the statehouse. Karen and I had considered thirty artists before picking Mark Dillman. His work with the brushes sealed the deal, but it helped that he's from the south side of Indianapolis, where our family once lived, and that he had supported me since the 1988 campaign. The portrait is going to hang in the statehouse for a long time, and I wanted it to be painted by someone who knew and liked me. I also wanted it to reflect the foundations of my life and work: my faith and my family. The artist worked from a photo taken at the vice president's residence. I was sitting on my desk, and to my right was a photo of Karen and the kids, next to my Bible, opened to Jeremiah 29:11. To my left were Dad's three law books and at my back the American and Indiana flags. We took dozens of photos during the sitting and were not happy with any of them. The setup was perfect; I was the problem. I just couldn't relax and smile. Then, as the photographer clicked away, Karen came down the stairs and peeked around the corner to see how the process was going. She caught my eye, and I looked away from the lens and broke into a smile. The camera caught it. That photo became the inspiration for the portrait.

As happy as I was with the portrait, I had some apprehensions about returning home. The Comey firing, the Russia investigation, the fire and the fury—it had been a rough-and-tumble year, even for someone accustomed to the give-and-take of national politics. I wasn't sure what type of reception was waiting for me in Indianapolis. When we arrived at the statehouse, there was a large and incredibly warm crowd gathered in its atrium. Walking into the statehouse, I joked with some old friends in the state police standing guard that it was good to be back because "I thought the next time I came here, I'd be horizontal." They laughed, "C'mon, Governor!" and escorted us backstage. Karen, Audrey, and I were joined by my mom on a small stage with Governor Holcomb and his wife, Janet, for the unveiling of the portrait. I was surprised by the crowd, moved by their support, and incredibly humbled. During my speech, I thanked my fellow Hoosiers and then turned to Karen and thanked her for "putting that smile on my face."

The morning before leaving for Colombia, I had the television on in my office at the vice president's residence, where I was doing some last-minute work. I looked up from my desk and caught coverage of the chaos unfolding in Charlottesville, Virginia, and my heart sank.

The previous day demonstrators had converged in the college town to protest the removal by city leaders of a statue of Robert E. Lee at Emancipation Park. Among them were members of White supremacist and neo-Nazi groups. That evening and then the following day, they clashed with counterprotestors. I watched on the television as radical right groups—Ku Klux Klansmen, neo-Nazis, and White nationalists—fought with Antifa and with counterprotestors who simply didn't want any of those extremists in their town. At the height of the violence, a man backed his car down a street at high speed, killing a thirty-two-year-old woman and injuring many more. Later, a helicopter monitoring the chaos crashed, killing the two police officers aboard. It was a sickening and tragic day. I sat there watching the coverage all afternoon, over and over. Trump was at Bedminster, I knew, signing a veterans bill and planning a small press conference for the new law. He made a practice of playing a round of golf most mornings when he was away from the White House, and I wondered if he had the time to fully see what the rest of the nation was seeing on the news, how truly horrified the country was—including our supporters. It was important, I thought, for him to make a definitive statement condemning the violence and the hatred. As the TV screen turned to an empty podium awaiting the start of the press conference, I thought of calling him but didn't have the chance. I will always wish I had.

Trump's opening statement condemned "in the strongest possible terms this egregious display of hatred, bigotry and violence on many sides," adding "no matter our color, creed, religion or political party, we are all Americans first." What was left out, though, was a condemnation of the racists and anti-Semites in Charlottesville by name. On top of that, he spoke of violence coming from "many sides," which was quickly reduced to a false equivalence between the protestors and the counterprotestors. The statement was immediately criticized by politicians and commentators on both the right and the left with emphasis on the fact that the president hadn't condemned the racists by name.

On Sunday, I was on Air Force Two on my way to Cartagena, Colombia. I had not been in front of a reporter or camera since the events in Charlottesville and Trump's public comments. I spent a great deal of time working on what I would say about it all. It was international news, and the president was taking fire from all sides. In fact, the headline was no longer the tragedy in Charlottesville; it was Trump's response. The reason my response was so important wasn't about me; it was about my job.

The president was under siege, smeared with allegations of sympathy for neo-Nazis and Klansmen. I was on my way out of the country, headed toward Latin America. It would have been easy enough and politically safe just to disappear there, avoiding any collateral damage to my own reputation.

But my job was to stick by the president, to be of help in times of trouble. I could do so, though, not just because of some reflexive loyalty but because I now knew Donald Trump. Through all the chatter about bigotry, racism, anti-Semitism—standard talking points of his opponents—it was never mentioned that his daughter Ivanka converted to Judaism. Her children are Jewish. I had seen him with them, and I knew how dearly he loved and cared for them. In all the time we spent together, I had never once seen him mistreat anyone on the basis of race, creed, or color. Donald Trump is not anti-Semitic. He's not a racist or a bigot. I would not have been his vice president if he was.

When we landed in Cartagena, reporters were waiting for me to comment on Charlottesville. "We have no tolerance for hate and violence from white supremacists, neo-Nazis or the KKK," I said. "These dangerous fringe groups have no place in American public life and in the American debate, and we condemn them in the strongest possible terms." That was our administration's policy; that was how we felt in our hearts.

The following Monday, the president delivered another statement that condemned the racist and neo-Nazi groups that had descended on Charlottesville by name. It still wasn't enough for his critics, who continued to ask if his early hesitation had been related to sympathy for those hateful groups. The following day, during an exchange with a reporter, Trump claimed that there had been "very fine people" on both sides of the conflict in Virginia. That was interpreted as another defense of White supremacists, even though he had condemned them by name the day before. Thus a narrative was set.

Two years later, when Joe Biden, never one for understatement, launched his campaign for the presidency, he claimed that Charlottesville had been a defining moment in the history of the nation, one that had "shocked" America's conscience. But I will always believe that what Trump meant was that it was possible that the debate at the center of the march on Charlottesville over the fate of a statue of a historical figure is one that could indeed have well-meaning Americans on both sides.

America has a painful past of slavery and racism, but tearing down monuments and erasing our history is not the pathway to a more perfect union. In the years ahead, that would become more obvious to millions of Americans as the radical Left made efforts to tear down monuments to Thomas Jefferson, Abraham Lincoln, and Theodore Roosevelt.

During the two-day visit to Colombia, I focused on my mission, telling our allies that America First did not mean America Alone, that our economic interests and national security were linked. But I also made it clear that the failing state in Venezuela was a danger to the Western Hemisphere, encouraging drug trafficking and illegal immigration. I didn't back away from the president's claim that all options were on the table to deal with Maduro. President Juan Manuel Santos of Colombia and other South American leaders were none too pleased. We also took time to meet with refugees who had fled the Maduro regime. In a small shelter at a church near the border, Karen and I were deeply moved by a woman who had trekked across Venezuela to Colombia with her four grandchildren. She told us that food had been so scarce that she had been forced to send her grandchildren to wait in line from five in the morning until five in the afternoon for a single loaf of bread. We met a father surrounded by his wife and chil-dren who spoke of waking up hungry every morning. Ever the school-teacher, Karen had brought coloring books for the children. She sat with them, putting them and their families at ease. While Maduro's government released statements criticizing my visit to the region and claiming that the US government defended White supremacists, I was coming face-to-face with the victims of his dictatorship and seeing the real costs of socialism, the ones always carried by the citizens trapped by it, never the ruling class enriched by it.

At the same time, our longest war against tyranny was entering its sixteenth year and a major decision involving America's values was due.

CHAPTER TWENTY-NINE

Stay and Fight

Today you are going into battle against your enemies.
Do not be fainthearted or afraid.
—Deuteronomy 20:3

One of President Trump's campaign pledges was to end the United States' experiment with what he called nation-building in Afghanistan. He believed that after sixteen long years, it was time for US troops to come home. During the first year of the administration, there was considerable debate among the national security team about when and how and if we should withdraw them. On August 18, Audrey's birthday, I helicoptered to Camp David for a meeting of the president's war council: Secretary of Defense Jim Mattis, Chief of Staff John Kelly, Secretary of State Rex Tillerson, CIA director Mike Pompeo, Chairman of the Joint Chiefs of Staff General Joseph Dunford, Jr., and National Security Advisor H. R. McMaster. H.R. had joined the administration in February, replacing Mike Flynn. He was a capable, highly intelligent career military officer who had written an important book about leadership in the Vietnam War. He was blunt and positive and served the president well throughout his tenure.

They all brought their best counsel, but now it was decision time. For my part, I had supported the war in Afghanistan from day one. I had been on Capitol Hill on September 11, 2001. I remember the smoke coming from across the Potomac, rising from the Pentagon. I had cast a vote authorizing the use of force in 2001. Over the years I had traveled to visit soldiers serving there on numerous occasions and spent time with the families of the fallen in Indiana. I still believed that it was in the United States' national security interest that Afghanistan remain out of the hands of terrorists—in recent months the Taliban, the group that had given sanctuary to Osama bin Laden, had been making territorial gains against the Afghan government. We had ample reason to stay and fight.

The decision, of course, was not mine. Trump's instincts, as a candidate and still more as president, were to bring US troops home. And I understood. I never saw him so impatient about our presence in Afghanistan as when he returned from visits to Walter Reed National Military Medical Center, having spent time with wounded soldiers. He had a visceral reaction to putting Americans in harm's way without a clear mission or identified goal. After a visit to Walter Reed, he would tell me of a "beautiful" young person who had lost his or her arm or leg, having been terribly maimed in Afghanistan. "What are we doing there?" he asked. As a parent of a service member, this is the attitude you want from a commander in chief. You want him to think about servicemen and -women as if they were members of his own family. And Trump did.

If only the decision had been so simple. At Camp David, our national security team laid out the choices for the president. He heard them out. They told us that a rushed exit from Afghanistan would be dangerous. The United States had exited Iraq hastily in October 2011, creating a vacuum that had led to the rise of ISIS. I was always impressed with Jim Mattis's rapport with the president. He had an easygoing western style and a slow delivery. He had a confidence that appealed to the president. Mattis believed that there was no task too great for the US military. He had a plainspoken approach after a long career in the military. Trump wanted straight answers to his questions, and Mattis gave them. Regardless of how hard Trump pushed or pushed back, Jim was unflappable.

Ultimately, it came down to this: Trump had campaigned on a promise to bring the troops home. But he had also pledged to fight terrorism. The war council presented the facts: leaving Afghanistan now would be dangerous; it could hand the country back to the terrorists who had planned 9/11. Mattis explained that a forward deployment of additional troops could help the Afghan National Army turn the Taliban back. Meanwhile, Tillerson would apply diplomatic pressure on Pakistan to play its part in bringing the Taliban to heel. The president believed that it could work. He knew that it would be difficult and the country was weary of war, but it was the right thing to do. It reminded me of another time and another president.

I had been in the White House when President George W. Bush, against tremendous political pressure after the bruising 2006 mid-terms, had decided to keep fighting to win in Iraq. Bush had called a group of House and Senate Republicans to a meeting in the Cabinet Room to inform us of his decision and ask for our support. I remember when he looked around the table and said, "I'd be a hero in every newspaper in the country if I announced we were pulling out of Iraq tomorrow—but I've decided not to lose." He informed us of a plan to surge forces in Iraq led by a brilliant tactician, General David Petraeus. That actually had succeeded in bringing the violence to an end and achieved real stability until President Obama had withdrawn our forces in 2012, opening the door to the rise of ISIS. It was a courageous decision by a US president who would not let the sacrifices of our soldiers and their families be for naught. I thought it was his finest hour, and I saw President Trump's decision on Afghanistan as a similar moment of leadership.

Men and women seek office promising to govern according to a certain worldview or ideology. They make pledges that reflect the desires of the people who elect them. And that does indeed guide the best leaders once in office. But there are times when the view from behind the desk doesn't match the one on the campaign trail. Trump understood the gravity of the situation in Afghanistan; he listened to his advisors and decided to try to win. He made a decision based on US security. "My original instinct was to pull out—and, historically, I like following my instincts," he admitted when he announced his decision at Fort Myer Army Base in Arlington, Virginia, on August 21. "But all my life, I've heard that decisions are much different when you sit behind the desk in the Oval Office." It was a moment that reflected the gravitas and lived expertise of the administration's national security team and the seriousness with which Trump took the role of commander in chief. I was proud to be seated just offstage for his nationally televised address. In essence, that day a president became a commander in chief.

Trump's Afghan strategy was unveiled, fittingly, just weeks before the anniversary of 9/11. On the day itself, Trump was scheduled to speak at the Pentagon. I was to travel to Shanksville, Pennsylvania, to participate in a ceremony honoring the forty men and women who died in a field there after redirecting a plane destined for Washington, DC. I was humbled to be asked to pay tribute to the heroes of United Airlines Flight 93, but as I prepared my remarks, my mind went back more than a decade. I had been there once before.

It was the spring of 2002; Karen and I were driving the kids back to Indiana for Easter when I decided to detour off the turnpike and find Shanksville, Pennsylvania. It was only months after 9/11. Michael was eleven, Charlotte nine, Audrey eight. I wanted them to see it; I hoped they would remember it for the rest of their lives. I wanted them to understand what those passengers had done. We pulled the minivan off the highway, found Shanksville on a map, and headed into the countryside. We found our way to the site, pulled into a gravel parking lot, and got out of the minivan. We walked toward a makeshift memorial. It was covered with flags, teddy bears, rosaries, and other mementos mourners and well-wishers had left. Way off in the distance beyond a chain-link fence, there was a small white wooden cross marking the point of impact. It was spring; the weather was warming and nature was just stirring itself back to life. We stood there as a family, quietly. As we were getting ready to leave, I noticed two plywood panels on the memorial. One listed the names of the lost. The other had a timeline of Flight 93. There was no one else around other than a park ranger. Noticing us looking at the timeline, she approached and walked us through. As she spoke, I recalled that morning, standing in front of the Capitol as the chaos unfolded. I remembered exactly what time it had been: 10:20. "If the Capitol was the target," I asked, "what time would it have hit?" She replied that judging from the speed and the distance, it had been estimated as "between ten and ten thirty." The plane loaded with fuel, crashing into the Capitol, would have detonated like a bomb. It was in that moment I realized that among the many lives the crew and passengers had saved that day by their selfless courage, those brave Americans might well have saved my own life. I grabbed Karen's hand, looked down at my children, and thanked God for the heroes of Flight 93.

In the sixteen years that had passed since our last visit, the temporary memorial at Shanksville has been replaced with a white marble wall containing the names of the passengers. A ninety-three-foot tower with forty wind chimes inside welcomes visitors to the memorial. I had given speeches for decades. I had spent most of the past nine months delivering remarks in nations I had never before set foot in, carrying the president's message to allies and foes, on occasion to less-than-friendly audiences. This, though, was on a whole different level. I stood there with the families of the people who had stormed the cockpit of that plane, who had perished in that field, so that others in Washington that morning, perhaps even including me, were able to go home and hug our families. For me, Flight 93 is personal. I struggled to read my speech, fighting back tears. There is little you can do to express gratitude to those loved ones on behalf of a grateful nation. Karen and I visited with the families afterward. They told me that they could tell I understood, that I was "one of them," that I would always be welcome in Shanksville. I will never forget it.

Before leaving, we walked through the visitor center. I noticed a small blue book, one of the few personal effects that had survived the crash. It was *A Life of Integrity: 13 Outstanding Leaders Raise the Standard for Today's Christian Men* by Howard Hendricks. The book had belonged to Todd Beamer, who had prayed with a phone operator before he had rallied his fellow passengers to storm Flight 93's cockpit with those timeless words "Let's roll!" When I got back to DC, I purchased a copy of the book, the same edition. Along with my Bible and Paul Johnson's *A History of the American People*, it was on Air Force Two for the rest of my vice presidency as a quiet tribute to the heroes of Flight 93. I never flew without it.

A week later, the president and I traveled to New York City to participate in the UN General Assembly. The annual four-day conference would be the largest stage yet for defining what America First truly meant, and Trump was planning to take full advantage of it. There was a great deal of anxiety among members of the United Nations. Trump, after all, had criticized the organization, pointing out rightly that the United States disproportionately paid 22 percent of its budget and calling it a club for people to get together, talk, and have a good time. He had also lamented its unfulfilled potential. For my part, I had long been skeptical of the United Nations, deeply concerned that it had too often been the "forum of invective" that John F. Kennedy had predicted, especially regarding Israel. When Trump arrived at 760 United Nations Plaza, the members of the other 193 national delegations were holding their breath.

The speech Trump delivered on September 19 was not for the faint of heart. In it he reaffirmed the United States' commitment to the United Nations, to leading the international community of nations. But he pulled no punches when it came to the crises abroad.

On North Korea and Kim Jong-un: "Rocket man is on a suicide mission for himself and for his regime. . . . If [the United States] is forced to defend itself or its allies, we will have no choice but to totally destroy North Korea."

On the Obama administration's deal to delay Iran's nuclear arms program: "An embarrassment to the United States."

He described the Syrian government as a "criminal regime" and said that the time had come to "expose and hold responsible those countries who support and finance terror groups like Al Qaeda, Hezbollah, Taliban, and the others that slaughter innocent people."

Watching from the floor of the United Nations, I heard gasps, *oohs*, and *aahs*, saw grimaces and smirks, and heard occasional muted applause from the same crowd that had chuckled and cheered when Hugo Chávez had stood at the same podium and called George W. Bush the Devil, the same organization that had declared that Zionism was racism, that had produced a publication claiming that Israel was guilty of apartheid, and whose Human Rights Council included nations such as Afghanistan and Somalia. But the United States wasn't going to abandon the world, and our fellow UN members, as shocked by Trump's language as they were, knew that. Indeed, the most telling moment was when he articulated the essence of America First. "As President of the United States," he explained, "I will always put America first, just like you, as the leaders of your countries will always, and should always, put your countries first." For that line, there was applause.

CHAPTER THIRTY

Promises Kept

When a man . . . takes an oath to obligate himself by
a pledge, he must not break his word.
—Numbers 30:2

There were a lot of long faces. In the summer of 2017, after health care reform crashed and burned, I joined a meeting at the National Republican Senatorial Committee near the Capitol. The NRSC is the wing of the party responsible for recruiting and running Senate candidates. Cory Gardner, a senator from Colorado, chaired it at the time. He and the committee staff explained that Republican voters and the party's financial supporters were furious. The party had majorities in Congress and held the White House and still couldn't deliver on its long-standing promise to repeal and replace Obamacare. Donors were outraged and had stopped sending checks. Fundraising numbers had fallen off a cliff. Activists were demoralized and threatening to stay home in the 2018 election. The odds of the GOP holding the Senate looked bleak—unless Congress and the White House could deliver on at least one of the big promises that had put them into power in the first place. The good news was that the work was already under way.

The White House and Congress were busy putting together the tax cuts that the president had wanted in the first place. That issue, right out of the gate, was less of a lift than health care reform. Regarding replacing Obamacare, there was little agreement other than the baseline of reforming the system. On tax cuts, though, Republicans, no matter their stripe, were in agreement. It was a matter of putting together a package that could pass both chambers.

But as legislators went to work on tax relief in the fall of 2017, it was a heartbreaking time for Americans. Hurricanes raked the Caribbean and made landfall over Florida, and California's most deadly and destructive wildfire season eventually took forty-four lives and destroyed thousands of homes.

On October 1, 2017, a coward opened fire from a hotel room on the thirty-second floor of the Mandalay Bay hotel on a country music festival under way on the Las Vegas Strip below. Sixty people were killed and more than eight hundred wounded.

And then, on November 5, a gunman cold-bloodedly killed twenty-seven worshippers, old and young, at First Baptist Church in Sutherland Springs, Texas, before taking fire from a member of the congregation and fleeing. Like the shooter in Las Vegas, he murdered the defenseless and then cravenly took his own life rather than face justice. Those incidents and an equally horrific school shooting in Parkland, Florida, in February 2018 would precipitate a national outcry for action.

In the midst of those difficult times, looking forward to a moment of respite, we planned to attend an Indianapolis Colts game on October 9. We had actually been invited by the team two months prior. It was a special occasion for the team and the city: Peyton Manning, the franchise's storied quarterback, who had led the team to a Super Bowl victory in 2006, was going to be inducted into its Ring of Honor before the game. And a statue of Peyton was set to be unveiled on the plaza across from Lucas Oil Stadium, where the Colts play. I still remember a day in March 1984 when the Colts arrived in Indianapolis from Baltimore, a caravan of Mayflower trucks driving through a snowstorm in the middle of the night. Indianapolis mayor William Hudnut III, one of the city's great leaders, presided over an improvised press conference to herald the news. I was a second-year law student, and after seeing the news on TV, I walked from campus to the Colts' new home, the Hoosier Dome, for the event. I've been a fan ever since.

In 2017, a trend sweeping across the NFL, started by San Francisco 49ers quarterback Colin Kaepernick during the previous season, was for players to take a knee in protest against racial inequality while the national anthem played. I believe in freedom of expression. But as the son of a combat veteran and the father of a marine, I also believe in standing for "The Star Spangled Banner" and respecting the flag. Honoring the flag is a way of keeping our promise to honor those who serve beneath it, especially those who have died defending it.

President Trump had weighed in on the matter the month before, tweeting to players who didn't want to stand for the anthem, "YOU'RE FIRED." But regard for Old Glory wasn't something I had just discovered. In 2003, I had introduced an amendment to the Constitution in Congress prohibiting desecration of the American flag.

The Colts game happened to be against the 49ers, even though Kaepernick was no longer on the team. It was likely to make news if the players took a knee, regardless of my reaction. I called Trump before the game to let him know I was going. "If they do the kneeling protest," I told him, "I'm going to have to leave." I wanted him to know. "You should definitely do that," he responded. My hope was that neither team would take a knee. We flew to Indianapolis from Las Vegas the night before and overnighted downtown. We arrived at Lucas Oil Stadium around noon. I met with Peyton Manning and talked to the Colts' general manager, Chris Ballard, before the game. "Your guys are not going to put me in a tough spot, are you?" I asked. "None of our guys will," Ballard said. We took our seats in the box. When the national anthem began, I stood and placed my hand on my heart. Looking out over the filled stadium and onto the sidelines, I could see 49ers taking a knee. I turned to Karen and said, "Let's go." A half hour later, I tweeted out my reasoning: I believe that Americans should rally around the flag, and I didn't think it was too much to ask NFL players to respect it and our national anthem. I wasn't the only one tweeting, however. An hour later, Trump sent out his own statement, saying, "I asked @VP Pence to leave stadium if any players kneeled, disrespecting our country. I am proud of him and @Second-Lady Karen Pence." He called me later to say it was the biggest story in the country. "Well, Mr. President, I felt strongly about it," I said. I took no joy in leaving the game. And the media promptly started to mock our action, suggesting that we had walked out only because Trump had told us to. Truth is, I left the game not because he told me to but because my heart for Old Glory and all those who have defended it told me to.

When we landed in California later that day, we were greeted by a group of weary firefighters on the tarmac. "Thanks for walking out of that game," one of them told me while his friends nodded in agreement. "We used to watch football at the station on Saturdays and Sundays. Now we just watch it on Saturdays." They weren't the only ones: NFL ratings dropped by double digits in 2018. The league then changed its policies, requiring players to stand for the national anthem and show respect for the flag. I tweeted just one word in response: "Winning."

Another win and another promise kept: during the 2016 campaign, Trump promised to relocate the US Embassy in Israel to Jerusalem. There was nothing unique about that; presidents dating back to Bill Clinton had been pledging the same thing. And in 1995, Congress had passed an act stipulating that the US Embassy be relocated from Tel Aviv to Jerusalem by May 1999. During trips to Jerusalem while I was in Congress, my hosts would point to a vacant lot surrounded by a chain-link fence and say, "That's where they are going to build the US Embassy." Of course, as with most things in Washington, there was a way to avoid doing it and thus igniting a controversy, and in that case, the act allowed presidents to delay the move with a waiver. That was what they had done for more than twenty years.

Trump was eager to keep his promise. Most of his administration was less eager. The State Department and intelligence agencies were against the move. Rex Tillerson encouraged the president to wait. So did Mattis. They argued that it would lead to violence. Foreign heads of state felt the same. During a gracious call, French president Emmanuel Macron told Trump that moving the embassy couldn't be done. But there were a few members of the administration who felt differently, including Nikki Haley and our ambassador to Israel, David Friedman, a brilliant real estate lawyer, the son of a rabbi, and a longtime friend of the president—and Jared Kushner, who had a great heart for Israel. I supported the move as well.

"We'll see. We'll see," he said when warned about the danger of relocating the embassy. He and Friedman also saw moving the embassy as part of a larger strategy, a new approach to achieving peace between Israel and its neighbors, which had been elusive so far. Like so many of Trump's attitudes toward governing, it came from his business background. To get a deal done, you take the one thing that is nonnegotiable off the table, in this case that Jerusalem is the capital of Israel. At one point he looked at me and asked, "You still think we should do this, right?" My answer was "Right." I saw God's providential hand at work. I felt that my career—much of my life, really—had prepared and led me to that moment, put me into the position to sit by Trump's desk when the decision was made. I remembered the horrors and sadness I had felt during visits distant and recent to Dachau, what I had learned about the incredible spirit of the Jewish people, who had endured centuries of persecution, from my late sister-in-law Judy and her family and my lifelong friend Tom Rose, and my travels to Israel while in Congress and as governor. When almost everyone—his cabinet, the diplomatic team, the national security advisor, allies in Europe and the Middle East—discouraged Trump from moving the embassy, I was able to provide reassurance and reinforce his resolve. The truth, though, was that he never wavered; he knew it was the right thing to do.

During a meeting late in 2017, the president went around the large oval table in the Cabinet Room, asking each member of his team for his opinion on recognizing Jerusalem as Israel's capital. The majority, including Tillerson and Mattis, were against it. It would create chaos and lead to violence, they argued. As was his custom, Trump asked for my opinion last. I told him that it was the right thing to do historically, that Jerusalem is the eternal capital of the Jewish state, that he had promised to recognize it as such, and that he would be the first president to honor that promise. On December 6, Trump officially recognized Jerusalem as the capital of Israel. Tellingly, given the sparse support for the move, when the president made the announcement from the Diplomatic Reception Room of the White House, I was the only one who joined him. Behind us was a portrait of George Washington by Gilbert Stuart. I thought of his legendary letter to the congregation of Touro Synagogue in Newport, Rhode Island, in 1790, with its wish of goodwill for "the Children of the stock of Abraham."

As 2017 drew to a close, when I was not on the road, I was often at the Capitol working to help pass tax cuts. The president was heavily engaged in that, and so was I. He turned on the charm with legislators and lobbied them respectfully, listening to their objections. "I hear you, but we can get this done?" he would ask. I would talk and listen to members of Congress as well, asking what their issues were. Let me go to work on it, I'd say. I met often, not just with conservative Republicans but with moderates as well. I invited them to the vice president's residence for meetings and working sessions. I met with and pursued support from outside organizations that advocated tax reform, including Grover Norquist's Americans for Tax Reform, the Heritage Foundation, and the Club for Growth. I talked to governors, many of whom I knew from my time leading Indiana, catalogued their ideas about what tax reductions would best impact their states, and conveyed their concerns as well.

It was an all-out coordinated effort, supported greatly by the work of Representative Kevin Brady of Texas and Senator Pat Toomey of Pennsylvania. The two men, both of whom I had known during my time in the House, steered the tax bill through the House Ways and Means and Senate Finance Committees. They helped reconcile the party's competing populist and more traditional supply-side impulses. The House passed its version, which reduced taxes for almost all Americans and cut the corporate tax rate from 35 percent to 20 percent, on December 20 with little drama. The vote was 224–201.

Passage in the Senate was going to be a bigger challenge, of course. Three senators were uncertain as the final bill came up for a vote. One of them was Susan Collins, a moderate from Maine who was holding out for changes to the bill. As the Senate leadership worked with her, Ivanka Trump, who had asked early on if she could help with the effort, partnered with Collins. The two worked together to secure an expansion of the child tax credit in the bill, and Ivanka traveled to Maine, joining Collins for forums on the tax bill. When the senator announced her support for the bill on December 1, Ivanka had played a large part in securing it.

Bob Corker, a plucky senator from Tennessee, had a rocky record with Trump. Corker had interviewed with Trump in 2016 for the vice presidential nomination and had then been considered for secretary of state, a position he wanted. A few months into the administration, however, he turned critical, complaining about what he considered to be "chaos" in the White House. A back-and-forth between Trump and the senator followed before a thaw and then another round of adversarial Twitter exchanges between the two during the summer of 2017. Corker's votes followed a similar trajectory: originally a no, he flipped to a yes at the last minute. That left one holdout.

Over the years, Jeff Flake and I had followed different paths: in 2013, I had left Congress to return to Indiana; that same year, he had moved from the House to the Senate. When Trump nominated me as running mate, one of the earliest trips I made was to Arizona to meet with Jeff and John McCain, both of whom were Trump-skeptics. We were still good friends; that never changed. But Jeff couldn't support Trump. One issue was immigration. Jeff, who represented a border state, simply objected to Trump's hard-line, harsh language on illegal immigration. A devout Mormon, he objected to Trump's blunt style. He said he would support me but not Trump. I wasn't running for president, though. I don't think he ever really gave Trump a chance.

As voting began on the bill, Jeff was noncommittal. He was concerned about the bill's potential to increase the deficit. And, I think, he wasn't so eager to give Trump a victory. On the night of December 19, I called Jeff from the vice president's residence. Members of Congress are given the option of buying their desks when they leave office. Though I hadn't originally been interested, Karen had persuaded me to purchase the desk I had worked from during my time in the House. Talking to Jeff, I sat at that desk, the same one we had huddled around back when we had been rebel congressmen, Butch and Sundance. Talking to him was a walk down memory lane. But it was also business. We had both worked for years to lower taxes and reform the tax code. We were the ones who had thought George W. Bush's tax cuts were too small in 2001! Whatever his issue with President Trump, I told Jeff, "This is what we came here to do." He didn't disagree. He wanted to work with the administration on immigration reform, on finding a solution to Deferred Action for Childhood Arrivals (DACA), a program created by an executive order by President Obama that had delayed the deportation of children brought to the country illegally. I didn't make him any promises, but I said I would try. He didn't give me any commitment on the tax bill. He later informed the Republican leadership that he was a yes. The Senate passed the bill, the Tax Cuts and Jobs Act, by a vote of 51–48 on December 19. I presided over the vote. It cut taxes across almost all brackets, dropping the top individual rate from 39.6 percent to 37 percent and reducing the corporate tax rate to 21 percent. It was the Trump administration's first major legislative victory and a big, though hard-earned, one. And it was a victory for the American people.

As the year came to a close, our attention turned to Afghanistan.

H. R. McMaster had asked me to have regular calls with the president of Afghanistan, Ashraf Ghani, following the announcements of the president's new military strategy earlier in the fall. He told me that the president was not inclined to participate in routine calls with heads of state, reserving them for times when issues needed to be discussed. But our goal was to maintain a strong relationship, and I readily agreed to the outreach.

In the fall, my staff had proposed that I travel to Afghanistan right before Christmas to visit with the troops executing the United States' new military strategy. They observed that no one in the West Wing had gotten a firsthand look at our progress. And with the president's ongoing desire to ultimately bring our troops home, it was important that someone go.

The following Monday at our weekly luncheon, I told the president that my team had put together a detailed proposal for a trip and slid a copy of the itinerary in front of him. As the president looked at the proposal, to the dismay of my chief of staff, who had planned the trip, I told him that I was willing to go but said, "You should do it." That was in keeping with my practice of always deferring to the president. He seemed intrigued by my suggestion. I told the president, based on my earlier travels as a congressman and governor, how important I thought visits to our troops were and that I thought the commander in chief should go first. With that we walked through the whole plan and the president said that he would think about it and let me know. In the end, he would travel to visit troops the following year, and he directed me to make the trip. But deferring to him and having him make the decision for me to go were important to me—and to him.

On December 22, Karen and I left for Afghanistan, flying in the belly of an anonymous C-17 transport plane. Inside it was a retrofitted Airstream trailer with an office and a pullout bed. The trip, for security reasons, was top secret. Only a handful of administration officials and the press flying with us knew where we were headed. My wife had first traveled with me following the end of major combat operations in Iraq and had been a great encouragement to our troops and their families everywhere she had gone.

When we arrived at nightfall at Bagram Air Base after a stop to refuel in Germany, it was the same scenario I was used to by now: when I arrived in a potentially dangerous area, military officials always wanted to place me in a secure conference room, keep me there, hold meetings there, and then fly me out safely. But I am a big believer in walking the ground and being seen. If you are going to fly the flag, fly it. We were closer to victory in Afghanistan than ever before. I wanted to fly into Kabul and land at the presidential palace, and I let that be known. My staff said it wasn't possible. When I protested, they said I should talk to the general. The general was John Nicholson, Jr., who was commanding the US forces in Afghanistan. He explained to me that because of fog and clouds, visibility was poor and landing at the palace, in the center of Kabul, might be impossible.

"Sir, we can get you up," he explained, "but there's no guarantee we can get you down."

"Well, General," I answered, "one thing I know for sure: if we don't go up, we for sure won't get back down." He smiled. "You got a point." If I was willing to try, so was he. I put on a bulletproof vest and a Kevlar helmet and buckled up inside a heavily armed Chinook helicopter. During the thirty-minute flight into Kabul, the cabin remained completely dark. We got down, and when we arrived in a courtyard outside the presidential palace, Ghani was there waiting. He projected a quiet strength that belied the underlying weakness of his government. The tenuous nature of the Afghan government was evident, though, when I realized that Ghani's main political rival, Abdullah Abdullah, was the nation's chief executive, a position equivalent to the American vice president. He joined our meetings at the presidential palace. As someone who now understood a bit about vice presidents, that struck me as an impossible arrangement. In the early days of our republic, we, too, had had an unworkable system: the runner-up in the Electoral College had become the vice president. When the Afghan government collapsed amid the disastrous withdrawal of American forces under the Biden administration, I knew my suspicions had been correct.

I delivered remarks to the soldiers in a hangar back at Bagram, and the mention of Trump's name elicited thunderous applause. They knew their commander in chief had their back, that he was going to get them the resources to get the job done and return home. When the trip received significant media coverage, the president was very pleased that he had sent me. It was a privilege for Karen and me to be among those American heroes.

The White House had originally planned to host a Rose Garden signing ceremony for the tax bill in early 2018. But Trump had promised to deliver the cuts before Christmas. On the morning of the twenty-second, before we left for Afghanistan, he called me to talk about signing the bill. He told me he wanted to do it now, not wait. Planning a formal ceremony would take too long. An Oval Office event was quickly arranged that morning, and the bill, the administration's most significant domestic accomplishment of its first year, was signed. It was done with little fanfare, but it did keep a promise.

The year 2017, then, ended much the way it had begun. On the first day of the year and the administration, my son, Michael, had remarked that the president had kept his promise not to reduce the military. Now, on one of the last days of the year, he kept his promise to cut taxes before Christmas. As Michael remarked, the little things are the big things.

CHAPTER THIRTY-ONE

On a Foundation of Faith

Now faith is the assurance of things hoped for,
the conviction of things not seen.
—Hebrews 11:1 (ESV)

Karen and I spent New Year's in Colorado, catching our breath after a busy but amazing first year in the vice presidency. We had stopped off in Columbus on our way back to the capital to celebrate her birthday with her family. My wife was the first little girl born in Kansas in 1957. Then it was back to work, another year with an ambitious agenda—we were going to keep the economy roaring, secure our border, reform the country's criminal justice system, confront the growing threats to the world's safety from North Korea, and take the upper hand in the competition against China. And I was going to do everything I could to help the president achieve all that.

After takeoff, Air Force Two took a hard turn and banked to the left. The sky was clear; I could see for miles in all directions. I shifted in my seat, leaned toward the small window, and looked down on Columbus. I oriented myself, then realized I could see my elementary school, Parkside. Then I spotted what seemed from so high above like just feet from it, the street I grew up on, Hunter Place, the home I had left to go to college. I hurriedly snapped photos with my phone. Then the Boeing 757 leveled and jetted east, back to Washington. In a few minutes my hometown was out of sight. I couldn't forget the view, though, or how blessed our family was by the assignment, even with its thorns. It was a uniquely American moment: a small-town kid from southern Indiana flying high above his home in that blue-and-white jet.

One of my first tasks in 2018 was an easy one. On January 3, I was back at the Capitol to swear in a new senator from Minnesota, Tina Smith. I was joined for the ceremony by former vice president Walter Mondale, who was, of course, also from Minnesota, and Joe Biden. After the ceremony I visited with the two former vice presidents, who were affable and funny. We bonded over the peculiar position in the US government we had in common. I had not previously met Mondale and took the opportunity not only to tell him that I have great respect for his career of service but I also joked that I hoped he wouldn't be offended to know that I had actually voted for him—and Jimmy Carter—in 1980. He was shocked. I also recalled how he had flown into Columbus as vice president on Air Force Two in 1978. He had come to town to campaign for Phil Sharp, the same congressman I would run against early in my political career. His motorcade had departed from the airport and driven into Columbus. I was working at Ray's Marathon, pumping gas, when I saw the limo approaching. It came swinging by on South Central Street and turned onto Highway 31. The procession of cars slowed as it neared downtown. I stood there in my blue Marathon shirt with my first name stitched on my pocket and stared into the rear window of the limousine. I raised the hand that wasn't on the gas pump and waved at him. He waved back. It was the greatest moment in my young life! He wasn't a remote official; he was a fellow citizen. Even if it was just a few seconds, and a quick wave, it was a connection.

Now, some forty years later, as we sat around a coffee table in the vice president's ceremonial office, I recounted the story for Mondale. "Well, to be honest with you, I don't actually remember that," he confessed with a smile. Everyone laughed. Then he grew philosophical and looked at me sincerely. The most important thing public servants do, he observed, is to show kindness to the people we serve. And he was right. As vice president I always kept my eyes out of the window of the car, always made eye contact, always waved at the people on the other side. I shook every hand I could. In the United States, public men and women owe the people respect, not the other way around—because someday a kid standing on the sidewalk waving will be riding in that car, and the vice president waving back will return to being a private citizen. History has shown us that it is those ordinary Americans who often change the course of our nation for the better.

When I had been in Congress, I had always made a point of attending Martin Luther King, Jr. Day events back in Indiana. For King's holiday in 2018, Karen and I invited to the White House the leaders of the Indianapolis TenPoint Coalition, a nonprofit whose leaders directly engage with youths in some of the city's most troubled neighborhoods. By walking the streets, often late at night, talking and praying with people, and working on conflict resolution, the coalition had been able to reduce violent crime in Indianapolis. We saw King's holiday as a time to discuss his legacy and work on ways to end violence and stop poverty with people doing that work today. And we did it in the same office in the Eisenhower Executive Office Building where King had once met with Lyndon Johnson. Later in the day, Karen and I joined the president in placing a wreath on the Martin Luther King, Jr. Memorial in Washington. It was a small gesture, but I have always believed in maintaining civic ritual as a way of demonstrating the importance of memory and a reverence for inspiring historical figures. But nothing is ever that simple.

A few days before the MLK holiday, while the president was meeting with a group of bipartisan legislators on immigration reform, he allegedly referred to El Salvador, Haiti, and several African nations that were receiving preferential treatment in immigration policy, as "s—hole countries." He denied having used those words but admitted to having used "tough talk" during the meeting. With the MLK holiday looming, the media predictably went into a frenzy. The UN Human Rights Office joined in, saying that the comments were "shocking and shameful" and "racist."

On the Sunday of MLK weekend, we had made plans to attend a service at Metropolitan Baptist Church in Largo, Maryland, a predominantly black church just outside Washington. Secretary of Agriculture Sonny Perdue and his wife had been attending services there and encouraged us to attend as a way of honoring the memory of Dr. King and worshipping with fellow believers.

Things had reached a fever pitch as we arrived at the church, where we were greeted by Reverend Maurice Watson. After being warmly welcomed by the congregation, we took our seats in a pew. Reverend Watson took to the pulpit and, without mentioning the president by name, denounced the "visceral, disrespectful, dehumanizing adjective to characterize the nations of Africa," adding "Whoever said it is wrong. And they ought to be held accountable."

The traveling press corps reported that I was "red-faced." But I wasn't. Reverend Watson had graciously warned me that he was going to speak out. I had long since learned to take such moments in stride. But I was honestly moved as we left the sanctuary by the handshakes and warm looks that we received from many people present. I think they were genuinely grateful that we had come. I had the impression that whatever they thought of whatever Trump had said, they knew I wasn't him. We had a common admiration for Dr. King. And I sensed that they appreciated our sincere efforts to strengthen ties on our shared foundation of faith.

Two weeks later we were back in the Middle East, my first trip as vice president to the area. The culmination of the planned trip was a visit to Jerusalem, where I was invited to speak in front of the Knesset, the Israeli parliament, to make the formal announcement of the United States' recognition of Jerusalem as the nation's capital and the relocation of the US Embassy there. Before doing that, however, I made stops in Egypt and Jordan, where the leaders of those countries voiced their formal displeasure with the move. They were publicly against it but not outraged. When I met with Egyptian president Abdel Fattah el-Sisi at the presidential palace in Cairo, his staff refused to let the press, who had traveled so far, into the meetings. I objected. Sisi, a former general, explained that he didn't give press access to presidential meetings.

"Well, we do," I said. "These people traveled a long way. It would mean a great deal to me if you let them in." He thought about it for a few seconds, then signaled to his staff to let the reporters in. Later at an ornate banquet in the presidential palace, Sisi, who was seated next to me, leaned in. In a quiet voice he asked me if I was a man of faith. "I am," I replied. He expressed his respect. He said that I was a Christian, he was a Muslim, that we were both men of faith.

In Jordan I was reunited with King Abdullah, whom I had always gotten along with well. We had something in common as well: he is a former fighter pilot, and my son is a fighter pilot. Like Sisi, even if King Abdullah wasn't enthused about the relocation of the US embassy, he was supportive of President Trump and had other issues he wanted to discuss during our meeting. Jordan was accommodating refugees coming across its border, fleeing from Syria's civil war, and helping rebuild the Christian communities on the Nineveh Plain in northern Iraq, which had been destroyed by ISIS. When I thanked the king for supporting the minorities in the region, he told me of his desire to build a strong Christian community in the Middle East, explaining that it is part of the fabric of who they are.

I felt then that his words represented a genuine moment in the Abrahamic tradition—one that recognizes the contributions of Abraham to three religions. Egypt had long before recognized the right of Israel to exist, and I sensed that there was an opportunity for other countries to do so as well; that despite all the dire predictions of bloodshed following the relocation of the US Embassy, there was a chance for peace in the region among Abraham's children.

Then it was on to Israel. Speaking at the Knesset and formally informing the Israeli government of the relocation of the US Embassy was one of the high honors of my career. During the trip Karen and I visited Yad Vashem, the country's memorial not of the Holocaust but of the 6 million men and women murdered in it. Shortly after, in keeping with tradition, I slipped a prayer into a crack in the Western Wall, the remaining limestone fragment of the ancient wall on the Temple Mount. Prime Minister Benjamin Netanyahu hosted us on that trip.

The first time I met the Israeli prime minister, in the same small conference room where I had visited with Ariel Sharon, Bibi, as he is known, showed me a 2,500-year-old coin that had been excavated on the Temple Mount. It bore the name of one of the ministers in the king of Israel's court, Netanyahu. With a wry smile he told me his family has been at this for a long time.

In Congress I gave pro-Israel addresses so often I was asked if there was a big Jewish community out in rural Indiana. I had Jewish constituents, yes, but I was expressing my support for Israel as an American believer—not simply because Israel is the lone democracy in the Middle East but because its existence is proof that God's promises are true. Its creation and survival so soon after the Holocaust are miracles.

I took to the podium in the historic Knesset chamber and said, "We stand with Israel because Israel's cause is our cause, we stand with Israel because we stand with right over wrong, good over evil." I explained that in the story of the Jewish people, we have always seen the story of America: a journey from persecution to freedom, a story that shows the power of faith and the promise of hope. I mentioned President Trump, to applause, but also presidents Washington and John Adams. Since our nation's founding, Americans have cherished the Jewish people; we were the first nation on Earth to acknowledge the state of Israel, and now we were the first to acknowledge Jerusalem as its capital. By doing so we were simply acknowledging a historical fact, righting a seven-decades-long wrong. And I believed at the time that we were setting the stage for a real peace. The children of Abraham have a common forefather, I said, and they can live together. I was humbled by the ovation that followed my address and left Israel with a sense of optimism about the prospects for a new beginning for peace.

Previous administrations had sought to resolve the violence and political turmoil across the region by prioritizing a two-state solution between the Israelis and Palestinians and engaging in diplomatic and military efforts to improve the conditions in Middle Eastern nations. In 2005, in his second inaugural address, President George W. Bush laid out an idealistic strategy to "expand freedom" around the globe, predicting that the spread of American-style democracy into the Middle East would bring peace and stability and end terrorism. I was in the audience on that January day and found the strategy impractical. Despite the courageous efforts of our troops in Iraq and Afghanistan to support the fledgling governments in those nations, democracy never spread across the Middle East.

President Obama concentrated on improving relations with Iran, the largest sponsor of terrorism and violence in the region. His administration signed the Joint Comprehensive Plan of Action with Iran in 2015, a compact that delayed but did not stop Tehran's nuclear ambitions in return for financial rewards in the form of cash payouts and lifted sanctions. Obama hoped that the arrangement would normalize relations with Iran, which would then spend its rewards internally improving the lives of its citizens rather than financing terrorism across the Middle East. Not only did Iran regularly break the rules of the agreement, denying International Atomic Energy Agency inspectors access to sites and continuing to run its reactors, as a regional strategy, it didn't work; when Trump took office, Iran's proxies and allies were fomenting violence in Syria, Iraq, and Lebanon. And separately, ISIS, the terrorist group that Obama had labeled "JV," emerged from the vacuum caused by the United States' departure from Iraq and held large parts of that nation and Syria—more than twenty thousand square miles.

Trump, as he did in so many policy areas both domestic and foreign, changed course. Our administration unapologetically supported Israel, deemphasizing the two-state solution, and not only acknowledged Jerusalem as its capital but also recognized the Golan Heights, territory won from Syria during the Six-Day War in 1967, as part of the Jewish state. But our administration also strengthened relations with other Middle Eastern nations, such as Saudi Arabia—the very first country Trump visited as president in 2017—and Egypt and Jordan as well. Trump gave our commanders in the field greater control over military decisions, and they took the fight to ISIS—destroying the caliphate and liberating the ISIS capital, Raqqa, in our first year in office. In 2018, he pulled the United States away from Obama's nuclear deal with Iran, calling it "one of the worst and most one-sided transactions" in US history. In doing so, he reimposed harsh sanctions on the country, causing negative economic growth and a 40 percent inflation rate, isolating Iran, and opening the door to an alliance among the United States, Israel, and other Arab nations.

The optimism I felt during that trip and the wisdom of our administration's approach would be confirmed three years later, in September 2020, when President Trump completed the Abraham Accords, a historic peace agreement between Israel and two of its former enemies, the United Arab Emirates and Bahrain. It was the first Middle East peace agreement since 1994. It didn't just establish diplomatic relations between the nations but also opened channels for trade and economic partnerships between them. The bulk of the credit belonged to Jared Kushner and Ambassador David Friedman. Trump had placed Kushner in charge of the peace process, and with the president's encouragement, he had promptly dispensed with the conventional wisdom when it came to brokering peace in that region. Instead of tying peace to the recognition of a Palestinian state, the administration maintained that by standing with Israel and normalizing relations between Israel and its Arab neighbors, Middle East peace was more possible. I believe that history will record that it was one of the Trump administration's most important accomplishments.

After I had delivered my address before the Knesset, I called the president from my hotel room. While we discussed how the speech had gone, Trump segued into a discussion of the US Embassy building itself. He had heard from the State Department that it would take up to a decade and cost a billion dollars to build one on the land owned by the United States and long designated for that purpose. He was disgusted. "Call David Friedman and get him to do it," Trump said. "David will get it done." And he did for pennies on the dollar. David Friedman, the US ambassador to Israel, was Trump's former lawyer. He, too, knows a thing or two about real estate. In May 2018, a few months after the president gave the order, the embassy opened—but not on the site originally chosen. Friedman decided instead to convert a building already owned by the United States that had been used to process visa and passport applications. Two years later, during a trip to Israel, we headed for the new embassy. During the visit, I posed with Netanyahu for photos outside the building's front door. While we were smiling for the cameras, I noticed the building's tan cornerstone. There, between President Trump and Ambassador Friedman's names, was my own. David Friedman had put it there.

CHAPTER THIRTY-TWO

Maximum Pressure

Have no fellowship with the unfaithful works
of darkness, but rather expose them.
—Ephesians 5:11

Karen and I returned to Washington just in time for another speech, the president's first State of the Union address. Trump's speaking style is improvisational and freewheeling. It is part of his appeal. But when the occasion required, working with his speechwriter Stephen Miller—no other writer better understood how Trump communicated—he soared. The president put a tremendous amount of effort into formal speeches, none more so than the State of the Union address. Though I didn't often help with them, I would review a draft of each once-a-year address and sit in on his rehearsals in the Map Room of the White House. Trump would have half a dozen speechwriters and policy staffers seated around him as he stood at a podium and rehearsed the speech with a teleprompter. Invariably, he would edit almost every other line on the spot and have them retype it. "No, say it this way."

The State of the Union address he delivered on January 31, 2018, like his previous address to Congress, was optimistic. And a year into the administration there was plenty to be optimistic about. US employers had created 2.4 million jobs since we had arrived in the White House, African American unemployment was at a forty-five-year low. A giant new tax cut was on the way. Billions of dollars had already been invested in the United States by companies like Apple since the tax bill had passed. AT&T had distributed bonuses to its employees around the country following the tax cut. Abroad, though, as the president noted, we still faced challenges. One tradition of the State of the Union address, dating back to the presidency of Ronald Reagan, is that the president invites American heroes—firefighters, policemen, and the widows of fallen soldiers—to the gallery of the House of Representatives, where the speech is delivered. During the course of the speech the president often tells their inspiring stories and asks them to stand, to a rousing ovation. In 2018, the president invited the parents of Otto Warmbier.

Otto was a twenty-one-year-old college student from Cincinnati, Ohio. He was curious and bubbly—a smart and funny kid. He never missed a day of school or had a grade below an A. No wonder: he studied seven hours a day. By the time of his junior year he had enough credits at the University of Virginia to earn a degree. More important, his parents loved him deeply, and they loved watching him grow into a man. Then in 2016, while studying in Hong Kong, he traveled to North Korea as part of a tour group. On his way out of the country, on January 2, 2016, he was arrested at Pyongyang International Airport and charged with treason for allegedly stealing a propaganda poster. He was subsequently given a sham trial and sentenced to fifteen years of labor for a crime against the state. His parents' efforts to gain his release were frustrated by the Obama State Department, which encouraged them to keep quiet, not wanting Otto's story to anger the North Korean government. To be fair, its approach was in keeping with the one deployed toward the Kim regime by every other administration: to kowtow to the North Korean government in the hope that it would abandon its nuclear program.

In June 2017, the State Department, led by Rex Tillerson, helped gain Otto's release. He was flown back to the United States in a vegetative state and died in a Cincinnati hospital days later. His parents, Fred and Cindy, went through hell. They took it upon themselves to persuade the US government to designate North Korea as a state sponsor of terrorism. It had been removed from that list by the Bush administration because Kim had supposedly met the requirements of a disarmament arrangement. When Trump put North Korea back on the list in November 2017, the Warmbiers had helped put it there. When Trump spoke of Otto during his State of the Union address, they stood with tears streaming down their faces and heard a rousing ovation. Next to them in the gallery was Ji Seong-ho, who had defected from North Korea, after having been tortured by the North Korean gestapo. He had defected by walking thousands of miles on crutches—the result of his legs having been run over by a train as a teenager. When Trump singled him out, Ji defiantly held his crutch high in the air. Republicans and Democrats alike stood in applause. The Warmbiers had spent the day of the speech in Washington, visiting with members of the administration. I spent time with them in my office and instantly developed a bond with the family. After the State of the Union address and a short stay in Washington, Karen and I were scheduled to return to South Korea, where the Winter Olympics were to kick off in the city of PyeongChang early in February. The United States sent a delegation to the Games, and I was asked by the State Department to lead it. As it turned out, Fred Warmbier also attended, making sure that the world did not forget about Otto. I asked him to join our delegation on the trip, and he agreed. We were not just going to the Olympics to root on America's athletes.

After a year of aggressive overtures, missile tests, threats, and insults, Kim Jong-un's tone shifted in the new year. At his request, North and South Korea agreed to have their athletes compete under one flag at the winter Games, the first time since 1994. The South Korean government, continually threatened by its northern neighbor, was eager to defuse tensions. In another diplomatic overture: Kim's sister and right-hand woman, Kim Yo-jong, planned to attend the opening ceremonies, the first time a member of North Korea's ruling family had set foot in South Korea since the end of the Korean War. The Games were supposed to unfold as a public relations coup for the Kim family, participating in the Olympics with the rest of the world and pretending to be part of the civilized order of nations—all while they continued to torture and starve the country's citizens and develop its nuclear arsenal. It was clear, though, by his willingness to talk with South Korean president Moon Jae-in, that Kim was rattled by Trump. For years his family had played US and world leaders perfectly. Now there was an unpredictable US president, and the North Koreans were worried. By sending his sister to the Olympics and playing nice with the South Koreans, Kim was not only playing nice with the world community but also hoping to make a propaganda coup. I wasn't going to the Olympics to play along.

On February 6, en route to the Olympic Games, we stopped off in Tokyo to make a call on Shinzo Abe, Japan's prime minister. A man of few words and also incredibly tough, Abe stood strong against North Korean provocations and led an administration preparing to amend Japan's post–World War II constitution to allow the expansion of its military. His father, Shintaro, had been Japan's minister of foreign affairs. The younger Abe applauded Trump's hard line on China and North Korea. He was a supporter of our foreign policy, and, though he spoke little English, we developed a close relationship quickly. He was in agreement that any peace talks or even any talk of lifting sanctions on North Korea was dependent on Kim's giving up his nuclear weapons. After all, just the year before, one of Kim's missile tests had streaked across the skies of northern Japan. After Abe and I met, I announced that the United States was readying another round of economic sanctions on North Korea. The United States and its allies would continue to isolate the Kim regime until it abandoned its nuclear program.

After Karen and I arrived in South Korea the next day, we made a point to visit the Cheonan Memorial, honoring the forty-six sailors who had perished when their warship had been sunk by a North Korean submarine in 2010. Sitting in the Cheonan Memorial Hall under the two salvaged pieces of the ship, we were joined by Fred Warmbier and met with several North Korean dissidents. One woman wept as she recounted having been forced to have an abortion in prison. Even the grizzled press was moved to silence. When Warmbier saw Ji Seong-ho, who joined the meeting, the two men embraced. By standing with Abe in Japan, looking over Japan's missile defenses, and meeting with men and women who had been brutalized by Kim's police forces, I was hitting a contrary note: the global media may have been fascinated by the North Koreans' participation in the Olympics, but the United States was not going to let them ignore the country's ongoing threats to the rest of the world and its leaders' barbaric treatment of their own people.

There was a touching moment during our time with Fred. When

he and his wife, Cindy, attended the State of the Union address, Karen, artist that she is, noticed the pendant on Cindy's gold necklace. It was a gathering of circles and bars that spelled "Otto." "I know exactly what that is," Karen told the Warmbiers. During our time in South Korea, Fred had presented Karen with a replica of the necklace, which, as it turned out, had been made by a Holocaust survivor, Aaron Rubinstein. It was a beautiful gesture and a sign of how close our families had grown in a short amount of time. Karen wore it throughout the Olympics. A couple of years later, when we were in Cincinnati, Ohio, Karen stopped by Rubinstein's shop to meet the man who had made that beautiful tribute to Otto.

South Korean president Moon's priority was Korean reunification, so he was eager for me to engage with Kim's sister and Kim Yong-nam, North Korea's ceremonial head of state and the highest-level official ever to go to the South. Before the opening ceremony, there was a large reception and dinner for the two hundred national leaders in attendance. As choreographed by Moon, both the North Koreans and I were at the head table. A group photograph was arranged at the outset of the banquet. Both Abe and I arrived intentionally late and didn't participate. By the time we arrived, the doors to the banquet hall were closed, so we waited for Moon, who eventually escorted us in. It was evident that he wanted to politely force a meeting between Kim Yong-nam and me. That would have been a huge symbolic victory for North Korea. No chance. Moon walked Abe and me and our wives into the banquet hall, guiding us toward Kim. I kept my distance, though, shook hands with every other leader in the room, and then walked out the door. When the dignitaries sat down for their dinner, there were two empty seats. The place cards read "Vice President Pence" and "Mrs. Pence."

While the Olympic festivities began the following day to a worldwide audience, the North Korean government was making back-channel overtures to me about having a meeting. I relayed the information to Trump. See what they have to say, he told me. If the meeting can be arranged, take it. I wasn't going to shake Kim's sister's hand in public, but if the North Koreans, away from the cameras, wanted to send a message, if they had something to say to President Trump, I was willing to listen.

As a possible meeting was negotiated through officials on both sides, the opening ceremony began. Abe and I were staying at the same hotel. Before we left to head to the Olympic arena, we met briefly in a conference room at the hotel and I asked if he wanted to ride to the event with me. He said yes. This time I angered the executive protection teams of two nations, both the US Secret Service and Abe's security detail; two world leaders riding in the same car is highly unusual.

A box had been reserved in PyeongChang Stadium for world leaders. Kim Jong-un's sister, who had been dubbed "the Ivanka of North Korea" by a fawning international press, was the first member of North Korea's ruling dynasty to set foot in South Korea since the Korean War, and she was sitting in the box. Despite the press coverage, I knew that the woman had been complicit in a regime that had murdered and oppressed tens of thousands of citizens, including a member of her own family. Both Abe and Moon were seated there as well. Another arrangement was offered to me, but I wanted to be there to stand, or rather sit, with Abe and Moon, to show that the United States, Japan, and South Korea were united against North Korea's aggressions. When Karen and I arrived in the box, Moon and his wife were to our left and Abe and his wife to our right. In the row behind us and to our right was Kim's sister. I ignored her.

Karen and I were returning to the United States the following day. The clock was ticking on a possible meeting, and it appeared to be a go: we would meet the following day in the Blue House, the South Korean equivalent of the White House. Two hours before the meeting was set to begin, we got word that the North Koreans were no longer willing to participate and we were told that the order "came from Pyongyang," leading to speculation that Kim Jong-un was irritated by my refusal to engage with his sister while the cameras clicked and the world watched. Trump was fine with it. The press saw my trip as a provocation—standing with Abe, traveling with Fred Warmbier, meeting with the North Korean defectors, refusing to socialize with Kim's sister or cheer on the North Korean athletes. North Korea had the rest of the world on the razor's edge, and I had made matters worse, the commentators groused. But the North Koreans got the message that this administration wasn't going to roll over like all of those before it. Sometimes the most reasonable thing is to be unreasonable.

A few weeks later, I was sitting in the Oval Office, the outrage about my presence at the Olympics still fresh, when a visiting South Korean delegation arrived with a message for the president: Kim Jong-un wanted to speak face-to-face with Trump, and he was suspending North Korea's missile tests and nuclear program as a precondition of the dialogue. It was proof that the North Koreans had been shaken. From punishing sanctions to Trump's tough, even shocking, talk of "fire and fury" to our strong posture during the Olympics, the administration had exerted maximum pressure on the Hermit Kingdom, and its leaders were unsure how to react. The same old games weren't working. Now they wanted to talk. And Trump was willing. Arrangements began between the two nations for a historic summit. Nothing was guaranteed, though, and the nation's attention was soon focused elsewhere.

CHAPTER THIRTY-THREE

Heal Our Land

The Lord is close to the brokenhearted.
—Psalm 34:18

On February 14, shortly after returning to Washington, we learned that a gunman had killed seventeen people and injured seventeen at Marjory Stoneman Douglas High School in Parkland, Florida, near Miami. It was the third mass shooting in less than a year, and Americans were still reeling from the shootings in Las Vegas and in Sutherland Springs, Texas.

I have always believed that leaders need to be present after a tragedy. The perspective they get by doing this can help inform and better direct government responses. But just as important, it means a great deal to grieving families and weary first responders to see and talk to their elected officials. You give them your condolences and assure them of your prayers. But I learned a long time ago that there isn't much you can say to lessen the pain.

When someone who is grieving meets someone in my position, they just want to tell you about their loved one. I learned to simply say, "Tell me about them." I hope it was a comfort. Heartbroken families deserve to know that their loved ones mattered and would never be forgotten. I did it when President Trump and I met with survivors and families of the Stoneman Douglas High School and Sandy Hook Elementary School shootings at the White House that week. And I had done it when we had traveled to Las Vegas and Texas the previous year.

When Karen and I arrived in Sutherland Springs in November 2017, the First Baptist Church, where the shooting had taken place, was sealed off, so we met with families and survivors in a local high school that had been converted into a response center. Karen and I went from table to table, spending time with everyone there. She is always great in such moments. In times of hardship, she sets people at ease and comforts them. Her presence in Las Vegas and Sutherland Springs—and at Walter Reed National Military Medical Center—always left a mark on the people she met.

There have been times in my career when my Christian faith was the subject of criticism or mockery. But maybe because of this, people in tragic settings know that we share something. Karen and I immediately formed a connection with the congregants of the First Baptist Church. I remember visiting the military hospital where the victims were being treated. We met with a man who had been shot repeatedly. Lying in his bed, he told me that men from the church came to the hospital and they had an impromptu Bible study. Before we left his side, he asked if we could pray together. And we did so right there in his hospital room, his little granddaughter holding his hand with her head bowed.

We visited another victim, a young man named Kris Workman. Texas governor Greg Abbott was with me outside his hospital room when a doctor came out with a pained expression on his face. Kris had just learned that he would be paralyzed from the waist down for life because of his wounds. The doctor said that the young man was devastated but still wanted to meet me. I walked in alone, extended my hand, and told him I was happy to meet him. Then Governor Abbott, who was paralyzed when a tree fell on him as a young man, wheeled into the room. "I just want to meet a future governor of Texas," he said with a smile. Kris lit up, and I stood back. "I know you got bad news," he said. "I got that same news long ago. It didn't stop me. It won't stop you." I know he was right. Those were little moments but among the most important parts of the job.

In the days following the Parkland shooting, the country was heartbroken and asking why so many innocent lives had been taken and what we could do to prevent it from happening again. There were calls for new gun control measures from politicians on the left and even on the right, as well as from survivors and their families. I understood their anger and frustration.

President Trump, Secretary of Education Betsy DeVos, and I held a listening session with Parkland students and families at the White House on February 21, 2018. Emotions were raw, and the stories told—of high schoolers losing classmates, of parents losing children—were devastating. There were deeply sincere and pained calls for more gun control and more school safety. Parents such as Andrew Pollack, a strong supporter of the president, called for more school safety. "Fix it," Andrew told us. "She's in North Lauderdale at whatever it is, King David cemetery; that is where I go to see my kid now." The president and I listened with compassion and with open minds.

In the wake of such a painful, unspeakable tragedy, the first impulse is to react, to take action, to do something to prevent it from happening again. I understand. But my belief is that if we create new laws, they must not infringe on the constitutional rights of Americans and must actually address the problem at hand.

I am as passionate about the Second Amendment as I am about the First Amendment. That is because of both my upbringing and my love for the Constitution. My dad, a combat veteran, a US Army infantryman, taught us boys how to handle and fire a gun. He taught me and my brothers that a gun was a tool, not a toy. We had guns in the house, and we went bird hunting from time to time. Guns were an ordinary but respected part of my life growing up in rural Indiana.

The Founders enshrined the right to bear arms into our Constitution because they believed that doing so was indispensable to the maintenance of liberty. Alexander Hamilton, in *The Federalist Papers*, wrote, "If the representatives of the people betray their constituents, there is then no resource left but in the exertion of that original right of self-defense." But the United States' first statesmen also recognized that the right to bear arms was a means by which law-abiding citizens could protect themselves, their families, and their property from those who would do them harm. Thomas Jefferson approvingly quoted a passage about gun laws from the writings of an Italian Enlightenment thinker and politician, Cesare Beccaria, in his commonplace book. The existence of gun laws, Beccaria wrote, "certainly makes the situation of the assaulted worse, and of the assailants better, and rather encourages than prevents murder, as it requires less courage to attack unarmed than armed persons." That was true then, and it's true now.

Restricting access to firearms by law-abiding citizens is not the answer. In many cases, the existing laws on the books are not fully obeyed or enforced. The shooter in Sutherland Springs, for example, had a criminal record that the air force did not submit to the FBI. Had the air force done so, the record would have appeared on a standard background check run by a gun shop. In the case of the Parkland shooting, the shooter had posted videos on YouTube talking about mass shootings. His behavior had been reported to the FBI, to local law enforcement, and even to the school resource officer at Marjory Stoneman Douglas. None of them acted on the information.

There are 450 million firearms owned across the United States, most by law-abiding citizens. The truth is that any solution to mass shootings is going to be complicated. So-called gun safety laws, as they are billed, have little impact on violent crime and often lead to further restrictions of the Second Amendment. That does not mean that we can't act, that we can't find solutions. Which was exactly what we did in the wake of the Marjory Stoneman Douglas shooting.

Shortly after the tragedy, the president convened members of Congress for bipartisan meetings at the White House. During one of the meetings, on March 1, the president made off-the-cuff remarks with the press present about increasing background checks and raising the age for rifle purchases. He also quipped to Republican senator Pat Toomey that he was "afraid of the NRA."

I knew the president was searching for solutions. I encouraged him to meet with the National Rifle Association, and we sat down in the Oval Office with Chris Cox, the executive director of the NRA's Institute for Legislative Action, who, acknowledging our support for the Second Amendment, said that we all want safe schools and mental health reform and to keep guns away from dangerous people.

The first thing that crossed my mind after the Parkland shooting was the Sandy Hook Elementary School shooting in December 2012, when another monster with a gun had killed twenty-six people, almost all of them children, at an elementary school in Connecticut. I was just transitioning into the Indiana Governor's Office at the time. I remembered the anguished families, the entire nation in mourning. I wanted to know, once I became governor, what Indiana could do to keep its schools safe. Mass killers are cowards. They will always target schools, concerts, or houses of worship, places where they know or think that no one will shoot back. Out of the gate, during my first year in office, I signed a school safety bill. It distributed safety grants, helping schools hire trained guards (many of whom were former policemen) who could not only protect students but also serve as resource officers.

In the weeks following, Congress came together around a similar focus on school safety and passed the STOP Act, which President Trump signed into law in March 2018. The law allocated $50 million a year to train teachers, students, and law enforcement officers to spot and stop school violence before it occurs. The bill was supported by Sandy Hook Promise, a gun reform group led by parents of some of the children killed in 2012, and the NRA, proving that we can find common ground when it comes to protecting our kids.

But there is more we can do. Currently, schools can apply for grants from the School Violence Prevention Program, funded by the STOP Act. But, as I learned through conversations with law enforcement officials after the law was passed, the application process for the grants is cumbersome. Congress should simply provide the necessary funds. We are the most prosperous nation in the world, and I say this as a fiscal conservative; there is no reason that cost should be a barrier to securing every single school in the United States.

We also need to make a commitment to ending the mental health crisis in our country. Fueled by the opioid addiction epidemic and made worse by the covid pandemic, mental health issues not only result in homelessness and deaths but are often a factor in mass shootings. There is no excuse for evil, but clearly the great majority of mass shooters are also suffering from mental illness. If there is a way to find these people treatment before they act, we have to pursue it.

We must create institutions in our society that give families with a relative manifesting mental illness a place to go. The Parkland murderer had left a trail of clues: he had held a gun to his brother's head and expressed his desire to kill people. Resources should have been available for his family to more easily find him some sort of treatment.

Already recognizing the need to address the situation when I was governor of Indiana, in December 2015, we broke ground on the state's first new mental health hospital in over twenty-five years. The Trump administration's Department of Health and Human Services made it easier for states to provide mental health care and increased funding to Certified Community Behavioral Health Clinics, which help states treat mental and substance abuse disorders.

Ultimately, governments have only so much power to address the causes of mass shootings. For all of America's blessings and despite the goodness of our people, there is a sickness across our land: broken families, broken homes, broken souls. The ties and bonds that hold communities together are giving way to isolation and anger, while our popular culture too often glorifies violence. There are few laws government can pass to stem this; the source of the pain is in the spirit.

So although allusions to "thoughts and prayers" are often demeaned in the wake of tragedies, we need to pray for our country, pray for the families that have suffered loss, pray for the safety of our schools and places of worship. And remember the promise in 2 Chronicles 7:14: "If my people, who are called by my name, will humble themselves and pray and seek my face and turn from their wicked ways, then I will hear from heaven, and I will forgive their sin and will heal their land."

CHAPTER THIRTY-FOUR

Blessed

Bless those who persecute you; bless and do not curse.
—Romans 12:14

On February 21, 2018, Billy Graham, the towering evangelical preacher whose ministry for the gospel of Jesus Christ had changed so many lives, died at the age of ninety-nine. What an incredible life. I never met Reverend Graham. Graham had first preached in Indiana in 1959, the year I was born. Karen and I had attended his last crusade at the Hoosier Dome in 1999 and took our son, Michael, along. When Graham made his altar call, with the hymn "Just as I Am" filling the stadium, thousands began streaming down the aisles. "You just get up and come," he said in that Tarheel accent. At that, Karen nudged me and asked, "Where's Michael?" We looked around and spotted our eight-year-old boy halfway down the steps to the floor. I ran after and caught up with him, explaining, "This is for those who want to make a decision to pray to receive Jesus Christ." "Dad, I want to go down," he assured me. It was one of the sweetest moments of my life. I grabbed his hand, and down we walked. Like millions of others around the world, my family owes an incalculable debt to Billy Graham.

Trump and I both traveled to Charlotte for Graham's funeral. Though I had never known Graham personally, as it turned out, Trump had. His father, Fred, had been a supporter of Graham. The younger Trump was a great admirer of Graham and had attended his revivals at Madison Square Garden. Graham inspired him. One Sunday at his Bedminster resort, the president invited Karen and me to attend services at a small nearby chapel with a sermon delivered by a local reverend. "Nice service, but he's no Billy Graham," Trump whispered to me as we walked out the door.

On St. Patrick's Day that month, Karen and I welcomed Leo Varadkar, the new Irish taoiseach (prime minister), to the vice president's residence for our traditional St. Patrick's Day brunch. Joe Biden had established the tradition, given his Irish heritage, and given ours, we readily continued it. As he was Ireland's head of state, we had much to discuss. But the media—predictably—focused on the fact that he was the first openly gay taoiseach and looked for some evidence of controversy between us, given my Christian views about traditional marriage. We addressed the media outside the vice president's residence but would forgo the usual press presence during the breakfast so we could enjoy the time together. I think the taoiseach appreciated meeting with us, but frankly, it was my mother who charmed him the most. We had some differences, but Irish mothers are universal. Varadkar was smart and gracious. In the end we got along famously. As he left, Karen insisted that he bring his partner to the next annual brunch, and he seemed genuinely touched. It was another noncontroversy for the ever-divisive press.

Apart from the international statecraft, the spring of 2018 was a special time for the Pence family. Since we had arrived in Washington, Marlon Bundo, the little black-and-white bunny rabbit we had inherited from our daughter, had been an object of playful fascination to the press.

Marlon, whom Charlotte famously dubbed "BOTUS" (Bunny of the United States), struck a chord of gentleness in an otherwise contentious time. Our imaginative daughter launched an Instagram account for the rabbit that drew thirty thousand followers and went on to write three children's books about Marlon that were beautifully illustrated by her mother.

The first book was published in March 2018. I was incredibly proud of Charlotte. It was a truly special moment for her. She put a great deal of work into *Marlon Bundo's A Day in the Life of the Vice President*. The day before it was to be published, another book about Marlon Bundo, the work of the comedian John Oliver, appeared. That Marlon Bundo, though, was gay. The parody book was clearly intended to mock our belief in traditional marriage and our Christian faith. I didn't care about that. If I became discouraged every time someone misinterpreted and mocked my beliefs, I would have retreated from public life decades ago. I had grown a tough skin over the years and learned not to take insults personally. But when it comes to attacks on my wife and children, that's another matter. I'd like to say I can brush those off, too, but that would be a lie. Karen and I are protective of our kids and their private lives. If they are part of our public lives, it's because they want to be, not because we ever required it.

My brothers often say that I have the worst temper but the longest fuse. That may be true. It takes a lot to get my Irish up. But when a book Charlotte and Karen had worked so hard on, a book about a little bunny rabbit, was ridiculed by a mean-hearted parody, I was angry. I think any dad would be. It was a humbling moment. I may have held a high office, but there was little I could do to protect my family in such a situation. Now I knew how Harry Truman had felt when a *Washington Post* critic panned his daughter, Margaret's, piano recital. In response to the nasty review, Truman wrote a furious letter calling the critic an "eight ulcer man on four ulcer pay." He also threatened to break his nose! I love Harry Truman.

Amazingly, Charlotte wasn't upset about the parody book. The proceeds from her book went to anti-human-trafficking efforts and a children's cancer program. The proceeds from Oliver's book went to LGBT charities. As my daughter reasoned, both books helped good causes. "The only thing better than one bunny book for charity is two bunny books for charity," she explained with characteristic grace. That's our girl. Besides, the publicity for Oliver's book drove up the sales of Charlotte's book and made it a *New York Times* best seller. Thanks for the assist.

More animal history. Midterm elections would take place in the fall; primary season got under way in the spring. I was traveling the country selling the tax cut and campaigning for Republican candidates, one of whom was Andy Barr, a congressman who represents a district in Kentucky that includes the horse country around Lexington. When Karen and I were in Kentucky, the congressman asked if we would like to visit Ashford Coolmore Stud, a horse farm not far from Versailles and the home of American Pharoah, the 2015 Triple Crown winner. I grew up watching the Kentucky Derby—Louisville is just a couple of hours south on I-65 from Columbus—and my parents attended it often. Karen and I love horses. We were excited to have an audience with a legend. When American Pharoah trotted out from his barn, I asked the farm manager if I could hold his reins; the reporters stood ready with their cameras. The manager warned that Pharoah was a little spirited that day. Not to worry, I insisted, I'm a horse guy. I smiled for the camera with the bridle in my right hand. As I petted Pharoah with my other hand, he turned his head and chomped my left forearm. It wasn't a nip, it was a bite. And it hurt. It happened so quickly that nobody noticed. The cameras clicked while I stood there with a frozen smile on my face, in a fair amount of pain. I got back into the limousine afterward, rolled up my sleeve, and discovered a blue welt in the shape of a horse's incisors. The moral of the story? If you stand next to a Thoroughbred, expect to get bitten from time to time. Words to live by.

I don't think American Pharoah meant any harm. I can't say the same about the journalists, celebrities, and elected officials whose fixation on my Christian faith reached a mania early in 2018. Maybe it was a slow news month or two. Articles with mocking titles such as "God's Plan for Mike Pence," which featured a drawing of me complete with billowing robes and a halo, appeared in the *Atlantic*, using terms such as "theocrat" and "Christian supremacist" to describe me. "What did you think of that?" Dick Durbin, a Democrat senator from Illinois, incredulously asked me during a visit to the White House. "I'd love to know which parts of that article are true and which aren't." I told him I hadn't read the article but "assumed virtually none of it was true."

In late 2017, White House Chief of Staff John Kelly had relieved Omarosa Manigault of her duties as a White House staffer for, among other things, reportedly misusing the White House car service. She was a former contestant on Trump's TV show *The Apprentice* who had joined the administration as communications and public engagement director. I had met her briefly during the campaign at Trump Tower. She made a point of mentioning our common Christian faith. Though we didn't often interact, she was always solicitous and kind. Then, in February 2018, two months after her White House departure, she published a book and turned against Trump and the administration.

While appearing on that forum of thoughtful debate *Celebrity Big Brother*, she said of me, "He thinks Jesus tells him to say things." Immediately reporters stuck their phones into my face and asked if it was true that Jesus spoke to me and instructed me what to say. "Well," I answered truthfully, "I try to read the Word every morning, and sometimes it does speak to my heart." Blank stares. "So Jesus does tell you what to say?" A few days later, Joy Behar, a comedian and cohost of the talk show *The View*, weighed in. "It's one thing to talk to Jesus," she said. "It's another thing when Jesus talks to you. That's called mental illness, if I'm not correct."

The vast majority of Americans are people of faith. The denominations are various, the degrees are different, but Americans are a deeply religious people. And these days they are regularly insulted for it. The late Chuck Colson once explained to me the hostility toward people with a Christian worldview by pointing out that it has always been a characteristic of the left-leaning elite. He said that India is the most religious country in the world—98 percent of its citizens participate in some faith—and Sweden is the least. "We are a nation of Indians governed by Swedes," he opined. Joy Behar's comments were emblematic of the intolerance of a minority of Americans toward a majority of their countryman. I call it "the intolerance of tolerance." In the name of tolerance, the Left heaps scorn on believing Christians. But this time it backfired.

I called her and her network out during an interview, saying, "It's simply wrong for ABC to have a program like that that expresses religious intolerance." A few days later, Behar called my office and said she wanted to talk. I said I'd be happy to take the call. I believe in grace; I believe in forgiveness. She couldn't have been more kind. She wanted to apologize. We talked about her religious upbringing, and she told me she had not meant to show a lack of respect toward me or my faith. I told her I wasn't offended that she had insulted me; I was offended for all the people of faith she had demeaned by her comment, and I thought she owed them an apology. She agreed and actually apologized on the air. I appreciated that. It's never easy to admit you're wrong. And I give her a lot of credit. As I traveled the country, I would often meet other Americans who felt their faith was misunderstood. "I'm praying for you," they would tell me. "I don't know how you put up with it," they would say. "Yeah, you do," I would always answer, sometimes with a glance to the skies. The warm smiles I got in return told me they knew exactly who I meant.

CHAPTER THIRTY-FIVE

Peace Begins with Strength

Be strong and courageous, and do the work.
—1 Chronicles 28:20

As the collusion saga dragged on, the United States and Russia had their first military altercation since the end of the Cold War. On February 7, a battalion of Syrian and Russian soldiers attacked a US-Kurdish base in the Deir ez-Zor region of Syria. The US forces repeatedly warned off the Russian military. When they approached anyway, artillery and airpower wiped out the Syrian-Russian force, killing hundreds of Syrians and Russian soldiers. Vladimir Putin would later claim that the Russians had been mercenaries, not acting on behalf of his government. They were in fact military contractors connected to the Russian government; the casualties were downplayed and obscured by the Kremlin.

Two months later, on April 7, Syrian warplanes bombed Douma, a town east of Damascus and a stronghold of the rebels in that country's civil war. Shortly afterward, citizens began streaming into hospitals with foaming mouths and scorched retinas. Bashar al-Assad had launched another chemical attack on civilians, killing innocent children with nerve gas. In the face of images of bodies stacked in the basement of an apartment building, Assad denied the use of chemical weapons. His ally Vladimir Putin backed the claim. Russian soldiers on the ground supposedly verifying the attack almost certainly tampered with evidence. Trump had expressed his desire to pull the two thousand US troops in Syria out of the country, but the news of another chemical attack outraged him. When Putin's government warned against any Western missile attacks on Assad's chemical weapons facilities, Trump took to Twitter to respond: "Get ready Russia, because they will be coming, nice and new and 'smart!' You shouldn't be partners with a Gas Killing Animal who kills his people and enjoys it!"

On April 13, the missiles were launched, destroying Syria's chemical weapons facilities. The strike on Syria came at the time Trump was set to travel to Peru to attend the Summit of the Americas, so I was asked to step in at the last minute to cover for the president in Lima. I went there to meet with the heads of state of Latin and Central American nations and also to bring a message on behalf of Trump directed at Venezuela. That once wealthy nation, not long before a flourishing democracy, had collapsed into tyranny and socialism. I laid it all at the feet of the dictator, Nicolás Maduro. And I asked the other nations in the region to help his people with aid and to end his reign through diplomatic isolation. Maduro himself was not invited to the conference—he was refused an audience—but the representative of Cuba, an ally of the Maduro government, attacked the United States, and specifically condemned our attack on Syria's nuclear program.

We were pursuing change abroad in 2018, but there was plenty of it in the White House. One of the most unusual features of Washington, at least of the Trump presidency, was the president's willingness to fire people at the top of his administration. If a cabinet secretary wasn't working out or working well with Trump, he didn't hesitate to dismiss him or her. This is much closer to how business is conducted away from Washington: if an employee isn't getting the job done to the employer's expectations, he or she usually has to find work elsewhere. Trump, it's worth remembering, had turned "You're fired!" into a catchphrase during his career on television. In DC, though, the departure of a cabinet member is viewed as a sign of chaos or failure. And if you fire someone, the person is sure to write a scathing and self-vindicating tell-all book about the White House.

In March, National Security Advisor H. R. McMaster tendered his resignation. He had never hesitated to tell the president what he thought and provided clear-eyed recommendations from the National Security Council in a measured delivery befitting a retired US Army lieutenant general. It was quite a contrast from Trump's freewheeling style, and as time went on I would increasingly see Trump look at me with an eye roll after the general departed a briefing. For my part I developed a warm personal relationship with the general, which I enjoy to this day. But in the end, the president lost enthusiasm for McMaster's steady counsel and was drawn to a more pugilistic national security expert who was a frequent defender of our administration on television.

As a sign of how respected McMaster was, White House staffers lined the sidewalks on either side of West Executive Avenue, the street running between the West Wing and the Eisenhower Executive Office Building, clapping as he walked to his car on his final day of work. He was replaced by John Bolton, who had served in the State Department during the presidency of George W. Bush and been appointed but never confirmed as Bush's ambassador to the United Nations.

Bolton had had an America First approach to foreign policy before Trump had emerged as the GOP's leader. Democrats despised him for it. He was also notable for his round glasses and bushy mustache. In 2010, he considered running for president. During a cattle call of potential candidates in Chicago that we both attended, I joked that not since Teddy Roosevelt had spectacles and a mustache caused so much anxiety on the world stage. Bolton had been a great champion of Trump and the administration on television and radio. McMaster is a great man and public servant and did an incredible job for the president. But Bolton's worldview was more in line with Trump's. He understood the president and seemed perfectly suited to carrying out his national security strategy.

Secretary of State Rex Tillerson also left in March. Rex, I thought, had been a creative pick to lead the State Department. He wasn't a politician or even a career diplomat, but as the head of a major corporation with holdings around the globe, he knew the world and he knew world leaders. Rex had done a yeoman's job carrying out bureaucratic and budget reforms at the State Department, and I believe he tried his best to express the president's opinion abroad. He was well informed and never hesitated to give the president his opinion. The problem was that although he and the president were both businessmen, they came from very different parts of the business world:

Trump was the CEO of an entrepreneurial family business, whereas Rex was the CEO of a publicly held multinational corporation. Trump was a pirate; Rex was a three-piece-suit company man. That difference is why, I believe, the relationship ultimately didn't work. Plus, going from being the head of one of the world's largest companies to being the subordinate of the president of the United States could not have been easy.

Rex was also often frustrated by the president's confrontational style of running meetings. I have great respect for Rex, his career, and his leadership at the State Department and from time to time made a point to encourage him after a particularly lively meeting. But the tension occasionally spilled out in the press, such as with an erroneous report that Rex had referred to the president as a "moron" after a meeting at the Pentagon in the summer of 2017. But I don't believe it. Whatever differences he had with the president, the secretary of state was a class act.

At the end of March, Trump dismissed Tillerson via a tweet. I was disappointed in the president for dismissing him in that manner. The rumor was that Tillerson, suffering from a stomach ailment, had learned about his firing overseas in the bathroom on the State Department plane. I didn't think it was funny.

Trump also announced Tillerson's replacement, Mike Pompeo, via a tweet. I knew Mike a bit from Congress: we had served one term together, passing like ships in the night. His résumé was already impressive: West Point graduate, captain in the US Army, successful businessman. He's also a devout evangelical Christian. I didn't know him very well, though he had helped brief me for my vice presidential debate in 2016. His name had appeared on the short list to lead the CIA in 2017, and I had endorsed him. When he came to the White House for meetings with the president, he would often stop by my office. We developed a warm personal relationship, and he impressed Trump. He was a strong replacement for Rex. Mike understood the president, and I knew he would be a great secretary of state. And he was.

If US relations with authoritarians in Latin America, the Middle East, and Eastern Europe were fraught, there was surprising progress in Asia—surprising because after a year of Trump's tough talk and un-predictability and my delivery of his message at the DMZ and at the Olympics, plans were moving ahead for a summit between Trump and Kim Jong-un in Singapore in June.

As a gesture of goodwill, Kim released three Americans impris-oned for "hostile acts" and espionage against North Korea: Kim Dong-chul, Kim Hak-song, and Tony Kim, who had taught at a uni-versity in Pyongyang funded by evangelical Christians. Mike Pompeo flew to North Korea to secure the three men's release and flew with them back to the United States. They landed at Joint Base Andrews in the early-morning hours of May 8.

When they arrived at two in the morning, Trump and I were there to welcome them home. The president climbed up the stairs of the plane to meet them, accompanied by the first lady. When they came down the stairs and set foot on American soil again, I shook their hands. When the freed men, two of whom spoke very little English, came off the plane, they handed me a card. "Mr. Vice President Pence, Thank you for your role in bringing us home," read the front. On the back was Psalm 126: "When the LORD restored the fortunes of Zion, we were like those who dreamed." It was a deeply emotional moment. I had grown close with Otto Warmbier's parents and had heard first-hand of the barbaric treatment of North Korea's prisoners. And I was deeply invested in achieving peace on the Korean Peninsula, six de-cades after my father had fought there.

The morning the prisoners returned, I sat for an interview in an airplane hangar for NBC's *Today* with Andrea Mitchell. Just moments after the three men had returned home, a huge step in the thawing of relations between the United States and a hostile power with nu-clear weapons, I was asked questions at three in the morning about—what else?—the Trump campaign's alleged collusion with Russia and Robert Mueller's ongoing investigation, which had now lasted a year. After confirming that we had been fully cooperating for more than a year and had provided more than 2 million documents to the special counsel, I offered that, "In the interests of the country, I think it's time to wrap it up." And that was the headline.

The investigation hovered over everything we did in 2018. Out of necessity I had sought legal counsel when the investigation had begun and made my lawyers available to Mueller and his team. My legal team had shared my recollections of Comey's firing—notably that the president had not fired him to end the Russian investigation; in fact, he had been warned explicitly that firing Comey would trigger the appointment of a special counsel, but he had decided to do it anyway because, as he said, it "was the right thing to do for the country." I learned later that others in the White House at the time had told Mueller's office the same thing. After that, my office was never contacted by Mueller or any of his agents. Inexplicably, the investigation would go on for another year with continuous unproven accusations by Democrats of collusion and obstruction of justice that nonetheless cast a pall of illegitimacy over the Trump administration. It was an absolute disgrace.

For the most part, moving the president's legislative agenda became much more difficult as the election approached; Democrats, making use of the filibuster, were not eager to give him or Republicans a legislative victory to campaign on. Trump had wanted $5 billion in funding for a border wall and an infrastructure package, but the votes weren't there. That led to the president urging House and Senate Republicans to do away with the filibuster during a meeting at the White House in June.

But I informed the president that based on my regular luncheons with the Senate Republican Conference, it was clear that the majority of Republicans in the Senate would oppose doing away with the filibuster. I explained to him that the legislative filibuster is a historic element of the Senate, protects minority rights, and exists to facilitate consensus in the lawmaking process. Trump wasn't convinced. He would often say that Chuck Schumer would try to do away with the filibuster as soon as the Democrats took over. Trump was right about Schumer; but I was right about the filibuster.

Despite the Democrats' obstruction, we never slowed down. In the spring, I received a visit from Jordan McLinn and his wonderful mom, Laura. Jordan, who had been born with a rare form of muscular dystrophy, had been a driving force behind Indiana's Right to Try legislation in 2015. It gave patients battling terminal diseases access to experimental, not yet federally approved medications. Forty states have enacted Right to Try laws. They are not promises that diseases will be cured or that new drugs will save lives. But they give people early access to therapies that stand a chance of curing or turning back their illnesses. It's a humane and compassionate thing to do, though not un-complicated. Pharmaceutical companies, understandably, are reluc-tant to give access to their medicines without the shield of a rigorous investigation and approval by the Food and Drug Administration. It is extremely difficult to provide liability protection for drugmakers, but Indiana got it done. After we had passed the bill, I had told Jordan and his mom that if there was ever anything I could do for them to call me. And they did. In 2018, they made their way to Washington to encour-age Congress to pass a federal Right to Try law. It was already on our agenda; at a rally in Lancaster, Pennsylvania, during the presidential campaign, I took a question from an eleven-year-old boy named Zack Mongiello: "Will you and Donald Trump, when you are elected, will you support the Right to Try? My father and our friend Matt, they both have ALS, so they are dying." I told him we would take it to DC and get it done. I hadn't even talked to the president about it, but I knew he would support it, and he did.

During our second year, we worked with Congress; this time both parties participated, and the bill was passed. Huge credit was due to Oregon's Greg Walden, the chairman of the House Energy and Com-merce Committee, who worked through iterations of the bill and with patients, regulators, and drugmakers to create a law that would bal-ance access to drugs that did not yet have FDA approval with liabil-ity protection for manufacturers and hospitals, and protect patients. The final bill passed the House on May 29, bearing both Jordan's and Zack's dads' names.

The president signed the bill in a small theater in the Eisenhower Executive Office Building across from the White House. Jordan, wear-ing a suit and bow tie, was to Trump's left. After the president signed the legislation, he began handing out pens that he had used during the signing, a presidential custom. While the president shifted around, Jordan got up from his wheelchair and leaned in for a hug. Trump, busy passing out pens, didn't notice. Then Jordan went for in for a hug again. Trump, who was addressing reporters, didn't see it the second time. Jordan then played it cool and leaned on the desk, propping his chin on his hand. Then the president noticed him and gave him a big bear hug and a kiss. It was a sweet moment. Jordan and his mom, and Zack and his dad, had made it possible.

The Trump administration had been in office for little more than a year, but another election was already approaching. Every two years, voters have a chance to give their representatives a thumbs-up or turn them out. By the spring, I was on the road often, campaigning for congressional candidates and touting the Trump tax cuts.

Back in the summer of 2017, I had set up a political action committee, or PAC, to help Republican office seekers and defray some of the costs of my political travel. When I registered my PAC on July 9, 2017, the *New York Times* reported it as something unusual, hinting that I was putting together the infrastructure for a "political future, independent from Trump." That greatly irritated the president, who called me that Sunday morning after the story broke to say how bad it looked. "Fake news," I told him. And I promptly tweeted that the article was "disgraceful and offensive to me, my family, and our entire team." The idea was contrary to my very approach to the vice presidency. It was also one of the oldest games in the political gossip mill: driving a wedge between the president and vice president. The Washington media wanted to push Trump's buttons, and it worked. I'd had a PAC when I'd been in Congress. It is a good way for supporters to donate to candidates and help out the party. After we talked, Trump understood. Or so I thought.

Now, a year later, with midterm elections a few months off, the president's political advisors asked if Corey Lewandowski could join my PAC as an employee. Corey had been Trump's first campaign manager; he had been with the president since the beginning of his journey to the White House. The problem was that he was currently working for the president's super PAC. The laws governing these political organizations are different; employees of a super PAC are unable to interact or travel with candidates. This is not the case for the staff of a regular PAC. The idea was to move Corey over to my PAC so he could interact and travel with the president. It was straightforward. I never had a cross word with Corey and knew he was a good friend of the president. I was happy to bring him on if the president wanted it. Eating burgers with the president in the small dining room off the Oval Office, I told him about the idea of moving Corey over to my leadership PAC. Trump agreed to it and thought it was a good idea.

Two weeks later, on the morning of May 15, Trump and I drove together to attend the National Peace Officers' Memorial Service, an annual ceremony honoring fallen law enforcement officers on Capitol Hill. The Secret Service prefers that the president and vice president not travel together in the same car for reasons of security and continuity of government, but Trump often asked me to get in with him anyway and did so once again. During the drive to the Capitol, Trump was reading a newspaper when he saw a story about Corey joining my PAC. "This looks bad. This looks really bad," he said to me angrily, holding the newspaper in front of me. "You told me to do it," I reminded him. "I never told you to do it," Trump pushed back. "It looks bad, like my guys are leaving." By that point I was angry. "Over lunch two weeks ago, you told me to do it," I said, my voice rising. I didn't lose my cool, but I was firm. He put the paper down and shrugged. I probably could have been more patient.

By now the president's patience with Attorney General Jeff Sessions was growing thin, and Sessions knew it. In what I always interpreted as an effort to regain favor with the president, he was the driving force behind a zero-tolerance immigration policy that the administration carried out from April to June 2018. The policy, enforced by the Department of Homeland Security and the Department of Justice, called for arresting and imprisoning parents of families illegally crossing the United States' southern border. That had the effect of separating mothers and fathers from the children traveling with them. It had been done previously, as a pilot program under the Obama administration but had never generated a firestorm of anger.

I first learned about it after Sessions announced it in a speech. I could appreciate the way such a policy could discourage families from making the long and dangerous journey to our southern border, but heartbreaking images of crying children, separated from their parents, quickly turned the entire nation against the policy. In the end, it was First Lady Melania, upset by the stories of stranded children, who weighed in and convinced the president to end the policy. The administration was actively combating the flow of illegal migration across the border, and it's true that traveling with children created a form of immunity for people breaking US laws, as Jeff would say years later. But the policy was poorly coordinated among agencies, it shouldn't have happened, and the president was right to end it.

Democrats and their allies continued to denounce conditions for families and children on the southern border while refusing to fund additional beds for Customs and Border Protection.

The following year I toured the border in Arizona but thought it was important to lead a delegation to a detention facility for families and children in McAllen, Texas. There we saw compassionate care for those swept up in the wave of illegal immigration coming across the US border. We visited the large, well-lit, air-conditioned facility and spoke with women and children who told us they were well cared for. I was proud of the service of the members of Border Patrol and Customs and Border Protection who were facing those overwhelming circumstances. With senators, members of Congress, and the media along, we also went to an adult detention facility where adult men, many of whom had been arrested multiple times, were waiting to be processed. They were in the temporary holding area, which was at capacity, because Democrats in Congress had refused to fund additional bed space.

While we were flying back on Air Force Two, we watched as CNN played video of the men in the temporary facility. They didn't play any footage of the family facility, refusing to broadcast the full story of the compassionate care the American people were providing to vulnerable families. I had to call them out. I typed the tweet myself: "CNN is so dishonest." Remarkably, CNN's Washington Bureau soon reached out to apologize, admitting that the network hadn't told the whole story, and began to run footage of the well-lit family facility that we had gone to Texas to see. Twitter really does work.

A summit between Trump and Kim Jong-un was scheduled for June in Singapore, but it was tenuous. We didn't have much trust in the North Korean regime. The engagement between the two nations was based on promises by Kim to denuclearize—promises that had been broken by the Kim family for decades. In April, during an interview with CBS News, National Security Advisor John Bolton alluded to the Libyan model, referring to the 2003 agreement that had led to the dismantling of Muammar Gaddafi's nuclear program. It didn't go over well with President Trump, who knew that Gaddafi had eventually been brutally overthrown after forfeiting his nuclear weapons and said in the Oval Office that "the Libya model isn't a model we have at all." As the president suspected, what the North Koreans pulled from the mention of Libya was the end of the Gaddafi saga, when the dictator had been deposed, dragged through the streets of Tripoli, and then shot in the head.

During an interview on Fox News I tried to clarify the issue, saying, "There was some talk about the Libyan model last week," adding "As the president made clear, this will only end like the Libyan model ended if Kim Jong-un doesn't make a deal." The North Korean government was enraged. A North Korean official called me a "political dummy" and said the comment was "ignorant and stupid."

The North Koreans were so incensed that they threatened to pull out of the summit. Trump was irritated by Bolton's Libya comment but even more angered by North Korea's threats and insults. If anyone was canceling the summit, it was going to be the president. And on May 24, he did exactly that, sending a letter to Kim informing him that the meeting was off. No nation was going to speak about his vice president like that. It was another moment, not unlike his dismissal of Michael Flynn early in the administration, that demonstrated a level of mutual loyalty. He did, however, leave the door open for a resumption of diplomatic discussions. "We'll see what happens, we'll see," as the Trump motto went.

In June, the roller-coaster ride with North Korea continued. Negotiations with its government resumed. A presidential advance team was on its way to Singapore to scout out locations for the meeting, and a high-ranking North Korean official, Kim Yong-chol, was on his way to Washington, after a stop-off to meet with Pompeo in New York. Kim Yong-chol was a former spy master and a general in the North Korean military. Now he was standing in the Oval Office, posing with the president under a portrait of Thomas Jefferson. I wasn't crazy about the venue. The dissonance of what I perceived as a henchman for one of the world's most inhumane dictators posing in the shadow of the author of the Declaration of Independence was not lost on me. The Oval Office isn't sacred ground, but the right to enter it should be reserved for those with fealty to what the United States represents: life, liberty, and the pursuit of happiness. Still, I understood fully why the president had welcomed Kim Yong-chol to the White House, why in the face of the insults and the threats from Kim Jong-un he was spending so much energy and time pursing diplomacy with North Korea. In time he would make a pitch to Kim Jong-un: Give up your nuclear weapons, give your people rights, enter the order of civilized nations, and the world is your oyster with investments and development to follow. But we knew who we were dealing with: an oppressive concentration camp state run by a family dynasty. Our real goal, above all else, was to end North Korea's nuclear program. The fear was not just that North Korea had nuclear weapons that could obliterate our allies in Asia or even reach the United States; it was also that North Korea could sell a weapon to ISIS or Al Qaeda, groups that would not hesitate to use a suitcase-size nuclear device on US soil. That is how great the stakes were.

That was why Trump strode across a stage in Singapore and shook Kim Jong-un's hand, the first time the leaders of the two nations had ever met. It was a historic event and happened only because Trump refused to continue the cycle of kowtowing to North Korea's threat, and because he had called Kim's bluff.

When Trump met Kim, the president would later tell me, he presented him with a CD of Elton John's "Rocket Man," good-naturedly reminding Kim that he had borrowed the title of John's song to taunt him. Trump told me Kim made a point to say he hadn't called him "rocket man," he called him "*little* rocket man." I remained in Washington during the summit and was regularly on the phone with the president, giving him the view of the meeting from back home.

The summit did yield some progress. Kim agreed, in theory, to end his nuclear program and, at the president's request, to return the remains of Americans missing in action during the Korean War. More than three hundred thousand of our boys had fought along the South Koreans against Communist North Korea. Nearly forty thousand had died in action, and more than five thousand had been lost in North Korea, disappearing into prisoner-of-war camps and remaining unaccounted for on battlefields. Though some of the remains had been returned over the years, repatriation had become difficult because of the hostility between the US and North Korean governments over the Kim family's nuclear program.

But a few months after the summit, in July 2018, North Korea released the remains of fifty-five Americans lost in the war, near the sixty-fifth anniversary of its end. They were flown first to South Korea for a formal repatriation and then on to Hickam Air Force Base in Honolulu. The president asked that I be there when the remains arrived. At Hickam I met Rick Downes, whose father, Hal, had been lost on a night bombing run over North Korea. And I met Diana Salazar, whose father, First Lieutenant Frank Salazar, had been shot down on New Year's Eve 1952 while flying a reconnaissance over enemy territory. We picked up Diana on Air Force Two at the very same air force base in California where, as a little girl, she had said goodbye to her daddy for the final time. She had not been back since.

Like most days in Hawaii, it was a beautiful day, but it was also an incredibly somber one. I delivered nationally televised remarks at the ceremony but was really just speaking to the families of lost Korean War veterans who were there and looking on. I said, "Some have called the Korean War the 'forgotten war.' But today we prove these heroes were never forgotten. Today, our boys are coming home." After I finished speaking, the cargo hold door of the transport plane that had arrived from South Korea lowered. A member of each armed service—army, navy, air force, and marines—walked up into the plane and returned back down the ramp with a coffin draped in an American flag. Four by four the coffins were brought into a hangar, where I stood, my hand on my heart, until all fifty-five were back on American soil. I was never more sure that my dad was smiling in Heaven. I thought about him the entire time. If he had lived, I have no doubt that that would have been his proudest moment in my service as vice president. He would have been on the plane with us.

Upon my return to Washington, the president talked about how moved he had been watching the ceremony on television. He commented on my remarks, which he said had gotten across how personal the war was to me. I always had the impression, though, that the president regretted that he had not been able to be at Hickam Air Force Base that day. I did, too. It was, after all, his accomplishment. Thanks to President Trump, our boys were home.

In February 2019, the president would hold a second summit with Kim Jong-un in Hanoi, ending the meeting early due to the unreasonable demand by North Korea that all sanctions on the nation be lifted. But they would meet again at the demilitarized zone in June. Applying maximum pressure had worked. President Trump's willingness to answer threats with counterthreats of fire and fury had worked. Kim Jong-un came to the negotiating table and never returned to the missile-testing and nuclear threats while we were in office. Our administration created a pathway for the denuclearization of the Korean Peninsula. When a new US president took office, Kim Jong-un returned to missile testing and his old pattern of provocations and threats. Weakness arouses evil. Our administration proved that peace begins with strength.

CHAPTER THIRTY-SIX

Righteous Indignation

For by your words you will be acquitted.
—Matthew 12:37

At the end of June 2018, Supreme Court justice Anthony Kennedy announced his retirement. It wasn't a shock. During a casual brunch at the vice president's residence early in our administration, I had sensed that Justice Kennedy might retire but that he wanted to know what type of judge the president would appoint before making his decision. The appointment of Neil Gorsuch, who had clerked for Kennedy, gave him early confidence. Kennedy had been appointed by President Reagan and had developed a moderate record during his decades on the court. I sensed that Kennedy would be more comfortable retiring if he knew his replacement would be someone with impeccable conservative credentials.

This was the president's second Supreme Court selection in little more than a year. It wasn't new terrain for the administration. When the president received word from Kennedy that he was retiring, the White House counsel's office took the lead, vetting candidates from the president's formal list of prospects. I was tasked by the president with meeting the finalists. Two of them made their way to my brother's summer home at Lake Maxinkuckee in northern Indiana, which we use for July Fourth family reunions. I took a break from the Pence clan and went a few doors down the road to meet the finalists in the home where the Secret Service had set up its headquarters for the visit.

Judge Raymond Kethledge came from Michigan. I was impressed with him during the time I spent with him and his son, who came along for the visit. He had written a book on the value of solitude to leaders, which I subsequently read and deeply enjoyed. I'm a fan of Judge Kethledge.

Amy Coney Barrett, a judge of the US Court of Appeals and professor at Notre Dame University, had a shorter drive to the meeting. She is a fellow Hoosier, so we made a quick Indiana connection, and I was immediately impressed by her intellect and temperament. When the president had nominated her to the US Court of Appeals in 2017, during her confirmation hearing, Senate Democrats had attacked her Catholic faith, painting her as an extremist unqualified for a federal judgeship. "The dogma lives loudly within you," California senator Dianne Feinstein had claimed. She had endured the outrageous attacks with great poise and won admirers around the country. At the end of our conversation, I asked the question I had asked in 2017 when interviewing potential Supreme Court justices: "If the president were not to choose you, who would you recommend that he choose to fill this Supreme Court seat?" Barrett did not hesitate. "Brett Kavanaugh," she said and alluded to the fact they had become friends and she had great confidence in his conservative convictions.

Interviews continued after Karen and I returned to Washington after the holiday. I spoke with Kavanaugh, a rock-solid conservative who had been appointed to the US Court of Appeals by George W. Bush. We sat in the sunroom in the vice president's residence for the better part of an hour, we spoke about our families, and I was struck by his humility and intellect. I also met with Judge Tom Hardiman, who sat on the US Court of Appeals for the Third Circuit and came highly recommended by Pennsylvania senator Rick Santorum.

The president had interviewed all of the candidates before I did, but he wanted my opinion on them. And I gave it to him and never gave it to anyone else. Suffice it to say, he wasn't surprised by who I recommended when another Supreme Court seat became vacant in the fall of 2020. The prevailing view in the White House was that Kavanaugh would be the safest bet and the easiest confirmation. Little did we know.

Shortly after nominating Kavanaugh, Trump traveled to Helsinki on July 16 for his first meeting with Russian president Vladimir Putin. In a press conference during the summit, the president, when asked about Russian interference in the 2016 election, appeared to give Putin the benefit of the doubt. "My people came to me . . . they said they think it's Russia," the president told reporters. "I have [asked] President Putin. He just said it's not Russia. I will say this: I don't see any reason why it would be." The press and political establishment went wild. It sounded as though the president was taking Putin's side over that of his national intelligence officials. Former CIA director John Brennan said it was "nothing short of treasonous" and "imbecilic" and that the president was "wholly in the pocket of Putin." Nancy Pelosi and Chuck Schumer both suggested that the statement was evidence that the Russians had compromising information on the president. Republican senator Bob Corker said it "made us look, as a nation, like a pushover." Even Lindsey Graham said it had been a "missed opportunity" that would be "seen as a sign of weakness" by Russia.

The next day, I strongly encouraged the president to clarify his remarks in a private conversation before a meeting in the Cabinet Room with members of Congress. Later, with the press in the room, the president acknowledged a need for "some clarification" and said that he had meant to say, "I don't see any reason why it wouldn't be Russia." The president also tweeted that he had "GREAT confidence in MY intelligence people." He continued that we could not exclusively focus on the past, tweeting "as the world's two largest nuclear powers, we must get along."

I knew what Trump was trying to do; he was eager to get along and stabilize relations with Russia, the world's other largest nuclear power. But I had always known it wasn't going to work. I had always seen Putin as a pariah and had referred to him as a "small and bullying leader" during the 2016 campaign. I didn't need to look into Putin's eyes or see his soul: "tyrant" was stamped on his face.

US-Russian relations had been on a downward slide ever since Bush had looked trustingly into Putin's eyes. First, Putin had invaded the country of Georgia. The Obama administration had attempted a "reset" since the invasion. Hillary Clinton, then the secretary of state, had even given her counterpart, Sergei Lavrov, a yellow box with a red button with the word PEREGRUZKA stamped at the top of the box. Clinton's people had thought it translated to "reset." As Lavrov pointed out, it actually meant "overcharge." By the end of the Obama administration, Russia had annexed Crimea.

I had seen the same intelligence reports the president had about Russia's meddling in the 2016 election. Its mischief had not elected Trump president. But its interference, which was online and through social media, was an attempt to sow discord, to destabilize US democracy, to spread false information across both left-wing and right-wing platforms so as to turn Americans against one another. I always had the impression that the president felt that acknowledging Russian meddling would somehow cheapen our victory. But in my view, there was no reason for Trump not to call out Russia's bad behavior; it wasn't an admission of collusion but a declaration that our intelligence services knew what Putin's regime had been up to. I had no problem calling Russia out.

At the National Cyber Summit, a gathering of government, telecom, and energy leaders held in New York City on July 31, I said that although other nations had possessed the cybercapability, "Russia meddled in our 2016 elections." That was the judgment of our intelligence community, and the president had accepted it. I described Russia's actions as "an affront to our democracy." We weren't going to allow it.

For all the criticism leveled at the president, the record shows that our administration's efforts—canceling the construction of the Nord Stream 2 pipeline, which was to have carried natural gas from Russia to Germany, expelling sixty Russian officials from the United States following the poisoning of a former Russian spy in Great Britain, dropping out of the Intermediate-Range Nuclear Forces Treaty following Russia's continued violations, killing more than a hundred Russian soldiers in a military engagement in Syria—served as a deterrent to the Russian aggression experienced by previous and future administrations. Say what you will about President Trump's approach to Russia, ours was the only administration in the twenty-first century during which Russia did not attempt to redraw international borders by force.

One of the sharpest critics of Trump's comments in Helsinki was John McCain. He described them as one of the most "disgraceful moments" in US presidential history. No love was lost between the Arizona senator and the president. We would soon learn that John was nearing the end of his battle with cancer, but he was as sharp-elbowed as ever. He died the following month, on August 25. The last time I had seen him had been that early morning in the Capitol when he had given the thumbs-down to the health care bill. It had been a gut punch to the administration. But to me, that represented just a fraction of my relationship with John. And in its way, giving his party the middle finger—or the downturned thumb—was pure John.

When he died, I lost a friend, but America lost a heroic servant. I first met John in 2000, when I was running for Congress. He had just ended his own rebellious bid for the Republican presidential nomination, losing to George W. Bush. John swung by Muncie and then came to Anderson to campaign with me. He participated in a breakfast at the Paramount Theatre, and then we visited Stepping Stones for Veterans, a shelter for homeless veterans. It was a great day and a tremendous boost to my campaign. During our time together, I asked him to sign and inscribe a copy of his book *Faith of My Fathers*, which I had recently read. He did, only he signed it not to me but to my son, Michael, who at the age of nine was already dreaming of becoming a pilot and whom McCain had met that day: "To Michael, with best wishes to a fine young man." I put the book back on my shelf after returning home, and it wasn't until years later that I discovered that he had inscribed it to Michael. When I did, I put it into my suitcase and took it to him during a visit while he was at flight training school in Pensacola. Michael later moved to Naval Air Station Meridian in Meridian, Mississippi, the home of McCain Airfield, named for John's grandfather, Admiral John S. McCain. During my first year in the vice presidency, I called John to chat about legislation. During the conversation I mentioned to him that my son was now training at the airfield named after his grandfather. "That's great," he said. "Just tell him to do better than me." "Well, Senator, I don't know if I can tell him that," I stammered. "No," the old flyboy explained, "tell him to do better than me and have as many landings as takeoffs."

Despite their antagonistic relationship, Trump approved of the state funeral for John, ordering that flags across the country be lowered to half-mast in honor of him. Presidents usually speak at such events. But Trump and McCain were at loggerheads, and John's family didn't want the president to participate. So I delivered a tribute in the Capitol Rotunda on August 31, surrounded by the McCain family and John's old colleagues in Congress. When I recounted how he had been better to enlisted personnel and harder on generals than anyone else I had ever traveled with, the Joint Chiefs of Staff, seated nearby, nodded in unison. McCain's farewell was a touching moment for the country and a unifying one as well. But any type of détente in the nation's capital doesn't last long, and this one didn't, either.

On September 5, the *New York Times* published an op-ed claiming that there was a small band of presidential appointees within the administration who were working together to thwart the president and save the United States. They were, said the article, the "adults in the room . . . trying to do what's right even when Donald Trump won't." Those particular adults did not even have the courage to identify themselves; they called themselves "Anonymous." The *Times* billed the author of the op-ed as a senior member of the administration. The author had spent most of his time in the administration as a deputy chief of staff at a government agency. What a farce.

That wasn't something I had a great amount of time to contemplate. But one particularly bizarre theory floated on Twitter was that I had been the author of the op-ed. The reason was that one of the words used in the essay—"lodestar"—was one I had used in the past. I was flattered that the people on Twitter were interested enough in my speeches to parse them for a single word. And I had no idea that I alone was associated with its use. The episode caused more hysteria outside the White House, with the press and rival politicians speculating on who Anonymous could be; Nancy Pelosi also suggested that it had been me. But the White House described in the *New York Times* by the mystery author—a place that was chaotic, with subordinates attempting to check the president's so-called worst impulses and bad ideas—was simply not the place I worked at every day for four years. The president was demanding, no doubt, and the environment was entrepreneurial and competitive. But the White House and president described by Anonymous didn't exist. Two years later, the author finally came forward, and even many in the media acknowledged that he was hardly a senior member of the administration. When his name was printed, I didn't recognize it. If he had been in any meetings with the president, they had been few and far between. For the sake of his phony narrative, Anonymous should have remained anonymous.

Shortly before the Senate began its confirmation hearings for Brett Kavanaugh in September, a professor of psychology at Palo Alto University named Christine Blasey Ford sent a letter to California senator Dianne Feinstein. In it she alleged that Kavanaugh had sexually assaulted her while they were in high school. Feinstein and her staff did not make the letter public. Kavanaugh sat for hearings in the Senate for four days starting on September 4, during which there was no mention of Ford's letter or the sexual assault allegations. Then, on the sixteenth, the *New York Times*, likely tipped off by Democratic Senate staffers, broke the news of Ford's letter and its allegations. That was, it must be remembered, in the middle of the "Me Too" movement. Allegations of serial sexual assaults were being made against numerous powerful men in Hollywood, in the media, and of course in politics. And as evidence to back those accusations accumulated, the men were stripped of their posts of influence and power and drummed out of society. Rightly. So when allegations of sexual abuse were leveled against a potential Supreme Court justice, the country took them seriously. And it wasn't just the initial allegation made by Ford; soon two other, even more damaging, accusations were made about sexual misconduct in Kavanaugh's past.

Senator Chuck Grassley, who chaired the Senate Judiciary Committee, scheduled another hearing so that both Ford and Kavanaugh could testify. A few nights before Kavanaugh testified, he and his wife, Ashley, sat down for an interview with Martha MacCallum on Fox News. Watching from the vice president's residence, I thought Kavanaugh did fine. He and his wife remained calm. He denied the allegations, explained that he had no recollection of meeting Ford, had never been to the party she described. He had never sexually assaulted her or anyone, not in high school, not ever. But he was understated.

I thought he needed to show more fire, more righteous indignation. I called him that night and told him so. After all, this was a man with an unimpeachable record, admired by colleagues both male and female, and he had been accused of sexual abuse with no corroborating evidence, no witnesses. No one, not even Ford, could remember exactly where the party had taken place.

So I told him that he had done well on television but suggested that when he testified in front of the Senate, he shouldn't hesitate to defend his reputation more forcefully. I don't pretend that I was the only one who made that suggestion to Kavanaugh. But when he testified before the Senate, he was emotional, fighting back tears and pushing back against senators who clearly believed the worst about him. Ford's own testimony had been moving, but there wasn't a shred of evidence to support it. Quickly the additional accusations of sexual misconduct fell apart. The *New Yorker*, which had printed the second account, quickly had to concede that its reporters could not secure any eyewitness account of Kavanaugh being at the party where the alleged transgressions had taken place. A third, even more lurid accusation of gang rape fell apart as well. Democrats, seeing the lack of evidence against Kavanaugh, claimed that his charged testimony was proof of an inadequate temperament. No legal observer had ever questioned Kavanaugh's temperament during his career. Only after he had passionately defended his name and family in the face of outrageous allegations did the accusation arise, out of desperation. I was outraged by it. And as the process played out, many Americans were as well. In one of Lindsey Graham's finest moments, the senator delivered a barn-burner speech to the Senate Judiciary Committee. Lindsey has an old-school approach to Supreme Court nominees: he votes on their qualifications, not on party lines. In fact, he had voted to confirm Obama's two picks, Sonia Sotomayor and Elena Kagan. But on that day, he condemned his colleagues for trying to ruin Kavanaugh's life and said that tarring candidates for the high court was "going to destroy the ability of good people to come forward because of this crap." He was right. On October 5, the committee, in a party-line vote, moved Kavanaugh's nomination forward. The following day, after an FBI investigation had cleared Kavanaugh's name, the Senate confirmed Kavanaugh's nomination as the newest associate justice on the Supreme Court, and it was my honor to preside over the vote and announce it to the nation.

Instead of simply reporting the vote count and hammering the gavel, I announced, "The nomination of Brett M. Kavanaugh of Maryland to be an associate justice of the Supreme Court of the United States is confirmed."

The place thundered with applause.

CHAPTER THIRTY-SEVEN

Dialogue Is Good

For God has not given us a spirit of timidity,
but of power and love and discipline.
—2 Timothy 1:7

One of the defining features of Trump's candidacy was his willingness to speak truth about America's relationship with China. Since the beginning of the twenty-first century, the West had believed that giving China open access to its economies, welcoming it into the World Trade Organization, and creating an economic relationship grounded in fairness and reciprocity would lead to greater rights for the Chinese, including freedom of expression and worship, and government transparency. Looked at in the light of 2018, that was a distant dream and had been a giant miscalculation.

At the end of the second decade of the new century, China's economy had grown ninefold in twenty years, becoming the second largest in the world, in large part because of US investment. As Trump would say, "We rebuilt China." I'd often correct him and say, "Actually, we *built* China, Mr. President." In return, the United States was subjected to intellectual property theft, currency manipulation, and punishing tariffs on the part of China. Previous administrations had ignored those acts of aggression and turned a blind eye. The rise of Donald Trump spelled an end to that. He had won the presidency on a platform that promised a new era in US-China relations in which China's government would be held responsible for its bad actions.

By the end of 2018, Trump had met with Chinese president Xi Jinping twice. The meetings were cordial. The two men got along well. But although Trump was happy to build friendly relations with leaders such as Xi, he had no intention of letting them pursue their nations' interest at the expense of the United States'.

On October 4, I was preparing to deliver what amounted to the first full-throated articulation of the Trump administration's China policy. It was to be held in Washington at the Hudson Institute, a think tank and research center with a focus on foreign policy, which had for years called Indiana home. I knew that the speech was an important one, and so did the president. When some of the cable business news channels started to speculate about the content of the speech a few weeks beforehand, the president took note of the coverage and I suggested that it would be a good idea to review the speech with him in detail. He agreed. With a draft of the speech and my chief of staff in tow, we sat opposite the president in the Oval Office and went through the entire speech line by line. When the president was distracted by a phone call or interruption, I would respectfully point at the draft on his desk and say, "Back to the speech." I wanted to make sure that the message to China was just right and that Americans understood how the president was honoring his word to stand up to the country. Under his leadership, the US military had been given the largest increase in funding since the Reagan presidency. He had slapped $250 billion in tariffs on Chinese goods. Besides enumerating China's economic offenses, I reminded the world of its military expansion in the South China Sea, the state censorship blocking the flow of liberating information to its citizens, the persecution of Chinese Christians, Muslims, and Buddhists, and the Chinese government's attempted interference in the US midterm elections. When the speech received an outsized amount of attention in the business press as an important statement of administration policy and the president wondered aloud why he wasn't the one giving the speech, I reminded him, "You read every word of it." He paused, nodded his head, and said, "You're right." And that was that.

Months after the speech, when I arrived in Japan on an official visit, I was greeted by our ambassador, Bill Hagerty, who said, "I just wanted to welcome the second most popular American in Japan." My speech had been reprinted in every newspaper in Japan and welcomed by every freedom-loving country in the Asian Pacific.

The midterm elections arrived in November with an unpleasant thud for Republicans. The president and I had campaigned across the country for candidates, but the writing was on the wall, and it didn't carry positive news. Historically, the party of the president doesn't fare well during midterm elections, especially when that party has unified control of government. Americans like a divided government. The president was far more optimistic than I was about the prospect of Republicans' keeping control of Congress. The economy was strong, unemployment was low, and he had delivered on a promised tax cut, was standing up to China, and was making historic progress in denuclearizing North Korea. He thought that the GOP would be rewarded for those things. But there was also the constant speculation over collusion with Russia and the impending Mueller report.

If the Democrats did win back Congress, Trump often speculated, it wouldn't necessarily be all bad for his administration and the country, suggesting he might be better able to "make deals" if one chamber went for the Democrats. I strongly disagreed. I had been in the minority in Congress. I knew Nancy Pelosi and what she was capable of. Handing her the speaker's gavel would put the Trump presidency into political peril. On the night of the election, members of the administration watched the returns come in in the East Room of the White House. Chairs were placed informally; large television screens were set up on stands around the room. The president and I were sitting next to each other when Newt Gingrich came by. Trump asked him to settle our argument. "Hey, settle this for us, Newt," he said to Gingrich. "I think it might still be okay if the Democrats win the House. Mike says no." Newt didn't need a second to contemplate his answer: "Your vice president is right." An hour later, the news stations called the election: the Democrats had won back the House of Representatives, and Nancy Pelosi would be speaker of the House for the next two years of the Trump term. It was a wipeout in the House, where the Republicans lost thirty-eight seats. There was some positive news floating in the blue wave: the GOP had managed to hang on to the Senate, even picking up seats in Indiana and North Dakota.

And there was a personal note of pride for the Pence family: my older brother Gregory was elected to represent Indiana's Sixth Congressional District, the seat I had held for twelve years. Over the years he had been one of my greatest supporters. He had served in the military, built businesses, and raised a beautiful family. I'd never thought he would enter politics or run for Congress. But I was glad he had. Members of Congress equipped with a lifetime of experience better understand and are better qualified to serve their constituents. That was Gregory. And, he could brag that unlike me, he had been elected to serve our hometown in Washington on his first try. Brothers.

The following day, Trump took questions about the election results from reporters at the White House. With the midterms now on the books, the political press focused on the next election, the presidential one. "Will the vice president be your running mate in 2020?" a reporter asked the president. "Well, I haven't asked him, but I hope so." Then he found me in the audience, sitting to his right. "Mike, will you be my running mate?" he asked. I nodded. Then he jokingly asked me to stand up and raise my right hand. "Will you?" he asked again. I put my right hand up. "Thank you, okay, great. Yeah, the answer is yes. That was unexpected, but I feel fine" with a smile and a gesture my way.

Two years in, victories and defeats, I felt fine, too. There wasn't much time not to.

In a few days I was on Air Force Two, headed to Singapore to represent the president at the Association of Southeast Asian Nations (ASEAN) conference, a biannual meeting of Southeast Asian nations where discussions on economic and national security are held. Trump was never big on those types of meetings. He didn't much like the socializing and schmoozing, the elaborate banquets. He much preferred to talk to other world leaders one-on-one, preferably on the phone. I was honored to go in his place.

The second day of the conference, I took my seat at the head of the four long, joined tables forming a square around a room in a convention center in Singapore. The plenary session, a meeting of all the member states of the association, the ten-state economic union of Asian nations, was beginning. I felt a tap on my left shoulder. It was Vladimir Putin.

He strutted through the crowd of translators, advisors, and diplomats with a confident bearing and took his seat. He quickly stood back up and came my way for a handshake. I stood up and shook his hand, and we chatted briefly before the session began. He offered help in combating the wildfires currently impacting California; I told him the president would meet with him at a summit in Argentina later in the year. I noticed that Putin projected a familiarity toward me. It came, I concluded, from his friendly meeting with Trump earlier in the year. It was as if we were old acquaintances. I didn't return the favor. I kept my expression firm and fixed, and the photo of me looking down at him with a furrowed brow and a grim expression was published around the world, just as I'd hoped it would be. When I came back, Trump had seen the photograph, and he told me that I had looked too harsh. When I told him that it was intentional, he said, "Sometimes it shows more confidence when you're friendly." I liked the photograph.

After the session ended, the Russians requested a brief meeting, and I knew it was an opportunity to lay down a marker when it came to meddling in US elections. As the leaders got up from their seats, both our staffs motioned Putin over to a corner, where we stood together, surrounded by security and aides. Putin was just inches from me, expecting a friendly chat. He spoke of his desire to restart nuclear nonproliferation negotiations. After he finished, I said I had something I wanted to say to him. "Mr. President, we know what happened in 2016, and it can't happen again." Though Putin speaks English, he listened as his translator leaned in, relaying my message. His expression grew incredulous. He turned with a question to his foreign minister, Sergei Lavrov, presumably asking what I was talking about. The only word I recognized was "elections." Then he spoke through his translator, saying Russia had nothing to do with the election. To which I responded, "Mr. President, I'm very aware of what you've said about that, but I'm telling you we know what happened in 2016, and it can't happen again." Putin seemed taken aback. Then he shrugged and changed the subject back to his upcoming summit in Argentina.

There was one more line to draw before leaving Singapore. At the conclusion of the ASEAN meeting, the world leathers gathered for a group photo. Afterward, as the crowd broke up, Li Keqiang, the Chinese premier, stopped me as I was stepping off the stage. He was aware of the tough speeches on China I had given at the Hudson Institute and at this conference. He pleaded China's case against the hard line the Trump administration was taking against its government, repeating his belief that China was a "developing nation." I listened to him as he explained to me that a different set of rules applied to China and the United States should be willing to accommodate its status as a "developing nation." I looked him in the eyes and said, "Mr. Li, things have got to change." And as the translator converted my words to Chinese, I said it again slowly: "Things have got to change." And we parted ways—in more ways than one.

A few days later, I was standing in the conference room of a cruise ship moored in the harbor at Port Moresby, the capital of Papua New Guinea, where China's President Xi and I would address US-China relations at the 2018 Asia-Pacific Economic Cooperation (APEC) meeting. "The US will not change course until China changes its ways," I said to the leaders gathered. During my speech, in which I leveled another broadside at China's trade abuses and military provocations, the transmission suddenly cut out. It was an audio glitch, not the Chinese government's doing. Or so I was told. President Xi had already made his case in a speech earlier in the conference, warning that confrontations and cold or trade wars have historically produced "no winners."

A grand banquet was held on the final day of the conference. Before taking our seats, the leaders gathered for a "family portrait." But one head of state was late for the photo. Karen and I waited in the reception room for more than an hour, along with Japanese prime minister Shinzo Abe, Australian prime minister Scott Morrison, and others including Dmitry Medvedev, Russia's prime minister, representing Putin, who had not attended. We all wore coordinated silk short-sleeve shirts, some red, some yellow, with black pants. Red, yellow, and black are Papua New Guinea's national colors. Since the 1990s, when Bill Clinton handed out leather bomber jackets during an APEC meeting in Seattle, attendees have donned shirts or other garments native to the host country as a form of tribute. As we milled around and chatted, the room suddenly grew quiet, and the chatter died down. A staffer nudged me, and I saw Xi Jinping enter the room. He isn't a particularly tall man, but he is an imposing figure. The crowd parted as he walked in the room, and he strode between the sides it formed. It was quite an entrance. He came to the area where I was standing. When he recognized me, he walked up with his interpreter (Xi doesn't speak English) and acknowledged me as the vice president. I told him it was an honor to meet him. He asked if I had ever been to China and I replied that I had, as governor of Indiana. He invited me to return and I said it would be an honor to do so.

The pleasantries over, it was time to talk business. Before I had left for Asia, I had met with Trump in the small dining room near the Oval Office and asked him if he had any particular message for Xi. "Yeah, okay," he had said before sharing the message. I had pulled out a note card and pen, jotted down what he told me, and brought it with me. With only a few minutes to talk before the leaders would pose for the group photo and sit for dinner, I said to the Chinese leader, "President Xi, President Trump gave me two messages for you." He nodded, with some apprehension. "First, he wanted me to tell you that he likes you very much." After the translator relayed the first message, Xi softened and smiled. Growing animated, he told me he liked Trump very much, too. Right then the crowd began moving; it was time to snap the photo and have dinner. We parted ways.

During the dinner Karen and I sat next to Prime Minister Morrison. We bonded over our Christian faith and conservative values. He told me that his party would win the upcoming Australian elections against all odds. And it did. After a long trip, Karen and I were watching our energy and decided to turn in before dessert was served. As we said our goodbyes, I made my way down the banquet table to where President Xi was sitting, five chairs away. "Mr. President, excuse me for interrupting, but I want to get my wife some rest," I told him. He stood up, shook my hand, and then said I had told him there was a second message from President Trump. Right. "President Trump said to also tell you that you have to open your markets. When you see him in Argentina, you need to be prepared to open your markets." The two would meet at the G20 Summit in Buenos Aires later in the month. With a furrowed brow he replied that dialogue is good.

CHAPTER THIRTY-EIGHT

Go Fix This

Do your best to present yourself to God as one approved.
—2 Timothy 2:15

In 2018, our son, Michael, now a first lieutenant in the marines, made his first tailhook landing. It's difficult and risky, guiding an aircraft onto the small space of an aircraft carrier and snagging the plane's tail on cables stretched across the deck. The ship he landed on was the USS *George H. W. Bush*, a *Nimitz*-class carrier. Michael was set to graduate from flight school in August. A month before his graduation, I sent President Bush a photo of the landing. I wasn't writing as a vice president to a former president but as a proud dad to a former aviator. Could you sign this picture for him? I asked.

Shortly afterward we received the signed photo in the mail, accompanied by a letter dated August 29. "The road to becoming a Marine Corps aviator," it read, "is long and arduous and requires grit and determination, qualities I am sure you learned from your parents." President Bush gave us perhaps too much credit. In closing, the former president wrote, "Though we have not met, I share the pride your father has for you during this momentous occasion. I wish you many CAVU days ahead." CAVU is an old aviation acronym for "ceiling and visibility unlimited." Bush had known it ever since he had joined the navy at the age of eighteen.

Michael was thrilled by the letter. Not long after it arrived, I learned from Bush's chief of staff that the former president, who was legendary for his letter writing, was writing only two or three a day because of his failing health. Bush never wrote an autobiography, so the story of his life in his own words is spread out across the countless letters he wrote, including the one he sent my son. I remember meeting him in 1988 as a twenty-eight-year-old congressional candidate, during the same trip to Washington when I met President Reagan. If sitting across from Reagan was like looking at Mount Rushmore, spending time with Bush was like being with an old friend. And his vice presidency—a loyal counselor and advisor to an outsider president—was an influence on my own.

After Bush died, on November 30, the Bush family asked me to deliver a eulogy. I told Bush's sons George W. and Jeb about the letter to Michael, and they urged me to share it when I spoke in the Capitol Rotunda on December 3. Surrounding the president's flag-draped casket that day were generations of leaders, Democrat and Republican, who had paused their partisanship to salute one of their own. It didn't last long. A few weeks later, the longest government shutdown in US history began.

During our conversations leading up to the election, the president and I had debated how bad a Nancy Pelosi speakership might be for the administration's agenda. We were about to find out. In the closing weeks of the year, Congress worked on an appropriations bill to fund the government. During the campaign Trump had promised, in an effort to curb illegal immigration, that he would build a "great, great wall" on the southern US border. Though he had taken executive action to initiate construction of the wall during our first year, Democrats in Congress had successfully postponed funding of the wall in previous spending bills. But this time Trump was adamant that he would not sign the annual appropriations bill if it did not include funding for a border wall.

The House, still controlled by Republicans until the end of the year, scrapped an initial bill, then passed a stopgap measure to fund the wall that Democrats in the Senate filibustered, causing an impasse. Pelosi was set to assume the speakership on January 3. The president now had to negotiate with the new speaker and Senate minority leader, Chuck Schumer, to keep the government running. And he was not about to give in on the wall or much of anything else. The morning of December 11 was a preview of things to come.

Pelosi, the speaker-designate, and Schumer came to the White

House to meet with the president and me. I spent the morning preparing for a phone call with Iraqi prime minister Adil Abdul-Mahdi. After the conversation concluded, I joined Trump, Pelosi, and Schumer in the Oval Office. The meeting had been planned to be closed to the press, but Trump invited reporters and their cameras into the Oval Office. To my right was Pelosi, seated on a couch. Across from her, to the president's left, was Schumer on another couch. The meeting got off to a pleasant enough start. "So the wall will get built, but we may not have an agreement today," Trump began before turning to Pelosi. "Nancy, would you like to say something?" It was all downhill from there.

For nearly twenty minutes, she and Schumer argued with the president, interrupted, even insulted him as the nation watched on live television. Early in the meeting, Pelosi mentioned the "Trump shutdown," and claimed that Americans were losing their jobs; the unemployment rate was 3.6 percent. Schumer claimed that there was no support in Congress for the border wall and reminded the president that "elections have consequences." Trump thought for a second, then shot back, "And that's why the country is doing so well," making the point that his election had left the country in a much better place.

Eventually the meeting fell apart over the fact that Trump would not sign any appropriations bill that did not fund the border wall and Pelosi would not include a border wall in any budget. The two Democratic leaders were clearly uncomfortable with the on-camera arguing, but Trump relished it. "Oh, it's not bad, Nancy, it's called transparency." I didn't say a word. And I couldn't have gotten a word in edgewise anyway.

My view was that it was not my job to direct traffic when the president was driving the conversation. My silence, and probably my somewhat pained expression, was quickly turned into a meme: Twitter equated my performance with the classic holiday toy Elf on a Shelf, the rosy-cheeked, button-eyed messenger from the North Pole that families place on shelves or elsewhere around the house at Christmastime. "Pence on a Shelf" briefly became a thing. There were even a few tweets with a photoshopped picture of the meeting with me in a red elf suit with a pointed hat. Always happy to provide a laugh.

After Pelosi and Schumer departed, the president looked at me and said, "Mike, go to Capitol Hill, fix this."

I may have been silent during the meeting, but from that point on I was busy during the long shutdown. Democrats scoffed at the idea of a border wall, but there were thousands of illegal immigrants pouring across the US southern border, more than sixty thousand a month as 2019 began. The volume was higher than ever and the immigration patterns had changed. Twenty years ago, the majority of migrants apprehended at the border had been from Mexico and usually on their own. That had made it much easier to return them to their native country. Now entire families were traveling from across Central America up through Mexico, making their return far more challenging. Mexico wasn't particularly cooperative with us, interested in taking the migrants, or doing anything to block their path.

The president called it a crisis, and in his view, the wall was one way—he never claimed the only way—of dealing with it. In fact, Schumer, Obama, Biden, and Hillary Clinton had all voted for the Secure Fence Act of 2006, funding seven hundred miles of fence along the southern border. So the Democrats' argument was never about the effectiveness of a wall in deterring illegal immigration; it was about denying Trump a victory, about humiliating the president.

So the government closed. And negotiations began. Karen and I canceled our holiday travel plans and remained in Washington over Christmas. Trump called off his trip to Mar-a-Lago, where he usually spent the holiday. One day during Christmas week we were talking on the phone, discussing negotiations to reopen the government, when he asked me what I was doing that night. Karen and I have a Friday-night routine of ordering pizza, one we continued while living in the vice president's residence. When I shared our plans, he asked if we could get together that night. And so Donald Trump, accompanied by Jared Kushner and Mick Mulvaney, now the acting White House chief of staff, came over to our house for pizza. We set up a small table in the dining room on the first floor of the Naval Observatory. When Karen learned that Melania wasn't coming, she sat that one out. It was just four guys having pizza on a Friday night. Mulvaney said the grace over the meal, and we dug in. We had a relaxed and wide-ranging discussion. The president had the ability to drop the formidable persona when he wanted to—or when he was tired—and be just one of the guys. That was one of those times. The only thing missing was a deck of cards.

When the New Year began, I led the White House delegation, joined by Kushner and Homeland Security Secretary Kirstjen Nielsen, in meetings on Capitol Hill, often accompanied by my favorite wingman, Michael J. Pence, who was home for Christmas. We met not just with members of Congress but also with staffers, twice on Saturday and Sunday, the fifth and sixth of January, in the vice president's ceremonial office in the Eisenhower Executive Office Building. Pelosi's position was that she would not negotiate on the border wall until the government reopened. The president wanted $5.7 billion for the wall. After two weeks of negotiating, the president offered the Democrats a deal: temporary amnesty for "dreamers" in exchange for $5.7 billion for the wall plus $800 million in humanitarian aid for the border. I wasn't surprised that Trump was willing to offer asylum for the dreamers; he had given a speech in Arizona during the 2016 campaign in which he had outlined a ten-point immigration plan that stipulated that after building a border wall and dealing with illegal immigrants with existing criminal records and those with visa overstays, he would work to reform our broken immigration system. There was always much more to Trump's immigration policy than the wall. He led with law and order but was prepared to follow with compassion. In any case, it was a fair proposal. The Democrats refused it.

On the twenty-fifth, the president agreed to reopen the government—with a commitment to continue negotiating over the wall for the next three weeks with the threat of another shutdown if no progress was made. But the Democrats were never going to give in. It was left to Jared Kushner, working with Patrick Shanahan, now the acting secretary of defense, to find a solution. On February 15, the president would use his executive authority granted by the Constitution to declare a national emergency at the southern border. That allowed the administration to use $8 billion already appropriated for military spending to build the wall. Congress quickly passed a joint resolution ending the national emergency. Trump vetoed it in March. It was the first veto of his presidency.

With funding for the border wall secured, President Trump continued to press for policies that would end the crisis on the US southern border. Cartels, which make as much money on human trafficking as on trafficking narcotics, were hauling humans up north to the border for $5,000 apiece. When the illegal immigrants reached the border, they applied for asylum, claiming persecution in their native country. They then would be given a hearing date, usually in a year and a half. Then, free to go, they disappeared into the United States. But our administration believed that forcing them to wait in Mexico for that year and half would discourage them. Secretary Nielsen had reached an agreement with the Mexican government at the end of 2018 that required illegal immigrants entering the United States from Mexico to remain in Mexico while their cases proceeded. But that agreement had never been enforced.

During an Oval Office meeting in late May, the president was presented with the latest illegal immigration figures. He was furious. He stood up from the Resolute Desk and paced around the room. "Here's the thing," he warned me and Nielsen and her staff, "you just need to tell 'em I am going to tax everything coming across the border at five percent until they agree to do their part. Just tell them that." Then he turned to me. "Mike, you get with the Mexican officials tomorrow, you meet with them and tell them how it's going to go down." Then he pulled out his phone and tweeted, "On June 10th, the United States will impose a 5% Tariff on all goods coming into our Country from Mexico, until such time as illegal migrants, coming through Mexico, and into our Country, STOP."

Upward of 80 percent of Mexico's exports are shipped to the United States. The tariff would have devastated the country's economy. It wouldn't have been great for our country's, either. The next day I gathered in the Roosevelt Room with Mike Pompeo and US trade representative Robert Lighthizer, sitting across the table from the Mexican ambassador, Martha Bárcena Coqui; Mexican foreign secretary Marcelo Ebrard; and the nation's foreign policy team. They pulled out charts and graphs with elaborate explanations for why Mexico didn't have the infrastructure or capacity to hold the immigrants while the United States processed their cases.

I waited until they finished their presentations and listened patiently to their explanations. "Are you guys done?" I asked across the table. Yes, they said, they just needed President Trump to understand that Mexico couldn't hold the migrants. "Okay, President Trump wanted me to meet with you about this and all have to say is . . . he really means it," I warned. "I've been working with him for three years. He's not bluffing. He really is going to do it. And we have until Monday to get this figured out. And if we don't, he really is going to impose a five percent tariff and ratchet it up to twenty-five percent." Pompeo piled on: "The vice president is right, it's going to happen." The Mexican delegation was stunned. Pompeo suggested that the ambassador and foreign secretary go to the State Department with him and hash out an agreement in writing. The next day he came back to the White House with one. Trump wasn't surprised.

Remain in Mexico, as it was called, reduced illegal immigration at the US southern border by 90 percent. It was a classic example of Trump's hardball approach and our ability to leverage his unorthodox style. When he made threats across the table, the United States' negotiating partners flinched because they knew he meant them. I played my part, as usual, by delivering the message with a smile and then closing the sale.

CHAPTER THIRTY-NINE

Changing of the Guard and Walking in the Ruins of Evil

Remember the days of old; consider the generations long past.
—Deuteronomy 32:7

The new year began with thunder. And more comings and goings. After two years of valuable service, Jim Mattis tendered his resignation at the end of 2018. It was a stand on principle: the president was committed to withdrawing US troops from Syria, but Mattis, who had fought alongside the Kurds, believed that removing US forces would leave them at the mercy of the Syrian and Russian armies. He understood that the president wanted to bring the troops home, and rather than fight, he stepped down. It was an honorable thing to do. At first the president graciously accepted his resignation and said he was retiring with "distinction" at the end of February. But when his resignation letter became public, it was seen as being critical of the president, who quickly tweeted that he had "essentially" fired Mattis and announced that he would be removing him from office two months before his planned departure. I would have preferred, in the words of Douglas MacArthur, that the old soldier be allowed to just fade away.

Also, since becoming chief of staff, John Kelly had brought order and structure to a White House that was often freewheeling. He had created a process for managing the Oval Office. He and the president had a very good and successful working relationship. In their time together, they had won tax cuts, confirmed a Supreme Court justice, and overseen a diplomatic breakthrough on the Korean Peninsula.

But with the midterm elections over and the president's campaign for reelection beginning, I perceived that their relationship began to cool. Kelly's service wasn't political, he wasn't partisan—it was duty to country, to the president. But as 2019 began, it was clear that the president wanted a new chief of staff, someone with political experience as the election year and our own reelection campaign approached. Mick Mulvaney, a former congressman from South Carolina who had served as the president's director of the Office of Management and Budget, stepped in as acting chief of staff when Kelly left in January.

There are few people in public life I admire more than Jim Mattis and John Kelly. As Mattis told me back in 2016, they rode for the brand, the brand being America. Mattis had overseen the destruction of ISIS. Kelly was a superb chief of staff and a much-needed gatekeeper, much to the president's benefit. In the waning days of the administration, one of his successors, Mark Meadows, a congressman from North Carolina, would fling the doors to the Oval Office wide open, allowing people in who should not even have set foot on the White House grounds, let alone have access to Trump.

To no one's surprise, Jeff Sessions also resigned following the 2018 elections. Trump replaced him with Bill Barr, a brilliant lawyer who had served as attorney general for President George H. W. Bush.

There were also changes in my office. My chief of staff, Nick Ayers, the father of triplets, was ready to return home to Georgia with his wife. I was able to entice Marc Short to come back from the private sector, where he had gone after helping us pass the tax cuts in Trump's first year, to replace him. He had started the administration as the president's legislative director but had left after the tax cuts had gone through. I had known Marc for years, dating back to when I had chaired the Republican Conference in Congress, where he had been my chief of staff. I had actually met him when he had been working for Kay Bailey Hutchison, when I had worked with the Texas senator on our immigration plan. John Boehner had originally been skeptical when I hired Marc to run the Republican Conference. It wasn't personal, the speaker just didn't know how good a fit a guy who had worked in the Senate would be in the different environment of the

House. But six months later, Boehner would admit that he had been wrong, saying, "You will never make a better hire in your life than Marc Short." And he was right.

In February, I traveled to Poland to participate in the Warsaw Conference. Mike Pompeo had organized the summit, centered on fighting terrorism and forging peace in the Middle East. More than sixty nations attended, coming from western and eastern Europe and the Middle East as well, including not only Israel but also Jordan, Saudi Arabia, and the United Arab Emirates. One of the central threats to peace in the Middle East was the largest state sponsor of terrorism, Iran. President Trump had withdrawn the United States from the Iran nuclear deal in 2018 and isolated Iran as never before. One of the central goals of the conference was to further rally the United States's allies to isolate the regime in Tehran.

During the trip we also made our first visit to Auschwitz, the largest of the Nazis' concentration camps, established in the town of Oświęcim after Germany invaded Poland. It was not my first visit to such a place. In 1983, I had backpacked across Europe with my brother Thomas. Our travels had taken us to Germany. We had read about the concentration camp at Dachau and wanted to see it for ourselves. We were staying in a bed-and-breakfast run by an elderly woman. The morning we made the trip, she asked about our plans for the day, and when I told her that we were going to Dachau, a look of hatred came over her face. "Lies. All lies," she said, pointing her finger in my face. "There is nothing to see there." We ignored her. When we arrived, there wasn't a formal museum, just some overgrown fields, the barracks, and a memorial erected in the late 1960s. We moved across the camp where 41,500 souls had been murdered. For years I never forgot seeing the iron gate the prisoners had marched through with its cruel inscription ARBEIT MACHT FREI—"Work sets you free."

Thirty-four years later, during my first year in office, I returned to Dachau with Karen and Charlotte. We wanted Charlotte to see and understand the evil of anti-Semitism, the horrors of Nazi Germany. In the years since Thomas and I had visited, the camp had been turned into a historical landmark, capturing for all time the Nazis' horrors, including its crematoriums. We walked the grounds with the memorial's director and Abba Naor, a former prisoner who now lives in Israel, where so many survivors have found new lives, where the Jewish people of Europe founded a democracy. It was foggy and cloudy, a dour day. We were mostly silent. Karen and I placed a wreath on the memorial at the center of the camp and said a prayer. As Naor recounted the horrors of Dachau, he trailed off. With evident emotion in his voice he said, "Then the American troops came." I was never more proud.

As terrible as Dachau was, nothing, though, could prepare me for what I witnessed this day. At Auschwitz, trapped in time, were the ruins of evil on an industrial scale. The magnitude was staggering; it was hard to talk about it then and still is today: 1.1 million people were murdered in that ghastly complex of brick and wood buildings. There were the two bombed-out gas chambers collapsed onto themselves, the guard towers, hundreds of yards of fencing. There the Germans had created a facility to destroy a people. If not for the Allied war efforts, they might well have succeeded.

We were joined there by Polish president Andrzej Duda and first lady Agata Kornhauser-Duda. The trip was especially meaningful to Karen and me because we were also accompanied by Jared Kushner, whose grandparents had been resistance fighters in the Holocaust, and one of my oldest friends, Tom Rose, a devout Jewish conservative from Indiana whom I had met thirty years before and had come to rely on for his insights and counsel. To be there with them as free men arriving in a motorcade, where generations ago innocent Jewish families arrived in boxcars, and to be standing in a free Europe on top of the ruins of the Nazi regime was an experience I carry with me still.

The Nazis transported prisoners packed by the hundreds into suffocatingly small boxcars. At Auschwitz, one remains, sitting motionless on the rails crossing the camp. There is an ancient Jewish tradition of placing a stone or pebble on the headstone of a loved one. I walked to the boxcar to place a pebble on the steps prisoners had climbed to enter the boxcar. Then I was overcome with emotion, dropped to one knee, fought back tears, and said a prayer.

I was not just in Poland to remember, though. Iran is a nation that denies the Holocaust but seeks to author a second one. The visit to Auschwitz was a reminder of the incredible evil tyrants are capable of. The mullahs' vile anti-Semitic rhetoric echoes the Nazis'. To be there just steeled my resolve to confront hateful dictators and regimes—and not just the one in Iran but also its oil-rich ally in South America, Venezuelan dictator Nicolás Maduro.

On February 25, I flew to Colombia for a meeting with President Iván Duque, an American-educated conservative, and a Venezuelan leader I had not yet met, Juan Guaidó. The backdrop of the summit in Colombia was violent clashes between Maduro's state police forces and pro-democracy protestors contesting his disputed election in 2018. Dozens of citizens had been killed and hundreds arrested by the dictator's police forces. Challenging the legitimacy of Maduro's election, Guaidó, the president of Venezuela's National Assembly, had assumed the role of interim president in January, and the Trump administration had recognized him as president, with more than sixty nations to follow.

Just days before our meeting, more protestors had been killed. For three years the United States had opposed and sought to isolate Maduro. Guaidó was well aware of that and appreciative. He was young—only thirty-five—but a remarkable soul. When we first met, he took me down a hallway to meet with a group of Venezuelan refugees. Across the wall were boxes filled with food and humanitarian aid, labeled with an American flag. The people waiting there recognized me politely as the US vice president, but when they saw Guaidó, they began to cry. I could see that he was a symbol of hope for those people, whose lives had been upended, who had fled their homeland because of hunger and fear. I watched as Guaidó walked around the room, speaking with each family and embracing them. He was closer to a pastor than a president. From that moment I was an advocate for him.

During the rest of my time in office, we spoke regularly by phone. When you call into Venezuela, national security personnel make it clear that Maduro's government will be listening to your conversation. On every call, I told him that we would pray for him and his wife and their little daughter. And I would sign off as a warning for Maduro, "You may be assured that your personal safety is a great priority to the United States." He would express his gratitude, but I would repeat myself: "No, I mean your safety is really a great priority." I knew that the other side was listening: Don't touch this guy, or there will be consequences.

CHAPTER FORTY

No Collusion, No Obstruction

Then you will know the truth, and the truth will set you free.
—John 8:32

After nearly two years, Robert Mueller was wrapping up his investigation into the Trump campaign's supposed collusion with the Russian government. The Democrats and the media believed that any day now, the special counsel would deliver its report and the walls would close in. Then, on April 18, after all the speculation, the predictions of damning evidence and inevitable impeachment, Mueller's report landed. With a whimper. Its conclusion? The special counsel "did not establish that members of the Trump Campaign conspired or coordinated with the Russian government in its election interference activities." In other words, there had been no collusion. The final report, issued in two volumes, also addressed whether the firing of Comey had been obstruction of justice, since the former FBI director had been leading the investigation into Russian interference when Trump had dismissed him. One of the central arguments against that was that a president could not obstruct justice while executing one of his constitutionally delegated duties, such as dismissing a director of the FBI. It was an argument my lawyers had made to the Mueller team in 2017. On that topic Mueller wrote that "while this report does not conclude the president committed a crime, it also does not exonerate him."

On March 24, Bill Barr had sent a cover letter to Congress, sharing the findings of Mueller's report and concluding that the president had not obstructed justice. Barr was maligned for his decision, but making it was his job, not Mueller's. Unlike Comey, Barr understood that investigators investigate and prosecutors decide whether to prosecute.

Attending a state dinner in honor of the French president and his wife on April 24, 2018. My wife, Karen, charmed the Macrons with her French.

Walking with the president along the West Colonnade at the end of another day at the White House. He was my president and he was my friend.

"Life is winning in America," I announced as the first vice president to address the March for Life rally on the National Mall, with Charlotte and Karen at my side, January 27, 2017.

Karen visiting veterans in the art therapy program at Walter Reed National Military Medical Center. As second lady, she championed art therapy programs throughout the Department of Veterans Affairs and across the country.

Chairing the inaugural Space Council meeting in Chantilly, Virginia, on October 5, 2017. The council had not met in decades when President Trump tasked me with leading the administration's space policy and reviving American leadership in human space exploration.

On horseback at the Crow Reservation in Montana, May 12, 2017, with Secretary of the Interior Ryan Zinke.

Surveying damage at Iglesia Santa Bernardita in Puerto Rico after Hurricane Maria, October 6, 2017.

At Mt. Pleasant Baptist Church in Opelousas, Louisiana, visiting with the pastors, the congregation, and local leaders following church burnings in the area, May 3, 2019.

At Old Faithful in Yellowstone Park with Secretary of the Interior David Bernhardt on June 13, 2019, promoting the passage of the Great American Outdoors Act. Old Faithful erupted right on cue as I started my speech.

Backing the Blue at a roll call at the Youngstown Police Department in Youngstown, Ohio, June 25, 2020.

Visiting the ruins of Flora Westbrooks's salon, which was burned down during the riots in Minneapolis following the death of George Floyd, with Secretary of Labor Eugene Scalia, September 24, 2020.

Cheering on NASA's SpaceX launch of American astronauts on an American rocket from American soil with Karen and President Trump on May 30, 2020. Karen's gesture says it all.

Karen and me enjoying a light moment with our pets Harley and Hazel, in the vice president's West Wing office.

Looking across the DMZ from South Korea on April 17, 2017, with General Vincent K. Brooks. I'd gone to deliver a message that things were going to be different, and I wanted the North Koreans to see my face.

Visiting the Western Wall in Jerusalem with Israeli prime minister Benjamin Netanyahu, January 23, 2020.

My encounter with Russian president Vladimir Putin at the ASEAN Summit in Singapore, November 15, 2018.

Karen and me touring Auschwitz with President and First Lady Duda in Poland on February 15, 2019. Seeing the ruins of this industrial-scale evil only steeled my resolve to confront hateful regimes.

Meeting with the president of Ukraine, Volodymyr Zelensky, in Warsaw on September 1, 2019. From our first encounter, I saw glimmers of the courageous leader the world would marvel at following the Russian invasion of 2022.

Meeting with Prime Minister Boris Johnson at 10 Downing Street in London on September 5, 2019. The prime minister broke protocol by walking out of 10 Downing Street to meet me, a tradition reserved for heads of state.

With Secretary of State Mike Pompeo and National Security Advisor Robert O'Brien at the home of the US ambassador to Turkey in Ankara, discussing cease-fire negotiations with Turkey, October 17, 2019.

White House Coronavirus Task Force briefing in the White House Briefing Room, March 2, 2020.

Leading a White House Coronavirus Task Force meeting in the White House Situation Room, March 2, 2020. Our team met daily throughout the early days of the pandemic, and we met weekly with America's governors.

Karen and me receiving the covid-19 vaccine on national television on December 18, 2020.

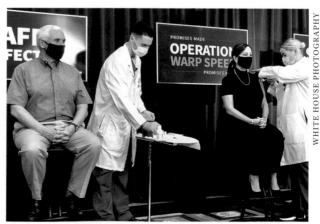

Walking to a secure location in the US Capitol after leaving our ceremonial office in the early afternoon of January 6, 2021.

Receiving a security update from lead Secret Service agent Tim Giebels in the parking garage of the US Capitol on January 6, 2021.

Monitoring developments from a secure area in the parking garage under the US Capitol with Karen and Charlotte on January 6, 2021. They wouldn't leave.

Working the phones on January 6, 2021, from the parking garage under the US Capitol. I spoke with congressional leaders, the Department of Defense, and US Capitol Police as efforts were made to secure the Capitol and end the violence.

Conferring with US Capitol police chief Steven Sund in the parking garage below the Capitol on January 6, 2021.

Returning to my ceremonial office near the Senate after the US Capitol was secured, around 7:00 p.m. on January 6, 2021.

Waiting in my Senate ceremonial office in the US Capitol as the Senate prepared to reconvene on January 6, 2021.

Charlotte and me drafting the statement I read on the Senate floor when we reconvened on the evening of January 6, 2021. All three of my children offered input.

Praying with Senator Tim Scott and Senator John Barrasso moments before returning to the Senate floor on the evening of January 6, 2021. There's always time for prayer.

Returning to the House floor from the Senate for the Joint Session of Congress in the early hours of January 7, 2021. Violence never wins. Freedom wins. And this is still the people's house.

Closing prayer by Senate chaplain Barry Black at the end of the Joint Session of Congress on January 7, 2021. I could think of no better man to have the last word on January 6.

Back home again among friends and family at Columbus Municipal Airport on January 20, 2021. There's no place like home.

Michael and Sarah's wedding at the Governor's Residence in December 2016.

Charlotte and Henry's wedding at the US Naval Academy chapel in December 2019.

Audrey and Dan's wedding outside a federal court-house in Washington, DC, in November 2020.

Our family at the US Marine Corps War Memorial after our marine, Michael, completed the Marine Corps Marathon in October 2019. A photo of the memorial has hung in all my offices since I arrived in Congress in 2001.

A casual brunch with the whole gang on the veranda at the vice president's residence at the US Naval Observatory, June 9, 2019.

I believe Bill Barr did the law and the nation a great service by looking at the facts assembled in a two-and-a-half-year investigation and confirming that there had been no collusion, no obstruction. Case closed.

I wasn't surprised at the conclusion, to put it mildly. I knew what I had seen during our campaign, and I believed what the president told me, that the entire thing had been made up. I'd always known that the truth was our friend. Trump associates and other people who had worked on the campaign for a short duration or in peripheral roles had been picked off during the investigation. Paul Manafort, who had chaired the campaign for two months while managing the Republican National Convention in the summer of 2016, was indicted for tax evasion and bank fraud. Roger Stone, a political operative and friend of Trump, was indicted for making false statements to Congress. He had had no formal role in the campaign. I had met him once, in Cleveland during the 2016 Republican National Convention. I had run into him in a restaurant, where we were introduced. The white-haired Stone had looked me over warily and said only two words: "Nice hair." That was it. George Papadopoulos, a low-level campaign aide arrested for false statements, I had never met. I had never even heard of him. In the end the president pardoned all three.

After two and a half years of constant conspiracy theories trafficked by mainstream politicians and media outlets that should have been relegated to the bowels of the internet, after millions of documents provided and millions of taxpayer dollars spent, there were no regrets, no apologies—not to Trump or to the country. Adam Schiff, a California congressman and former colleague, is a good example of the reckless behavior by the opposition during the Trump presidency. For years he had told reporters that he had seen ample evidence to indict Trump on collusion charges, that there was a smoking gun, that the size of the scandal dwarfed Watergate. On March 3, just weeks before the findings of the special counsel were released, he gave a fiery speech on the House floor to that effect. Then, when Mueller's report was released, incredibly, he kept at it, maintaining that there was indeed evidence of collusion while never actually providing it. It reminded me of my favorite Marx Brothers quote: "Who you going to believe, me or your own eyes?" Schiff, Rachel Maddow, John Brennan: they never let the facts get in the way of their attempt to overturn the 2016 election.

And that was what the Russia collusion hoax was all about: removing Donald Trump from power by any means possible. The collusion peddlers never for a moment stopped to consider the consequences of insisting that the duly elected president of the United States had been put into power by a hostile foreign power. They never gave any thought to the anxiety they were causing the American people, the damage they were doing to our institutions and the credibility of our elections. The collusion crowd had no regard for the environment they were creating, one in which hyperpartisans could look at a dishonest attempt to overturn an election and wonder why they couldn't do same thing.

As the country would learn after our administration left office, another crucial piece of evidence emerged to show that the collusion story had been made up. The Special Counsel's Office, led by John Durham, who had been appointed by Attorney General Bill Barr, discovered that the "Steele Dossier"—the document full of lurid allegations about Trump, the one presented to Trump by James Comey during our transition that was the basis of the Trump-Russia investigation—was nothing more than fraudulent opposition research paid for by the Hillary Clinton campaign.

Throughout the Russia investigation, I never once saw the president despair about its outcome. He never stopped fighting. But for those of us working in the White House, there was a sense of relief that it was finally over. It was time for the entire country to move on.

CHAPTER FORTY-ONE

Onward and Upward

The Sovereign Lord is my strength . . .
he enables me to tread on the heights.
—Habakkuk 3:19

With the Russian collusion saga concluded and the midterm elections past, I entered the spring of 2019 with optimism. With less than two years left in the president's term, work remained to deliver on some of the major promises of his first campaign, among other things, reforming the North American Free Trade Agreement (NAFTA) and accelerating the United States' manned exploration of space. It was onward and upward. Very much upward . . .

A few days after news of the Mueller Report broke, Air Force Two rolled into Huntsville, Alabama, an early hub of US rocket engineering. A month before, in an optimistic Oval Office ceremony, the president had signed Space Policy Directive-4, establishing a new, sixth branch of the US military: Space Force. There was still the matter of organization and earning congressional approval. Much work remained to be done. The idea of Space Force wasn't exactly original to the Trump administration. A military presence in space had been an ongoing concern dating back to the end of World War II. As recently as 2017, congressmen Mike Rogers, a Republican from Alabama, and Jim Cooper, a Democrat from Tennessee, had proposed a space agency called Space Corps. But it came to reality in a typically Trump way. "Maybe we need a new force. We'll call it the Space Force," the president had said, thinking out loud, to a crowd of marines in San Diego back in 2018. Then he had warmed up to the idea in real time. "What a great idea," he had told the marines. "Maybe we'll have to do that. That could happen. That could be the big breaking story." The marines had roared.

The revival of the Space Council was a means of reasserting the United States' role in manned space exploration. An American had last set foot on the moon in 1972. Since then NASA's work had remained in low Earth orbit, never straying far from the planet. There was important scientific work being done aboard the International Space Station, but on the fiftieth anniversary of Apollo 11 and Neil Armstrong's "One small step for man," I wanted to encourage our astronauts and engineers to make their next giant leap and return Americans to the moon. I was in Huntsville to chair the fifth meeting of the council in March 2019 not only to name the first commander of the Space Force, General Jay Raymond, but also to make it official that we planned to send the "next man and first woman" to the moon in five years in American rockets launched from American soil. Not just that, but the astronauts would be landing on the moon's south pole, where no American had ever gone.

The United States didn't have a rocket capable of sending astronauts to the moon, but instead of lamenting that and postponing the country's return there, the president and I were encouraging NASA to do what our administration had done elsewhere—with the economy, on foreign policy: shrug off compliancy, cut the red tape and unnecessary regulations, and, as I said that day, think bigger, fail smarter, and work harder. And do it with urgency.

A few months prior, China had become the first nation to land on the far side of the moon, all while Russia was charging the United States $80 million for a ride to the International Space Station. Trump liked to quip that "Rich guys love rockets," a reference to the generation of entrepreneurs investing in commercial space flight, including Elon Musk and Jeff Bezos. If their companies' technology could get Americans back to the moon, NASA shouldn't hesitate to work with them. During the transition I took a call from Bezos. When I congratulated him on his rocket innovation, he told me, "Mike, I started Amazon just to feed my space habit." With entrepreneurs such as him and Musk, the US space revival was well under way. And the country had a president who was a builder, who always wanted to go farther, faster, and higher in every endeavor.

As the year drew to a close, Congress would pass the National Defense Authorization Act, officially establishing Space Force as a new stand-alone branch of the military, the first one in more than seventy years. Each branch of the service had elements committed to space across sixty departments. The Space Force would be a place where all of the United States' space assets could be concentrated. It could meld the space projects and programs into a single chain of command. That would be no easy task.

Initially our efforts were met with the usual institutional opposition in the Senate and the Pentagon. Secretary Mattis wrote to Congress in 2017, "I do not wish to add a separate service that would likely present a narrower . . . approach to space operations." In August 2018, expanding on President Trump's statement "We are going to have the Space Force, separate but equal," I took the unusual step of delivering a speech at the Pentagon. A few days later, Secretary Mattis announced that he was "not going against setting up a Space Force."

At Joint Base Andrews on December 20, the president announced the official formation of Space Force. In the middle of his speech, he veered off his text, saying, "I particularly want to thank Mike Pence; he was so involved in this with me." He referred to "the spirit and love" we shared for Space Force because "we realized how important it is to our military, to our future, to our defense."

History may well record Space Force as being one of the most consequential achievements of our administration: providing for the common defense in the boundless reaches of space.

CHAPTER FORTY-TWO

Trade and Travel

The wealth of the nations will come to you.
—Isaiah 60:5

By the spring, the presidential election was kicking in. Despite squawking from a few Republicans, including my old friend Jeff Flake, about running against President Trump in the Republican primary, it was obvious that the nomination was Trump's; he continued to enjoy astronomical approval ratings among GOP voters. He was already on the campaign trail, holding rallies across the country.

On the Democratic side, a number of contenders were inching toward declaring their candidacy and heading to the early primary states of Iowa and New Hampshire. One of them was my predecessor in the vice presidency, Joe Biden, who had been so gracious and helpful during the transition. In March, he had even said I was a "decent guy." That turned out to be an unforced error. When the outraged liberal Left lashed out at Biden for the faint praise, he quickly retracted it. I'd been in politics long enough not to take either the compliment or its withdrawal personally. It was a sign to me that the Democratic Party Biden sought to lead was a far different, far more radical, far more intolerant one than the one he had belonged to for more than fifty years. And that he would bend as far leftward as it wished.

One big focus of our administration from the outset was renegotiating the North American Free Trade Agreement, the Clinton-era (though its creation really dates back to the Reagan presidency) trade pact cosigned by the United States, Canada, and Mexico in 1993, linking the three nations' economies and goods. Despite its congressional authors' intentions, NAFTA hadn't worked exactly as planned.

Mexico's and Canada's manufacturing had grown at the United States' expense, flooding the US market with their products, including steel and aluminum, costing jobs, and hurting entire communities. I witnessed entire Indiana communities shuttered as jobs moved south of the border to Mexico. Anderson, Indiana, went from having ten thousand GM employees to having two. By the time Trump ran for president, the United States, in no small part because of NAFTA, had a trade deficit of $576 billion. He called it a "politician-made disaster." And he was right.

During a conversation in his penthouse apartment the day before I was announced as his running mate, Trump made a persuasive case that multilateral trade agreements were not in the interest of American workers. Since my days in Congress and as governor, I had supported free trade. I had always said, "Trade means jobs." Indiana is the second leading export state in the country, and I was convinced that opening up foreign markets through trade agreements would benefit Hoosier families. I had voted for permanent normal trade relations with China. And as governor I had expressed support for the Trans-Pacific Partnership agreement, a multination pact among Pacific nations and the United States designed as a counterweight to China's economy. Standing by one of the large picture windows overlooking Central Park, Trump said to me, "I'm not against free trade," but added, "I just think when a country enters into a trade agreement with lots of other countries, you lose leverage." He told me that he thought trade agreements should be arm's-length negotiations between trading nations, adding "If it doesn't work for one of the countries, they can just get out." In the years ahead, I would see the president engage in tough negotiations that would improve trade agreements to benefit American workers. Trump convinced me that trade means jobs only if it's free and fair. And he would go on to change the consensus in the Republican Party as well, setting the stage for the largest trade deal in US history.

As a candidate Trump had promised to rethink NAFTA or, if necessary, withdraw the United States from it. The message resonated, especially in places such as Pennsylvania, where more than three hundred thousand manufacturing jobs had disappeared after 1993.

Negotiations among the three nations on a new agreement began in the summer of 2017, and the following year, a new trade agreement, the United States–Mexico–Canada Agreement (USMCA) was reached. That was in no small part due to the work of US trade representative Robert Lighthizer. It created comprehensive labor protections, removed trade barriers to American farmers accessing Canada's markets, and created new rules on intellectual property, protecting American innovators and businesses. It was projected to generate $235 billion in economic growth and 589,000 jobs. And it unified the United States, Canada, and Mexico against China's unfair trade practices.

But there were bumps along the way. One of the primary disagreements was over Canada's protected dairy industry, which was exporting inexpensive dried milk powder products, undercutting America's dairy farmers. In the fall of 2018, during one of the culminating moments in the negotiations, Trump pressed Canadian prime minister Justin Trudeau to give American dairy farmers better access to Canada's market. Trudeau wouldn't budge. "Okay, then, I am just going to tax all the cars you ship across the border to us," Trump said, preparing to end the conversation. Astonished, Trudeau replied that that would destroy their economy. "It probably would," said Trump and continued, "I don't want to do it, but if you won't give in on dairy, we will go another direction, and we will just use tariffs." Trudeau changed his tune, and we soon reached an agreement with Mexico and Canada on the USMCA.

The Canadian prime minister might have been surprised by Trump's blunt negotiating style, but I wasn't. I had seen it many times before, including during a state visit by the prime minister of Japan to the warm clime of Mar-a-Lago. It was in April 2018, when Shinzo Abe traveled to Florida for meetings with the president about trade between our two nations and an upcoming summit with Kim Jong-un. During Abe's stay, there was a classic Trump moment.

On the afternoon of April 18, there was a working lunch attended by the president, our cabinet, and Abe and members of his government. The Americans sat on one side of a large table covered by a white tablecloth, a row of potted roses running down its center, in front of a backdrop of Japanese and American flags. I was sitting to the president's right, John Bolton and John Kelly to my right. Abe and his ministers were across the table. Trump opened the lunch formally and graciously. He spoke kindly of Abe, the great round of golf they had played earlier, how much Melania admired his wife. Then, without taking a breath, he said, "But, Shinzo, you're killing us on cars, and it's over."

The men to Abe's left and right gasped, their eyes widened. "I mean, how many Buicks are there in Tokyo?" Trump continued. "But I don't blame you—we have had stupid people running this country for years. But not anymore." Though all his ministers and aides were shocked, Abe's expression was unchanged. I assumed that that was because he had heard the same kind of thing already over the eighteen holes of golf with the president earlier that day.

Afterward the president asked me how I thought the meeting had gone. "We shouldn't have kicked the press out," I answered. But that was Trump. He was the same on or off camera, at a huge rally or in a small meeting. The language he spoke, calling out the Japanese prime minister on behalf of the American automobile industry, was something the guy on a bar stool at the local bar would have cheered on. But he was also invested in building relations with world leaders, and they took him seriously. As was once observed, the media took Trump literally but not seriously; the rest of the world took him seriously but not literally.

The USMCA was done. But trade deals must be ratified by Congress. And that was where Speaker Pelosi came in. The passage of the USMCA would be a major win for the president with an election drawing near, and the speaker was loath to give it to him. But members of her caucus, vulnerable Democrats from swing districts in states hurt by NAFTA, places such as Wisconsin, Michigan, Pennsylvania, and Minnesota, were inclined to vote for the USMCA. We needed to win their support, pry them away from Pelosi. And if they refused or dragged their feet, we would make sure that their constituents heard about it. In 2019 my itinerary was full of stops with that mission in mind: Eau Claire, Wisconsin, to tour J&D Manufacturing, which makes ventilation systems for farmers; oil fields in Artesia, New

Mexico, situated in the Permian Basin, a center of the US energy re-
naissance; Gerdau Ameristeel in Newport, Minnesota, where I made
a surprise stop at the North Pole Restaurant to pick up some malts;
Lamb Farms in Lebanon, Indiana; a Tyson Foods plant in Nashville,
Tennessee. On May 22, our motorcade was driving through Union
County, North Carolina, in the town of Waxhaw, when we passed by
a group of elementary schoolkids from the Big Blue Marble Academy
standing in the grass next to the road, waving flags. I asked the Secret Service to stop, jumped out of the car, thanked them, snapped
some photos, hopped back into the limo, and headed to a nearby tex-
tile mill. It was good old-fashioned politicking, talking and listening
to farmers, steelworkers, autoworkers, and roughnecks, reassuring
them that the days of undermining US manufacturing were over, that
we were fighting for trade deals that would put America first. And it
ultimately paid off. We built what Lighthizer described as a coalition
across parties and across industries that would help pass the USMCA
in the House by the end of the year. The Senate followed in early 2020.

On July 3, I was sitting on the tarmac at Joint Base Andrews, moments
away from departing for New Hampshire. As part of the administration's efforts to fight the opioid epidemic, I was scheduled to visit the
Granite Recovery Center in Salem. As I sat in my seat, going over
my briefing materials, a Secret Service agent approached me. There
was a problem. A contact at the Justice Department had just phoned.
Though the details were few, one of the attendees at the event, who
was going to be onstage, was suspected of trafficking drugs. A federal
arrest was imminent. If I still wanted to attend the event, I could, but
it was important that I know what I was getting myself, and possibly the entire administration, into. The person in question was going
to join me onstage at an event with an audience of more than two
hundred people. Sitting there on the tarmac, waiting for takeoff, we
decided to cancel the trip. I didn't want to embarrass the president or
the administration. We disembarked from Air Force Two and headed
back to the White House.

When my staff relayed the information to our team member in

New Hampshire, he had a bit of an Alexander Haig moment. In 1981, Haig, as secretary of state, had claimed, "I'm in control here" after Ronald Reagan had been shot, suggesting a transfer of power and causing panic. To be fair to my staffer, it was a difficult situation, and he couldn't tell the crowd why I had canceled, lest the investigation be compromised. He was put into a tough spot. "I have some bad news at this point," he said after stepping to the podium. "Air Force Two was headed this way. There's been an emergency." He inexplicably told the crowd that we had turned the plane around in midair, suggesting a crisis back in the capital. "We'll just ask that you all calmly go ahead and have all of you leave the room." The crowd immediately wondered: Was the president okay? Was the country under attack? The press did not take the announcement calmly, either. What was behind the mystery of the canceled trip? My team tried to clear it up and explain that there was a problem on the ground in New Hampshire, but out of necessity, the mystery remained.

When I walked into the Oval Office, where my emergency "midair turnaround" was on the television in the small dining room, I ran headlong into an irritated president. "What's going on?" he demanded. "It's like they are saying something happened to me!" I explained the situation to Trump, who eventually calmed down. "There was a very interesting problem that they had in New Hampshire," Trump told curious reporters afterward. "I won't go into what the problem was, but you'll see in about a week or two." Sure enough, later that month the employee of the recovery center was arrested for selling fentanyl. Looking back, the firestorm of speculation was unfortunate but not unjustified. It was unfortunate because it transferred attention away from a very real national crisis, the opioid epidemic, to yet another nonexistent one involving the executive branch.

We didn't make the trip out east, but we did go westward. While our kids were growing up, Karen and I had taken them on summer trips to national parks. Great Smoky Mountains, Yosemite, we knew it was important to expose our children to the incredible beauty of this country. These natural wonders are America's national treasures. State parks, too. As governor I was always proud to point out that Indiana has the United States' most popular and most frequently visited state park system, and I had made investments in and improvements to the state parks during my term. I am a Teddy Roosevelt conservationist. Like TR, I believe we have a responsibility to protect and pass on America's most beautiful places. Trump agreed. But by 2019, the National Park System had a $12 billion backlog of maintenance projects to be carried out. The president wanted to boost the funding of the Department of the Interior, which houses the NPS. We were building an infrastructure fund using half of the revenue from energy leases on federal lands to relieve the parks' maintenance backlog. During the visit to Yellowstone National Park to drum up support for the president's plan, Karen and I hammered some nails into a pedestrian walkway and watched Old Faithful erupt—right on cue as I was beginning my speech to park employees. It was fortuitous: the following year Trump signed the Great American Outdoors Act, which appropriated $1.3 billion to repairs at our national parks. It also created a new national park at the dunes of Lake Michigan in northern Indiana. It's good to be vice president.

For a year that had opened with the longest government shutdown in US history, by the summer of 2019, the country was humming along and the White House was optimistic. The economy was roaring. The administration was moving forward on the USCMA, negotiating with Democrats in Congress. Robert Mueller testified before Congress on July 24, an event that Democrats hoped would revive the collusion narrative. Instead of breathing new life into the impeachment crusade, in his testimony before the House Judiciary Committee, Mueller often seemed tired and not fully conversant with his own report. He made no new revelations, did not add anything beyond what he had written. Whatever slim hopes remained of impeachment ended. I was energized by the past few months, the travels across the country to promise our new trade pact, the beauty of Yellowstone National Park. And I knew the president was upbeat as well; he always was, he couldn't be anything other than optimistic. And our working relationship, three years in, was strong.

In the middle of all that, an op-ed was printed in the *Wall Street*

Journal encouraging the president to dump me from the ticket in 2020 and to run instead with Nikki Haley, who had left the administration at the end of 2018 and had returned to private life. Swapping me for Haley, the author, Andrew Stein, argued, would help the president win back suburban women who had voted Democrat in the 2018 midterm elections. It's a free country; everyone is entitled to offer political advice and every politician is entitled to advance his own interests. Two months after the *Journal* piece appeared, Haley issued a statement via Twitter saying enough with the rumors, that she and I were dear friends. But the Washington wags kicked the rumors around a bit and then asked the president directly if I would be his running mate, which he confirmed. I never gave the notion that Trump might replace me on the ticket much credence or felt the need to wage any sort of campaign to stay there or to plant stories in the press. I had a peace about where we were and what we were doing. I felt called to be there, called to serve. I had not sought the job in 2016, and I wasn't going to seek it in 2020. I had put it into the Lord's hands, and I was going to leave it there. That attitude ultimately came from my faith and from my friendship with the president. You always knew where you stood with Trump, and we were okay. When you don't have a good relationship with Trump, you know it. And of course, he paid as little note of the rumors as I did. In our conversations he dismissed them out of hand, saying, "I know who my vice president is."

CHAPTER FORTY-THREE

A Less-than-Perfect Phone Call

Set a guard over my mouth, Lord; keep watch
over the door of my lips.
—Psalm 141:3

In late August, Karen and I traveled to Vermont to spend the final days of summer with friends, as we had done the previous year. During the trip I joined, via a secure phone, a meeting of the president's national security team in the Situation Room. At the time, another major decision about Afghanistan was looming.

Back in 2017, President Trump had sent more US troops into the country to turn back the Taliban and help stabilize the Afghan government. Nearly two years later, though violence had decreased across the country, we were receiving briefings showing that despite the assistance of US soldiers, the Afghan National Army was yielding ground to the Taliban, who were in control of increasing parts of the country. Trump had wanted to get the United States out of Afghanistan when he had run for president in 2016. In 2017, he had decided to send more troops. But now, after three years of meeting wounded soldiers and standing at Dover Air Force Base with the families of the fallen, he wanted to bring Americans home.

Over several months, Mike Pompeo, along with Zalmay Khalilzad, an Afghan-born US diplomat, negotiated a peace settlement with the Taliban: the United States would reduce its troop levels if the Taliban ended its attacks against Americans, denied Al Qaeda and ISIS operations bases in the country, and agreed to work with the Afghan government. The question of leaving a residual force was the subject of debate within the administration. I had always held the view that if we ended our mission in Afghanistan, some small force should be left behind to support counterterrorism efforts. By the end of the summer, an agreement was taking shape. The president agreed that the United States would draw down troop levels in Afghanistan from 14,000 to 8,600, and the Taliban would agree to a cease-fire with the Afghan government.

During the call on the thirtieth, the president's national security team discussed the treaty and whether the president should sign it. Pompeo and Khalilzad were in the Situation Room with the president, along with our new secretary of defense, Mark Esper. National Security Advisor John Bolton, who was in Poland, joined via conference call. In the middle of the discussion, the president proposed that we bring Taliban representatives to Washington for talks, even suggesting that the meeting could take place at Camp David, and asked for my opinion. I thought it was a bad idea but weighed my words carefully. "Mr. President," I said, "we should reflect on who they are and what they've done and if they have truly changed. These people are animals." The president kept at the idea; I wasn't opposed to his meeting with President Ghani and other representatives of the Afghan government, but the Taliban had no place in the US capital, let alone the historic grounds of Camp David.

After a terrorist attack killed an American soldier in Afghanistan in early September, Trump abandoned the idea. As the call was ending, Bolton asked with some urgency, "What about Ukraine?" The call continued. Trump was dragging his feet on releasing $250 million in military assistance for Ukraine that had been earmarked by Congress. It was the first I had heard about the matter.

Over the prior two administrations, Russia had sought to redraw international borders by force. First it had rolled tanks into Georgia during the Bush administration, and then it had taken Crimea and infiltrated eastern Ukraine during the Obama presidency. When our administration arrived, we reversed the Obama-era policy of not providing lethal military assistance to Ukraine. Our administration was determined to provide military aid to Ukraine from the outset. In our first year in office, we approved of the largest sale of defensive weapons since 2014, including sniper systems and ammunition, and in 2018 we approved the sale of 210 Javelin anti-tank missiles and 37 launchers to Ukraine. In my meetings with President Petro Poroshenko, who led the country when we took office, he expressed profound gratitude for the US assistance. I'd met Poroshenko in Munich in 2017, and after a meeting I had with him during his visit to the White House in June of the same year, I'd walked him down to the Oval Office, where the president invited him for an unscheduled meeting. When the president waved the press into the room, Poroshenko commended the president's leadership and called Trump and the United States Ukraine's "most reliable strategic partner."

In 2019, Congress earmarked $250 million in additional aid to Ukraine, but President Trump was skeptical. The lack of European support for Ukraine was a source of irritation for him. Shortly after taking office, he related to me his first conversation with German chancellor Angela Merkel. She had asked him what he intended to do about Ukraine and pushed him to do more financially to help the country in its ongoing conflict with Russia. Trump had told Merkel that he would look into it. When he had, he had learned that Germany was giving Ukraine very little help and was pursuing Nord Stream 2, a gas pipeline that would make Europe even more dependent on Russia for natural gas in the years ahead. Trump had visited Ukraine years earlier on business and had often reflected about how corrupt the country was following the fall of the Soviet Union. When I learned about the stalled assistance package, I read it as part of his concerns with Ukraine and his desire to get the United States' allies to play a larger role in defending it. After Bolton's comments during the August 30 call, I asked my national security advisor, General Keith Kellogg, to get some answers about the Ukrainian assistance from the president's advisors. They explained that Trump was concerned about corruption in Ukraine and wanted to know why other European countries were not doing more to help. That lined up with what I had heard and also with his healthy skepticism about foreign aid. He looked at every dollar coming out of the Treasury as if it were coming out of his own bank account.

On September 1, I flew to Poland to attend a ceremony marking the eightieth anniversary of the beginning of World War II. Trump had originally been scheduled to attend, but with Hurricane Dorian approaching the East Coast, he elected to change plans and remain home, and I went in his place. It was a last-minute rearrangement; I had previously been scheduled to visit Ireland, Iceland, and the United Kingdom, all of which had to be changed in order to accommodate the stop in Warsaw. While there, I held a bilateral meeting with the new Ukrainian president, Volodymyr Zelensky, who was also attending the ceremony.

Zelensky, a television star and comedian with a law degree who had played a schoolteacher turned president on a TV show called *Servant of the People*, had been elected in April 2019. After his victory, Zelensky had invited Trump to attend his inauguration. The president, following protocol, had told Zelensky that he would send a delegation in his place. My office had then worked with the US ambassador in Ukraine to see if we could schedule my attendance. The difficulty was that unlike in the United States, where presidential inaugurations are on January 20 every four years, in many European nations with parliamentary or snap elections, inaugurations are not planned out long term and are scheduled after the votes are counted. On May 13, the Ukrainian government had still not picked a date for the inauguration, so my office had informed the State Department that I would not be able to attend and would instead travel to Canada to work on the USMCA. We had never confirmed the trip, and there had been scheduling complications. During that time I had called Zelensky to offer my congratulations and discuss his inauguration. Before leaving for Poland, I did what I always did before meeting with a foreign head of state: I asked Trump if he had a message he wanted me to convey. Yes, he said, he wanted me to ask Zelensky what he was doing about getting more support from Europe and what he was doing to fight corruption in Ukraine.

Back then, Zelensky was still something of a mystery. I was prepared to be unimpressed by a television comedian turned head of state, but I had the opposite reaction. From our first encounter at our meeting that day in Poland, I was struck by his affability and the confidence he exuded in his new role. My first impression was that this was a man who knew his people and understood his role. He expressed genuine appreciation for the military support our administration had made available, being well aware that the Obama administration had not sent lethal aid. I also sensed that he was aware of my long-standing support for democratically elected governments in eastern Europe and that I was there to help find a way to continue to expand US military aid to Ukraine. He also expressed his commitment to fighting corruption in his country. He addressed me with familiarity. He knew I was a friend.

In the days that followed, when he crossed a banquet hall at the United Nations to greet me and Karen, I knew we had made a personal connection. And when I saw the way that he respectfully addressed the impeachment trial that would follow, I saw the glimmers of a leader the world would marvel at following the Russian invasion of 2022: personable, intelligent, resolute, and courageous. He did not allow himself or Ukraine to be used as a foil against our administration during the impeachment trial. His statement that there had been "no pressure" during his meeting at the United Nations with Trump and in the days that followed showed integrity and poise.

The day after my meeting with Zelensky in Poland, which both Bolton and Rick Perry attended, I took questions from the press who traveled with our delegation. Robert Costa, a reporter for the *Washington Post*, asked if I had discussed Joe Biden with Zelensky and if the holdup of the military assistance to Ukraine had had anything to do with the attempts by former New York City mayor Rudy Giuliani to dig up dirt on the Biden family. "Well, on the first question, the answer is no," I answered before explaining that Zelensky and I had discussed the military aid and the president would soon make his decision on releasing it. The questions caught me by surprise. I had heard rumors that Giuliani was freelancing abroad for the president, but his activities were opaque. And the connection between the Bidens and the aid was new to me.

From Warsaw I went to Ireland. I was thrilled to be back in my grandfather's country and looking forward to meeting again with the Irish taoiseach, Leo Varadkar. The visit, though, turned into a "controversy." When I had stepped in for Trump in Poland, our schedules had been shifted. We had planned to spend a night in Dublin for diplomatic meetings and a night near Doonbeg, where my mom's family had come from. My mom had joined the trip, making it a homecoming for both of us. We decided to spend two nights there and to fly to Dublin for meetings.

When we arrived in Doonbeg, the street was lined with people cheering and greeting us, and my mother made a beeline from the motorcade to the rope line. Then we went into Morrissey's pub, where I had worked as a twenty-two-year-old following my grandfather's death, and were greeted by a roomful of distant relatives. It was a joy to be in Ireland with my eighty-five-year-old mom in the town where her parents had grown up, to see the buildings they had lived in still standing, to take in the cheering crowds, and to enjoy a vintage Irish meal down in a pub full of family.

It just so happens that one of Trump's golf resorts is in Doonbeg. The president had stayed there during a trip to Ireland just a few months earlier. When he had learned that I would be visiting, he had suggested that we should stay at the hotel, too. My team had already found a hotel in Galway, about an hour away from Doonbeg, but we eventually decided to stay in Doonbeg at Trump's resort, since the Secret Service had already vetted the site for the president's visit and there were only two other hotels in the small Irish hamlet, one of which is called Doonbeg Pods and Cottages. Despite the fact that the president had stayed there before and our stay had been fully approved by the State Department, it was depicted as a conflict of interest by Democrats. The media attacked our stay at Doonbeg, thinking we had done it for Trump. I stayed there for my mom.

Next was London, where I met with Prime Minister Boris Johnson on September 5. I knew the intentionally rumpled Johnson from meetings I had had with him at the White House during his time as the United Kingdom's foreign secretary and also from his brilliant biography of Winston Churchill. When I arrived at 10 Downing Street, the prime minister's residence and office, the prime minister greeted me on the sidewalk outside while the press snapped photos. After a discussion of trade between the United States and United Kingdom, my diplomatic aide told me that Johnson had broken protocol by walking out of 10 Downing Street to meet me; that was a ritual reserved for heads of state. I will never forget that sign of friendship and respect from Prime Minister Johnson.

After I returned to Washington, I met with Trump in the Oval Office to discuss the Ukrainian aid along with Ohio senator Rob Portman, who joined us by phone. Portman was a great champion of Ukraine and was also encouraging the president to release the funds. "Well, Mike wants it, too . . . done," Trump said.

So, on September 11, Trump released the Ukrainian aid. On September 18, with the money released, I made a follow-up call to President Zelensky during which he thanked me for what he perceived to be my personal role of securing the release of additional military assistance for Ukraine. I thanked him for the meeting in Warsaw, told him I had conveyed his commitment to fighting corruption to the president, and discussed his upcoming meeting with President Trump at the UN General Assembly. It was all standard stuff. On the nineteenth, the day after I talked via phone to Zelensky, the *Washington Post* ran a story about a whistleblower complaint that alleged that Trump had asked a favor of some world leader. More details emerged the next day, when the *Post* claimed that Ukraine was the country in question.

The next day I flew to Mackinac Island, Michigan, a charming island we had vacationed at as a family, for a political event sponsored by the Michigan Republican Party. Even that became a controversy when the Secret Service flew our cars in to transport us to the event. Mackinac has no motorized transportation, only bicycles and buggies. If I could have ridden a bicycle or a horse from the airport, I would have. Anyone who knows me knows I would have preferred either one to the motorcade. But the Michigan Democrats and the media made a fuss about it—right up until photographs of a barge carrying television trucks onto the island made its way onto the internet. Classic media moment: rules for thee but not for me.

On the flight back, my team heard from the White House: there was a problem. The House Intelligence Committee was going to release a whistleblower complaint filed by a government employee, citing the testimony of several officials present during a phone call on July 25, who alleged that the president had pressured Zelensky to interfere on his behalf in the upcoming election. I had not seen the record of the call. In fact, before leaving for Poland to meet Zelensky, I had not been informed of the whistleblower complaint, which had been filed on August 12 and which the White House legal team was aware of. Nor had I been supplied with a readout of Trump's call with Zelensky in my briefing materials. If the president had talked to a foreign head of state before I was set to meet with him, I was usually provided with a written record of the call for context. Not this time. To be fair, my trip to Poland had been planned at the last minute—I had been given the briefing materials prepared for Trump and even his speech, which I had had to Penceify before delivering it in Piłsudski Square. We took the terse prose drafted for the president, marking the eightieth anniversary of World War II, and added more sweeping rhetoric and my reflections on the role of faith in the cause of freedom. It aired around 6:00 a.m. Eastern Time on a Sunday morning. It was one of the greatest speeches never heard.

Over the following days, details emerged alleging that Trump had pressured Zelensky to investigate Joe Biden's son, Hunter, during the call. In 2014, the younger Biden had been given a seat on the board of Burisma, a Ukrainian gas company. It was a lucrative appointment with a $50,000 to $80,000 monthly paycheck. He had had no previous experience in the energy industry. And the appointment had been made while Hunter's father was leading the Obama administration's Ukraine policy—a responsibility Biden had told me about at great length when we met at his office in the White House during the transition in late 2016. In March 2017, he had bragged, on camera, that he had threatened Ukrainian president Petro Poroshenko that if he didn't fire a prosecutor general named Viktor Shokin, who was facing criticism for not doing enough to fight corruption in Ukraine, the United States would withhold $1 billion in US loan guarantees. But Shokin was in fact investigating corruption! He was investigating Burisma Holdings—the same company whose board Biden's son sat on. Poroshenko quickly fired Shokin. It stunk.

When I finally saw a readout of the call at the UN General Assembly, where Trump was set to make another major foreign policy address, I concluded that although it was not how I approached interactions with foreign leaders, the president had done nothing wrong. In all my interactions with heads of state, I assumed a disciplined posture, choosing my words carefully to align them with current US policy. The Trump who spoke on the call had used the freewheeling manner of conversation I had heard him use with other heads of state for the past three years.

Ordinarily when you are taking a call with a foreign head of state, your staff comes in and sets up the secure connection. Then a voice on the line will say, just for example, "Introducing his majesty . . ." The conversation begins. You have a card before you with talking points and prompts. "Your majesty, it's a great honor. I want to reiterate to you the commitment of the president . . ." You have your notes, and the other person has notes, too. "Mr. Vice President, we are grateful to you . . ." It is all choreographed. But that was not how Trump managed such calls. He was as informal in conversations with heads of state as he was with anyone else when he was on the phone or in face-to-face meetings. He was initially casual, asking about his counterpart's family. Then he would start in. "What about this treaty thing? What are we going to do about this?"

When I saw the readout of the call with Zelensky, it had the same spontaneous feel of other conversations I had heard him hold. He had mentioned Hunter Biden, the Russia collusion campaign, and a Ukrainian cybersecurity company called CrowdStrike, which he believed had been a conduit for pro-Clinton interference in the 2016 election. When we gathered in a holding room at the United Nations as the story broke, Trump assured me that there had been no quid pro quo, that he had not tied release of the Ukrainian assistance to Zelensky's investigating the Bidens. By that time Democrats in Congress were already clamoring for impeachment, and Nancy Pelosi had started an impeachment inquiry.

I have a view about interacting with foreign leaders: I let them handle their politics, and we handle ours. But I am also aware that heads of state are political people, and it's very common for world leaders to discuss their elections. Trump had said publicly that the conversation had been a "perfect call." It was a less-than-perfect call, but it was not an impeachable offense.

In point of fact, there was nothing illegal about what the president had said during his call with Zelensky. He had not conditioned release of the assistance to an investigation of the Bidens. It is worth noting also that Biden's poll numbers were falling in the summer of 2019, when the Trump-Zelensky call took place, with Vermont senator Bernie Sanders and Massachusetts senator Elizabeth Warren on the rise. It was less than certain that Biden was even going to be the Democrat nominee. So it's likely, given Trump's capacity to doggedly focus on past elections, that during the call he was actually focused on the last election and not the next one.

The White House, in a move to end the saga, released a transcript of the call and the whistleblower complaint, but the impeachment horses were out of the barn at that point and there was no turning around. There was a typical irony to all the timing. The call between Trump and Zelensky, the one that had triggered the impeachment inquiry, had taken place on July 25—the day after Robert Mueller's congressional testimony, which had driven a final stake into the heart of the Russia collusion conspiracy theories. The cloud of constant impeachment threats, which had hung over the administration for three years, had lifted in the spring, only to drift back over the White House in the fall.

No sooner had the White House released the transcript than Pelosi proceeded with impeachment—over a phone call. The truth is, Pelosi, Schumer, Adam Schiff, and their allies in the media had become consumed with impeachment for two and a half years and simply couldn't resist. It was absurd.

CHAPTER FORTY-FOUR

A Cease-Fire and Justice Served

But if you do wrong, be afraid, for rulers do not bear the sword
for no reason. They . . . bring punishment on the wrongdoer.
—Romans 13:4

Impeachment didn't pause the events beyond Washington, DC. In October, Trump announced that he was withdrawing two detachments of US troops from northern Syria, where they were supporting US-allied Kurdish soldiers, the Syrian Democratic Forces (SDF), which were positioned at the Syrian-Turkish border. The SDF had partnered with US forces against ISIS but had been deemed a terrorist organization by Turkey. Shortly after the US troops were removed from the region on October 8, Turkish president Recep Erdoğan launched an air and ground military offensive against the SDF, displacing two hundred thousand civilians and causing a potential humanitarian crisis. The campaign generated bipartisan anger in Congress and wide criticism of the president's decision.

The president called together the national security team and the secretary of state for a hurried meeting in the Oval Office and got Erdoğan on the phone. I was in my usual seat by the Resolute Desk. "You gotta stop," he told the Turkish president, who wasn't budging. Erdoğan explained through an interpreter that with terrorists on the border, he could not stop the military operation. "Can I send some of our guys over to talk?" Trump asked. Erdoğan agreed to meet, and with that Trump punched the mute button on his phone and looked at me across the Resolute Desk. "Can you go to Turkey today?" "I'm here to serve," I replied. Trump hit the mute button again. "Pence is coming over. Mike Pompeo is coming, too. They are on their way."

We had thirty-six hours to get there. A vice presidential foreign trip is normally a long-term planning engagement. The Secret Service has to go over in advance to scout and secure hotels. Thirty-six hours would not be enough time to produce safe accommodations. We would have to fly over, meet with Erdoğan, and then turn right back around and come back. And the prospects for success were not high.

We landed in Ankara late on the seventeenth, went to the presidential palace, and walked up the stairs through the emerald walls of the opulent 1,100-room building.

Upon my arrival Erdoğan asked for a short conversation, just the two of us with translators. The rest of the US delegation waited out in a hallway, cooling their heels, surrounded by Erdoğan's palace guards. Again and again he told me that he could not do it, just as he had rebuffed Trump's request for a cease-fire. "Mr. President, President Trump sends his regards," I said, "but I just have to tell you I have a list here of all the individuals and companies that will be sanctioned tomorrow if you do not agree to a cease-fire."

He shot back that he could not do it. "You can, you need to," I countered. He repeated over and over that it couldn't be done.

For more than an hour the back-and-forth bartering went on. Outside my staff had grown anxious; I was in the room alone with Erdoğan and no Secret Service. The atmosphere was tense. After more than an hour, I later learned, Secretary of State Pompeo, who had met privately with Erdoğan in the past, told the men guarding the door of the president's office that he needed "proof of life" and either they were going to open the door or he was going to break it down. Fortunately for all concerned, the meeting ended before an altercation ensued. I love Mike Pompeo.

Back inside the conference room, I continued to negotiate with the Turkish president. Finally, the "You can," "I can't" dialogue came to an end. Erdoğan paused, and with an exasperated sigh, asked how much time would the Kurds need to move out if a cease-fire was called. "You know, Mr. President," I answered, "I've got some very smart people with me who are knowledgeable about these things, and they can get you an answer." The doors of the room were opened, and the US delegation met with Erdoğan's ministers and hammered out a deal. As their meeting began, I asked for reporters to be let in. Erdoğan resisted at first and then relented, and our traveling press shuffled into the room to capture a few grim images of our team at the outset of the formal negotiations. The Turkish invasion would pause for 120 hours while the Kurds withdrew from the Turkish-Syrian border. If the cease-fire held, the United States would not leverage any additional sanctions on Turkey. Bleary-eyed, I phoned Trump on the way to the airport, where Air Force Two was waiting to take us back to Washington. "We have five days to move them out. Our teams will coordinate it," I told him. "What?" he responded. "That's great!" I had never heard him more elated. I suggested that he announce the deal. His response: "I'm going to tweet it out right now!" And of course he did.

Back in Washington, the impeachment inquiry moved along. On October 15, our old friend Adam Schiff, the chairman of the House Intelligence Committee and the Inspector Javert of the Trump era, was back on the case, requesting the transcript of my call with Zelensky from September. I had never discussed the issue of the Bidens with President Zelensky and had no objections to releasing a transcript of the call. One of the reasons such calls are not often released until after the people who made them are long gone—historians can now read the transcripts of all the calls between Franklin D. Roosevelt and Winston Churchill—is to give world leaders the chance to speak frankly to each other. If the calls are all made public, what world leader would want to speak to the president or vice president frankly? The solution was to place a staff member's testimony about my call with Zelensky in a classified room and give every member of Congress access to it. Apart from predictable complaints from Democrats about the call being classified, it generated little concern.

On the afternoon of October 27, with much of Washington preoccupied with a possible impeachment of the president, I was called to the White House. It was a Sunday afternoon, and there was a confidential gathering in the Situation Room. US Special Forces had located Abu Bakr al-Baghdadi, the leader of ISIS, the self-proclaimed caliphate of the Islamic State. He was the world's most wanted terrorist, a theocratic sadist who had presided over the rise and expansion of ISIS and its attacks not just in the Middle East but around the world. He was the heir to Osama bin Laden's leadership of the global war against civilization. His arsenal included blowing up children and stoning, hacking, or burying prisoners alive. Trump was presented with a mission to eliminate him. The national security team proposed a daring nighttime raid on a compound in northern Syria where Baghdadi was hiding. Trump heard the plan. He didn't deliberate or hesitate. He told the Joint Chiefs of Staff to go get him.

A few hours later, we gathered around the long table in the Situation Room along with Mark Esper, Chairman of the Joint Chiefs of Staff Mark Milley, and National Security Advisor Robert O'Brien. At the onset I asked if we could have a prayer for our soldiers. The national security officials, all hardened and imposing in stature, said they would be grateful for that. Heads bowed in the Situation Room, and I prayed for the safety and success of the mission and for justice to be served.

A large screen in the room carried a live satellite feed of the raid in grainy black and white. We watched quietly as helicopters descended to the ground and troops jumped out and moved toward Baghdadi's hideout. The president would interject with a question at times, but the room mostly remained quiet. We could see women and children exiting the house at the direction of our special forces. As our soldiers made their way toward the house, Baghdadi, coward that he was, grabbed a child and scurried like a rat into the basement of the building toward an underground tunnel. With a military dog named Conan in pursuit, the terrorist detonated a suicide vest, taking his own life and the child's. Shortly after that, we heard the mission commander's voice over the speakerphone in the Situation Room say, "Got him, one hundred percent confidence, jackpot." The president's facial expression, always stoic, never changed. I felt immense pride—not for a single person sitting there in the Situation Room but for the special forces, who, without one US casualty, had taken down the most ruthless terrorist in the world.

I thought about Peter Kassig—Abdul-Rahman Kassig—the Hoosier hero who had been murdered by ISIS in Syria in 2014. And about Kayla Mueller, the young aid worker murdered in Syria by ISIS in

2015; the operation had been named in her honor. The death of Baghdadi was little consolation for their loss, but it was justice served.

The only US injury in the raid was Conan, the big Belgian Malinois who had chased al-Baghdadi. He had run into some exposed electric wires but recovered, thankfully. In November, Conan made a special appearance at the White House so the president could introduce him to the world. When I walked into the Oval Office to meet the four-legged hero, a military advisor explained to me that this was a military dog and though they were aware I was a dog lover, he was an attack dog and I should be careful around him. Message received. Conan was on one side of the Resolute Desk, and Trump, who I don't think was a huge dog person, was on the other. I resolved not to treat Conan with the same familiarity with which I treated our dog Harley. Then Judge Jeanine Pirro, an ardent supporter of the president, burst into the Oval Office—you never knew who you would meet in the West Wing—and made a beeline for Conan. A great pet enthusiast, she got down on one knee and rubbed both of his jowls, at which point his tail started wagging happily. It was fine. So I felt comfortable walking over and petting Conan, too.

We went outside into the Rose Garden: the president, the first lady, Conan, his handler, and me. The press had gathered and were snapping photos. Usually, the president and first lady stand in the center for photos, but this time I was in the middle and Conan was next to me. Trump introduced Conan, talking him up and calling him a killer. All the while, the dog was nudging my hand. So I scratched him on the head. He nuzzled for more scratches. As long as Conan was in a good mood, I was going to keep him there. The result was one of my favorite memes from my four years in the vice presidency: a photo of Conan and me with the caption "Find someone who looks at you the way Conan looks at Mike Pence." When I got home that night, I could swear I saw a look of jealousy in Harley's eyes.

On December 10, House Democrats unveiled their articles of impeachment, alleging an abuse of power and obstruction of Congress. By that time, Gordon Sondland, the administration's ambassador to the European Union, had agreed to testify at the inquiry. Sondland had no background in diplomacy. He had joined our delegation in Poland but, as I heard was his custom on foreign trips, had ranged around trying to be relevant, sitting in meetings without contributing anything. When he testified at the House impeachment inquiry in November, he alleged that he had mentioned a connection between Ukrainian assistance and an investigation into the Bidens to me. Never happened.

There was a happy distraction away from my job late in the year—the marriage of our oldest daughter, Charlotte, which all started at her brother Michael's wedding. Michael and his girlfriend, Sarah, were married at the end of 2016 in a private ceremony in the Indiana Governor's Residence. The following year we had another, larger ceremony for friends and family in Brown County, Indiana. At that wedding, Charlotte met Lieutenant Henry Bond, who had trained with Michael at Naval Air Station Meridian, where they had been in Bible study together. Two years later, Charlotte and Henry were engaged. Henry is a third-generation Naval Academy graduate, a wonderful guy with a broad smile. They were married on December 28 in the chapel of the US Naval Academy in Annapolis, Maryland. Karen and I pulled up to the chapel in the presidential limousine, known as "the Beast," which President Trump had loaned us for the day.

I stood in the back of the church, waiting to walk Charlotte down the aisle. There were so many things going on in my mind, but I looked at Charlotte as we lingered in the anteroom and then it hit me: these were the last few minutes that I would ever be with Charlotte Pence. The emotion started to overwhelm me; everything else I was preoccupied with disappeared. My daughter slipped her arm under mine and asked if I was okay. I said no. The music began, and we headed down the aisle. The whole way down I was struggling, my face contorted to avoid breaking down in tears. And it's a long walk: the Naval Academy chapel is huge! As we approached the altar, I looked at Henry. I could see the same emotion on his face. He was just as torn up as I was. And in that moment peace descended on me. It gave me the greatest confidence that he was the right guy. My daughter had chosen well.

Our family would spend the holidays on Sanibel Island off the west coast of Florida. While there, I received a phone call from the White House. Following the successful military operation that had killed al-Baghdadi, the Pentagon had gotten intelligence on the location of the leader of the Iranian Quds Force, Qasem Soleimani. If Baghdadi had been the most notorious terrorist in the world, Soleimani was the most dangerous. In the years after the end of the initial combat operations in Iraq in 2003, hundreds of US soldiers had been killed and maimed by Shiite militias funded and equipped by a special forces branch of the Iranian military. Its leader was Soleimani. Under his guidance, the Iranian military had supplied terrorists in Iraq with the components to build powerful projectile weapons that were turned on American soldiers.

During my travels in Iraq in 2007, I had had an audience with Sheik Abdul Sattar Abu Risha in Ramadi. As the president might say, the leader of the Sunni tribes fighting Al Qaeda was a character out of central casting. Underneath his flowing robes was a crisply tailored business suit, and there was a Rolex on his wrist. Sheik Abu Risha had stepped forward to lead what came to be known as the Anbar Awakening, an alliance of Sunni Iraqis against the insurgency that was claiming Iraqi and American lives. For his courageous leadership he would be assassinated a few short months after we met—but not before he gave me an indelible insight into the source of violence across the Fertile Crescent. "Congressman, anybody who tells you the Iraqis don't like Americans is lying to you," he explained through a translator. "Your problem here is the Persians." I looked at the State Department attaché who accompanied us on the trip. "He means the Iranians." Sheik Abu Risha warned me that the United States' problem in Iraq was the Persians. Soleimani was *the* Persian.

With intelligence pinpointing Soleimani's travel plans and locations as he moved between Damascus and Baghdad, the president asked me to convene a series of calls with his national security team— Mark Esper, Mike Pompeo, Mark Milley, Robert O'Brien, and Gina Haspel, the director of the Central Intelligence Agency—to track developments. Intelligence indicated that Soleimani was planning attacks on US installations in Iraq that would put the lives of our military and diplomatic personnel in danger. The national security advisors believed that the military could execute a drone strike on Soleimani. In the Bible Jesus said that before you build a tower or go to war, you "count the cost." That was what we did. The group had several phone calls discussing the potential risks of killing Soleimani, which included an armed conflict with Iran. They carefully laid out the details to the president, who listened and asked questions. They presented a number of options other than eliminating Soleimani. There was not consensus among the group participating in the calls. There were reservations about the fallout from a possible strike. Earlier in my vice presidency, I had read an essay in a briefing book written by General Stanley McChrystal that I had thought expressed regret at not killing Soleimani when he had been head of the military's Joint Special Operations Command in Iraq in 2007—thirteen years earlier. I remembered standing with Gold Star families at grave sites of Hoosier soldiers lost in Iraq. Soleimani had been responsible for hundreds of American deaths. If we had the chance of preventing him from taking one more American life, we had to take it. After several calls, the president made the decision and gave the order to take Soleimani out. A few members of the team repeated the risks and possible fallout to the president. He understood. "Don't worry about it. Get it done, and let me know." He never wavered.

That afternoon, a Secret Service agent escorted me to our motorcade for a secure call. It was the middle of the night in Iraq. There had been an explosion at Baghdad International Airport, where Soleimani had just landed. The mission was a success. The president called shortly after. "Did you hear?" I congratulated him and thanked him. But I also had a sense of foreboding over what was to come. Following the strike, the repercussions echoed across the Arab world. Many nations maintained a stunned silence, while others openly commended the United States. The Iraqi government voted to expel five thousand US troops. And Iran threatened vengeance and retaliation.

Shortly after, Trump warned that any retaliation by Iran would be answered by US strikes on fifty-two preselected sites in Iran including cultural sites. When international condemnation followed in the press, the president said, "They're allowed to torture and maim our people, they're allowed to use roadside bombs and blow up our people, and we're not allowed to touch their cultural sites? It doesn't work that way." Classic Trump. We were not going to bomb the tomb of Cyrus the Great or the Dome of Soltaniyeh. But they didn't know that. What Trump made clear was that if Iran took any American lives, they would be hit hard.

On January 8, having returned to Washington, I was in my West Wing office when Robert O'Brien, the president's national security advisor, burst in. "Mr. Vice President, we need you in the Situation Room now!" I rushed down the narrow stairs that led to the room where the national security team waited. On the giant screens I saw missiles tracking out of Iran heading toward Ayn al Asad, the joint American-Iraqi air base in western Iraq. Karen and I had just been there, making a surprise stop to spend Thanksgiving with our troops. It's a huge facility; thousands of US soldiers, sailors, airmen, and marines are stationed there.

The president joined us shortly after I arrived. I prayed silently as we watched the missiles fly. We were informed by the Pentagon that the attacks were coming.

Most of the personnel stationed on the base were evacuated into the desert; the planes were ordered into the air. After the missiles hit, we waited in the Situation Room for a bomb damage assessment. Thankfully, there were no deaths. We would learn in time, though, that there had been more than a hundred injuries; many of the people who remained sheltered on base suffered concussions from the explosions and had to be treated. Various press outlets reported that the Iranian missile attack on Ayn al Asad had been an intentional miss. That was absurd. The Iranians had intended to kill Americans. But for the swift professionalism of our service members on the ground, they would have.

A short time later, we received indications from Tehran that the Iranians were done, not interested in escalation to a full-scale war with the United States. The president had acted decisively. Our troops had done their job courageously. Soleimani was gone. It was over.

In late December, the president and I lunched in the dining room in the back of the Oval Office, where we met so often, discussing our prospects for reelection. The economy was roaring, and unemployment was low. Impeachment was a distraction but not a great worry.

We were genuinely proud of what we had accomplished in three years, from tax cuts to military spending to two new justices on the Supreme Court. The passage of the USMCA was nearing. ISIS was devastated; Baghdadi was dead. We were rebuilding the US military and had created a new branch of it to compete with China and Russia in space. And as we looked at the numbers, the maps, and the Democratic competition, we had reason to feel confident about the coming campaign. We both thought things looked good, but I offered a cautionary thought: "Sometimes history shows up." Those were usually energetic conversations, with very few pauses or silent moments. But this time, the president grew quiet. "What do you mean?" he asked. I told him that unforeseen circumstances can change the world, scramble the most carefully laid plans, level the ambitions of leaders: Fort Sumter, Pearl Harbor, 9/11. These had all been moments when history showed up. He took it in and shot me back a look of knowing recognition.

As 2019 was winding down, Congress fought over what the impeachment trial would look like, when it would begin, who would testify. It was, I knew, a futile act of political theater. Democrats might impeach the president in the House, but the Republican-controlled Senate would acquit him. Whatever Republicans thought about the appropriateness of the Zelensky call, the overwhelming majority of them believed that it was not an impeachable offense. Congress was wasting the country's time. Meanwhile, a mysterious virus was spreading in Wuhan, China.

CHAPTER FORTY-FIVE

History Shows Up

You will not fear the terror of the night . . .
nor the pestilence that stalks in the darkness.
—Psalm 91:5–6

In the first weeks of 2020, my daily briefings contained more and more reports about a new coronavirus that was spreading in the city of Wuhan, China.

Government to government, the United States was told by China that the virus was contained. Doctors in China who attempted to speak out about how contagious the new coronavirus was were silenced. The Chinese government was denying to global health officials that there was evidence of human-to-human transmission. The World Health Organization (WHO) in Geneva, Switzerland, took the Chinese Communist Party at its word and repeated the claim—all while the disease was spreading across and beyond China, unbeknown to much of the world. The Chinese, incredibly, shut down travel within their country but not abroad. On January 3, Dr. Robert Redfield, the director of the Centers for Disease Control and Prevention (CDC), reached out to his Chinese counterpart, offering to send over US experts to help investigate the virus. He was rebuffed. The Chinese government shut down investigations and publications that would have helped the rest of the world develop a better understanding of the virus before it crashed on its shores. The information the Chinese did share was little more than lies. And after the WHO said that there had been "limited" human-to-human transmission of the new coronavirus, it quickly reversed course, presumably under pressure from China, tweeting that there was "no clear evidence" that covid-19 could spread between people.

On January 15, for the third time in US history, a president was impeached when the House of Representatives voted along party lines to impeach Donald Trump. Nancy Pelosi held a signing ceremony after the vote, investing great pomp in sending the articles of impeachment to the Senate, where the president would be tried. She needn't have bothered. The outcome was never in doubt. The Senate was going to acquit the president, and it did so three weeks later in two votes on the articles of impeachment of 52–48 and 53–47.

But as the impeachment trial got under way, the first documented case of covid-19 reached the United States in Washington State on January 17. The CDC started airport screening of passengers on flights arriving in California and New York from Wuhan. Knowledge of the virus was limited, though, because of the Chinese government's secrecy. The CDC was scanning arriving passengers for the symptoms commonly associated with the virus—shortness of breath, coughing— when, as the world would soon learn, many cases of the virus were asymptomatic.

On January 22, in an about-face, the WHO declared that coronavirus can be spread by humans. Now reports were arriving that in Wuhan a number of people had died because of it and hundreds more were sick. Its population, more than 11 million, was under quarantine. A week later, the WHO declared a global health emergency. In the days that followed, the numbers of both cases and deaths grew as the virus reached additional countries.

On January 29, President Trump created the White House Coronavirus Task Force. Prior to its creation, the federal government's response to the new virus had been led by the CDC, which is part of the Department of Health and Human Services (HHS). The president named Alex Azar, the secretary of HHS, chairman. Azar had replaced Tom Price in 2018 after the failed effort to replace Obamacare and a controversy over the secretary's travels. The task force unified the government's covid response and advised the president on covid policy. Two days later, the task force presented Trump with one of the most difficult decisions of his presidency.

On January 31, Azar brought the task force into the Oval Office to brief the president. By that point there were 10,000 confirmed cases of the virus in China and 200 deaths. There were 114 other cases in other nations. It was clear that the virus was transmissible from human to human. The virus was highly contagious, spreading rapidly around the globe from China, a country from which nearly 3 million people travel to the United States every year. There was no way to monitor every single one of them entering the country. There was a very real concern about the virus spreading through the United States and overwhelming the nation's health care system.

Surrounded by the nascent task force, Secretary Azar recommended that the president ban travel from China to the United States. That was a momentous decision to make and not one without major complications. Treasury secretary Steven Mnuchin reminded Trump of the economic cost of cutting off travel from China, the second largest nation in the world: possibly more than $10 billion in 2020 due to ending the flow of people and commerce. At the time, there were still very few cases identified in the United States. There was a spirited discussion about the benefits of and possible damage by a travel ban, with the public health officials in the room pushing for it and the economic advisors resisting it.

I sat in a chair next to the Resolute Desk in my usual spot and listened. I understood the seriousness of the moment and what the nation was facing. When the Middle Eastern respiratory syndrome, or MERS, had reached Indiana in 2014, it had been of a completely different magnitude, and though the virus had a mortality rate of 30 percent, the first thing the state focused on, working with federal health experts, was stopping its spread. If this virus, covid-19, was pouring out of China, we had to try to cut off its ability to reach us. I sensed, though, how unprecedented and likely subject to wide-ranging criticism doing that would be. As the conversation in the Oval Office reached its conclusion, for the president's benefit, I asked members of the task force, "Has any president in American history ever suspended all travel from another country?" The answer was no.

Trump sat back in his chair, pondered all that he had heard, and made a decision: the United States would temporarily suspend all travel from China. The following day, Joe Biden, still in pursuit of the Democratic presidential nomination, tweeted his disapproval: "We are in the midst of a crisis with the coronavirus. We need to lead the way with science—not Donald Trump's record of hysteria, xenophobia, and fear-mongering."

President Trump's decision to suspend travel from China saved countless American lives. It didn't stop the virus from arriving in the United States, but it likely delayed its arrival. Instead of spreading in mid-March, it would have been in the country a month earlier at least. The decision bought the government time to organize the greatest national mobilization since World War II.

On January 31, the Trump administration also declared covid a public health emergency. The CDC was at work quickly developing tests to send to labs across the country. Life still went on. With his impeachment trial under way, the president delivered his State of the Union address and made mention of the covid outbreak, saying that we were coordinating with the Chinese government and that the administration would "take all necessary steps to safeguard our citizens from the virus."

The evening was particularly meaningful to me because the president also presented Rush Limbaugh with the Presidential Medal of Freedom and invited him to sit in the House gallery. Rush was fighting cancer at the time and had only another year to live. He had helped shape the conservative movement, and, going back to my days as a broadcaster, I owed a great deal of my inspiration to him. It was heartening to see him with the medal around his neck and hear him receive a standing ovation in the Congress of the nation he loved.

When the address ended, to thunderous applause, I stood up and shook the president's hand. But I didn't look to my left to see the speaker of the House ripping up a copy of the State of the Union address on national television. It was, of course, a premeditated gesture. During the address, she had been slowly tearing into the printed document so that she could rip the entire thing in one flourish before the cameras. It was childish, the type of action Pelosi and other Democrats constantly accused Trump of while feigning outrage. It was beneath the dignity of the speaker of the House. And she knew better.

The following day, February 5, to no surprise, the Senate acquitted the president in his impeachment trial. There was not much time for celebrating in the White House, though. The covid-19 death toll in China was rising. Clusters of infection had formed in northern Italy. By early March the Italian government would lock the country down. Testing in the United States, as elsewhere, was scarce. The tests created by the CDC were flawed and in short supply. As the virus spread and our understanding of it grew, the federal response was still coming together across offices within the Department of Health and Human Services. By February 26, fourteen cases of the virus had been confirmed in eight states.

History had shown up.

Near the end of February, President Trump traveled to India, his first visit to the country. Before the trip, Mick Mulvaney, who was still acting White House chief of staff, told my chief of staff that we were facing a pandemic and that federal response needed to be housed in the White House. While the president was in India, my staff learned through back channels that the president planned to ask me to lead the nation's response to covid-19. It was likely a lose-lose assignment: if the task force was successful, I wouldn't get any credit; if it failed, I would get the blame. I understood that. But at a moment of incredible uncertainty and peril, credit or blame was irrelevant. I spoke at great length with Karen about it. We both agreed: there was only one answer.

After the president returned from India, we met in the Oval Office. He made clear that he wanted to elevate the importance of the task force by putting in charge someone inside the White House and with a higher profile than a cabinet secretary. "Is that something you could do?" he asked. And as I had done so many times over the last three years, I looked the president in the eye, nodded, and said, "I'm here to serve."

What gave me confidence was that I had been a governor and had gone through two different health crises, one including the first MERS case in the United States and the other an HIV/AIDS epidemic in a small Indiana town. I had seen firsthand how the state and federal governments could work together during a health crisis. I understood and readily accepted the challenge.

I stood up, walked out of the Oval Office, headed down the hallway, and pulled the team together in my West Wing office for my first meeting as head of the White House Coronavirus Task Force. Not knowing what lay ahead, we bowed our heads and opened that first meeting in prayer. From that moment a seriousness settled on me that was nothing short of God's grace. I didn't know what was ahead, but I knew America would rise to the occasion.

On February 26, 2020, the day President Trump appointed me to lead the White House Coronavirus Task Force, the first case of community spread of the virus was identified in California. An American who had not traveled abroad or knowingly come in contact with covid was discovered to be infected. The virus was moving across the land quickly. The United States was facing its greatest public health crisis in a century, and the truth was that we didn't have what we needed in terms of testing, medical supplies, or medicines to confront the rapidly expanding pandemic.

President Trump gave the White House Coronavirus Task Force one mission: to save lives. To do that, we needed every level of government—federal, state, and local—to rise to the task.

From the outset, I knew that the federal government alone could not meet the challenges ahead. That was not a criticism of its limitation but a realistic assessment that the sheer size of the nation and the scope of what we had to produce—from tests and needles to gowns, gloves, and masks—would require enlisting the full strength of the American economy. And of course the main challenge, which would have to be driven by the private sector, would be inventing and mass-producing a safe vaccine. The federal government could not go it alone; we had to work with industry but also partner with US governors. We didn't just need a whole-of-government approach, we needed a whole-of-America strategy for fighting covid.

As of late February, the federal government had fewer than three thousand tests that could correctly diagnose covid-19. Across the country there was a shortage of personal protective equipment (PPE) for health care workers treating patients and for the patients themselves. The national stockpile of ventilators, which could help patients with severe cases of this respiratory disease breathe, was also low. There was no vaccine for covid, no treatment, nothing in our medical professionals' arsenal to stop it. The government's few tools to respond to the pandemic were spread out across agencies and departments, and their deployment was slowed by red tape and regulations. Even with the fog of disinformation coming out of the Chinese government about the nature of the virus, its lethality, its contagiousness, even its origins just beginning to lift, health officials still knew very little about the virus.

The work was ten hours a day, seven days a week. We began the assignment with prayer and focused on the work. I often thought of what Chesley "Sully" Sullenberger had said when he had been asked if he had prayed when he was landing US Airways flight 1549 in the Hudson River: "There were a lot of people in the cabin doing that for me. I had to fly the airplane." Every day I prayed to put aside any anxious thoughts and work on the problem.

As other nations shut down travel in February, almost ninety-five thousand Americans were left stranded abroad. The task force launched a rescue mission to bring them home safely. A number of Americans who were unable to get back home were on cruise ships. The *Diamond Princess*, for example, was a British luxury liner stuck in quarantine off the coast of Japan after seven hundred of the four thousand passengers tested positive for the virus. The task force launched a complicated mission to evacuate the passengers, many of them elderly and vulnerable. We coordinated with air force bases in California, Texas, and Nebraska to receive the passengers, who had to be safely transported off the ship and into quarantine on the bases. Another cruise ship, the *Grand Princess*, was sailing from Hawaii to San Francisco when a number of passengers tested positive for the virus. While the ship sat in the waters off California, we worked with that state's governor, Gavin Newsom, and the federal Department of Health and Human Services to arrange for the ship to dock at the Port of Oakland and to safely bring testing and medical equipment on board. Under the capable leadership of Secretary of State Pompeo, the State Department, in a little over a month, repatriated sixty-two thousand Americans from a hundred counties on six hundred flights. By the end of 2020, more than ninety-five thousand were back home.

One of my early operational goals was to broaden the task force.

The president had already suspended all travel coming from and going to China, a decision with economic consequences. I knew that there would be additional decisions to make in order to slow the virus, and those would have even greater economic consequences. Other nations, such as Italy, were already ordering lockdowns and quarantines, shutting down entire regions and their economies. It was important, then, to have not just public health and national security officials involved in the decision-making but also members of the president's economic team. So I added Treasury Secretary Steven Mnuchin and Director of the National Economic Council Larry Kudlow.

When I took over the task force, one other person joined. Matt Pottinger, the president's deputy national security advisor, pulled aside my chief of staff, Marc Short, soon after I agreed to lead the task force. "We know this will be a heavy lift," he admitted, "but the best person in the world is on her way to help." That was Dr. Deborah Birx. She had led President George W. Bush's President's Emergency Plan for AIDS Relief (PEPFAR), a program I had supported passionately as a congressman. But her service went far beyond that; she had worked in some capacity as a public health official dating all the way back to the 1970s. She arrived with a to-do list.

From the outset, Dr. Birx told the task force that the CDC's testing was way off and needed to be overhauled. For two decades, she explained, the agency had built a surveillance system based on symptoms. She had already studied data from covid spread in China and Italy. She believed that the disease could appear without symptoms. On top of that, the covid tests that the CDC had developed could be done only in federal labs, state facilities, or community hospitals. That greatly lowered the number of tests we could conduct. The CDC model wasn't going to work. "This is going to be really bad" if we didn't have the tests, she said. She was right.

The members of the White House Coronavirus Task Force met around the table in the Situation Room every day, two to three hours a day, poring over the latest information on cases and hospitalizations, working to repatriate Americans stranded overseas and on cruise ships, monitoring quarantine at ports of entry, and standing up a whole-of-government response. It was an all-hands-on-deck affair, but I had peace that the American people and their government would rise to the challenge, thanks to the wisdom of the American founders in designing a system of federalism.

On March 2, I opened the first of more than forty weekly video-conference calls between the White House Coronavirus Task Force and America's governors in the Situation Room with the words "I've been in your chair." Each call went on for several hours and often involved all fifty governors. It was a chance for them to tell me what was happening in their state and what they needed. As a former governor, I understood that your first instinct is to look at the national stockpile and say, "One-fiftieth of that is mine. My state is entitled to it." But sitting in the Situation Room with all the governors displayed across the computer screens, I had to break the news to them: "Let me make this clear: you all are not going to get everything you want, but you are going to get what you need when you need it." If the governors heard me say it once, they heard me say it a hundred times over the next ten months. We directed testing supplies and medicines to the hardest hit and most-in-need areas first. And to their credit, America's governors understood and supported our approach.

On March 3, Secretary Azar and I took the task force to Capitol Hill to brief lawmakers on what the country was facing. We met with Republicans and Democrats in the House and Senate, and the environment was refreshingly apolitical. Impeachment, that exercise in partisan politics, was over. Now reality was about to hit the entire country hard. We were reminded again that at the end of the day, we were all on the same team.

It was an anxious time for the American people and their elected representatives. I believe, as the Bible says, that "a gentle answer turns away wrath." So from that very first briefing, I always sought unity on behalf of all the American people. Our meetings with Republicans and Democrats on Capitol Hill reminded me of the days following 9/11. As members of the task force briefed senators and congressmen, there was no grandstanding by the elected officials. We were all in this together, at least for now.

During a meeting that same day in the vice president's staff office just off the Senate floor, Dr. Birx returned to the issue of testing: "We are not going to have the testing capacity with what we have now using CDC and state labs." I asked how we could solve the problem. "You would have to get all the major testing labs in the country to work together and coordinate, and I have no idea how we are going to do that," she explained, looking right at me. "Why don't we get them on the phone?" I asked. "Get who on the phone?" Birx answered. "The CEOs of the diagnostic labs," I said. Birx wasn't buying it. "Well, these are CEOs of some of the largest corporations in the country." I asked her for a list of names, which she gave me. I picked up the phone, dialed the White House operator, gave her the names of the CEOs, and asked that she set up a conference with them all as soon as possible. I said thank you and put the phone down. Thirty minutes later, the CEOs of America's biggest testing companies were all on the line, including Labcorp and Quest Diagnostics. We explained the testing crisis and made it clear that we wanted the industry to work together. I told them that the pharmaceutical companies would have to create a consortium to work together to develop medicines and vaccines and I wanted the diagnostic companies to do the same. They were eager to help and said they would discuss it in a meeting of the industry to take place the next day. "Can you all be at the White House later this week?" I asked. They all said yes, they would be there. I hung up. Birx was in disbelief. "How did you do that?" she asked. "Welcome to the White House," I said.

Within two days we met around the small table in the Roosevelt Room with the CEOs of all the major diagnostic companies in the country. Adam Schechter, the new CEO of Labcorp, who was sitting to my right, gave me the good news. "Mr. Vice President, we formed a consortium to create new tests for the American people," he told me. I pumped my fist in the air and said, "That's great!" During the meeting, the CEOs of Labcorp, Roche Diagnostics, Thermo Fisher Scientific, Abbott, and Quest Diagnostics agreed to work together and pool their resources and expertise. I told them, "Make as many tests as quick as you can, and the federal government will buy them from you. Make a billion a month if you can." And with that we launched an effort to redesign testing. The first step was telling members of the task force that if there was red tape in the way of testing or creating new tests, to cut it and cut it fast. That opened the door for the Food and Drug Administration (FDA) to allow specially designated labs to conduct covid tests without waiting for the agency's approval. I charged Admiral Brett Giroir, the assistant secretary for health at HHS, with coordinating diagnostic testing efforts among public health service agencies, state and local public health authorities, and private and public clinical laboratories. He did a brilliant job.

Then we expanded the number of people eligible to take tests and allowed Medicare to waive the cost of tests. The next step was getting the private testing companies to kick into high gear. Less than ten days later, the FDA approved new tests made by Roche and Thermo Fisher. Hologic and Labcorp began work on a two-hour diagnostic test. HHS partnered with Thermo Fisher, providing funding and technical help for developing a thirty-minute test.

In just a few days, these great American companies were ramping up the testing and production of tests. By the end of February, between CDC labs and state public health facilities, the United States had performed only about eight thousand coronavirus tests. By June, we had conducted more than 23 million, roughly five hundred thousand tests a day. By the end of 2020, we had conducted 270 million, more than any other country in the world.

Later in the year, the journalist Bob Woodward would publish a book saying that Trump had admitted deliberately downplaying the covid threat. He quoted the president from a March 2020 interview as saying, "I wanted to always play it down . . . because I don't want to create a panic." I thought that mischaracterized the leadership that President Trump showed in the early, harrowing days of the pandemic.

Though I heard the president speak that way many times in my early days leading the task force, it never gave me pause. President Trump had, after all, suspended all travel from China, brought the federal response into the White House, initiated a national effort to secure testing and supplies, and directed shutdowns of large portions of the economy in mid-March to slow the spread of the virus. Those were not the actions of a president downplaying the threat. The president would later defend his words, saying that he saw himself as a "cheerleader" for the country, believing that part of his job was to project confidence, saying, "leadership is about confidence . . . confidence in our country." For me, it was important that Americans were confident that we were doing everything that could be done, and I welcomed the president's focus on national morale.

While we were immediately addressing testing, we also needed to fortify our healthcare system. As covid spread quickly, the health care system was short of vital supplies such as masks, gowns, gloves, and ventilators, and we needed to mobilize American industry to meet the need. One area where there was a shortage was the N95 face masks used by medical professionals. That was where it seemed as though Providence stepped in again.

With the campaign season under way, we had long planned to attend a political rally in St. Paul, Minnesota, on March 5. But as there was a severe covid outbreak in Washington State, I made plans to cancel my attendance at the rally and travel there to assess the emergency on the ground. As I was thinking about the nation's supply of personal protective equipment, I realized that Minnesota was home to 3M, which happens to be the nation's largest producer of masks. It was God's timing. I asked Birx and Stephen Hahn, the director of the FDA, to come along. We got onboard Air Force Two and landed in Minnesota on our way to Seattle. As Karen ably filled in for me at the scheduled political rally—the crowd was probably happy they had gotten her rather than me—Birx, Hahn, and I met with the state's governor, Tim Walz, and Michael Roman, the CEO of 3M. I knew Walz from Congress—we had been in the House together—and our governorships had overlapped. I asked them how 3M could increase its production of masks. Roman explained that the company produced 35 million masks a month, but only 10 percent were for hospital use; all the rest were for construction workers. "But are they essentially the same mask?" I asked. The answer was yes. "Great, then, can we just purchase those for hospital use?" No, I was told, the masks had not been approved for medical use by the FDA. The company could be sued if they were used in hospitals. "What's the answer here?" I asked. Roman explained that if 3M could be afforded legal protection by Congress, we could sell them across the country.

So after the meeting ended, I grabbed Walz by the elbow. I told him he would have to call Nancy Pelosi and Chuck Schumer—Congress was quickly putting together a covid emergency bill—and tell them we needed the Democratic leaders to put language into a bill that would provide temporary protection for companies such as 3M to sell their masks for medical use, which he did. With that reform alone we went from having 3 million N95 masks available to 20 million when Trump signed the bill a week later.

At that point, it must be recalled that due to the shortage of face masks, the government and public health officials were encouraging only Americans infected with the virus to wear masks in order to guarantee that enough would be available for medical workers. There was also much debate over the effectiveness of masks in preventing people from getting the disease. At that moment our focus was entirely on ensuring that health care workers and Americans with the virus had access to face masks, but as time went on and masks became more readily available, that debate died down and gave way to recommendations for nearly universal mask wearing and mandates. But that was never my position.

Later in the spring, during a visit to the Mayo Clinic, I elected not to wear a mask, since at that time our best science suggested that masks only prevented the spread of the virus. Since I was tested every day and knew I didn't have the virus, I explained to the local media that there was no need for me to wear a mask. The media furor that followed was an early indication that attitudes about mask wearing were becoming more about virtue signaling than about science. That said, it was an unnecessary distraction, and I should have worn a mask.

Shortly after I took over the task force, Jared Kushner approached me. He told me he was dropping everything he was working on to help me in whatever way I needed. He went to work on logistics, helping to develop what came to be known as Project Airbridge, which expedited the transportation of medical supplies, masks, gowns, thermometers, face shields, and stethoscopes from producers to hospitals and doctors. Two weeks in, on the evening of Sunday, March 15, he called me. When I heard his voice on the other end, I could tell he was discouraged about the challenges we were facing in ramping up testing, getting enough medical supplies distributed, and coordinating that effort at the ground level. "We can't do this from the White House," he confessed. "It's too much, we will never be able to meet the needs." "You want me to make you feel better?" I asked, not even waiting for his answer. "We don't have to," I said. "The framers of the Constitution gave us a system of fifty CEOs leading states across the country. . . . We just need to make sure they have what they need, and they will get it done." To that, he sighed in relief, saying, "I hadn't thought of it that way," adding, "You know what? You're right!"

Equipping governors was key.

CHAPTER FORTY-SIX

Only in America

Not looking to your own interests but each of you
to the interests of the others.
—Philippians 2:4

On March 13, President Trump declared a nationwide emergency under the Stafford Act and accepted the task force's recommendation to move the emergency response to the Federal Emergency Management Agency (FEMA). There was no other organization in government with the capability to manage an emergency response and allocate supplies in all fifty states and territories. And there was the great benefit that governors were well acquainted with FEMA's structure and its approach to natural disasters that was "federally supported, state managed, locally executed." FEMA administrator Peter Gaynor brought a cool head and a lifetime of experience to leading the coordination with the states, and Admiral John Polowczyk, perhaps the Pentagon's best logistics man, was detailed to FEMA to oversee the distribution of supplies.

With the tireless efforts of FEMA and an energetic effort organized by Jared Kushner to assemble a team who worked around the clock finding and purchasing medical supplies all over the world, our administration increased the supply of personal protective equipment by the billions. In partnership with private industry, as of June, we had delivered more than 143 million N95 masks, 598 million surgical and procedural masks, 20 million eye and face shields, 265 million gowns and coveralls, and 14 billion pairs of gloves. As part of the effort, Project Airbridge conducted more than two hundred flights bringing equipment from overseas. It was an unparalleled peacetime logistics feat.

Early on, Democrats began to focus on the Defense Production Act (DPA), a federal law that allows the national government to order industry to produce certain products during times of war or national emergency. Democratic lawmakers sent the president a letter demanding that he use the act, and presidential candidate Joe Biden also criticized the administration over the DPA, saying, "Step up and do your job." But what Biden and the Democrats failed to understand was that American industry was already stepping up without the heavy hand of government being necessary.

At a press conference in mid-March, the president was asked why he had not invoked the Defense Production Act, and after he said that our administration was looking into it, he quickly moved on. Walking down the hallway after the press conference, the president turned to me and asked with an impatient tone, "Why haven't we used the Defense Production Act?" I replied, "Because nobody said no." He responded, "What?" And I said, "Every company we have asked to do something has dropped whatever they were doing and gone to work to meet the need. Nobody said no." The president said, "That's a really great answer." I said, "Well it's the truth." The next day, before the press, the president gave a very similar answer, commending American businesses.

When it came to the matter of the nation's ventilator supply, we faced another shortage with dire consequences. In severe cases of covid, the patients' lungs become so inflamed that they can no longer deliver oxygen to the bloodstream. Ventilators provided a lifeline to the lungs while patients fought off the virus.

The Strategic National Stockpile hadn't been refilled since the H1N1 influenza outbreak in 2009, and at the outset of the year, we had ten thousand ventilators on hand. It wasn't nearly enough. In the first few weeks, we had requests for fifty-five thousand ventilators from the states. If there was anything that kept me up at night, it was the idea that any American who needed a ventilator could be denied a ventilator. That had happened in northern Italy, and the best way to prevent it from happening here, I knew, was to tap our great capacity for innovation. There were simply not enough ventilator makers in the country to meet the demand. That was when America stepped in again.

The American auto industry had the industrial scale with its factories to mass-produce ventilators. It did not have the expertise, though; it was no simple task to switch overnight from making cars to making medical equipment. So by the time the president invoked the Defense Production Act, requiring the automakers to mobilize in the fight against covid, Chrysler, Ford, and General Motors were already at work partnering with ventilator manufacturers such as Medtronic to mass-produce the machines. Auto factories that had been temporarily paused as the virus spread were opened back up and ventilators were soon rolling off factory floors, much in the way jeeps, tanks, and bombers did in the lead-up to World War II.

We found other ways to innovate as well. The surgeon general, Dr. Jerome Adams, was by training an anesthesiologist. While we strategized on the task force about how to ramp up ventilator production, Adams told us that anesthesia machines could be used as ventilators. But doing so would require a change of filter as well as a change in regulations because the FDA forbade their dual use. We remedied the problem quickly: in early April, the agency authorized the retrofitting of the machines. In the months ahead, our administration saw to the manufacture of a hundred thousand ventilators in a hundred days. Only in America.

Early in the pandemic, we convened the first televised White House Coronavirus Task Force briefing from the White House Briefing Room. As I had learned during health care crises in Indiana, communication is vital. There is an old saying that if you can't communicate, you can't govern. So I told the health experts on the task force that I thought it was important for the American people to hear from us, especially as our understanding of the virus grew and informed our recommendations. Americans were anxious and wanted information. We generally held the briefings after an extensive meeting of the task force in the Situation Room and, accompanied by Dr. Birx, Secretary Azar, Dr. Anthony Fauci, and others, I would present data and the latest trends on the virus and the progress we were making, as well as offer a reassuring word of compassion and faith.

Not surprisingly, those 5:00 p.m. press briefings reached a wide audience during those early anxious days. President Trump, who did not initially participate, asked me over lunch if I was aware of how many people were watching; I told him I was not. Millions of people were tuning in, he told me, and he wondered aloud if he should participate. I told him I thought it was always a good thing for the American people to hear from their president during a time of crisis. So in mid-March, he joined the briefings. In the beginning, the president encouraged me to open the briefings with a report on the task force's work. Then other members would speak about data, testing, supplies, and best practices, and at the end, the president would take questions.

In the first few weeks, the media representatives were on their best behavior and focused their questions on the pandemic. But as the weeks wore on, things got frisky. The press began to use the time to joust with the president on a broad range of issues. And the president seemed to relish the normal sparring in such unfamiliar times. I always thought that the public most needed information and reassurance. The president took a different approach, but there was a method to the way he handled the briefings. I think he felt that seeing him and the press argue was in some way reassuring to the American people that life was going on.

In the weeks ahead, the briefings became even more adversarial. The mood around Washington changed. Rather than uniting the country, the covid pandemic divided us even further. And maybe that was inevitable. The 9/11 attacks had happened in the first year of a new administration. The covid pandemic struck in the fourth year of an administration as the country geared up for a national presidential campaign. It's hard to imagine a worse time for such a crisis in the life of a nation. But I really didn't have time to think about it. I had a job to do.

At the task force press briefings, Tony Fauci emerged as an early star and a great source of comfort to millions of Americans. A well-known immunologist and decades-long public servant, Fauci had been on the medical and scientific vanguard in the early fight against HIV/AIDS. He had been one of Azar's original appointments to the task force. And I was glad he was there. He was a reassuring voice to the public; Mitch McConnell had advised me, correctly, that Fauci would be a valuable member of the team because of his stature. He and Dr. Birx had known each other for years; they had almost a mentor and mentee relationship. Fauci played an invaluable role in helping the president and our team understand the true scope of the threat, though I still don't understand why he was so insistent that covid-19 had not emerged from a Chinese lab. Dr. Robert Redfield of the CDC always held that it had, and the more we have learned, the more I believe that Bob was right.

I always worked well with Tony, as he was keen to stay in his own important lane. He offered his expertise and advice, but in all our dealings he always recognized that there were economic and social factors to consider in the president's decisions. I never thought his role was to lead the government's response to the pandemic or be its point person, and neither did he. Some in the media sought to portray him as a foil to Trump. But they initially had a very good relationship. When the president would bluntly challenge Fauci in the Oval Office, Fauci was unfazed. He understood the president: Trump is from Queens, Fauci from Brooklyn, and Fauci was not put off by Trump's New York brashness. He had grown up around it. He is a brash New Yorker, too. His input was important when balanced with that of the other members of the task force. After we left office, the Biden administration would more or less appoint Fauci to lead the federal response. And not surprisingly, our balanced, whole-of-America approach, focusing on business innovation and state-based solutions, went by the wayside.

From the early days of the Biden administration, it was clear that all the focus was being placed on vaccines, deemphasizing the development of therapeutics and lifesaving medicines. Instead of empowering states, as we had done from early in the pandemic, the administration virtually discontinued the weekly communication with the nation's governors that we had established and turned to vaccine mandates that would ultimately be struck down by the Supreme Court. Biden also deemphasized the partnerships we had established with businesses over the manufacture and distribution of testing and supplies. The government stopped purchasing tests, and when shortages emerged, the new administration attempted to run testing out of Washington, DC, and was forced to purchase tests from China with taxpayer dollars. Having promised to "defeat the virus" and having inherited from our administration ample test kits, supplies, therapeutics, and vaccines, the new president still failed. And the widening and heartbreaking loss of life in Biden's first year in office is evidence of his administration's flawed approach.

By the second week of March 2020, with cases on the rise in several major cities and the threat of an outbreak that could overwhelm our health care system, the task force took a plan to the president, developed by Fauci and Birx, to shut down much of the US economy for two weeks. We called it "15 Days to Slow the Spread." It was a mitigation tactic driven by the knowledge that the virus was extremely contagious. The president urged citizens who could stay home to do so and to avoid interacting with others, and temporarily shut down huge parts of the economy, other than businesses and workers deemed essential.

Ramping up testing, bolstering the nation's supplies of medical equipment, and getting it all to the states was an effort to save our medical system from collapsing under the weight of the virus. The goal of the so-called lockdown was never to stop the spread of the virus; it was to slow it to buy time for the US health care system while its innovators got to work producing supplies and developing a medical arsenal. Sadly, many Democrat-led states continued with lockdowns long after we had reinforced our health care system and even after we were distributing vaccines to millions of Americans.

The shutdowns hit the US economy hard, sending the nation into a recession. But I think they hit the American people harder. We asked people to upend their lives, abandon their schedules and routines. Long-anticipated events, weddings, and graduations were canceled. My own daughter Audrey's wedding was rescheduled three times, and we watched her graduation from Yale Law School online. It was still an incredibly proud day for our family. As she began her career, I gave her my dad's three old law books.

Businesses that were generations old and vital parts of their communities closed. The American people adapted and looked out for one another. Congress, so bitterly divided for the last three years, was able to come together and craft relief packages. Treasury Secretary

Mnuchin deserves great credit for crafting the Paycheck Protection Program, which provided financial lifelines to businesses forced to shut down because of covid. It saved millions of jobs.

It's fair to observe that during my time in Congress, I voted against bailouts for Wall Street and the auto industry, and I joined other fiscal conservatives in demanding that the Hurricane Katrina rescue plan be accompanied by corresponding budget cuts. After these battles against big government spending, some no doubt wonder how I readily supported trillions of dollars in government spending during the pandemic.

I believe in limited government; I am not anti-government. In the earlier instances, it's important to note, the government was "bailing out" industries that had made decisions, taken on risk in a competitive marketplace, and failed. But in the spring of 2020, as covid spread, businesses were forced to temporarily close and furlough employees by no fault of their own. The loss of revenue, even for a few weeks, was devastating and could cause many restaurants, stores, and other businesses to shutter for good and force them to let workers go.

This was not a "bailout." This was what government is for, to do what only government can do: provide help when there is no other recourse. And this is why governments balance budgets and live within their means in ordinary times: because history shows up, whether it be war, calamity, or pestilence. And when the unthinkable happens, government has to have the means to respond. And we did.

At the end of March, the president, like all of us, had hoped that fifteen days would be sufficient to tamp down the virus. But when the total US death toll reached more than 23,000, Birx and Fauci asked for a meeting with the president to present their projections of what Americans might experience if we did not extend the mitigation strategies for another thirty days. Trump had hoped to reopen the country by Easter. We arranged a time to brief the president in the Yellow Oval Room, a room on the second floor of the White House just above the Blue Room.

That Sunday afternoon, Birx and Fauci presented a staggering chart. They showed the president that based on current trends, even if the country did everything right from that point on—mitigation, production of personal protective equipment, and diversion of supplies to hot spots—we could still lose up to 240,000 people. The numbers were shocking, but they got worse.

They informed us that if we failed to keep the mitigation in place for another thirty days, up to 2.2 million Americans could die before the year was out. The graph presented two waves, the worst-case scenario in dark blue, the "if we do everything right" outcome in light blue. The former looked like a mountain; the latter was significantly smaller but still heartbreaking in size.

The president digested it all for a quiet moment. It was another hard decision, but he made it. On March 31, we presented the chart to the American people and extended the 15 Days to Slow the Spread protocol for another thirty days. In the early weeks of the pandemic, it was clear that what we most needed was time, and that measure was designed to buy it.

There were Americans who could not stay home. We called them essential workers, and they were on the front lines of the pandemic. They were hospital and nursing home staff, caregivers, and bus and train operators, along with our courageous medical professionals throughout our health care system and first responders. They were the men and women who stocked our supermarkets and stores, the ones who delivered food to people in their community, who kept our economy alive and our country afloat. And there were the small businesses that shifted quickly to join the fight: distilleries that produced hand sanitizer and often gave it away for free, apparel companies that made personal protective equipment. I was deeply moved by the compassion and selflessness shown by ordinary Americans and businesses large and small. At our task force briefings, I tried to make a point of highlighting those selfless Americans. They were the heroes of the covid pandemic. And I believe with all my heart that history will remember them as such. God bless them all.

Because of them, because of the collaboration between our government and our industries, and because of the mitigation strategies the American people followed, I know we saved millions of lives. The nightmare scenarios facing our health care system never came to pass. Only in America.

Through it all, the governors were our partners. As the pandemic spread across the country, the task force continued to host a weekly video conference call with the governors and their staffs from every state and territory. During the discussions, we pored over data indicating where the virus was breaking out and where we needed to increase resources, such as army personnel, testing, or supplies. It was a data-driven approach to pandemic management. Early on, it was clear that senior citizens and nursing home residents were particularly vulnerable to the disease, and my fellow Hoosier Seema Verma, leading the Centers for Medicare & Medicaid Services, which oversees long-term care facilities, worked with governors to increase standards and inspections and direct resources to our long-term care community.

Governors whose states had few cases were sending in appropriate requests for testing and supplies; others were overestimating the resources they needed. When New York governor Andrew Cuomo requested forty thousand ventilators, Dr. Birx looked at the data, shook her head, and said, "There is no way he needs more than ten percent of that. If the roof fell in on New York City, he might need four thousand." We got him six thousand. He ended up giving many of them away to other states. When New York City became an infection hot spot, we sailed a navy hospital ship with a thousand beds into New York Harbor and turned part of the Javits Center into a field hospital. Both went mostly unused. Cuomo was something of a covid celebrity early in the pandemic. When his daily press briefings became must-see television, he stopped participating in the task force's weekly calls with the governors. And although early on he thanked me and the president for having "moved quickly" and "delivered for New York," and even described our administration's response as "phenomenal" to the press, after the initial wave of infections passed in the New York area, his appreciation waned. He spent the summer writing an entire book on how he alone had led New York through the crisis. He later won an Emmy Award for his briefings. I was never really offended that he won it. He certainly deserved an award for "acting like an effective governor." Tragically, as the Javits Center and navy ship remained vacant, he returned covid-positive seniors to nursing homes, ignoring the directives that HHS had issued against the idea and undoubtedly costing lives.

Fortunately Cuomo was only the vice chair of the National Governors Association during the pandemic. The organization's chair, Maryland's Republican governor, Larry Hogan, is a personal friend whom I had supported from his first campaign. Governor Hogan helped organize and gather the governors every week. He was a terrific advocate for the states, often led our calls, and was a vital link between the White House and the statehouses. Though he and the president saw eye to eye on very few issues, he never let that affect our relationship or his work with the task force. Governor Hogan once said that I had "risen to the occasion" and "done a really incredible job." I could say the same of him. Early on I also focused on relationships with the states where covid infection rates were highest. New Jersey was especially hard hit. Its governor, Phil Murphy, a Democrat who had just recovered from cancer when covid hit, was a full partner in everything that we did. The same was true of Democratic governor John Bel Edwards of Louisiana, where New Orleans was a hot spot. He participated in every single conference call. He was interested in helping the people of Louisiana, not scoring points against the administration.

That wasn't always the case. Detroit was another early epicenter of infection. And around March 25, the city was dealing with more than three thousand infections and nearly a hundred deaths and was in need of medical supplies. In a phone call with Michigan's Democratic governor, Gretchen Whitmer, she told me exactly what she needed. I hung up the phone, and we got it to her. Within a day, eighteen-wheelers full of medical supplies were rolling into the city. The next morning Trump called me to say, "The governor of Michigan is killing us on TV, saying they are having to go it alone." Later that week, in a radio interview, she implied that the administration was intentionally withholding medical supplies from Michigan. In a weekend series of tweets, President Trump called her Gretchen "half Whitmer" and said she was "way over her head." At a Monday press conference, Trump said he told me not to call "the woman in Michigan." I called her. When I did, she said we had done a great job but she was going to keep pushing for more. I respectfully asked her to talk to me if she needed anything rather than take it to cable television. The next day, President Trump said he had had a "productive conversation" with Whitmer. Blessed are the peacemakers.

But peacemaking wasn't necessary for most governors, especially Republicans. Georgia governor Brian Kemp deployed the National Guard to sanitize nursing homes in Georgia, and Texas governor Greg Abbott issued guidelines specific to counties with a certain number of cases, inspiring other states around the country. Governor Ron DeSantis worked with us to surge supplies to nursing homes in Florida at a time when our administration was shipping personal protective equipment to all 15,400 nursing homes across the country. In May, he accompanied me to personally deliver supplies to a nursing home in Orlando, as the staff cheered us on from inside the lobby, and joined me for lunch at Beth's Burger Bar afterward, when we were opening up Florida and the rest of America. Governor Doug Ducey of Arizona worked closely with our administration during the summer surge in 2020 to ensure that hospitals and health care facilities were well supplied, saw his state and its economy through a truly challenging time, and still reopened Arizona's schools for in-person learning in August. Republican governors set the pace in engaging our task force and leading their states.

From the outset I told all the governors, regardless of their party or whether they had criticized our administration, that they could call me day or night, and many of them did throughout the year. I gave them all my longtime assistant Zach Bauer's cell phone number and told them if they had a need or a problem, they could call him virtually twenty-four hours a day to get a message to me. I'm not sure how jazzed Zach was about that. He had joined my team when I was a member of Congress, right after he graduated from college, and followed me to Indiana when I became governor. He became almost a member of our family and worked longer hours and harder than almost anyone else who ever served at my side. And he had a servant's heart, always willing to take on any task or follow up on any detail, no matter how small. Later in the year, when I was traveling the country, we learned that he was now something of a rock star. When we were on the road, governors regularly asked if they could meet Zach, who had been a helpful voice on the phone and an indispensable link between the state and federal responses. There's only one Zach Bauer.

All of us on the task force were there to make the governors successful. Our federal response to covid was going to be only as good as our state-level response. That was certainty true in the early days of the pandemic. Birx was following trends in the states and was in contact with the governors away from our regular calls. She kept a catalogue of new ideas governors were trying. Before our weekly conference call with the nation's governors, she would ask me to let this or that governor speak so they could share what they were working on so their colleagues might adapt it for their own state. We were not just communicating data but encouraging governors to communicate with one another. As the Bible says, "As iron sharpens iron, so one person sharpens another." When our press briefings waned, I encouraged Birx and Redfield to visit the states and meet with governors and health officials. I believed that our role was to give our best counsel but respect the state leaders—which we did without fail. Though some Republican governors came under fire for reopening their states, we made it clear that the decision was theirs to make and supported them.

As May approached, infection rates began to decline, and the White House worked with states to carefully reopen the country. We launched Guidelines for Opening Up America Again, acknowledging that although the virus wasn't vanishing, our health care system was now in a much better place to give the American people the care that we would want for any family member. It was a recognition that prolonging lockdowns carried its own damaging consequences to the mental health of Americans and their livelihoods. On Arbor Day in late April, Karen and I joined President Trump and Melania for a ceremony on the South Lawn of the White House. After the president and I made formal remarks about conservation and our progress in reopening the country, the president unexpectedly waved Karen to the podium. With no notes, she took the opportunity to talk about her work on mental health—a very real issue in the covid pandemic. She sent people to the PREVENTS program page, a suicide prevention initiative on Facebook that had been refocused on mental health issues, and ended with the words "We don't want anyone to feel like there isn't help, because it's okay to say 'I'm not okay.'" President Trump returned to the podium and said simply, "Wow." So proud.

By May, as Americans were moving forward with their lives, the media never let up, stringing daily infection and death counts across news shows at a time when cases in more than half of the states were dropping, and case rates were also in decline, numbering twenty thousand a day, down from thirty thousand in April. And the country was in a much better place in terms of fortifying its health care system than it had been at the height of the pandemic. I articulated that in an editorial printed in the *Wall Street Journal* on June 16, 2020.

I wanted the American people to know that we were all making real progress in mitigation and care, despite the incessant alarmism of the national media. I wasn't claiming that we had defeated the virus. Dr. Fauci had told me that, like the swine flu, it was possible that covid was seasonal and there would be a natural abatement during the summer. But as it turned out, people began to move indoors in the heat, and there was a summer surge in the South. Nevertheless, as I stressed in the *Journal*, because of the whole-of-America approach and our progress in increasing testing capacity, supplies of personal protective equipment, and ventilators, we were in a much stronger position to fight covid. We had, I wrote, "created a solid foundation for whatever challenges we may face in the future." Unfortunately, the paper placed a somewhat misleading headline on the essay, titling it "There Isn't a Coronavirus 'Second Wave,'" and medical experts and media outlets (who thought they were medical experts) called the op-ed "reckless anti-science optimism." I am an optimist, but they apparently never got past the headline.

As the country opened back up, the task force's work went on, but the press conferences, having become increasingly adversarial, wound down following some unfiltered musings by the president.

On April 23, our task force was given a briefing by William Bryan, the undersecretary for science and technology at the Department of Homeland Security. He had come to present information on the benefits of sunlight and disinfectant against the virus with the intention that he would present his findings at our press conference to encourage people to enjoy the outdoors and be confident that surfaces could be sanitized and safe.

After the task force meeting, we went to the Oval Office for a pre-brief before the press conference and introduced Bryan to the president, who was encouraged by his findings. Later, at the press conference, Bryan informed the public that the coronavirus weakens more quickly when exposed to sunlight, heat, and humidity, suggesting, as Dr. Fauci had told me, that the virus might be less contagious in warm weather. Things went downhill from there.

President Trump had a habit of thinking out loud in meetings, throwing out ideas just to get a reaction. I had seen him do it on countless occasions in the Oval Office. I always thought it was part of his process of reaching a decision. This time it got the better of him.

When the president took to the podium, he spoke with enthusiasm about Undersecretary Bryan's findings and mused about possible treatments, then asked if hitting "the body with a tremendous, whether it's ultraviolet or just very powerful light" could be beneficial. He then brought up disinfectants, asking, "I see the disinfectant, where it knocks it out in one minute. And is there a way we can do something like that, by injection inside or almost a cleaning?" Despite the fact that the president went on to say, "It wouldn't be through injections. . . . Maybe it works, maybe it doesn't work," the damage was done.

The hysterics in the media accusing the president of telling people to ingest bleach were deafening. Later that year, when Joe Biden accused the president of saying, "Maybe if you drank bleach you may be okay," even the liberal fact-checkers at PolitiFact wrote, "No, Trump didn't tell Americans infected with the coronavirus to drink bleach." Point of fact, the president was not telling people to ingest bleach. The reality was the president made an unforced error and his political opponents, including those in the media, never let it go.

In late April, Mark Meadows, who had become the White House chief of staff at the end of March, pushed for the president to end the task force briefings. That, I thought, was regrettable. My belief was that we should continue to communicate about the virus while the country reopened. I spoke to the president about it during the summer from time to time, but it was clear that Meadows had prevailed, and it was, after all, the president's decision.

The greatest challenge remained creating a vaccine. In early March, we had assembled a meeting in the Cabinet Room at the White House with leaders from the pharmaceutical industry. At the meeting, President Trump asked about the possibility of creating a vaccine. That would take five to seven years at least, one of them explained. "Not good enough," Trump shot back. It's true that the development, creation, approval, and mass production of a new medicine often take up to a decade. The president wanted us—the federal government, together with private research and drug companies—to get it done in less than a year. It was an unprecedented task, but no one blinked. The FDA, under the capable leadership of Dr. Stephen Hahn, a thoughtful and brilliant physician who had served as the chief medical officer at the University of Texas, allowed drugmakers regulatory flexibility without abandoning the agency's regulatory oversight. Any treatments for covid had to be safe and effective as well as delivered with record-breaking speed. Clinical trials, which prove a new medicine's viability, were accelerated and greatly expanded. Dr. Hahn, with his experience as both an administrator and a scientist, was an invaluable partner in achieving a medical miracle by year's end.

An already existing antiviral drug named remdesivir showed early promise in trials in helping covid patients recover. The FDA authorized its emergency use, and the task force increased the provision of its limited supplies of the drug to areas and communities most impacted by the virus. To combat the most severe symptoms of covid, the government also approved the emergency use of other drugs, including steroids, monoclonal antibodies, and convalescent plasma treatment. If a drug was safe and showed promise in treating the virus, we wanted to get it to doctors. In part because of our acceleration of those tools, measured against the peak in March and April, by the end of the year, the covid mortality rates declined by 70 percent among Americans age seventy and older and by 85 to 90 percent among Americans below seventy.

When it came to a vaccine, though, the United States had a running start: China had released the genetic sequence of covid-19 in January. Days later, the federal government was working with Moderna, a Massachusetts-based biotech company, on a vaccine. By March, the first clinical trial utilizing messenger RNA vaccines that teach our cells how to make a protein that will trigger an immune response was under way. That was incredible progress. But even if the vaccine proved effective, we would need to produce an incredible amount of it to make sure every American who wanted it could get it—all 330 million of them.

Drugmakers don't begin production while they are still in the testing stage for obvious reasons: the cost and risk of mass-producing a drug that is not yet approved make zero financial sense. But to meet the president's timeline, we needed to plan ahead. In March, the Department of Health and Human Services stepped in and provided the financial assistance—more than $400 million—to the drugmakers working on vaccines—not just Moderna but also Johnson & Johnson— to begin production while the trials were under way. That was the beginning of Operation Warp Speed. The outcome of the trials was far from certain. The rate of failure among new drug candidates is high. Knowing that, the government worked with a number of companies developing potential vaccines, and by May there were more than a hundred candidates. Fourteen promising vaccines emerged from those. By the fall the number was reduced to four. By the end of 2020, two, produced by Moderna and Pfizer, were approved. They were both nearly 95 percent effective against contracting covid. Thanks to Operation Warp Speed, millions of doses were already manufactured and ready to be distributed. To have two safe and effective vaccines available to the American people within nine months of the start of a pandemic was a medical miracle. While those research companies are to be commended, so, too, are the leaders of Operation Warp Speed, Moncef Slaoui and HHS assistant secretary Paul Mango, who shepherded the vaccines through the process in record time, and General Gus Perna, who worked with states and American companies such as FedEx to distribute the vaccine across the country before the year was out. The day we left office in 2021, we were vaccinating a million Americans a day. Only in America.

We did not end the covid pandemic, but we battled against it with everything our nation had. By the end of 2020, more than four hundred thousand Americans had lost their lives to the pandemic. Not a day went by when I wasn't thinking of the families who had lost loved ones, that my heart wasn't breaking over people who had not been able to say goodbye to loved ones because of hospital quarantine rules. At our press briefings, I always expressed my sympathies to those who had lost loved ones, and I prayed often for people who were suffering from loss. But I believe the work we did all across America made a difference: it bought us time, it gave us weapons, it saved lives. But the American people were the real heroes—people such as Leilani Jordan.

On Memorial Day, we visited Arlington National Cemetery with the president as he laid a wreath on the Tomb of the Unknown Soldier. Leaving the cemetery, I spotted a family visiting a fresh grave. Karen and I told our motorcade to pull over. When we approached them, we learned it was the grave of a young woman named Leilani Jordan. Part of a military family, she had been afforded a spot in Arlington among our veterans. Rightly so. Leilani, who had had cerebral palsy, had been a bagger at a Giant Food store in Largo, Maryland. Her family told Karen and me how after the virus hit, she had refused to stay home. Some of her coworkers had not been going to work, and she said she had to go. Her customers, many of them elderly, needed her. She wasn't going to let them down. While doing her job, she was infected with covid and died shortly after in her mother's arms.

I left Arlington, where so many heroes rest, humbled and full of gratitude: to Leilani and countless others all across this nation who had selflessly stepped forward in so many different ways—from rushing to treat patients without even the help of medicines to being there for neighbors cut off from family to innovating in record time to just showing up at work.

The covid pandemic was the worst health crisis to strike the United States in a century. Because of the dedication of countless federal officials, the agility and generosity of our businesses, and the selflessness of doctors, nurses, first responders, truck drivers, grocers, and everyday Americans who looked after one another, we got through the worst of it. For our part, I will always be proud of what the American people accomplished in those early days of the pandemic. We reinvented testing from a standing start, produced and distributed billions of pieces of personal protective equipment, and manufactured tens of thousands of ventilators. In nine short months we developed three safe and effective vaccines; when we left office in January 2021, we were vaccinating a million Americans a day. Together, we saved millions of lives in the greatest national mobilization since World War II. It took all of us, the whole of government, the whole of America. But we did it.

Only in America.

CHAPTER FORTY-SEVEN

Overcome Evil by Doing Good

Do not be overcome by evil, but overcome evil with good.
—Romans 12:21

When I arrived back at the vice president's residence on the evening of May 25, Karen was waiting with a question: "Have you seen the video?" I hadn't, and when I did, I was horrified. That morning in Minneapolis, George Floyd, a Black man, had been killed by a White police officer. In the middle of an arrest, the officer had pinned Floyd down, pressing his knee to Floyd's neck for nine minutes. And it had all been captured on video. Within hours, the entire shocked country saw Floyd die, crying for his mother, on a Minneapolis street.

I have supported the police for my entire career, and that will never change. The men and women who wear the badge consider our lives more important than their own every day, and they deserve our gratitude and respect. Nobody hates bad cops more than good cops do. There was no excuse on Earth for what happened to Floyd. The spectacle of a White police officer killing a Black man awakened memories of the racism and inequality in America's painful past.

The following day, Minneapolis residents took to the streets in protest over Floyd's death. The protests spread across the country over the following days as America's justice system worked: The police officer was fired and charged with third-degree murder. The other officers who had been on the scene and done nothing while Floyd was killed were dismissed as well.

But as the days passed, the peaceful protests deteriorated into broken windows, gutted and smoldering businesses, and cities turned into war zones. Though many of the Americans who took to the streets to protest during the summer of 2020 did so peacefully, others hijacked their cause as an excuse for violence and looting.

Some of it was sheer opportunism, a chance to ransack a Target, and some of it was fueled by radical politics, the violence eventually spreading to the toppling and vandalization of monuments and statues of historical figures deemed insufficiently enlightened, including statues of Frederick Douglass in Rochester, New York, and Abraham Lincoln in San Francisco.

The right to peaceable assembly is enshrined in the Constitution, but there is no justification for rioting and looting in the name of any political cause. And it does nothing but diminish and discredit that cause. The burning of buildings and the destruction of entire neighborhoods, owned by and lived in by people who had had nothing to do with Floyd's death, was not justice.

As rioting spread across the country in the summer of 2020, the government had the obligation to restore order and protect citizens and also to listen to the voices of the disaffected with open hearts. We could do both.

During the summer, elected leaders, public figures, and citizens began to take a knee in the name of racial justice. They said, "Black lives matter" rather than "all lives matter." Some of it was well meaning and charged by a real sense of outrage and desire for change. Much of it, however, was just political theater: Nancy Pelosi, Chuck Schumer, and fellow Democrats not only taking a knee in the Capitol but doing so while wearing kente stoles, ceremonial garments from the African nation of Ghana, was a symbolic gesture. I don't believe they furthered the cause of justice or equality.

Taking a knee, repeating a phrase: those were easy, cathartic responses to difficult problems. They didn't improve the lives of any Americans living in struggling communities. The truth was that for four years our administration had worked to improve the lives of African Americans. And we had made real progress.

In August 2016, during a campaign stop in Michigan, Trump had veered off his prepared remarks and made an unvarnished appeal to African Americans, asking, "What do you have to lose by trying something new like Trump?" It wasn't exactly Jack Kemp, and of course it produced the usual outrage in the media. But he was right to ask the question, to point out that for too long Democrats had taken African Americans and their votes for granted at all levels of government, resulting in disproportionally high rates of unemployment, failing schools, and communities with little opportunity for advancement in life.

It was also a recognition that if the party of Lincoln wanted to earn back the support of African Americans, it had work to do. And we went to it. By cutting taxes and regulations, we let the US economy and labor market kick into overdrive and saw the lowest unemployment rate ever recorded for African Americans. Labor force participation increased, resulting in more income for African Americans: during the first two years of the Trump administration, the median income of African Americans grew by 15.4 percent.

Opportunity Zones, a provision of our tax bill, also made a difference. Championed by South Carolina senator Tim Scott, the first African American member of the Senate from the South since Reconstruction, those designated economically struggling communities—with an unemployment rate nearly 1.6 times higher than the national average—were meant to benefit from private-sector investment encouraged by tax benefits. Former NFL great Scott Turner led our administration's effort to promote Opportunity Zones across the country. Through 2019, they attracted $29 billion in investments in impoverished areas across the country, according to the Government Accountability Office. And during our term multiple initiatives provided billions of dollars to help start and expand Black- and minority-owned businesses. We were improving economic opportunities for African Americans all across America.

And then there was criminal justice reform. Ever since Bill Clinton had signed the 1994 Crime Bill, African Americans had been disproportionately incarcerated and little progress had been made to solve the problem. But in December 2018, all that changed when Congress passed the First Step Act, the first major criminal justice reform in a generation. Jared Kushner and his right-hand man, Ja'Ron Smith, led the administration's efforts with Congress to rethink sentencing and incarceration in the United States.

Early on, Jared approached me for advice because Indiana had reformed sentencing laws when I was governor. I had always said that Indiana should be the worst place in America to commit a serious crime and the best place, once you've done your time, to get a second chance. But there were too few pathways to personal reform, and we were squandering the opportunity to help people lead productive lives once they left prison.

The bill I signed in 2013 had reformed sentences for nonviolent offenders and allowed Hoosiers to expunge their criminal record once they had demonstrated good behavior for a designated amount of time. But, as I explained to Jared, the only way we had been able to pass the first major reform of Indiana's criminal justice system since the 1970s was because we had worked with and earned the support of law enforcement.

During 2018, Jared hosted summits at the White House with law enforcement personnel and advocates of reform regardless of their political affiliation. A key supporter was former Obama administration official Van Jones. After a year of collaboration between Congress and the White House, when the president signed the bill, which allowed prisoners to earn time credits in order to earn early release from prison and created programs to aid in successful reentry, it was another instance when Trump had done what other presidents had promised but never accomplished. After the bill passed, Van Jones called it a "Christmas miracle" on CNN, adding "You had, for the first time in more than a generation, both parties coming together to do something for people at the bottom." And he was right.

It didn't end there. In 2019, Trump also signed a bill permanently providing more than $250 million a year to historically black colleges and universities. He reversed an Obama-era decision and doubled funding for Washington, DC's, school choice program. In our first three years, we had improved the lives of African Americans in tangible ways: more jobs; more investments; expanded opportunities in education; and criminal justice reform. The work was unfinished, to be sure, but we had made real progress, and when in 2020 our ticket received the highest percentage of African American votes of any Republican ticket in sixty years, it was evident that many African Americans knew what we had done. But it didn't seem to diminish what was to come.

On May 27, the president ordered the FBI and Justice Department to open investigations into Floyd's murder. But regardless of what the president did, Biden and the Democrats would try to make what had happened in Minneapolis about Trump; when riots erupted across the country in the summer of 2020, Joe Biden declared, "This is Donald Trump's America." In fact, as the leader of the party calling to defund the police and looking the other way at the violence engulfing our cities, it was a preview of Joe Biden's America.

During the weeks that followed, protests continued across the country. There was violence in Seattle, New York City, Chicago, Indianapolis, Portland, Oregon, and many other cities. All in all, there were more than five hundred riots in two hundred American cities, causing twenty-five deaths and more than $1 billion in property damage.

The first obligation of a government is to protect its citizens and secure its streets. Some sixty-two thousand National Guard were mobilized in response, but many mayors and governors were failing in those most basic responsibilities of governing.

If they wouldn't protect America's neighborhoods, we would. During the summer of 2020, the president deployed federal law enforcement personnel to stop the violence, and I supported him wholeheartedly. As the riots went on and cries from the Left to defund the police grew louder, I made a point of meeting with law enforcement officers as I traveled around the country. I spoke at "Back the Blue" rallies in Ohio, Pennsylvania, and Arizona before the summer was out. I spent time with law enforcement officers, attending a police roll call in Youngstown, Ohio, and visiting the Fraternal Order of Police Lodge #5 in Philadelphia. It was important that the men and women serving on the thin blue line knew that they had a president and a vice president who had their backs.

But I also knew that there were millions of Americans, incensed by Floyd's death, who had concerns about how our communities were policed. The president was leading on (and tweeting about) law and order. In June, he signed an executive order creating a database to track police officers with records of misconduct and abuse of public trust. But there was much more to do to move our nation forward.

With the blessing of the White House, our office opened a dialogue with inner-city Americans who wanted change for their communities but had had nothing to do with the rioting and had in many cases been hurt by it. So during the summer, I traveled the country, meeting with Americans to hear their ideas about how to reform community-police relations. The first thing I wanted everyone I met with to hear was that justice would be served for the man who had killed George Floyd. And that America could not ignore the historic, underlying inequities that have beset minority communities—particularly the African American community.

In Pittsburgh, where rioters had thrown rocks at police and beaten a cameraman, I met with Black faith leaders in Bishop Joseph Garlington's Covenant Church. I asked them to unburden their hearts, and they did. Cheryl Allen, a retired judge and Republican, told me that her sons had been stopped dozens of times by the police with no provocation. It wasn't just White officers, she told me, but Black ones, too. None of her sons had ever been arrested. She had even gone to the station to confront the police. But the violence and rioting were solving nothing, she said. "Just as murder is sin, so is violence, looting, and destruction."

"I'm tired. I'm mentally, physically, and spiritually tired," Pastor Ross Owens told me. He had grown up in one of the poorest areas of Pittsburgh, the Hill District, and he made clear: "I'm still tired because of the racism I see." When his children were in middle school, they saw so much racism at the ages of thirteen and fifteen that he had to comfort them when they came home every day. He rightly pointed out that covid was disproportionately impacting Black Americans and the local decision to shut down schools was causing children to fall behind in their education and development, particularly in disadvantaged districts with less access to the computers necessary for remote learning. "At the same time I'm optimistic," he continued. The church he attended had once been all White; Black people had been told to worship at a church down the street. But over the years it had integrated and was now equally split between the races.

The most tragic element of the strife that summer was that its greatest victims were people who lived and worked in minority neighborhoods that were left in ruins. Minority-owned businesses that had served their neighbors for decades were left boarded up, their shelves emptied. At Hope Christian Church in Beltsville, Maryland, I talked to Dr. Michael Kim and his wife, Joan. The children of immigrants, they owned four drugstores in the Washington, DC, area. They are the embodiment of the American Dream. During the pandemic, the White House Coronavirus Task Force directed covid tests to pharmacies in minority communities, including the Kims' Grubb's Pharmacy. It was one of only three drugstores in the city to offer covid testing. "We are there to help and serve the community and do whatever we can," Michael said. When riots broke out in Washington in early June, he and his wife had a late-night phone call from their alarm company. They rushed from their home in Maryland into Washington only to discover that two of their stores had been broken into. Over the next few nights, the rest of their stores were damaged and robbed. They watched it all on their surveillance videos. A U-Haul van had been driven through one store wall, and people had swarmed into the building, taking whatever they wanted, including the medicines that the Kims provided for people on disability and welfare.

Later in the summer, when I visited Minneapolis along with Ivanka Trump to attend a forum on community-police relations, I spent time with a wonderful African American woman named Flora Westbrooks. Since 1985, she had owned and run Flora's Hair Designs. More than a thousand Minneapolis businesses were damaged in the riots that erupted after George Floyd's murder; Flora's had been burned to the ground. I asked her to show me what was left of her shop. We jumped into the motorcade and drove to a vacant lot full of ashes and rubble behind a chain fence. Flora told me that in desperation someone had spray-painted "Black Owned" on her building, hoping that it would be spared by the rioters. It wasn't.

What inspired me was that the Kims and Flora weren't angry. They were heartbroken, yes, but not vengeful and not discouraged. It brought to mind what I had seen in April 2019 after an arsonist had set fire and razed three Black churches in Port Barre and Opelousas, Louisiana.

Flying to Louisiana, we had gone to what was left of Mount Pleasant Baptist Church in Opelousas and joined hands with the pastors and parishioners of the three churches. I could have been out of place, the conservative White Republican vice president coming to visit with the congregations of three largely Black churches. But I wasn't there as the vice president; I was there as a brother in Christ. And they knew it. After we exchanged a few words, there was a connection. I looked over the remains of the church; all that was left was a brick foundation, ashes inside.

Then as now, what struck me most about those communities was that after three churches were burned, there was no talk of retribution or anger. There were sadness and disbelief, but there was also a determination to rebuild. Two years later, Mount Pleasant Baptist Church was standing again, with donations from all fifty states, and of this writing was preparing to host services once again.

The Kims' customers and community had come together in the aftermath of the riots to raise money to repair the pharmacies. And Flora Westbrooks had raised more than $250,000 on GoFundMe by the next year to reopen her salon. Faith restores, faith overcomes. As Michael Kim said, "We need to do more good, to shine the light on the good that is happening," as he remembered Romans 12:21: "Do not be overcome by evil, but overcome evil with good." And that was just what America was doing: neighbors helping neighbors. This was America at its best.

Of course, the mainstream media continued to take every opportunity to divide us and make the strife across the country about Donald Trump. On June 1, I walked into a crowded Oval Office where President Trump, Ivanka, General Mark Milley, Mark Esper, and staff were gathered. There had been rioting across the street from the White House in Lafayette Park, and the historic St. John's Church, known as the church of the presidents, had been set on fire. Mark Meadows informed me that the president would be walking to Lafayette Park and visiting the church as a show of support. I thought it would be a strong symbolic gesture of our commitment to law and order and religious freedom, as my visit to the Black churches in Louisiana in 2019 had been. I asked the president if he wanted me to join him, but he waved me off.

Back in my office, I watched on live television as Trump crossed the park and held up a Bible. Soon thereafter I watched as the media went wild, suggesting that the US Park Police had tear-gassed protestors to clear the way for a photo op for the president and even saying that he had held the Bible upside down. A year later, the inspector general of the Department of the Interior, Mark Greenblatt, confirmed that the US Park Police had not used tear gas and had been planning to clear the area for days to allow contractors to safely install fencing in response to the rioting and attacks on police officers. The president hadn't held the Bible upside down, either.

Amid all the strife, there was a brief respite of inspiration at Kennedy Space Center on May 30. That day, for the first time in nearly a decade, American astronauts returned to space on an American rocket from American soil. Much as the space program in the 1960s had happened during times of civil strife, that launch took place while the nation was reeling from the murder of George Floyd and during a pandemic. I believe that Americans watching on their phones and computers were inspired in the same way a previous generation had been fifty years prior, watching the launch of Mercury, Gemini, and Apollo on their black-and-white television sets.

It was the culmination of three and a half years of incredible work, resulting from the revival of the Space Council, and the fruition of Trump's vision to usher in a new era of American space exploration. The rocket that carried NASA's astronauts to the International Space Station, though, had been built by a private company, SpaceX. It was the first time that America's astronauts ventured into space aboard commercial rockets. The president had made it clear when the Space Council announced the United States' return to space that if the private sector could get us there quicker than NASA's contractors could, we would collaborate. Elon Musk's company took us up on the offer. We streamlined the regulations for the commercial use of space, and our astronauts and engineers got to work.

Standing between Karen and the president, I watched the rocket, trailed by a white flame, climbing the blue sky. I'm not in the business of taking credit; that belongs to the men and women of NASA and SpaceX. But I couldn't help but think in my heart of hearts that that epic day had just a little something to do with a boy sitting raptly in front of a black-and-white television set in Columbus, Indiana, watching the moon landing in 1969. As the rocket launched, a White House photographer snapped a photo of Karen, Trump, and me from behind. Aware that the moment was being captured for posterity, the president and I remained stoic and still. Karen, on the other hand, didn't care. I think she captured the emotions of the American people that day, raising both her fists in the air triumphantly as the rocket rumbled into the heavens.

It was an important day in the life of the nation and one that was much needed. This was our America.

CHAPTER FORTY-EIGHT

Running the Race

Let us run with perseverance the race marked out for us.
—Hebrews 12:1

As the nation attempted to see its way through all those challenges—the pandemic, the riots and strife, the bitter election campaign—I was reminded that even when it doesn't seem that way, God is still working. In the summer of 2020, I received a letter from Chip DeWitt, a pastor who led a church not far from Jacksonville, Florida. In 1977, he and his new bride, he wrote, had been attending Asbury Seminary in Kentucky, where a Christian music festival was held each spring.

That year, he told me, the seminary had been considering canceling the next year's event, and DeWitt and his young wife had been asked if they would be willing to organize it. Even though they were warned by friends that it would be a great amount of work and hard on their new marriage, they answered the call. He told me they had worked the whole year arranging the festival in 1978. After all their efforts, he wrote, on the culminating Saturday night of the concert, clouds moved over and poured rain on the campground where the festival was taking place. As the young couple walked through the camp area, he recounted, they had been so disappointed. They thought it all had been for naught. Then he wrote words I will never forget: "That's because we didn't know a future vice president of the United States would be giving his life to Jesus Christ that night." He wrote that he could not "write that without tears," and I could not read it without tears because I remember that night, sitting in the rain, when I made a decision that changed my life. He ended the letter by telling me that learning of my experience on that rainy night had reminded him that "even when things aren't going like we expected, they are always going like He expected." It was just what I needed to hear.

Perhaps at some other time in our history the tragic events of the summer of 2020 would have pulled the nation together. Most Americans were angered over the murder of George Floyd. But there was a convergence of other factors. By May, covid infection rates had declined, and states were reopening. After almost three months of lockdowns and social distancing, Americans, many of whom had never lived through anything like the pandemic, were angry and anxious. And then there was the presidential election. It takes much more than a pandemic to stop politics in America.

Though Joe Biden's candidacy had seemed to be sinking in early 2020, when the first Democratic primary votes had been counted in Iowa and New Hampshire, he caught a second wind in South Carolina. He went on to win most of the Democratic primaries in the early spring. The party flirted with the socialist Bernie Sanders but eventually settled on the former vice president. He pitched himself, quite dishonestly, as a moderate who could beat Trump while the rest of his party drifted leftward. And with his well-worn working-class, lunch-pail-Joe persona, Biden appeared to be the Democrats' best chance to win back voters in Pennsylvania, Wisconsin, and Michigan who had supported Trump in the last election. Covid or not, the race was on.

The Republican National Convention, originally scheduled to take place in Charlotte—North Carolina was an important swing state—was canceled. The campaign couldn't agree with the North Carolina government on covid protocols at the Spectrum Center. The venue was switched to Jacksonville, Florida, but the president eventually decided that a series of outdoor venues was more practical. The party's formal nomination of the president and vice president was still scheduled to take place in Charlotte. At the last minute, Trump and I made plans to attend. My old practice-debate sparring partner, Scott Walker, nominated me from the floor in Charlotte. And the president and I were confirmed by acclamation.

Before we walked into the ballroom in the city's convention center, Trump and I stood behind a blue curtain, waiting to be introduced to the 336 delegates on the other side. He was composing himself to take the stage when I stuck my hand out. "Mr. President, I just wanted to say thank you." He looked at me, wondering what I was thanking him for. Then he got it. He smiled, stuck out his hand, and said, "You've earned it." It was unsaid, but we both knew what we were talking about. The journey had started four years before with a phone call promising that it was "gonna be great." For all the country had been through since we had taken office, and in that difficult year, he had been right; it had been great. Four years of promises made and promises kept for the American people. And now it was time for four more years.

When the party and the campaign had planned the convention, it had originally been suggested that my speech take place at the Soldiers' Home in Washington, DC, where Abraham Lincoln had drafted the Emancipation Proclamation. When that had proved to be logistically impossible, another hallowed space had come to mind. In early 2019, I had visited Fort McHenry in Baltimore, that symbol of American resilience that had inspired the words of our national anthem: "and our flag was still there." In a year that had so challenged the American people, I couldn't think of a better place to tout how far we had come, all we had accomplished, and all the work that lay before us. A week before, the Democrats had held their virtual convention, and unsurprisingly, it had been full of attacks on Trump. The speakers could barely bring themselves to say a charitable word about our nation or its history. In talking about America, the Democrats saw only darkness.

On August 26, Karen and I flew on Marine Two to Fort McHenry with Charlotte, Audrey, and Dan. I worked on my speech on the helicopter and backstage, finishing just before I took the stage behind the podium, in front of a redbrick archway. My first convention speech had been in front of a stadium full of people; this one was in a courtyard before a few hundred Americans under a starry sky. I used my speech to make the case for what our administration had accomplished in four years, and I asked what path the American people would choose going forward: the path of more freedom and opportunity with President Trump or the path of socialism and decline under President Biden. Where they saw darkness, we saw greatness—past, present, and future.

The Democrat had positioned himself as a "transition" president. Transition to what? I asked as much as I warned. Ultimately, though, the speech was inspired by its venue, a place where Americans had passed through the great test of our second war with Great Britain. America would pass its current test, too, with hands on hearts and eyes fixed on Old Glory and the author and finisher of our faith of freedom. The president and first lady walked onto the stage as Karen and I waved to the crowd, and we listened as Trace Adkins sang "The Star-Spangled Banner" at Fort McHenry. The moment still gives me chills.

The race to the election was on. It took a brief traditional pause on September 11. I traveled to Ground Zero on the nineteenth anniversary of that terrible morning. For the occasion, politics and partisanship were temporarily put aside. When the bell rang marking the time of the first plane hitting the World Trade Center, Karen and I stood in silence with Joe Biden, Chuck Schumer, and New York City mayor Bill de Blasio. As the service was ending, Biden approached me; we bumped elbows rather than shake hands and exchanged a mutual "Good to see you, Mr. Vice President." When I thanked him for saying hello, he slapped me on the shoulder. "Aww, come on," he said, "we are both old-school."

On the way out of New York City, Karen and I stopped by unannounced at Engine Company 10. When we arrived, the entire company was lining the street ten deep; they had been tipped off that we were coming. I stepped out of the car, took off my mask, said a few inadequate words of thanks, and then went down the line and shook every single hand. "Were you here that day?" I asked each one of them. "Yes, sir, yes, sir, I was." "Tell me someone you lost. Tell me their name," I said. And those big, burly New York firemen did just that, naming the heroes lost, with emotion evident on their face.

Just a few days later, on September 18, Supreme Court justice Ruth Bader Ginsburg passed away. I greatly admired Justice Ginsburg and her incredible life story and pioneering career. She had built a career in law when few opportunities existed for women and in doing so had paved the way for other women to follow. I didn't agree with her liberal judicial philosophy, but she served her country honorably on the high court. Ginsburg's flag-draped casket was placed on the West Portico of the Supreme Court. Karen and I made plans to pay our respects.

When we made the trip up to Capitol Hill, we were not alone. Our daughter Audrey and her fiancé, Dan, came with us. Audrey had recently graduated from Yale Law School and was practicing law in Washington at the time. A promising and brilliant (I'm her dad; I can say that—and it's true) young lawyer, she had looked up to Ginsburg as a judge and as a pioneering woman in the law. Audrey was the member of our family who had most often shied away from public events during the administration, but paying her respects to Ginsburg was so important to her that she didn't mind standing in front of the global media with her mom and dad. We were proud to honor the life and service of Justice Ginsburg, and it was a special joy to share that moment with a young woman in law who had been inspired by her example.

There was never any doubt, after Justice Ginsburg died, that Trump would nominate a successor. At that point the election was almost a month away. Compared to the two previous nominations, the process was compressed and quick. I didn't interview the candidates this time, but I did tell the president who my pick was. "You still think what you thought last time?" he asked, referring to 2018. "Yes, I do," I said with a nod. On September 26, the president nominated Amy Coney Barrett, and she was confirmed a few weeks later, on October 27. Her confirmation hearing when she was nominated to the US Court of Appeals had been rancorous; this time, with an election only a few months away and the memory of the disgraceful Kavanaugh hearings still vivid, the Democrats were more restrained in their questioning. But she mopped the floor with them anyway. My favorite moment was when one Democratic senator pressed Judge Barrett to show what was written on the notepad in front of her. When she held up a blank pad and smiled, you could almost hear conservatives across the country cheering.

When the White House held an event in the Rose Garden to introduce Judge Barrett on September 26, Karen and I attended along with a large crowd of elected officials and supporters. Afterward a number of attendees came down with covid, and the media promptly dubbed it a "superspreader event," despite the fact that many of the attendees had been tested and the event had been held outdoors.

As the season turned and fall arrived, covid cases were rising again. The task force was regularly in touch with governors, distributing tests, supplies, and new medicines as we drove toward the development of a vaccine by the end of year and even as I traveled across the country on the campaign trail at a breakneck pace.

On Thursday, October 1, I left Washington early for a day of campaigning. After a day of rallies, speeches, and interviews in Iowa, I got back to the vice president's residence by 10:00 p.m. Shortly after walking in the door, I got a phone call from the president. He sounded hollowed out. Absolutely uncharacteristic. "Hey, I want to tell you because it's going to be in the news in a little while," he began. "I got this." He had tested positive for covid. Although the first vaccines would not be available for a month, he assured me that he was doing fine. When he told me the news, I was not alarmed because I knew how vigorous he was. But I was concerned for my friend. I told him to take it seriously and that Karen and I would be praying for him. He appreciated it and knew we meant it.

The following morning, he flew to Walter Reed National Military Medical Center, where he recovered and convalesced. Trump had directed his own doctor to keep mine in the loop and I received regular reports on his condition, but I never really worried. Trump was the youngest seventy-two-year-old I'd ever met. His energy level was astounding. I gave the president twenty-four hours before calling, but after that we talked daily. When we spoke, he sounded much improved but admitted that he had been in "rough shape." He said that when the doctors had given him a cocktail of therapeutics developed during our administration, including remdesivir and dexamethasone, he had felt better "right away" and was ready to get back to work. Not surprisingly, after a weekend in the hospital, he was back at the White House on October 5, returning in dramatic fashion by landing on the South Lawn aboard Marine One, taking off his mask, and telling the country it would beat the virus.

My second vice presidential debate, in which I debated Biden's running mate, California senator Kamala Harris, approached. The preparation followed the same formula as the lead-up to my debate with Tim Kaine in 2016. There were rehearsals and more rehearsals in a large but spartan conference room in the Eisenhower Executive Office Building. Scott Walker oversaw the debate preparation, as he had done so well in 2016. Sarah Huckabee Sanders and Florida attorney general Pam Bondi stood in for Harris in the practice debates. Each session lasted ninety minutes, and both Sanders and Bondi stayed in character the entire time, attacking me relentlessly. Harris is a former prosecutor with an aggressive debating style. The high point of her ill-fated presidential run had been when she had lambasted Biden for chumming around with segregationist senators and chided him for having opposed busing in the 1970s. She basically accused him of racism, insinuating that he had been on the wrong side of the civil rights movement.

Bondi in particular, a former prosecutor herself, had watched Harris's debate performances and channeled the California senator well—almost too well. She threw and landed so many punches that she approached me after the mock debate and apologized. It was a useful practice. I'm still not over it.

The second time around, the vice presidential debate was in many ways more challenging. In 2016, I had been introducing myself to the American people. In 2020, we had a record that I was prepared to defend, but I knew I could also be asked to respond to the relentless attacks on the president of the past four years. Was I nervous the day before the debate? Absolutely. Fortunately, my family was there. Karen, Michael, Sarah, and Charlotte joined us for the trip to Salt Lake City, and Audrey flew in the night before, after sitting for the bar exam in Washington, DC. The day before the debate, we all went for a long hike on Ensign Peak, just outside Salt Lake City. It is an almost vertical, 384-foot ascent in one mile.

The day of the debate, October 7, I was still extremely anxious. I had been nervous back in 2016 because of the unknown; this time I knew what was coming, someone who had a record as a formidable debater. I was in for a rough night. Interestingly, right up until the last minute, it wasn't clear if there was even going to be a vice presidential debate. Twenty-four hours before the event, Harris's team had demanded that a Plexiglas wall be placed between us. Now we were appropriately socially distanced and tested for covid. Tony Fauci sent the debate commission a letter saying that the wall was unnecessary. It was just covid theater, a visual way of accusing the Trump administration of having unleashed the pandemic on the country and forever altering the way people interact. In the end, I didn't want to give Harris an excuse not to show up. I said, "Put up the wall, and we will see you at seven p.m." It didn't hurt anyone. It wasn't even tall enough to stop a fly.

We had a family prayer, and I walked out of the dressing room and onto the stage at Kingsbury Hall, a beautiful old building on the University of Utah campus. To my surprise, the Kamala Harris I had prepared to debate didn't show up. In 2016, Tim Kaine, whose forte is civility and thoughtfulness, had come out as an attack dog. I hadn't thought it suited him. In 2020, Harris largely avoided a confrontational prosecutorial style for one that was more measured. She kept to her script, criticizing the president's management of the covid pandemic and his comments after the tragedy in Charlottesville. I viewed the debate as a chance to press a warning about what a Biden-Harris administration would look like: a Green New Deal, higher taxes, the curtailing of American energy production, attempts to revive the terrible nuclear arms deal with Iran (everything that has actually happened on the Biden-Harris watch).

But there was one point I felt particularly passionate about during our debate. Operation Warp Speed was nearing the approval of covid vaccines and millions of doses were in production, but in early September, Senator Harris had cast doubt on their safety. When asked by a CNN reporter if she would take a vaccine, she said, "Well, I think that's going to be an issue for all of us. I will say that I would not trust Donald Trump." She was sowing distrust based on partisan politics about a medicine desperately needed in the fight against covid. When the debate moderator, Susan Page, asked Harris if Americans should take a vaccine approved by the Trump administration, she repeated the irresponsible answer: "If Donald Trump tells us that we should take it, I'm not taking it." I was outraged. We were going to have vaccines by the end of 2020, in record time. They would save millions of lives. And here she was, the Democrat candidate for vice president, undermining public confidence in that lifesaving medicine. I called her out. As the debate moderator attempted to move on from the issue of vaccines, I told the senator, "Stop playing politics with people's lives." It fell on deaf ears.

In the end I was content with my performance. I gave as good as I got. As I came off stage right, with my family waiting in the wings, after a few encouraging words about my performance, my daughter-in-law, Sarah, asked, "Did you see the fly?" I said I'd seen a large fly buzzing over the stage. That was when she asked, "Did you know the fly landed on your head?" I didn't. The memes began instantly. I figured that if all they could criticize in my performance was the fly, I might have done all right. But as I told my daughter Charlotte, someday in glory, after I thank God for all my blessings, I intend to ask Him, "The fly, was that really necessary?"

The president called me that night after the debate, when I was back at my hotel. He was happy. "You just make us look so solid." "Mr. President, your team is solid," I reassured him. "It's easy to brag on the record you've built for the American people." His first debate with Biden in September had been a wild punch-throwing affair. Neither of the participants' performances was well reviewed. "Melania says I gotta be more like Mike," he told me. I was actually told he had watched my debate a few times. And at his second meeting with Biden, later in October, his performance was more understated and effective.

In some ways the 2020 campaign was familiar. As in 2016, we were running not just against the Democrats but also against their allies in the press, who carried the water for our opponents with constant attacks on the president and our record and papered over what history would record were real controversies swirling around the Biden family. In mid-October, the *New York Post* broke a story about Biden's son Hunter's laptop, dropped off at and never picked up from a repair shop in Delaware. It contained emails confirming business deals with a Shanghai-based company with ties to the Chinese government. True to form, the Democrats' media allies immediately dismissed the story, fact-checked it as false, and dusted off all the old Russia collusion peddlers, including James Clapper and John Brennan along with forty-eight other intelligence officials who claimed the laptop had all the "earmarks" of a Russian disinformation campaign, an explanation Biden himself would repeat during a presidential debate with Trump.

Even big tech weighed in by censoring publication or discussion of the *New York Post*'s reporting on Hunter Biden's laptop in the weeks leading up to the election. In an interview on *60 Minutes*, Lesley Stahl chided the president for bringing up the laptop, saying, "There's no real evidence of that." It was *60 Minutes*, after all, and she was lecturing the president. "And we can't put on things we can't verify." A year and a half later, every major news organization in the country acknowledged that the laptop and emails were authentic. In the spring of 2022, the *New York Times* confirmed that the emails in question appeared "to have come from a laptop abandoned by Mr. Biden in a Delaware repair shop." My dad used to say that life isn't fair. The fair is what comes to the county in July. But it was still a disgrace.

In other ways, the 2020 campaign trail was quite different from any I had been on before. All the protocols were altered; Karen and I were tested for covid every day. There was no handshaking. Air Force Two would land at a rally, I would go down the stairs and walk across the platform, then run up to the podium, deliver my remarks, get the crowd going, and go right back to isolation in a cabin on the plane and be off to the next city. It was surreal. I missed the human interaction, one of the most important aspects of retail politics. Amazingly, though eight members of my staff caught covid, Karen and I never did. We viewed it as evidence of God's grace.

I had a habit of running up the steps and jumping onto the elevated platforms at the campaign events. It drove the Secret Service and my staff crazy. They pleaded with me not to jump and warned that the time would come when I would miss and injure myself. One morning during the summer, I woke up feeling great and energetic. We had a full day of campaigning ahead. The first stop was in Wisconsin. I arrived at Joint Base Andrews and went to the stairs leading up to Air Force Two. I had been having so much fun running up to podiums across the country and thought I could take those steps, too. I jogged all the way to the last steps with the door just feet away. Then *boom!* I wiped out. I bounced right back up, straightened my tie, gave the reporters a wave, and walked in to where the head of my Secret Service detail, Tim Giebels, was waiting. "Sir, I thought you were picking up a quarter," he deadpanned. We both laughed, I slapped him on the shoulder, and it was back to the campaign trail.

In 2016, the polls had said we lost before the votes were counted. But now the crowds and the excitement in the country told me otherwise—they were even bigger than four years earlier. The closing weeks of the 2020 campaign mirrored those of 2016. Even under pandemic conditions, as we had done in 2016, we outworked our opponent, who rarely left his Delaware home other than to get ice cream. The president even introduced—a first in US politics—Jumbotrons to his events. Meanwhile, Biden was holding rallies at drive-in theaters.

On the Monday before election day, we both spoke at several rallies, and we planned to meet up for one final rally in Michigan, where a huge crowd gathered before a brilliant red sunset in Grand Rapids. Speaking on the phone after my final solo rally of the day, I told the president that we had "finished strong." He replied, "We are gonna finish strong—and win, lose, or draw, I got the right guy."

When November 3 arrived I felt confident, but at peace, too. The outcome was no longer in our hands, and we would accept it, win or lose. I believed that we were going to win. Our kids had all come in from around the country to watch the election returns with us. Michael and Sarah joined us from their base in Arizona. Charlotte's navy husband, Henry, was deployed overseas, but she came to be with us, and Audrey and her new husband, Dan, were there, too, which ended up making things even more memorable.

Audrey and Dan had been planning a Hawaii wedding earlier in the year, but due to covid, like so many others, their wedding had been delayed three times. Audrey had the idea that since everyone was in town, they could just have a courthouse wedding with immediate family the Sunday before election day and plan a bigger celebration down the road. When she called two weeks before the election and asked what I thought, I said, "You know, that's two days before the election," but quickly added, "What a great idea!" I passed that "Dad test" with flying colors. On the Sunday before election day 2020,

I flew to North Carolina in the morning to attend church with Franklin Graham, Billy Graham's son, and returned to Washington in time to marry our daughter off in the afternoon. It was a beautiful sunset in downtown Washington, DC, that Sunday night.

Having our kids with us in those days made all the difference. Once the returns started coming in, we all headed into the White House and huddled in my West Wing office before joining the first family and key staff members. There was a war room set up in the basement of the White House filled with aides tracking results on laptops and numerous television screens on stands blaring out coverage. The early returns were promising: Florida, Texas, and Ohio all came in with strong margins of victory. Even after Fox News had called Arizona with a large number of votes still out, I spoke with Governor Doug Ducey, who, though not the election official in the state, assured me that his best estimate was that we could still hang on to a victory. After making our way to the main floor of the White House where much of the first family had gathered, I found myself standing next to the president in the Green Room watching returns coming in when things began to change. In several states where mail-in voting changes had been carried out, the results began to shift. Our lead started to vanish. The mood in the White House, initially ebullient, began to sour.

CHAPTER FORTY-NINE

Here We Go

Hope deferred makes the heart sick.
—Proverbs 13:12

November 3, 2020

It had never occurred to me that we could lose the election.

The enthusiasm and excitement I had seen on the campaign trail had given me the impression that President Trump and I would ultimately be reelected. And in the end, we received the largest vote total for a Republican ticket in history and 10 million more votes in 2020 than we had in 2016, a feat virtually unheard of in the annals of modern presidencies. But still we came up short under circumstances that would cause millions of Americans to doubt the outcome of the election and set into motion events leading to a tragic day at our nation's Capitol. And it all began after midnight on the first Tuesday in November.

It was then that vote counting appeared to slow or even stop in several key states, most notably Pennsylvania. In several states where mail-in voting changes had been implemented without the approval of state legislatures, things began to shift and the president was not happy. None of us were. But having experience with the slow count of absentee and mail-in ballots from many years in Indiana politics, I did not immediately assume the worst. There were still millions of votes yet to be counted in several states that would decide the election.

Joe Biden had addressed the nation after midnight, expressing confidence before calling it a night. A little before 2:30 a.m., Karen and I walked into the East Room of the White House with President

Trump and Melania to address the nation. After rousing the crowd with word that our results had been "phenomenal," the president laid out his concerns about the results before the nation. "We were winning everything and all of a sudden it was just called off," he said, labeling the process "a fraud on the American public." And then, despite the fact that millions of votes had yet to be counted and races in half a dozen swing states still had not been called, the president declared, "Frankly, we did win this election." When he finished, the president waved me to the podium. I obliged, thanking the more than 60 million Americans who had already voted for us. I promised that we would remain vigilant to protect the integrity of the vote and said I believed with all my heart that we were on the road to victory. And I did.

Exhausted from the long day and weeks of relentless campaigning, Karen and I gathered our family and headed back to the vice president's residence. The next several days were a little like the twilight zone. The result of the election was actually not called until Saturday, November 7, but our campaign was already going full steam ahead with lawsuits challenging the results in virtually every state.

Watching the returns come in, we saw our margin of victory slowly wither in Pennsylvania, Michigan, and Wisconsin, three states we had carried to victory in 2016. In an early-morning call on Wednesday, the president asked me to "study it up and let me know what you think," adding "We are gonna fight this."

Later that day, Corey Lewandowski called my chief of staff to ask if I would go watch the vote count in Philadelphia and participate in a hurriedly organized press conference on Thursday, November 5. I declined. Though the president never asked for my participation directly, Mark Meadows, who had been diagnosed with covid the morning after the election, did call to make a personal albeit weary plea. I explained that though I was fully supportive of the legal challenges, I did not think it was my place as vice president to directly participate in the event. He grudgingly agreed but said he had to ask.

By Saturday, the race was called for Joe Biden. That same day, the president called a meeting with his senior staff and went through all legal options for challenging the election results in court. Several approaches seemed promising, especially in Wisconsin, where it appeared that the Democrats in Madison had conducted an early-voting process outside of state law, and in Pennsylvania, where mail-in ballot rules had been changed without legislative approval. As I would say over the next two months, I shared the concern of millions of Americans about those irregularities, but I strongly believed that election challenges should be conducted according to state law and reviewed by the courts. I remained hopeful, as we all did, that those legal challenges would succeed.

Jared Kushner called me that day for advice. He asked if I thought that fraud had taken place in the election. I told him over the phone that "Democrats cheat" is virtually a proverb in Indiana, and although I was sure that some voter fraud had taken place, I wasn't convinced it had cost us the election. Later that day, Biden gave a lackluster acceptance speech, claiming some sort of mandate for action and pledging a return to civility that would never come. That night when the president called, I tried to encourage him as a friend. I told him he had reinvented the Republican Party to be more courageous and more diverse, with more Latino, African American, and working-class voters than ever before. I told him, "You took a dying political party and gave it a new lease on life." The words were true but seemed to be little consolation.

On the Monday after the election, it was back to work on the White House Coronavirus Task Force with the news that Pfizer had won FDA approval for the first safe and effective vaccine for covid-19. The timing was suspicious and infuriated the president, who believed that the Democrats and the FDA "didn't want to have me get a Vaccine WIN, prior to the election, so instead it came out five days later in a tweet." The FDA had required an additional round of testing, but I was hard-pressed to believe that Dr. Stephen Hahn, who had moved heaven and earth to streamline the approval process for vaccines and other medicines and treatments, would have allowed politics to affect his decision-making. He is a truly good man. The president was considering firing him, but I strongly counseled against it, and Dr. Hahn finished his distinguished term the day we left office. Now, with a vaccine from Operation Warp Speed available, the real work began: getting it to the American people. In the weeks ahead I would meet with

Dr. Moncef Slaoui, General Gus Perna, Secretary Alex Azar, and the entire Operation Warp Speed team for a briefing on our nationwide distribution plan.

As the election challenges moved through the courts, I lent my support through speeches to conservative groups where I promised that we would never stop fighting "until every legal vote is counted and every illegal vote is thrown out!" The ovations were deafening. We also made plans to travel to Georgia, where not one but two runoff elections would take place on January 5, deciding the fate of the Republican majority in the Senate.

On Wednesday, November 11, the president and I went to Arlington National Cemetery to mark Veterans Day. It was the president's first public appearance in six days, as he had spent the majority of his time focused on our efforts to challenge the election. After we returned to the White House, it was clear that he was not happy with the lack of progress and set a meeting for the next day to review legal challenges with the campaign's lawyers, Justin Clark and Matt Morgan. Justin is a smart, principled lawyer, and Matt had been my general counsel and part of the Indiana team that we had brought to Washington, DC. Matt is a true Hoosier, as honest as he is talented. I had great confidence in both men, but, as would become clear in a meeting in the Oval Office the next day, the president had his doubts about them.

What began as a briefing that Thursday afternoon quickly turned into a contentious back-and-forth between the campaign lawyers and a growing group of outside attorneys led by Rudy Giuliani and Sidney Powell, an attorney who had represented General Mike Flynn. After the campaign lawyers gave a sober and somewhat pessimistic report on the state of election challenges, the outside cast of characters went on the attack. I will never forget the look on Justin's face when Giuliani told the president over the speakerphone, "Your lawyers are not telling you the truth, Mr. President." Even in an office well acquainted with rough-and-tumble debates, it was a new low. Standing in the middle of the Oval Office, Justin, a normally restrained and affable man, lashed out harshly at both lawyers and said that neither of them knew what they were talking about. It went downhill from there. In the end, that day the president made the fateful decision to put Giuliani and Sidney Powell in charge of the legal strategy. Their antics at press conferences and conspiracy theories replaced the steady legal counsel offered by Justin and Matt. The seeds were being sown for a tragic day in January.

On Monday, November 16, the president and I met in the small dining room down a short hall from the Oval Office for our weekly lunch. I decided to tell him that if the legal challenges came up short and if he was unwilling to concede, he could simply accept the results of the elections, move forward with the transition, and start a political comeback, winning the Senate runoffs in Georgia, the governor's race in Virginia in 2021, and the House and Senate in 2022. That accomplished, I said, he could run for president in 2024 and win. He seemed unmoved, even weary, at the prospect. "I don't know, 2024 is so far off," he said before returning to the status of election challenges in various states.

As the lawsuits challenging elections played out in courts across the country, I returned to work on the White House Coronavirus Task Force with emphasis on the vaccine rollout and hit the campaign trail for the Georgia special election. And life went on. On the twenty-first, my son, Michael's, birthday, we held a Zoom reveal party where he and Sarah shared the news that we were going to have a granddaughter, our first grandchild. The next day, I spoke with the president again about the election challenges. I had been in touch with the governors of Arizona and Georgia, Doug Ducey and Brian Kemp, as both were looking into election irregularities in their states. I called simply to gather information and share it with the president. There was encouraging news from Wisconsin regarding a legal challenge to widespread early voting that would eventually come within one vote of prevailing on the Wisconsin Supreme Court. The US Supreme Court had also issued a preliminary decision, and it appeared that Justice Samuel Alito, Jr., who had granted the Republican Party in Pennsylvania time to separate late absentee ballots, wanted the Court to be heard on election irregularities. The campaign was right to defend the integrity of America's elections, I told the president. "You're the greatest," he signed off.

The following day, the twenty-third, the president told me that Jay Sekulow, his personal lawyer and staunch defender, wasn't optimistic about the election challenges. But the campaign pressed on with them.

We stayed in Washington with Charlotte over Thanksgiving as the president spent the holiday at Camp David. When he called to check in that night, I told him his vacation time was well deserved. He laughed and said sarcastically, "Yeah."

After December 4, we began nearly weekly visits to Georgia to campaign. By the end of December, I had been to three rallies across the state with our two incumbent senators, who were fighting to hold their seats and the Republican majority in the Senate. Along the way, I rallied the faithful around our record and our determination to defend the integrity of US elections. After the state of Texas filed a lawsuit making a constitutional challenge to the manner in which a number of states had changed their election rules without legislative approval, I thundered, "God bless Texas!" to the roaring approval of a crowd in Augusta in early December. There was still genuine hope among our supporters that one of the challenges would give us a fighting chance before the Supreme Court. It did not last, though.

The president was focused on contesting the election, but lawsuits and legal challenges were faltering by the day and being dismissed across the country. As the legal window narrowed, the widening circle of outside lawyers who had been leading the election challenges continued to promise success in court and allege evidence of massive voter fraud. Their promises never seemed to materialize. On December 1, Attorney General Bill Barr told an Associated Press reporter that the Justice Department had not found evidence of the kind of widespread fraud sufficient to change the outcome of the election.

On December 5, during a call, the president mentioned challenging the election results in the House of Representatives for the first time. I wasn't familiar with the Electoral Count Act, so I asked my general counsel, Greg Jacob, to brief me on procedures.

Under Article II, Section 1 of the Constitution, elections are conducted at the state level, not by Congress. The role of Congress with respect to the Electoral College is to open and count votes submitted and certified by the states. The vice president serves as the presiding officer of the joint session of Congress during which electoral votes are counted. The Twelfth Amendment, which was written after the controversial election of 1800, sought to clarify the Electoral College process. After another controversial election in 1876, which was ultimately decided by Congress, the Electoral Count Act was adopted and has been followed ever since.

Greg composed a memo describing the Twelfth Amendment and the Electoral Count Act, which, he opined, "as a constitutional matter" was not particularly clear. Whatever ambiguities there were in the Electoral Count Act about the role of Congress, there was no ambiguity in the Constitution or the law about the role of the vice president, and I never believed that the vice president's role was anything more than ceremonial.

My first instinct was that there was no way the founders of this country intended to give any one person the authority to decide an election. Since my college years studying the American Revolution, I knew that our forefathers had fought a war to win independence from a king. The last thing the framers of the Constitution would have intended would be to confer unchecked authority on one individual. The presidency belongs to the American people and the American people alone. Frankly there is no idea more un-American than the notion that any one person could choose the American president.

Nevertheless, by mid-December, the internet was filled with speculation about my role, which was accelerated by an irresponsible television commercial run by a group that called itself the Lincoln Project. This group of has-been Republican politicos, which had opposed the president from the outset, began running television ads suggesting that when I presided over the counting of the Electoral College, it would prove that I knew "it's over," and that merely by doing my constitutional duty on January 6, I would be "putting the final nail in the coffin" of the president's reelection. To my knowledge, it was the first time anyone had implied that I might be able to change the outcome of the election, and to this day those grifters have never been held accountable for promoting that lie. But it was designed to annoy the president. It worked.

During a December meeting of the cabinet, President Trump told me that he thought the TV commercial "looked bad for you." I replied that it wasn't true; I had fully supported the legal challenges to the election and would continue to do so. It didn't help. In late December, press outlets such as Axios began to print insider accounts of the president's frustrations with his allies for not doing enough to contest the election results. My name was among those mentioned as targets of his ire.

The idea that I could influence the outcome of the election began to spread across the internet. The president took note but wasn't consumed with the possibility at first. Over a Sunday night call on December 13, he told me I was trending number two on Twitter as people began speculating whether I was going to participate in the January 6 proceedings at all. Given the widening concern of so many people about election fraud, supporters around the country were arguing that I should decline to participate altogether. The president concurred. "If you want to be popular, don't do it," he suggested.

He then went a step further: I might convene the session and at some point walk out. "It would be the coolest thing you could do," he said jokingly, "otherwise you're just another RINO," referring to the political acronym for "Republican in name only." We both laughed at the controversy and his crack. At that point, there was no angst between us and there was no talk of rejecting electors or returning votes to the states.

There was a precedent for declining to participate, too: after he had lost the 1968 presidential election to Richard Nixon, Vice President Hubert Humphrey had declined to attend the official Electoral College count, saying that he "couldn't bear to be there." With two-thirds of Republicans telling pollsters that they believed the election had been rigged, it was becoming clear to me that Democrats were trying to goad me into doing less than my duty so as not to offend the president or our voting public. I hung up the phone with the president determined to study the evidence and do the right thing.

On December 14, states across the country certified their elections for president and vice president and sent copies of their Electoral College votes to Congress for the formal count that would take place on January 6, 2021. For all intents and purposes, at that point the election was over. But under the Electoral Count Act, members of Congress are permitted to raise objections to the count in any given state, and Democrats had actually filed objections in three of the last four presidential elections where Republicans had prevailed. Several House members had announced plans to object to certain state votes, and with the expectation that several senators would cosponsor those objections, the law allowed debate before the House and Senate and a vote approving or rejecting the electoral votes.

All along, the work of the White House Coronavirus Task Force soldiered on. I traveled to the headquarters of Operation Warp Speed in late November for a full briefing on planned nationwide vaccine distribution and on December 3 was in Tennessee to highlight our administration's upcoming partnership on delivery of vaccines by FedEx. So many American companies stepped up during the early days of the pandemic, but few did more to bring medical supplies from around the world and then lifesaving vaccines across the nation than Fred Smith and the incredible men and women of FedEx.

To encourage public confidence in the new vaccines, on Friday, December 18, Karen and I got our shots on national television along-side the surgeon general, Jerome Adams, and members of the White House Coronavirus Task Force. To be honest, at first I resisted getting vaccinated because I didn't want it to appear that we were "cutting in line" ahead of the American public, especially those who were more vulnerable to serious illness. In the end, it was my national security advisor, General Keith Kellogg, who persuaded me to move forward. He told me that my first instinct had been right, noting that the commanding officers in a war zone eat last in the mess hall, but, he added, "the commanding officers are always the first on the battlefield." That resonated with me. I was proud of having played a role in securing a vaccine for the American people in record time, and I could see how leading by example—getting vaccinated in public—might encourage others to take advantage of this lifesaving breakthrough. My only regret that day was getting the shot next to Jerome Adams. It had been more than a few years since my arms had seen the weight room on a regular basis. Jerome had arms that looked as though he worked out three hours a day. At the end of the press conference, I told Jerome that he had made great remarks but it was the last time we were both going to be "guns out" at the same time.

On Saturday, December 19, around dinnertime, the president called and, after telling me that we had "looked good" getting our vaccines on television the previous morning, he mentioned plans for a rally in Washington, DC, after the first of the year. It was the first I'd heard of it. He told me that the plan was to actually hold the rally on January 6, that he thought it would be a "big day" and it would be good to have lots of our supporters in town. My first thought was that a rally that day might be useful as a way to call even more attention to the proceedings on the floor of the House and Senate. I had spoken that day with a member of the Senate about the importance of vetting concerns about the election before Congress and the American people. Since so many of our lawsuits had been dismissed by the courts before even considering the evidence of voting irregularities, I said, "We haven't gotten our day in court," and "We need to get our day in Congress." Even though the Democratic majority in the House was "unlikely to change the outcome," I told the president, "let's have a debate."

The following Sunday night, *60 Minutes* ran a segment on our covid response featuring General Perna, the army logistics officer who was leading our nationwide effort to distribute vaccines. My impression was that the coverage wasn't that bad. The president had a different view, thinking that the liberal TV newsmagazine had not given our administration its due for its covid response. I told him, as a friend, "I don't think you are taking enough credit for the vaccine." He suggested a meeting with Perna and the team before Christmas that we worked to arrange the next morning.

On Monday the twenty-first, the president and I met for our weekly lunch in the small dining room just off the Oval Office. I sensed that he was growing increasingly frustrated with the lack of progress on any of the legal challenges to the election. He seemed sullen but not angry. I told him that I had been praying for him and said, not unkindly, that I understood that "if you liked to lose, you never would have gotten here." I encouraged him not to look at the election "as a loss—just an intermission." I told him he would do well to trust the

White House counsel's team, led capably by Pat Cipollone. Hoping to steer him away from the outside lawyers who had taken over the election challenges in November, I said, "You've got a good team at the White House," to which he grumbled, "No, I don't." If the president had chosen to listen to those good men and not the gaggle of outside lawyers who took over the election challenges from the campaign, things would have been very different.

Later in the day, I stopped by the Oval Office after the president met with Alabama congressman Mo Brooks and other members of Congress who were preparing objections to be introduced during the proceedings on January 6. After the meeting, a larger group of congressmen had huddled in the Cabinet Room for a planning session before leaving town for the holidays. I decided to drop by the meeting for a few minutes and was warmly greeted by my old colleagues in the House as I entered the room. Ohio congressman Jim Jordan, a close friend and strong Christian, was leading a discussion about plans to bring objections in the House, and I assured them that they would have ample opportunity to present evidence on the floor of Congress. Since I would be presiding in the chair that day, I promised them that all properly submitted objections would be recognized and fully debated. I was not going to allow the Democrats to disrupt the proceedings with deleterious motions or tactics designed to prevent a full hearing of objections and evidence. I told them what I had told the president just a few days earlier, that though we hadn't gotten our day in court, I would make sure we got our day in Congress. The group expressed their genuine appreciation and gave me a round of applause as I left the room. Several members appeared on television that night and echoed my remarks in explaining their plans to bring objections on the House floor. I was flattered and honestly felt that we were all on the same page, ready to take our case to Congress and the American people.

After walking back to the Oval Office, the president and I were wrapping up for the day when he stood up behind the Resolute Desk and began to head toward the back hallway, usually a sign that he was ready to call it a night. I stepped toward the opposite door to leave when he stopped in front of the desk. "What do you think we should do?" he asked. I put my hands on the back of the couch nearest to the door and told him that after we had exhausted every legal process in the courts and Congress, if we still came up short, he should "take a bow." "What do you mean?" he asked. I told him we should do a thank-you tour, just like we did after we won in 2016, remind people of everything we had accomplished in the past four years, and let them know that we had done it all together. "Take a bow, Mr. President, and after that, if you want to run again, run again," I advised. He nodded, pointed at me as if to say, "That's worth considering," and walked into the back hallway. I will always wish he had.

The next day, I traveled to West Palm Beach, Florida, for a youth conference sponsored by Turning Point USA. The convention center was packed, a rarity at the close of the first year of covid, and the enthusiasm was deafening. I took to the stage and spoke about our record, what we had accomplished together. Anticipating that many of those young people might be disappointed in a few weeks, I simply urged them to stay in the fight. "Stay in the fight for election integrity. Stay in the fight to defend all that we've done," I encouraged them.

On Wednesday, the day before Christmas Eve, our family boarded Air Force Two to spend Christmas in Vail, Colorado, at the home of some Indiana friends. Our entire family was there except for our new son-in-law, Henry, who was still at sea rounding out a long deployment aboard the USS *Nimitz*. Having time to huddle with our kids and almost all their spouses over Christmas was a blessing. We hit the slopes and had long conversations over breakfast and dinner about plans for the future: ours and theirs. The only decision Karen and I had made for sure was that, barring an unexpected turn of events in the election, we would be moving back to Indiana. As my son, Michael, had said a few weeks earlier, "We're hobbits, Dad, we go back to the Shire," referring to the *Lord of the Rings* books I had read to him as a little boy. We were going home.

As the Air Force 727 made its way across the American heartland en route to the Rocky Mountains, a tweet came across that was a harbinger of things to come. That night, President Trump retweeted on his @RealDonaldTrump account to nearly 100 million followers an obscure internet message without comment titled "Operation Pence

Card." The article alluded to the theory that if all else failed in election challenges in states across the country, there was still the "Pence Card," meaning that I could somehow alter the outcome of the election in my role as presiding officer over the counting of Electoral College votes submitted by the states on January 6. I showed it to Karen and rolled my eyes, thinking, "Here we go."

CHAPTER FIFTY

Standing Firm

Stand firm. Let nothing move you.
—1 Corinthians 15:58

That Christmas was one for the books. In the morning, we kept our tradition of reading Luke 2, about the birth of our Savior. Then we lost ourselves in piles of wrapping paper, presents, and laughter. I will always believe that those days with Karen, Michael, Charlotte, and Audrey were a gift from God that gave me strength for the days to come.

That afternoon, I kept a tradition of the past four years and called the president to wish him, Melania, and the Trump family a Merry Christmas. Not surprisingly, the conversation turned quickly to the election challenges. He told me that he had heard that Senator Mitch McConnell was pressuring senators not to cosponsor objections filed in the House. The Electoral Count Act required that any objection be sponsored by one member each of the House and the Senate, and at that time no senator had agreed to cosponsor an objection with the House.

I could tell that he was spoiling for a fight. I encouraged him to hold off criticizing the Senate Republicans, since we would need their support if we hoped to prevail on any of the objections in January. With that, the conversation turned to the process on January 6. "You play a big role," he said. "You know, I don't think I have the authority to change the outcome," I replied and reminded him that the House and Senate had the sole power to count or reject state electoral votes. But it was clear from our conversation he had been hearing something different.

Article II, Section 1 of the Constitution provides that the vice president, as president of the Senate, "shall, in the Presence of the

Senate and House of Representatives, open all the Certificates, and the Votes shall then be counted." No more, no less. The vice president as president of the Senate is afforded no authority to reject or return votes to the states, and no vice president in history has ever asserted that authority.

As we ended the call, he said with a sigh, "If we prove we won a state and Pelosi certifies anyway . . . I don't think we can let that happen." "You'll figure it out," he added.

As the days wore on, it was becoming clear that there would be a real cost to me politically when I presided over the certification of the 2020 election. I thought of the words of Edmund Ross, the lone Republican to oppose the impeachment of President Andrew Johnson: "Friendships, position, fortune, everything that makes life desirable to an ambitious man were about to be swept away by the breath of my mouth, perhaps forever." Ironically, I had written an essay about Ross for the *Wall Street Journal* in January a year earlier, never imagining that I might face a similar moment in my career.

During my devotions each morning, I prayed for wisdom to know the right thing to do and the courage to do it. I always knew that I did not possess the authority to overturn the election. I knew it would be hurtful to my friend for me to participate in the certification. But my duty was clear. I was determined to stop thinking about what it would mean to me and my future and just do the right thing. My family was incredibly supportive.

I also heard from family and friends who understood the position I was in and called with words of support. My mind was made up about my role and duty that day, but I still appreciated their kindness. Even my old friend Dan Quayle called as we were arriving in Colorado to encourage me. A book would be written in the following year that suggested that Vice President Quayle had had to talk me into doing my duty, creating an avalanche of ridicule from the snickering media. Dan dismissed all of it in an interview with the *Washington Post* later that same year, saying, "I did not notice any hesitation on his part," and adding "I interpreted his questions as looking for confirmation that what he was going to do was right."

While everyone I spoke with affirmed my view that the vice president's role was ceremonial only, some well-meaning friends were encouraging me to recuse myself from the proceedings on January 6 altogether, allowing Senator Chuck Grassley of Iowa, the president pro tem of the Senate, to preside. That just never felt right. The Bible says in Psalms that you keep your oath, even when it hurts. And talking it over with Karen and the kids, we all agreed that the only thing that mattered was my duty.

I had taken an oath to support and defend the Constitution of the United States. As my marine son reminded me, "You took the same oath I took, Dad." There is no hardship exception at the end of the oath we take. It doesn't say, "I will support and defend the Constitution unless the task is really hard." Every day, somewhere in the world, Americans in uniform are doing hard things without regard to their own personal safety. The Constitution tasked the vice president with overseeing the proceedings when the House and Senate open and count the Electoral College votes. Regardless of what it would mean to me, I would do my duty. It was settled—at least as far as I was concerned.

On December 28, Texas congressman Louie Gohmert and other Republicans filed a lawsuit in federal court asking a Texas judge appointed by President Trump to declare that I had "exclusive authority and sole discretion" to decide which electoral votes should be counted. Though it was immediately panned by legal scholars, I directed our staff to request that the Justice Department lawyers represent us in the case, which the department lawyers did without hesitation—to the consternation of the president, I would later learn.

The day the lawsuit was filed, my chief of staff, Marc Short, got a call from Kelli Ward, the chair of the Arizona Republican Party, who was also a plaintiff in the Gohmert lawsuit. She called to say that she had heard my family and I were in Vail and that Sidney Powell was also in Vail and wanted to meet for coffee. Incredulous, Marc replied, "You sued the vice president today." To which Ward replied, "That's Sidney's thing," adding "We wouldn't have done that without the president telling us it was okay." Things were coming into focus. Clearly the president's view of my authority on January 6 was hardening. I figured Sidney Powell was just trying to meet to serve me the papers in the lawsuit. I declined the meeting.

The Justice Department did yeoman's work opposing the lawsuit with my full support. Calling the Gohmert case a "walking legal contradiction," the Justice Department lawyers had the case dismissed by Friday, January 1, rejected on appeal just a day later, and ultimately dismissed by the Supreme Court on January 7. Gohmert described his effort to the media as a "friendly lawsuit," actually meant to help. I was unpersuaded. At such a serious time in the life of the nation, such a frivolous lawsuit only served to raise unrealistic expectations that I could change the outcome of the election on January 6. When I walked down the middle aisle on the floor of the House to begin proceedings on that fateful day, Louie Gohmert was standing two seats in on a middle row and reached out for a fist bump. I walked on by.

While still on vacation in Colorado, I began working on a statement that would explain my position on January 6. I thought that something I could read at the outset of the proceedings and publish afterward would be beneficial to the country. It was an opportunity to lay out the process, giving our voters confidence that I would ensure a full airing of the facts and reminding the country that the elected representatives of the American people have the sole authority to accept or reject any Electoral College votes.

By that point, the Supreme Court had thrown out two election challenges, one filed against Pennsylvania and a lawsuit filed by Texas against several contested states. The Court also took no action on a number of election cases, including those filed in Arizona and four cases filed by Sidney Powell, alleging fraud perpetrated with the Dominion voting machines. Having promised famously to "release the Kraken" at a November 2020 press conference and having taken her case for election fraud into the Oval Office, she accomplished nothing. A year later, she would admit in a lawsuit against her that "no reasonable person would conclude that the statements were truly statements of fact." Now she tells us. Overall, US courts, including many presided over by Trump-appointed judges, had rejected some sixty challenges filed in connection with the November election. The team of lawyers that had taken over the election challenges in mid-November had come up empty.

I could hear the weariness in the president's voice when we next spoke by phone. With plans to do my fourth rally for our Senate candidates in the Georgia runoff on the following Monday, I wanted to make sure that was okay with him, since he would be doing a large rally in Georgia that night. He didn't seem much in the mood to talk and replied only, "I don't mind." I also had plans to travel to Israel and the Middle East right after the proceedings on January 6, but on that the president said, "I don't think you should go . . . more important to have you here."

Over the next few days, I worked on my statement for the proceedings and spoke to Marc Short and Greg Jacob about preparation for the upcoming joint session of Congress. I also asked Greg to prepare a summary of alleged violations of election laws by state or local officials and any evidence of instances of election fraud in the six swing states that could be subject to objections in Congress on the sixth.

On December 30, Marc and Greg had been in touch with members of Congress who were planning to bring objections. The big news that day was that Missouri senator Josh Hawley announced that he would cosponsor objections brought by the House members, ensuring that there would be debate and votes on election objections in the House and Senate.

I had encouraged Senator Hawley to seek the Senate seat in Missouri back in 2017. A family man and strong Christian, Josh had called to ask how Karen and I had kept our family so close during our years in Washington, DC. I told him that our kids had been his kids' ages when we had first been elected to Congress and that we had moved our family to the nation's capital. We spoke for about an hour, and I was later told that the conversation had played a role in his decision to move forward in a successful campaign. That said, I welcomed Senator Hawley's decision not just because I felt an affinity with him but because it ensured that we were going to have a substantive debate in the Congress. I shared the concern of millions of Americans about allegations of fraud and irregularities in the November election and thought that a full airing of all the evidence to the country was in order. Without Hawley's support, I would have been required to dismiss each of the House objections without debate, something I really did not want to do.

The final day of the year, we hit the slopes one last time, and as we rang in the New Year, we also celebrated my wife's birthday. Karen was the first little girl born in Kansas in 1957, and every year, after we watch the ball drop at midnight, she opens her first present. We knew that 2021 would be a year of change. We didn't know what the future held, but we knew who held the future.

Karen and I were making plans to move home to Indiana; we were praying that Charlotte's husband, Henry, would return home safely from his long overseas deployment; our daughter-in-law, Sarah, and son, Michael, were expecting a little girl, our first grandchild, in April; and Audrey and her new husband, Dan, were beginning their lives together in Washington, DC. For all my blessings, I went to bed that night with a growing foreboding about the days ahead. I sensed that the president's attitude toward me and my role was changing. It didn't take too long for me to realize that I was right.

After a sleepless night, I woke up early on New Year's Day and soon heard the phone ring with a call from the White House operator, saying, "The president would like to speak with you." Grabbing a fresh cup of coffee, I headed to a back room in the condominium that had been set up for secure communications.

The president came on the line and came on strong. He wanted to know why we had filed a brief opposing the Gohmert lawsuit. "I don't want to see 'Pence Opposes Gohmert Suit' as a headline this morning," he said. The problem was, I said, that I did oppose it. "You are being savaged," he said. "If it gives you the power, why would you oppose it?"

I told him, as I had told him many times before, that I did not believe I possessed the power under the Constitution to decide which votes to accept or reject. He just kept coming.

"You're too honest," he chided, predicting that "hundreds of thousands are gonna hate your guts" and "people are gonna think you're stupid." Growing increasingly irate, he said, "That means we're gonna have a president who cheated," and asked, "You say that's okay?" When I replied with a simple "no," he railed about "massive fraud" and asked again, "You're okay with that?"

"No," I said. "I just hold the view that election disputes are resolved, under the Constitution, the Twelfth Amendment, and the

Electoral Count Act, by the elected representatives of the people, not by one person."

The president grew silent. I said sincerely, "You are my friend and you are my president, but I am persuaded that the oath I took to support and defend the Constitution informs me that the decision on objections to the Electoral Count belongs to the House and the Senate." As I had observed many times over the past five years, once he got things off his chest, he often softened his tone and moved on. It happened again that day. We finished up by discussing a few administrative items. With that the call came to an end, but I knew that that would not be the end of it.

On Saturday, January 2, after returning to Washington, DC, I was working from home on a planned statement outlining my position on my duty on January 6, when I got a call from my old colleague and former speaker of the House Paul Ryan. We talked about the election and the swirling controversies. He said he just called to thank me for all I had done and would do for the country. "The guy I know is faithful to the Constitution," he said.

That day my general counsel Greg Jacob, chief of staff Marc Short, and Matt Morgan came to the residence. I told them that I had decided to issue a statement, and we proceeded to review the facts, the law, and the process governing the proceedings just a few days away. We also learned that Senator Ted Cruz was working on a motion to establish a ten-day commission to review voting irregularities and had already recruited nearly a dozen Senate cosponsors.

Around five o'clock, President Trump called. He sounded pleasant but tired, much different from the day before. He informed me that he had spent the day speaking to a secretary of state, state legislators, and members of Congress, adding that he had learned of Senator Cruz's proposal for a ten-day delay. "You can make the decision" to delay the count for ten days, he said and referred me, for the first time, to an attorney named John Eastman, who I had the impression was advising him on that and other Electoral College matters. I did not know Eastman beyond that he had been the legal scholar behind the constitutional challenge filed by the state of Texas. The president asked if I would meet with him, and I said I would have Greg Jacob, my general counsel, do so.

The next day, as I had requested, Greg Jacob brought me a detailed memorandum outlining "unlawful election conduct in six states" to assist me in preparing to preside. We found that although the allegations of actual voter fraud were relatively small in number, there was strong evidence that state and local officials had committed numerous procedural violations that reduced transparency and favored Democrats.

Despite those voting irregularities, Democrats and their allies in the media had taken to ridiculing members of Congress for filing objections under the Electoral Count Act, even though members of their party had filed objections to Electoral College votes the last three times a Republican had been elected president. The hysterics and hypocrisy on the part of some Democrats who had voted for objections were pretty rich, even by Washington standards. I thought it was important that I weigh in.

That night, I instructed Marc Short to issue a statement supporting the right of members to bring objections under the Electoral Count Act. "Mr. Pence welcomes the efforts of members of the House and Senate to use the authority they have under the law to raise objections and bring forward evidence before the Congress and the American people on January 6th," the statement read. By Sunday morning, the headline "Pence Welcomes Congressional Republicans' Bid to Challenge Electoral Votes" was everywhere.

When the president called me that morning, his mood had brightened. He had seen the coverage of our statement and was very pleased. "You have gone from very unpopular to popular!" he exclaimed. He immediately returned to his argument of a few days before, saying, "You have the absolute right to reject electoral votes," and alluded to actions taken by Vice President Thomas Jefferson when he had chosen electors who had given him a victory in Georgia in 1800. The fact that no one had questioned that Jefferson had won Georgia or that his action had taken place prior to the adoption of the Twelfth Amendment was not especially persuasive to the president.

"You can be a historic figure," he said, his tone growing more confrontational, "but if you wimp out, you're just another somebody."

"Mr. President," I said, "you know me, I'm going to do the right thing," adding "I praised the House and Senate members for bringing objections because that's what the Constitution and the law allow." Returning to the topic from the beginning of the call, I reiterated that I didn't understand why even some Republicans were criticizing members for using their authority under the law to bring objections.

Later on Sunday, I met with the parliamentarian of the Senate, Elizabeth MacDonough, to discuss the procedures for the upcoming joint session on January 6. MacDonough had been appointed to her position in 2012, and I had always found her to be a straightforward and honest public servant. Sitting in my ceremonial office just off the Senate floor, we reviewed the history of election disputes and the procedures for the day.

I asked her a direct question: "Are there any alternate electors from any state?"

She told me there were not.

I mentioned that I had heard that some alternate electors had been sent from several of the disputed states, and she told me that Congress always receives miscellaneous slates of electors every four years but that there was no alternate slate bearing what was known as a certificate of election from any competing state authority from any of the disputed states.

"We should say that," I told her.

She seemed surprised. The "script" for the proceedings had been used for decades without any changes. But given the controversy surrounding this election, I thought we should make it clear in the record that there were no alternate electors, and she agreed to draft the language.

In the end, we added forty-three words that were based upon the language of the Twelfth Amendment and federal law. After every slate was brought before the joint session, I would announce aloud not only that it was "regular in form and authentic" but also as "the parliamentarians have advised me is the only certificate of vote from that state, and purports to be a return from the state, and that has annexed to it a certificate from an authority of that state purporting to appoint or ascertain electors." It was a formal way of confirming, in the *Congressional Record* forever, that there were no alternate electors from any state in the 2020 election. I thought it would help calm the waters around the impending proceedings. It did not.

On Monday morning, I was off to Milner, Georgia, for my fourth "Defend the Majority" rally for our two candidates who were facing a runoff election. Standing on a platform in a packed arena, I talked about our record and the fact that Georgia Republicans needed to "hold the line" and win the two Senate seats on the ballot the next day. With the election controversy hanging in the air, I spoke about my faith. I told the audience about the letter I had received from the pastor in Florida and the night I had come to Christ, reminding them, "Even when it doesn't seem like it, God is always working." I assured them that I shared their concern about voting irregularities and promised, "Come this Wednesday, we'll have our day in Congress. We'll hear the objections. We'll hear the evidence, but tomorrow is Georgia's day." The response of the crowd was thunderous.

On the flight back to DC that afternoon, Marc Short got a call from Mark Meadows, saying that we needed to be at the White House for a meeting in the Oval Office with a long list of attendees, including Rudy Giuliani, John Eastman, and everyone else working on the increasingly desperate legal strategy for January 6. When Marc pushed back on the idea that we would air out our differences in front of a room full of staff and lawyers, Meadows said, "I'll take care of it."

We arrived in the Oval Office in midafternoon and greeted the president and Eastman. The president had been touting Eastman's credentials to me for weeks relating to his role in the Texas lawsuit. The meeting began cordially as the president introduced Eastman, who made his pitch. I listened respectfully as he argued that I should modify the proceedings, which require that Electoral College votes be opened and counted in alphabetical order, by saving the five disputed states until the end. Eastman argued that I had the authority to simply direct that electoral certificates not be counted and instead order that they be returned to the states until each state legislature certified which of the competing slate of electors for the state was correct. It was the first time I had ever heard anyone suggest that we send votes back to the states. The president and many of his defenders later repeatedly made the case that that was all I had ever been asked to do. It wasn't.

Since I had already confirmed that there were no legitimate competing electors, I was tempted to dismiss Eastman's proposal out of hand, but I let him drone on. He repeatedly qualified his argument with the words that it was just a legal theory, and I decided it was necessary to press him in front of the president. I was seated in my usual chair to the right of the president near the Resolute Desk, and Eastman was in the next chair to my right. I turned to him and asked, "Do you think I have the authority to reject or return votes?"

He stammered, "Well, it's never been tested in the courts, so I think it is an open question."

At that I turned to the president, who was distracted at the time, and said, "Mr. President, did you hear that?" He turned his attention to me, and I said, "Even your lawyer doesn't think I have the authority to return electoral votes." The president nodded. As Eastman tried to get out some explanation, the president replied, "I like the other thing better," presumably referring to his previous opinion that I could simply choose to reject electoral votes altogether.

Marine One was on the South Lawn, and the president needed to depart for a final rally in Georgia. As he was leaving, he asked that my guys just meet with Eastman and hear him out. I told the president that if he wanted my staff to meet further with Eastman, they would do so, even though I was confident that I did not possess the authority Eastman said I had. The president seemed content with that and made his way out of the Oval Office to the waiting Sikorsky helicopter.

That night, I made a point, as I often did, of watching the president's rally in Georgia on TV. I heard him make remarks that gave me hope that we were getting to a better place. At the opening of the rally for our two Senate candidates, the president returned to the 2020 election, repeating his message about election fraud. Then he said, "I hope that our great vice president comes through for us!" to the cheering crowd. He then said, "Of course, if he doesn't come through, I won't like him so much," but quickly added, with a smile, "No, the one thing you know about Mike, he always plays it straight," and at that the audience broke into applause. I was touched by the evident support in the crowd, but I actually hoped it also meant that the president was coming my way and might get to a place where he realized that whatever difference of opinion we had, he could trust me to do what I thought was right.

On the morning of January 5, I decided to work from home at the vice president's residence and scheduled a meeting of the White House Coronavirus Task Force on the progress with vaccine distribution. I pored over drafts of a statement to Congress and the country explaining my role as presiding officer of the joint session of Congress and addressing the controversies that had arisen in recent days.

As the president had requested, Greg Jacob and Marc Short met for more than an hour with John Eastman about his proposal for returning electoral votes to state legislatures. Greg later informed me that Eastman had continued to make his case for returning electoral votes so that state legislatures could decide whether to certify an alternate slate of electors—although, Greg said, he had acknowledged that most Republican legislative majorities in the disputed states had signaled that they had no intention of doing so. But soon Eastman's theory gave way to another, the one the president had argued for all along.

As I made my way to the White House for the task force meeting, I got an urgent call that the president was asking to see me in the Oval Office. Unbeknown to me at the time, Eastman had just called Greg to inform him that the president's lawyers were now requesting that I simply reject the electors. That was a significant change of posture, for although the proposal to return electoral votes to the states or even Senator Cruz's proposal for a ten-day delay to review allegations of voter fraud would likely not have changed the outcome of the election, for the vice president to simply reject electoral votes on the floor of Congress would have the potential to overturn it.

Under the Constitution and federal law, if no candidate for president receives 270 electoral votes, the election is resolved by a vote on the floor of Congress. Though the Democrats held a majority in the House at the time, under the Constitution, Congress would vote by state delegations, a majority of which were controlled by Republicans. In sum, if I were to reject the state electoral votes so that neither Joe Biden nor President Trump received 270 votes, the election would go to the House and the majority of Republican delegations could presumably vote to reelect the president. But that was never going to happen.

I had told the president many times that the vice president, as president of the Senate, is afforded no authority to reject or return votes to the states and no vice president in history had ever asserted that authority.

I later learned that even Eastman had conceded to Greg Jacob that rejecting electoral votes was a bad idea and any attempt to do so would be quickly overturned by a 9–0 vote on the Supreme Court. This guy didn't even believe what he was telling the president of the United States of America. Nevertheless, that afternoon, the president tweeted, "The Vice President has the power to reject fraudulently chosen electors" to millions of his followers.

Arriving at my West Wing office, I told the staff to inform the task force members that I would be delayed in coming to the Situation Room, and, sensing that things had taken a decidedly difficult turn, I breathed a quick prayer and made my way down the short hallway to the Oval Office.

When I walked into the president's office, there were several senior staff milling about, including Meadows. The president began by talking about the size of the crowd already forming on the Ellipse just off the South Lawn of the White House for the next day's rally. "You need to get more National Guard out there," Trump said, turning to Meadows, suggesting that the crowd could be one of the biggest ever for a Trump rally. "I'll take care of it," Meadows told the president. With that he and the others walked out of the room as if on cue, leaving the president and me alone in the Oval Office.

"I think you have the power to decertify," he began.

"I don't believe the Constitution or the law gives me that authority," I countered. "That belongs to the elected representatives of the people."

The president again referred to the crowd outside. "Those people love us," he said and suggested that I could not let them down.

"Those people love you, Mr. President," I said. "And those people also love the Constitution."

At that his mood darkened. "These people cheated, and you want to play by Marquess of Queensberry rules." It was "bad for the country," he went on, "and bad for you."

"I'm less concerned about the latter," I explained and then reminded him, "Our duty is to support and defend the Constitution."

Seated behind the Resolute Desk, he waved his hand dismissively and said, "You are naive." Referring to the objections that would be raised, he said, "Pelosi will vote it down. How can you certify a fraud?"

"Mr. President, I don't question there were irregularities and fraud," I said. "It's just a question of who decides, and under the law that is Congress."

With that, the president said that he guessed it probably just "takes courage," implying that was what I lacked. I paused before replying and, facing him from my seat in front of the Resolute Desk, said firmly, "Mr. President, I have courage, and you know that." And as he looked me in the eye, I repeated myself, saying, "I wouldn't be here if I didn't have courage, and you know it."

Hearing that, he relented and said with more than a little sadness, "Well, I'm gonna have to say you did a great disservice."

With that I stood up, buttoned my jacket, and said, "Mr. President, you need to say what you need to say, but you know, other than your family, no one in this administration has been more loyal to you than me." Turning, I walked out of the room.

Returning to my office, I shut the door and sat down behind my desk. The conversation had exhausted me. I took a moment and looked around the room at the portraits of Lincoln, Jefferson, Adams, Coolidge, and Teddy Roosevelt. I thought of the "cloud of witness" passage from Hebrews 12:1: "Therefore, since we are surrounded by such a great cloud of witnesses, let us throw off everything that hinders and the sin that so easily entangles. And let us run with perseverance the race marked out for us." Surrounded by those portraits and remembering all those who had gone before, I bowed my head and with folded hands prayed that God would give me the grace and the courage to do my duty.

The president called twice more before the day was out, the first time with John Eastman continuing to make his case to me and my senior staff. Back at the Naval Observatory that evening, I was seated at my desk in my second-floor study, working on the draft statement that I would release in the morning, when my military aide delivered a copy of a letter from a group of Republican members of the Pennsylvania legislature urging Congress to return the state's electoral votes. It was far from a formal request and was not even signed by a majority of the Republicans in the statehouse. The president called after 9:30 to make sure I had seen the letter, seeming to shift back to his earlier argument about returning votes to the states. "You gotta be tough tomorrow," he admonished. I assured him that I would do my duty.

Right before going to bed, I saw that the Trump campaign had issued a statement, apparently in response to a *New York Times* story that I had told the president that I did not believe I possessed the power to block congressional certification of President-elect Biden's election. Which, of course, was true. Regardless, the Trump campaign issued a statement saying that I had never said that and calling the report "fake news."

"The Vice President and I are in total agreement," the statement read, "that the Vice President has the power to act," adding "Our Vice President has several options under the U.S. Constitution. He can decertify the results or send them back to the states for change and certification. He can also decertify the illegal and corrupt results and send them to the House of Representatives for the one vote for one state tabulation."

I couldn't believe what I was reading. The campaign had issued a statement directly contradicting what I had told the president just a few hours earlier. When Marc Short called the campaign's communications director, Jason Miller, he apologetically said, "I had no choice, Marc." Given the lateness of the hour, there was little else I could do for the time being. I've always said that truth is a force of nature. I figured the American people would know the truth soon enough, so I put the whole matter in the Lord's hands and tried to get some sleep. I had a feeling that January 6, 2021, was going to be a very long day.

CHAPTER FIFTY-ONE

So Help Me God

Who keeps an oath even when it hurts.
—Psalm 15:4

I rose early on January 6, 2021, and began my day in prayer. Over the mantle of our home ever since I had first won the trust of American voters is a framed parchment quoting Jeremiah 29:11: "For I know the plans I have for you, says the Lord . . . plans to give you a future and a hope." That morning I claimed that ancient promise and then went to the desk in my study to ponder the many drafts of the statement I would later issue to Congress.

For me, there is no good writing, just good rewriting, and I labored over my words to make sure they conveyed my position clearly and my determination to fulfill my oath under the Constitution that day. I addressed it to the members of the House and Senate, but my true audience was the American people.

For starters, my statement sought to explain the proceeding, saying, "Today, for the 59th time in our Nation's history, Congress will convene in Joint Session to count the electoral votes for President of the United States," adding that under our Constitution, it would be my duty as vice president and president of the Senate to serve as the presiding officer.

From there I made it clear that "After an election with significant allegations of voting irregularities and numerous instances of officials setting aside state election law, I share the concerns of millions of Americans about the integrity of this election." As presiding officer, I promised to "do my duty to ensure that these concerns receive a fair and open hearing in the Congress of the United States." I assured the

Congress and the American people that "Objections will be heard, evidence will be presented, and the elected representatives of the American people will make their decision."

Given the controversy surrounding the previous year's election, I noted that "some approach this year's quadrennial tradition with great expectation, and others with dismissive disdain." I wrote that "Some believe that as Vice President, I should be able to accept or reject electoral votes unilaterally. Others believe that electoral votes should never be challenged in a Joint Session of Congress," but noted, "After a careful study of our Constitution, our laws, and our history, I believe neither view is correct." I then addressed each argument head-on, one at a time.

I wrote, "The Presidency belongs to the American people, and to them alone," and that when disputes concerning a presidential election arise, under federal law, "it is the people's representatives who review the evidence and resolve disputes through a democratic process."

Harkening back to my early days studying the Constitution in the Columbus public library, I wrote, "Our Founders were deeply skeptical of concentrations of power and created a Republic based on separation of powers and checks and balances under the Constitution of the United States. . . . As a student of history who loves the Constitution and reveres its Framers, I do not believe that the Founders of our country intended to invest the Vice President with unilateral authority to decide which electoral votes should be counted during the Joint Session of Congress, and no Vice President in American history has ever asserted such authority."

I quoted Supreme Court Justice Joseph Bradley, who had written following the contentious election of 1876, "The powers of the President of the Senate are merely ministerial. . . . He is not invested with any authority for making any investigation outside of the Joint Meeting of the two Houses. . . . [I]f any examination at all is to be gone into, or any judgment exercised in relation to the votes received, it must be performed and exercised by the two Houses."

And I also quoted a statement from the former US Court of Appeals judge J. Michael Luttig. Judge Luttig had been a favorite of conservatives when George W. Bush had chosen Chief Justice John

Roberts for the Supreme Court. In response to a request from my outside counsel Richard Cullen, Judge Luttig had recently written, "The only responsibility and power of the Vice President under the Constitution is to faithfully count the Electoral College votes as they have been cast," adding "The Constitution does not empower the Vice President to alter in any way the votes that have been cast, either by rejecting certain votes or otherwise."

Against that weight of history and recognized authority, I wrote, "It is my considered judgment that my oath to support and defend the Constitution constrains me from claiming unilateral authority to determine which electoral votes should be counted and which should not." In short, I did not have the power to overturn the election.

I pledged to Congress and the American people that I would do my duty to preside when Congress convened in joint session to count the votes of the Electoral College to the best of my ability and asked only "that Representatives and Senators who will assemble before me approach this moment with the same sense of duty and an open mind, setting politics and personal interests aside, and do our part to faithfully discharge our duties under the Constitution," reminding them of the words of John Quincy Adams, who had said, "Duty is ours; results are God's."

I closed the letter with words that I hoped would make it clear to the American people that I felt compelled to discharge my duty because of the promise that I had made to them and to Someone else:

> Four years ago, surrounded by my family, I took an oath to support and defend the Constitution, which ended with the words, "So help me God." Today I want to assure the American people that I will keep the oath I made to them, and I will keep the oath I made to Almighty God. When the Joint Session of Congress convenes today, I will do my duty to see to it that we open the certificates of the Electors of the several states, we hear objections raised by Senators and Representatives, and we count the votes of the Electoral College for President and Vice President in a manner consistent with our Constitution, laws, and history. So Help Me God.

Ending with that prayer, I felt that I had gotten the wording just right.

I started to close the document but thought that since there had been so many versions, maybe I should print it first just in case. So I hit "Print" and then thought I saved the document on my desktop computer. But when I tried to reopen the draft, as I had feared, it had not been saved and all the changes I had made since the day before were completely gone. It was around 10:30 a.m., with the joint session scheduled to begin in just a few hours.

I dashed to the printer in the family room of our private quarters at the vice president's residence, and, to my relief, there sat the final draft printed out. But with less than an hour to when we were scheduled to depart for the Capitol, I didn't know exactly how I was going to get it retyped in time, since my staff was not set to arrive for another hour. My daughter Charlotte, the writer in the family, stepped in. She typed as I read it aloud and helped me with some needed edits. My family saved the day once again.

Marc Short and Greg Jacob arrived at the Naval Observatory in the late morning and were ushered into the downstairs library by the naval enlisted aides who managed the residence. They had received the final draft of the statement by email, and, after we took a moment to pray, we began discussing the address. When the phone rang a little after 11 a.m., it was the president. With his rally on the Ellipse south of the White House scheduled to begin at eleven, I had assumed he was already at the podium.

Walking upstairs to our private quarters, I picked up the phone and the White House operator, always pleasant and professional, greeted me with a friendly tone and said, "Please hold for the president." That was when the friendly part of the call ended.

When Trump asked where I was on the upcoming session, I replied firmly, "Despite the press release you issued last night, I have always been forthright with you, Mr. President," adding "I do not believe I possess the power to decide which electoral votes to count; that resides with the elected representatives of the American people."

When he began to object, I said, "As I have told you, I don't have the authority" that he had been convinced I had and said I would be issuing a statement to Congress confirming that before the joint session started.

With that the president laid into me. I was unmoved. "You'll go down as a wimp," he predicted, adding "If you do that, I made a big mistake five years ago!"

But when he said, "You're not protecting our country, you're supposed to support and defend our country!" I calmly reminded him, "We both took an oath to support and defend the Constitution."

With exasperation in his voice, he said, "You're listening to the wrong people," to which I replied, "I'm listening to my heart and mind."

With that, the call ended.

After I shared a few private moments with Karen and Charlotte, we headed to the Capitol. Though I would ordinarily have had the television on to monitor a Trump rally, that day I made a conscious decision not to watch. I wanted to stay focused on the task at hand and "guard my heart," as the Bible says, against any distractions outside my duty to preside over the joint session of Congress.

Maybe I should've watched.

As I would learn later, President Trump took to the stage almost an hour late, wearing the long overcoat that he invariably wore against the cold. There he told the thousands gathered on that frigid day, "I hope Mike is going to do the right thing. I hope so. I hope so. Because if Mike Pence does the right thing, we win the election." Repeating the argument made by the crank lawyers standing just offstage, he said, "All he has to do, all this is, this is from the number one, or certainly one of the top, constitutional lawyers in our country. He has the absolute right to do it. We're supposed to protect our country, support our country, support our Constitution, and protect our Constitution. States want to revote. The states got defrauded. They were given false information. They voted on it. Now they want to recertify. They want it back. All Vice President Pence has to do is send it back to the states to recertify and we become president and you are the happiest people."

He then acknowledged our phone call and said, "Mike Pence is going to have to come through for us, and if he doesn't, that will be a

sad day for our country because you're sworn to uphold our Constitution."

After a final prayer with Karen and Charlotte upstairs, we made
our way to the waiting motorcade. We had hoped to send the statement to members of Congress after the president finished speaking,
but with the joint session scheduled to begin at 1:00 p.m., I gave the
go-ahead to send the statement to the email account of every member
of the House and Senate around 12:45, as our motorcade took a wide
route to Capitol Hill, avoiding the crowds and closed streets associated
with the president's rally. We actually drove by our daughter Audrey's
apartment, and she later sent us a picture of her fingers making a circle
around our motorcade, which is a family tradition signifying a silent
prayer for safe travels. In a matter of minutes, the news was breaking
everywhere: "Pence Rejects Trump's Call to Overturn Biden Election."

As our motorcade arrived at the East Front of the Capitol, I saw
thousands of protestors standing peacefully on the East Lawn just past
a rope line opposite the entrance to the Senate. My heart went out
to them. I felt compassion for all the good people who had come to
our nation's capital having been told that the outcome of the election
could be changed. They were cheering as our Suburban wheeled into
the carriage entrance beneath the Senate steps. I turned to my daughter and said with a sigh, "God bless those people. They're gonna be so
disappointed."

As we made our way into that historic building, I had no idea
that what was later described as a "wall of people" had arrived about
a block west of the Capitol. My legislative director, Chris Hodgson,
and my brother Congressman Gregory Pence were waiting in my office when we arrived. After a short pep talk from my older brother,
I went over floor procedures with Chris and stepped into the Senate Chamber, where senators were gathered for the ceremonial walk
across the Capitol to the House Chamber, where joint sessions of
Congress take place. As I proceeded through the crowded Senate
aisles, everyone became unusually quiet. One senator after another
shook my hand and patted me on the back or whispered a word of
thanks, presumably referring to the statement they had received just
moments ago.

I led the Senate members onto the House floor and was greeted by the traditional applause the chamber offers to visiting guests. But the mood was solemn. There was no indication of the mayhem unfolding just outside the Capitol. Everyone appreciated the gravity of the moment. Walking up to the rostrum to the seat reserved for the vice president, I was greeted by the masked face of Speaker Pelosi and gaveled the chamber into session a little after 1:00 p.m.

The process under the Electoral Count Act provides that when an objection is raised, the joint session of Congress is suspended and House and Senate members return to their respective chambers to debate the motion. When the electoral votes for the state of Arizona were opened, Congressman Paul Gosar rose to raise the first objection of the day, which had been cosponsored by sixty members of the House. When I formally asked if the motion had been cosponsored by a Senator, Senator Ted Cruz rose from a seat to Gosar's right, and the Republicans in the chamber gave them both a standing ovation.

With that, I adjourned the joint session and accompanied members of the Senate back to their chamber, oblivious to the widening riot outside the Capitol. As the Senate convened to debate the objection to the Arizona electoral votes, I took my traditional seat as president of the Senate to hear the debate.

For nearly an hour senators rose to speak about the election. Mitch McConnell, who spoke first, described the vote ahead as the most important in his career. He acknowledged that there had been irregularities in the voting but noted that there was no proof of the massive scale of fraud that the president and his legal team had alleged and that judges appointed by the president had rejected those claims. Chuck Schumer followed, saying that Congress does not determine the outcomes of elections in America; the people do. Then Ted Cruz told his colleagues that nearly half the nation believed that the election had been "rigged." Senators, both Republicans and Democrats, stood to make their case.

Forty minutes into the session, Republican James Lankford of Oklahoma had the floor, speaking solemnly about vote counts, when the Senate parliamentarian, Elizabeth MacDonough, who was seated just a few feet in front of me, leaned back in her chair and whispered through her face mask, "Mr. Vice President, protestors have breached the building's doors on the first floor. Just informing you." It was around two in the afternoon.

As Lankford's speech headed toward its conclusion, I could see his colleagues anxiously glancing at their cell phones. And I saw the ever-capable Max Millian, one of the men on my Secret Service detail, walk onto the Senate floor, straight to my chair, and heard him say, "Mr. Vice President, we gotta go."

He told me that protestors were on the move in the Capitol, that we needed to leave the building. I was confident that the US Capitol Police would soon have the situation in hand, so I told him we would just wait in the nearby ceremonial office reserved for my use as president of the Senate.

Since the 1850s, the small, elegantly appointed chamber a few steps from the Senate Chamber has served as an office of sorts for the vice president. The room is full of history, and the only addition I had made to the decor during my time as vice president was a quiet Hoosier landscape by T. C. Steele.

My senior staff was waiting in the small office, and my wife, Karen, and daughter Charlotte joined us shortly after. Along with my brother Gregory, we stood together in that cramped office and watched the mayhem unfolding inside and around the Capitol on a small television set. The scenes were alarming, but having served in the House for twelve years, I had every confidence that the US Capitol Police would soon have the situation under control.

Soon my lead Secret Service agent, a large, confident man named Timothy Giebels, walked through the doors of that crowded office and said, "Sir, we've got to get you out of the building." He informed me that the protestors who had smashed their way into the House side of the Capitol were now heading for the Senate Chamber. They had come to protest and prevent Congress from fulfilling its responsibility to open and count the Electoral College votes. And, as I later learned, many had come looking for me.

I have often told our three children that the safest place in the world is to be in the center of God's will. I knew in my heart that we were where we were supposed to be, doing what we were supposed to be doing. I felt resolve and a peace informed by my upbringing in Indiana, my faith, my family, a lifetime of service, and a lifelong love of the Constitution. I felt no fear. I told my detail that we would hold there until the Capitol was secured. I was not leaving my post.

I was not afraid, but I was angry. I was angry at what I saw, how it desecrated the seat of our democracy and dishonored the patriotism of millions of our supporters who would never do such a thing here or anywhere else. To see fellow Americans ransacking the Capitol left me with a simmering indignation and the thought: Not here, not this . . . *not in America.*

Responding to a muffled roar in the distance, my wife closed the drapes over the large windows facing outside to the north as our lead Secret Service agent returned to make one more urgent plea for us to leave.

The rioters had reached our floor. We had to leave the building at once, Tim said. I pointed my finger at his chest and said, "You're not hearing me, I'm not leaving! I'm not giving those people the sight of a sixteen-car motorcade speeding away from the Capitol."

"Okay," he answered in a voice that made it clear that it wasn't. "Well, we can't stay here. This office only has a glass door, and we can't protect you," he continued, motioning at the entranceway. My daughter Charlotte, sensing my frustration, then asked, "Isn't there somewhere else Dad can go that is still in the Capitol?" With that Tim said we could move, temporarily, from the vice president's office to the Capitol's loading dock and garage, a few stories below. I agreed.

The door to the office opened. A path was cleared in the corridor to the stairwell descending to the garage. The steps were secured. "Sir, we have to go now!" Tim shouted. I stood up, placed my hand on Karen's arm. Charlotte was at our side. I looked at them and said, "Let's go."

We walked out into the hall slowly. As we headed down the stairs, I glanced behind me to make sure that my brother was along with us. All around us was a blur of motion and chaos: security and police officers directing people to safety, staffers shouting and running for shelter. I could see the intensity in the eyes of the Secret Service detail; it was audible in the voices of the Capitol Police. I could hear the falling of footsteps and angry chanting. Making our way to the basement of the Capitol took a few extra minutes because I insisted that we walk, not run, to the secure location below. The Secret Service team begrudgingly accommodated me.

Arriving in the loading dock beneath the Senate side of the Capitol, we saw that our motorcade had been repositioned with all the cars pointed toward a ramp leading out of the building. As we walked into the poorly lit garage area, Tim Giebels began to escort us toward our cars; the doors on either side were held open by a waiting Secret Service agent. As we approached, I saw that the lead police car was slowly beginning to move up the ramp, and I stopped, turned to Tim, and said, "I'm not getting in the car." Sensing my point, he replied, "Sir, we're just going to have you wait in the car, but we are not leaving the Capitol." To that I replied, "Tim, I believe you. You're a man of integrity, but you're not driving that car." It wasn't my first rodeo. I just knew that if we got into the car and that two-hundred-pound door shut, somebody was going to tell the driver to get us out of the building. I turned to Tim and asked, "Is this area secure?" He replied, "It is for now." I said, "Well, then, we're staying here for now." End of debate. It was around 2:15 in the afternoon.

Now settled in a secure location, we started to talk about what was happening above us. We had no access to televisions in the garage area, so my staff and our security team briefed me on the situation using police radio communications and, of course, Twitter. The leaders of the House and Senate had been whisked away to a secure location off Capitol Hill, but I learned that members were actually barricaded in the House chamber as US Capitol Police worked to hold back the mob. I couldn't believe what I saw unfolding in images on the internet. The video of rioters smashing and climbing through a first-floor window of the US Capitol was playing all over social media. It infuriated me. Something needed to be done.

I directed my chief of staff to reach out to the congressional leadership and arrange a call. Around that time, my assistant Zach Bauer, an unflappable young man who had been my personal assistant since my days in Congress, walked up sheepishly and handed me his phone. The president had sent out a tweet at 2:24 saying, "Mike Pence didn't have the courage to do what should have been done to protect our Country and our Constitution, giving States a chance to certify a corrected set of facts, not the fraudulent or inaccurate ones which they were asked to previously certify. USA demands the truth!"

My wife was standing looking over my shoulder; my daughter was next to me. My staff was waiting for my response. I just shook my head. "It doesn't take courage to break the law, it takes courage to uphold the law," I said. Charlotte nodded slowly. "Write that down," I told her. And she did.

The truth was, as reckless as the president's tweet was, I really didn't have time for it. Rioters were ransacking the Capitol. Some of them, I was later told, were chanting, "Hang Mike Pence!" The president had decided to be part of the problem. I was determined to be part of the solution. I ignored the tweet and got back to work.

Marc Short had arranged for a conference call including senators McConnell and Schumer, Speaker Pelosi, and Leader Kevin McCarthy. Leaning against the concrete wall of the loading dock and spreading out my papers on the deck, I told the leadership that I was still in the Capitol and asked what they were hearing. McConnell told me that they were not getting straight answers about when the Capitol would be secure. Pelosi said that she had been told it would be three days before the Capitol could be reopened. That was unacceptable to everyone on the call. McConnell made the point that it was imperative that Congress reconvene as soon as possible to complete the count of the Electoral College vote. There was unanimous agreement on that. For my part, I recalled 9/11 and said, "The best thing we did that day was gather on the steps of the Capitol and sing 'God Bless America,'" proving that Congress was still intact and on the job. Everyone agreed.

Though I was the presiding officer of the joint session, I still thought it was proper to ask the House and Senate leaders if they wanted me to get involved. They all emphatically said yes, and I promised to try to get some answers and get back with them after making some calls. After receiving reports of the ongoing mayhem on the floors above us, I told Karen and Charlotte that they might want to go back to the residence. They weren't having it. My daughter had planned to come and observe the opening of the session only. But the two of them stayed until the final gavel fell in the early morning hours of the next day. I am a truly blessed man.

By 2:38 p.m., it appeared that cooler heads had prevailed at the White House. The president tweeted, "Please support our Capitol Police and Law Enforcement. They are truly on the side of our Country. Stay peaceful!" A half hour later, he urged the rioters to "remain peaceful. No violence! Remember, WE are the Party of Law & Order—respect the Law and our great men and women in Blue." But it was clearly not strong enough.

I felt compelled to offer a tougher message, so at roughly 3:30 p.m., I sent a tweet that read, "The violence and destruction taking place at the US Capitol Must Stop and it Must Stop Now. Anyone involved must respect Law Enforcement officers and immediately leave the building," adding "Peaceful protest is the right of every American but this attack on our Capitol will not be tolerated and those involved will be prosecuted to the fullest extent of the law." And I meant every word.

Over the next few hours, I spoke to the acting secretary of defense, Christopher C. Miller, and the chairman of the Joint Chiefs of Staff, Mark Milley, both of whom assured me that the National Guard had been mobilized and would be on the scene shortly. I spoke to the acting attorney general, Jeffrey A. Rosen, and his staff about additional Justice Department personnel that I was told were already on the scene with more to come. And I talked to the chief of the Capitol Police, Steven A. Sund, who gave me an update on the riots and the lengths his officers were going to, to secure the Capitol. He sounded weary and defensive. Clearly our courageous Capitol Police had been caught off guard by the magnitude of the riot, but help was on the way. I reported back what I had learned to the congressional leadership and went back to fielding calls about law enforcement's efforts to quell the ongoing riot just above us. At 4:17 p.m., the president issued a video telling the rioters, "I know your pain, I know your hurt... but you have to go home now, we have to have peace."

By late afternoon, Chief Sund called with an updated timetable. I asked him to come down to the loading dock to brief me personally.

Standing among the police cars parked in the garage and officers who were making their way through the garage, I had a distinct sense that we had turned a corner. Sund informed me that the Capitol was being secured and we would be able to reconvene the joint session of Congress that night, possibly as early as 7:00 p.m. I thanked him and the officers who accompanied him for their efforts and then noticed that one of the officers had a cut above his eye from an altercation with rioters. I asked the White House physician with me to attend to him and placed a call to the leadership with the news that we would be able to reconvene safely that day.

By 7:00 p.m., we had been cleared to return to my office just off the Senate floor, which we had been forced to abandon as the riot unfolded. Before heading up the stairs, Marc Short suggested that I stop and speak to the press about the events of the day. I thought it was too serious a moment for off-the-cuff remarks, so he suggested that I consider making a statement on the Senate floor when we reconvened in an hour. That felt right.

Arriving in my ceremonial office, we went to work on an opening statement. With Karen and Charlotte looking over my shoulder, I drafted what I hoped would be a comfort to the nation troubled by the loss of life and vandalism that had taken place at our Capitol that day. My family knows my heart and mind better than anyone else in the world, and in that hour I took suggestions from Karen and Charlotte and by phone from Michael and Audrey to get the statement just right. And I hope we did.

Walking out of my office on my way to the Senate floor, I was met by senators Tim Scott and John Barrasso, two good men and close friends thanks to our many years of service together. They thanked me for the role I was playing that day.

As my staff was making its way toward the Senate floor, Tim asked, "Is there anything we can do for you?" I had met him when he was a young state legislator in South Carolina. He had come to an event where I was speaking and said he wanted to meet me, as he was a fellow conservative and a Christian. I have taken great satisfaction seeing his deserved rise through the House and Senate.

"Pray for me," I said.

"You want to pray now?" Tim asked.

At that my staff said, "Sir, we don't have time. The senators are all in their seats waiting for you."

I smiled and said, "There's always time for prayer." And so we all bowed our heads as Tim appealed to Heaven to help us finish that trying day. I will always be grateful for that moment of grace.

As I walked onto the Senate floor, you could hear a pin drop. I stepped up to my chair at the front of the chamber, struck the gavel, and asked for leave to address the chamber. It was granted.

Looking out across the Senate to faces of leaders clearly still dealing with the unimaginable events of the day, I began to read:

> Today was a dark day in the history of the United States Capitol. But thanks to the swift efforts of U.S. Capitol Police, federal, state, and local law enforcement, the violence was quelled. The Capitol is secured, and the people's work continues.
>
> We condemn the violence that took place here in the strongest possible terms. We grieve the loss of life in these hallowed halls, as well as the injuries suffered by those who defended our Capitol today. And we will always be grateful to the men and women who stayed at their posts to defend this historic place.
>
> To those who wreaked havoc in our Capitol today, you did not win. Violence never wins. Freedom wins. And this is still the people's house. And as we reconvene in this chamber, the world will again witness the resilience and strength of our democracy, for even in the wake of unprecedented violence and vandalism at this Capitol, the elected representatives of the people of the United States have assembled again on the very same day to support and defend the Constitution of the United States. So may God bless the lost, the injured, and the heroes forged on this day. May God bless all who serve here and those who protect this place. And may God bless the United States of America.

I closed the folder holding my remarks and said, "Now let's get back to work." With that, the usually reserved Senate burst into applause, and Republicans and Democrats together rose to their feet in a standing ovation, not for me but in celebration of our democracy and all who had defended it that day. It was a deeply inspiring moment that I will never forget.

When we reconvened, everything changed. Many members withdrew support for objections that had been properly filed, and the process took on the feel of a slow march to the inevitable. On the floor of the Senate, leaders and many members rose to express disdain for the violence and vandalism of that day, but a few of them spoke in generous terms about their gratitude for our service, none more eloquently than Lindsey Graham of South Carolina.

I had first become aware of Lindsey during the Clinton impeachment hearings and saw him as a fierce conservative champion in the House. During my time in the House, I had come to know him as a friend, had traveled overseas with him and John McCain, and felt him to be a reliable ally in many conservative fights. During our administration, we had become even better friends, and he was probably the most stalwart supporter of the president and our agenda in Congress. I like and respect Lindsey, but I never expected the words he spoke in the Senate that day.

Rising on the floor of the Senate, he began with a brief history lesson on the origins of the Electoral Count Act, explaining why he did not support objections but saying that those who had brought them "were not doing anything wrong." Then he spoke about the president, whom he called a "consequential president" but added, "All I can say is count me out." He took on the claims of fraud. He then turned to me, seated in the chair at the front of the chamber, and said, "Vice President Pence, what they're asking you to do, you won't do because you can't." He continued, "If you're a conservative, this is the most offensive concept in the world that a single person could disenfranchise 155 million people." Quoting the Constitution, he said, "Where in there does it say if Mike can say I don't like the results, I want to send them back to the states, I believe there was fraud?"

Then he addressed me directly, saying, "So, Mike, Mr. Vice President, just hang in there," adding "All of us can count on the vice president . . . you're gonna do the right thing, you're gonna do the constitutional thing." Then he got personal, and I got emotional. Senator Graham said, "You got a son who flies F-35s, you got a son-in-law who flies F-18s, they're out there flying so we can get it right here!" In the Senate gallery, Karen put her arm around Charlotte at the mention of Charlotte's husband deployed so far away. And the mention of my son and son-in-law brought a tear to my eye as well.

Lindsey Graham gets it, and I will never forget those words.

For the remainder of the night, we worked through the process, until the wee hours of the morning. Some members withdrew their objections. Others soldiered on, bringing objections and arguments to the floor of the House and Senate, but the nation had tuned out. Beyond the tragic loss of life and destruction of property, the January 6 rioters had also managed to drive the debate over election irregularities into oblivion. The robust debate, the "day in Congress" I had promised the American people, was rendered null and void.

At around 3:40 a.m., with Karen and Charlotte looking on from the gallery in the House chamber, Senator Amy Klobuchar of Minnesota read the results of the 2020 election: Joe Biden and Kamala Harris had received 306 Electoral College votes to Donald Trump and Mike Pence's 232. It was met with muted applause by Democrats still awake on the floor of the House. With the words "The announcement of the state of the vote by the president of the Senate shall be deemed a sufficient declaration of the persons elected president and vice president of the United States," it was over. And I signaled the chaplain of the Senate, Barry Black, to come to the podium with a prayer of benediction.

I could think of no better man to have the last word on January 6.

Stepping off the rostrum in the House chamber was a blur. Members approached me with words of thanks, but all I could think of was finding Karen and going home. I made my way into the Speaker's Lobby off the House floor, and there she was. Ignoring all the others speaking to me, I walked up to my wife, and as we hugged, she looked up at me with teary eyes and said, "I'm proud of you."

On our way out of the Capitol, I realized that I had lost track of my chief of staff, Marc Short. Pulling my phone from my pocket, I typed a quick text, saying, "I lost you and just wanted to say thanks for everything." As we walked down the steps to the waiting motorcade, I saw that he had replied simply "2 Timothy 4:7." When we sat in the car, I looked up the verse, which reads, "I have fought the good fight, I have finished the race, I have kept the faith." As the motorcade pulled away, I reached over to hold Karen's hand, and with one more look at the Capitol dome against that early-morning sky, we went home.

CHAPTER FIFTY-TWO

The Calm After the Storm

*Everyone should be quick to listen, slow to speak
and slow to become angry.*
—James 1:19

On January 7, 2021, the morning came too quickly. Karen, Charlotte, and I had arrived home from the Capitol at around 4:30 a.m. With less than four hours of sleep, I was just getting coffee when the White House operator rang. Speaker Pelosi and Senator Schumer were trying to reach me, she said. The day before, we had worked together without partisanship, but I knew that would be short lived.

I placed a call to my chief of staff, Marc Short, who was equally weary, and asked him to find out what the Democratic leaders wanted. He called back to say that they wanted to discuss invoking the Twenty-Fifth Amendment to remove the president of the United States. "Here we go again," I thought.

The Twenty-Fifth Amendment was ratified in February 1967 and created a process whereby the vice president can become the acting president when the president "is unable to discharge the powers and duties of his office." It was an effort to clarify the rules of succession; it was not a substitute for impeachment, and the two Democrats knew it. It was pure political theater and a gross distortion of a provision in the Constitution. I didn't take the call.

As the day wore on, I was humbled by calls from family, as well as from friends in the cabinet and Congress. All expressed their support and appreciation for the stand we had taken at the Capitol. Some of them were quite public about their support; others were more discreet. I will always remember and cherish every call.

I neither had nor sought any contact with the president. But that afternoon, he issued a useful recorded statement in which he condemned the "heinous attack on the United States Capitol," saying that the demonstrators had "defiled the seat of American democracy." He delivered a stern message to those who had broken the law, saying, "You will pay," and then, in a measured tone, he defended having "vigorously pursued every legal challenge to the election," adding that it was imperative to reform our election laws.

Perhaps of greatest importance, the president said that "Now that Congress has certified the results, a new administration will be inaugurated on January 20," and that his focus would be on ensuring a "smooth, orderly, and seamless transition of power." He said everything that needed to be said. We were back on track, at least at our end of Pennsylvania Avenue.

On Friday morning, I spent some quiet time in my devotions and read from James 1:19, "Be quick to listen, slow to speak and slow to become angry," and I tried to do just that. But the truth is, I was angry. Having weathered the storm of events, I was encouraged that the president had denounced those who ransacked the Capitol and had committed to an orderly transition, but I was still angry at how his reckless words had endangered my family and all those serving at the Capitol. President Trump was wrong, I had no right to overturn the election, and in time I trust that most Americans will recognize that our actions were consistent with the Constitution and the laws of our country on that tragic day.

That said, I believe in forgiveness. My faith instructs me to "forgive those who trespass against us," and the Bible also admonishes to "forgive as the Lord forgave you." I have been shown grace in my life. So that morning I prayed for the strength to meet the remaining days of our administration in that spirit. But that was easier said than done.

Karen and I spent the weekend packing up our things at the Naval Observatory and preparing to move into a rental home in northern Virginia where we would live as we looked for a house in Indiana. We were emotionally drained, so some lifting and packing were just what the doctor ordered.

Over the weekend, the Democrats' push to use the Twenty-Fifth

Amendment to remove the president began to drive the news. Nancy Pelosi introduced a resolution in Congress calling on me to invoke the Amendment. She wouldn't let it go. It was time for another written statement to Congress, my second in as many weeks.

On Monday, I met with Marc Short and Greg Jacob in my West Wing office to discuss drafting another formal message to Congress, to be delivered just prior to an expected vote on the Democrats' Twenty-Fifth Amendment resolution the next day. I chaired a meeting of the White House Coronavirus Task Force that afternoon and learned that Jared and Ivanka wanted to meet. I remain very fond of both of them and value their friendship, so I readily agreed.

Arriving back in my office in the late afternoon, Jared and Ivanka informed me that the president wanted to meet and wondered if I would be willing to sit down with him before going home for the day. It had been five days since January 6, and the president had made no effort to contact me in the midst of the rioting or at any point afterward. Truth is, I had felt no obligation to initiate a meeting, but if the president had something to say to me, I assured them that I would be willing to hear him out. They told me he was available right then.

Walking down the narrow hallway between the Vice President's Office and the Oval Office, I didn't know what to expect. I made my way to the small dining room where we had met for lunch every week for the past four years. There on the wall in the hallway, along with a few historic photographs, was a framed picture I had given the president on his birthday during our first year in office. It showed Karen, Charlotte, and me with him and Melania in the sunshine at Bedminster the weekend I had interviewed for the ticket in 2016. He had displayed that photo of the five of us just outside the Oval Office for four years.

When I walked into the back room, Mark Meadows was there but made a hasty exit as the president invited me to come in and sit down. He looked tired, and his voice seemed more faint than usual.

"How are you?" he began. "How are Karen and Charlotte?" I replied tersely that we were fine and told him that they had been at the Capitol on January 6. He responded with a hint of regret, "I just learned that." I told him they were there the whole night; they wouldn't leave.

He then asked, "Were you scared?"

"No," I replied, "I was angry. You and I had our differences that day, Mr. President, and seeing those people tearing up the Capitol infuriated me."

He started to bring up the election, saying that people were angry, but his voice trailed off.

I told him he had to set that aside, and he responded quietly, "Yeah."

I said, "Those people who broke into the Capitol might've been supporters, but they are not our movement." For five years, we had both spoken to crowds of red hat–wearing Americans who were the most patriotic, law-abiding, God-fearing people in the country and who would never do anything like what those people did that day.

I told him that I had prayed for him for the past four and a half years, and I encouraged him to pray. "Jesus can help you through this," I said. "Call on Him."

He didn't say anything.

I asked him what his plan was for the next eight days. He told me he intended to "lay low and give a few speeches."

With genuine sadness in his voice, the president then mused, "What if we hadn't had the rally? What if they hadn't gone to the Capitol?" Then he said, "It's too terrible to end like this." To which I replied, "It's not over yet."

I told him that we had eight days left to serve the country and we should focus on finishing what we started. I told him I had plans to visit military bases to thank our troops and would be going to the inauguration. He replied that he had "no problem with that."

I encouraged him to make a farewell address to the country, as every president since George Washington had done. He could show sadness for what had happened, express anger toward those who had desecrated the Capitol, and speak up for the millions of our supporters who were being unfairly maligned because of the despicable actions of a few thousand rioters. In the end, I thought he should simply thank the 74 million Americans who had stood by us and our record after four years of incessant attacks by the Democrats and their allies in the press. He listened to my thoughts without interruption.

We talked alone for more than ninety minutes, and as I stood up to leave, I said, "You know, I did what I believed the Constitution and the law required me to do," to which he gently waved his hand, saying, "I know, I know." As I left, I urged him one more time to take time to pray.

On Tuesday, January 12, a certain quiet seemed to descend on Washington, DC—everywhere but on Capitol Hill, where Nancy Pelosi was pushing her resolution demanding that I take action under the Twenty-Fifth Amendment to remove the president from office. That was really no surprise. Pelosi and the Democrats had spent the last four years trying to remove the president from office, and with eight days left until the end of our term, they were going to give it one more shot.

As we had done the week before, my team and I prepared a message to Congress to be delivered before the vote.

After expressing appreciation for the actions of the leaders of both parties for reconvening on the very same day of the attack on our Capitol, I informed the speaker that I did not believe that invoking the Twenty-Fifth Amendment would be "in the best interests of the nation or consistent with the Constitution." I reminded her that just a few months earlier, when she had introduced legislation creating a Twenty-Fifth Amendment Commission, she had said, "A President's fitness for office must be determined by science and facts," insisting that we must be "[v]ery respectful of not making a judgment on the basis of a comment or behavior that we don't like, but based on a medical decision." I reminded her that under our Constitution, "the 25th Amendment is not a means of punishment or usurpation. Invoking the 25th Amendment in such a manner would set a terrible precedent."

I had not yielded to pressure to exert power beyond my constitutional authority to determine the outcome of the election a week earlier, and I was not about to yield to similar efforts by Democrats in Congress to achieve their own political ends. That night, all but one of the House Republicans, including some of the president's harshest critics, voted against the Twenty-Fifth Amendment resolution. Case closed, or so I thought. The very next day, Pelosi and the Democrats in the House voted to impeach the president for the second time.

Late in the day on Thursday, I stopped by the Oval Office and found the president working quietly in the back room. He had delivered an address to the nation the night before from the Oval Office. He had unequivocally denounced the violence at the Capitol and called for calm and national unity. Sitting for a few moments at the small table where we had spent so much time together, I congratulated him on his address, to which he responded, "I knew you'd like it." He seemed discouraged, so I reminded him that I was praying for him. "Don't bother," he said.

As I stood to leave, he said, "It's been fun." I said, "A privilege, Mr. President," to which he replied, "Yeah, with you." Walking toward the door leading to the hallway, I paused, looked the president in the eye as he was seated at the end of the table, and said, "I guess we will just have to disagree on two things." "What?" he asked. I referred to our disagreement about January 6 and then said, "I'm also never gonna stop praying for you." He smiled and said, "That's right—don't ever change."

Inauguration Day was cold and muted by the tragic events of earlier that month and by the smaller crowd and the masks adorning all the dignitaries on the platform. Waiting to be formally introduced over the public address system, Karen and I stood, holding hands, in the historic hallway through which presidents come and go in the peaceful transfer of power. We didn't say much to each other, but just before we were introduced, I looked down at my wife, and as our eyes met, she gave me that "You're going to be okay" look I've seen a thousand times. I squeezed her hand as my eyes welled with tears, our names were called, and we walked into the sunlight of the January day in Washington, DC.

Epilogue

There is a time for everything, and a season for every activity under the heavens.

—Ecclesiastes 3:1

By the time the winter of 2021 had given way to spring, Karen and I were settled back home in Indiana: our eighteenth move. We welcomed our beautiful granddaughter, Avery Grace, and quickly realized that the reason we had children was to have grandchildren. In the days that followed her arrival into our lives, Avery's dad, our son, Michael, was deployed overseas, while Charlotte's husband, Henry, came home from a long deployment, and Audrey and Dan finally had that long-delayed wedding, surrounded by family and friends.

We had come full circle, back to where we began, private citizens once again, with a farm field beside our home, the blue and gold of Indiana's flag fluttering beneath the Stars and Stripes just outside the window. The entourage of staff, a constant in our life for eight years, was gone. We will always be grateful for their work, but I didn't mind being able to drive my own car and mow my own lawn again.

I always tried to remind myself how important it was, as vice president or governor, to take time to connect with the people I met along the way. I could always tell how much it meant to them to meet someone in my position, but I knew it wasn't about me. I never saw high office as anything other than a temporary cloak I wore. I knew that once I took it off and another put it on, that effect would wane. As it should. As our founders intended. "We draw our presidents from the people. It is a wholesome thing for them to return to the people," Calvin Coolidge wrote. The same holds true for congressmen, governors, and vice presidents.

Since leaving office, people have often asked me about my relationship with President Trump. I tell them I will always be grateful that he chose me to be his vice president. He was my president and he was my friend. For four years, we had a close working relationship. It did not end well. But as you have read on these pages, we parted amicably when our service to the nation drew to a close. In the months that followed, we spoke from time to time, but when the president returned to the rhetoric that he was using before that tragic day and began to publicly criticize those of us who defended the Constitution, I decided it would be best to go our separate ways.

President Trump and I may never agree on the events surrounding January 6, but I will always believe, by God's grace, I did my duty that day, and I will always be proud of our record and the good work we did for the American people.

In four short years, we rebuilt our military, secured our border, revived our economy, unleashed American energy, and, most important of all, gave the American people a new beginning for life. The Supreme Court's historic decision to overturn *Roe v. Wade* righted a historic wrong by returning the question of abortion to the states and the American people. The fact that three of the five justices who joined that opinion were appointed during the Trump-Pence administration makes all the hardship we endured from 2016 forward more than worth it. Restoring the sanctity of life to the center of American law has been the calling of my life. Now our movement has the opportunity to save countless innocent lives and come alongside women facing crisis pregnancies as never before, supporting the unborn and the newborn with generosity and compassion. To have had the privilege—along with generations of pro-life champions—to have played some small role in that victory for life will be something I cherish for the rest of my days.

The road wasn't always easy, and I can't claim perfection, but I have no regrets for setting out on this journey with all of you.

What I do regret is watching so much of what the Trump-Pence administration accomplished overturned or eroded in the months that followed our departure: the economy, ready to rebound after the pandemic, dragged down by inflation; US energy production, soaring under President Trump, stifled in favor of green extremism; the hard-earned tools and knowledge in the fight against covid wasted as the pandemic continued; a crisis at the southern border and a disastrous withdrawal from Afghanistan, emboldening the enemies of freedom from Eastern Europe to the Asian Pacific; and a steady assault on the liberties and traditional values of millions of Americans.

But as disheartening as these events have been, they are only the reflections on a passing American government, not the American people.

My faith in the American people and our Constitution will always be boundless. No system has ever been more perfectly designed to protect freedom, no people have ever done more good for mankind. Someday—and soon—we will once again have a government as good as our people. And when we do, the time we are passing through today will be only a footnote in our history. What we did once, we will do again.

There was another painting by the Hoosier artist T. C. Steele, one that I placed on the blue wall in the Vice President's Office in the West Wing. I looked at it almost every day for four years. It wasn't a narrow road winding off out of view but a wide landscape, humble in its Hoosier way, the low hills of southern Indiana rolling far into the distance, as far as the eye can see, a vista of endless possibilities. And in the vast sky overhead, a patchwork of bluish-red clouds, their tint leaving the viewer wondering which part of the day the painter had captured, sunrise or sunset? But I never wondered; it's not dusk, it's dawn—the sun is always rising in America.

Michael R. Pence, Zionsville, Indiana, June 2022

Acknowledgments

This is the first book I have ever written, and there are so many to thank for their role in my life and their generous assistance in bringing our story to the written word. Given the number of people I am indebted to, a name or two will no doubt be neglected. In the case of any oversight, allow me to apologize in advance and assure all those who have made a difference in our life and career, you will always be in our hearts.

To my agent, David Vigliano, my most sincere thanks for believing in this book from the very beginning and providing steady counsel along the way, insisting that the book aspire to a literary quality and helping us find the right publisher and the right team to bring our story to the American people. I hope we came close to your vision. Over the past two years, David became my agent and my friend, and I am grateful for his support and prayers. Thanks also to his assistant, Tom Flannery, for bringing his considerable writing talents to shape the outline of the book from early on and for his friendship to me and my family.

To my publisher at Simon & Schuster, Dana Canedy, my gratitude for her passion for this project, support, advice, and encouragement. Dana's inspiring example, professionalism, and kindness combined to bring us together, and I will always be grateful for her confidence. I was impressed with her distinguished career long before her best-selling book and major motion picture and appreciate her encouragement in our shared faith as well. I have also come to strongly agree with her maxim: Writing a book isn't cathartic; finishing it is. Thank you, Dana, for believing in me.

To my editors, Priscilla Painton and Robert Messenger, who are as talented as they are patient, all my thanks. Whatever success this book may enjoy will be as much owing to their talent for bringing the written word to life as any effort on our part. It was a privilege to work with you both. To Jonathan Karp, the president and CEO of Simon &

Schuster, thank you for the opportunity to tell my story under the imprint of this historic publishing house. You also have my admiration for standing up for freedom of expression over the course of this project and providing valuable insights all along the way.

Perhaps the greatest joy I have had in writing this book has come from working with Ryan Cole, who helped me get this story onto the page and stayed faithful to our vision to make it as much about Indiana as about us. Ryan is a fellow Hoosier and a published historian from a storied Indiana family who brought his formidable research and writing talents to this project every day over the past year, and I know it is but the latest of many important works that will benefit from his insight and talent. Special thanks also to his dedicated wife, Jamie, who supported our efforts every step of the way as well. Ryan was recommended by the great American historian Amity Shlaes, whose enthusiasm for this work and guidance over the past year were of immeasurable value. For recommending Ryan, for her confidence and counsel, and for her matchless pen, my admiration and thanks.

This book would not have been possible without the generous contribution of time and memories by those whom I had the privilege of working with during my years in Congress, as governor of Indiana, and as vice president.

Special thanks to Marc Short, who served as my chief of staff when I was House Republican Conference chairman from 2009 to 2010, was legislative director for the Trump administration, and would serve as my chief of staff in the Vice President's Office during the tumultuous days of 2019–2021. The Bible says, "There is a friend who sticks closer than a brother," and Marc Short is such a friend. Marc is a man of faith who is deeply committed to the conservative agenda and was an invaluable support throughout our more than a decade of working together in this movement. His recollections and his counsel were also invaluable in assembling this work. Some of the most momentous days in this story happened with him at my side, and I will always be grateful to him, his wife, Kristen, and their entire family.

Very few people have played a larger role in my career than Bill Smith of Elwood, Indiana. Bill managed my first successful campaign for Congress, served as my chief of staff for more than a decade, and would go on to serve as chief of staff in the governor's office. Bill is a man of faith and integrity whom I came to rely on during some of the most contentious days of my service in Congress and as governor. In many ways, the record we built of consistency to principle was as much owing to his faithfulness and prayers as to my own. For his help with this historic record and for his friendship and seminal role in my life and career, thank you, Bill, Karen, and the entire Smith family for your years of faithfulness to the Lord and our family.

Thanks also goes to my two other chiefs of staff during my years as vice president, Josh Pitcock and Nick Ayers. Josh Pitcock is a fellow Hoosier who was my last chief of staff when I was in Congress, represented Indiana in Washington, DC, during my years as governor, and would become my first chief of staff at the White House. Josh is a consummate professional and man of great character who assembled our team during the transition of 2016 to 2017 and did a remarkable job. His generosity of time and recollections for this project have been invaluable, given his long time of service, and I will always be grateful to him and his wife, Katie, for their friendship and years of dedicated service to Indiana and America.

Nick Ayers and I became acquainted when I ran for governor of Indiana in 2012 and have been close ever since. Nick had served as executive director of the Republican Governors Association at a young age and emerged as one of the bright young talents in the Republican Party. Nick took responsibility for coordinating our vice presidential campaign in 2016, and in 2018 would become my second chief of staff at the White House. Nick's memories of our days together on the campaign trail and during his time at the White House gave real richness to this work. We are grateful to Nick, his wife, Jamie, and their family for their dedication then and now.

Marty Obst served on our campaign for governor and was instrumental in our successful campaign for vice president in 2016. Marty was there in the run-up to my selection as vice president and was so generous with his time and recollections throughout this project. Marty is like a member of our family and one of the great political talents of his generation. We could not have told this story without his input. Thanks for everything, Marty.

Greg Jacob was my general counsel during the final year of the administration and demonstrated his legal insight and loyalty to the Constitution as few others in his position had ever been called upon to do. Greg's recollections of the final weeks of the administration were of incalculable value as we captured those days for this history. Greg's principled devotion to the Constitution was a lodestar, and he, Corey, and the family will always have my respect and thanks.

Matt Morgan is another dedicated Hoosier, who served as our campaign attorney when I ran for governor, served as general counsel in the Vice President's Office, and would go on to serve as counsel to the Trump-Pence campaign. Matt is a brilliant lawyer and a truly good man. His assistance in helping us sort through my years as governor and time at the White House was indispensable. Karen and I so admire Matt and Nicole for their integrity and service.

Thanks also go to former Virginia attorney general Richard Cullen. Richard served as my personal attorney throughout the administration, assisted in negotiating our contract with the publisher, and was an invaluable resource as we labored to put the story of our efforts through the independent counsel investigation onto the page. Richard is a man whose integrity and judgment I have come to rely on and whose friendship I will cherish the rest of my life. God bless Richard Cullen, Aggie, and their entire family.

During my time in the White House, I had the good fortune to come to know Fred and Cindy Warmbier, who tragically lost their son Otto after his detention and abuse by the North Korean regime. Their assistance in preparing this manuscript was invaluable, but their contributions to strengthening the resolve of the American people to stand up to the brutality of the Kim regime will be remembered for generations.

Jarrod Agen joined our staff early on as our communications director and would go on to serve as my acting chief of staff in early 2019 before returning to the private sector. Jarrod has a reputation for great integrity that served our office well in all our dealings with the Washington press corps, and Karen and I will always be grateful to Jarrod and his wife, Bettina, and their family for years of dedicated service.

Zach Bauer came to work for me straight out of college when I was a member of Congress; he followed me back to Indiana during my years as governor and returned to Washington when we went to the White House. Zach served as what is commonly known as my "body man" and was with me continuously throughout my years of service. His willingness to be available throughout this process, to share memories as we researched one moment after another, added immeasurably to this work. Zach is one of the best young men I have ever known, and I count it a privilege to have had him at my side all those years.

Thanks also go to Lani Czarniecki, Jennifer Pavlik, Paul Teller, Aaron Chang, Marc Lotter, Devin O'Malley, Hannah MacInnis, Lieutenant Colonel Andrea Thompson, General Keith Kellogg, and Emily Lair for their years of service and their encouragement over the past year. Lani has modeled the heart of a servant throughout our twenty years together, and his faith and friendship will always inspire. Emily Lair deserves special mention, as she routinely coordinated research and editing sessions in the midst of my otherwise busy schedule. Thanks for making everything work, Emily.

Jim Atterholt was my chief of staff during the final two years of my governorship and steered our staff through health care innovation and controversies, and was a rock of stability during the national campaign of 2016. Jim lent great insight to this book as he recalled our years together, and I will always be grateful for his faith, his professionalism, and his friendship. I also express my appreciation to my former deputy chief of staff in the governor's office, Danielle McGrath, for her assistance with this project and exceptional public service.

Chris Atkins was the director of Indiana's Office of Management and Budget during my years as governor and guided our passage of the largest income tax cut in Indiana history and the adoption of balanced budgets with record investments in education. Chris's assistance in assembling documentation and recollections for this project were instrumental in re-creating my record as governor. Not only is Chris a brilliant fiscal expert but he is also a man deeply dedicated to his faith and family. I will always count it a privilege to have served Indiana with Chris Atkins at my side.

Working on a book that includes my twenty years of public service has reminded me of the extraordinary dedication of so many men and women who served alongside me in Congress, the statehouse, and the White House. To all of you who were part of Team Pence all those years, know that you will always be in our hearts.

Special thanks also to the members of the White House Coronavirus Task Force and industry leaders, many of whom provided assistance in re-creating the story of our nation's response to the worst pandemic in one hundred years. I am grateful for your service to the nation and your assistance in telling our story.

Thanks to the White House photography office, including D. Myles Cullen, Delano Scott, Andrea Hanks, Tia Dufour, and Joyce Boghosian, and to the Indianapolis Museum of Art for loaning the Vice President's Office the Indiana landscapes *Road Through the Woods* and *Blue Hills in the Distance* by T. C. Steele and for permitting us to reprint them in this book.

Beyond all the former staff who made this book possible, I will always be grateful for the support and prayers of lifelong friends who assisted in crafting our story.

Jeff Brown and I have been friends since junior high; he was the best man in my wedding and is a dear friend to this day. Jeff's willingness to share his memories of our early days in Columbus, including the days following my decision to put my faith in Christ, were a real blessing.

Jay Steger and I have been friends from our college days and remain close. From our college days with Dr. Curtis to the day I met Karen to the early campaigns, his willingness to share stories and memories added greatly to this book even as his friendship has added to my life. Love ya, buddy.

I met Tom Rose in 1991, and we have been close friends ever since. We collaborated on many of my major speeches in Congress, and he would serve on the foreign policy staff of the Vice President's Office. A fellow Hoosier, a friend, and a mentor, he is dedicated to his Jewish faith and has a great love of both America and the Jewish state of Israel. There is no one like Tom Rose.

Former Indiana secretary of state Ed Simcox was a mentor through all my years as governor, and his assistance in re-creating this story of some of our more challenging days was beyond helpful, a real answer to prayer.

To the families who were there with us from the very beginning of our political career and stayed with us through lessons learned and dreams fulfilled, we owe so much. To Van and Margaret Smith, Fred and Judy Klipsch, the late Dick and Ruth Johnson, and the late Wayne and Jane Vincent, we offer our love and thanks for believing in us and never giving up. Thank you for helping set this story into motion with your friendship, generosity, and prayers.

And for the prayers and friendship of Fred and Sue Schwein, Phil and Diane Bond, Captain Tom Joyce, Rex and Nancy Bennett, Bill and Linda Armstrong, Jim and Jane Wainwright, Mark and Julie Brown, and Jeff and Lynn Brown, we will always be grateful.

To my family, I owe the most for who I am and for our ability to tell this story.

I will always be grateful for the time my brothers took early on to share stories of our upbringing with Ryan, with my brother Edward even taking him on a guided tour of Pence family homes in Columbus. My younger brother, Thomas, spent hours sharing stories of us growing up, and Gregory, now a congressman, spoke of our boyhood days and the time we had served together on opposite ends of Pennsylvania Avenue. Thanks also to my two sisters, Annie Poynter and Mary Walsh, who have unfailingly supported their brother through all his years of service even as they built careers and families. To my siblings, their spouses, Denise, Kim, Melissa, and Kevin, and their families, thank you all. I love you.

And to my mother, Nancy Pence Fritsch, thanks, Ma. Thanks for making time to help with this book and for cheering me on over the past year. You believed in my dreams but always told me just what you thought. You shaped me more than anyone else in this world, and I hope in this book you see a part of your legacy of love, strength, and faith. Love ya, Ma. Thanks also to my mother's husband, Basil Fritsch, for your support and for loving my mom so well these past eighteen years.

To Karen's late mother, Lillian Barcio, her stepfather, Bernie, and her sister, Cyndi, our heartfelt thanks for your love and support throughout the years. In the early days of our marriage, you were all a constant source of love and support, and after Lillian left us, you always remained faithful and encouraging. We love you.

And finally, to the most important people in my life, Karen, Michael, Charlotte, and Audrey, I owe so much, not just for this book but for living it with me. Thank you for being my toughest editors and adding so much to the story of our family's journey.

To Captain Michael J. Pence, Sarah, and little Avery, thank you for being such an inspirational family and taking time to make sure your old dad was telling our story just right. We are proud of you all. Michael, you will always be my favorite guy.

To Charlotte Pence Bond and Lieutenant Henry Bond, thank you for your good advice as this project began and your prayers over the past year. Charlotte, special thanks for helping us bring the manuscript to a close in the waning days of this project. I hope this book lives up to the high standard you set in *Where You Go*. You will always be the best writer in this family.

Audrey Pence Tomanelli and Dan Tomanelli, thanks for letting us share part of your story in this book. Audrey, your careful edits and suggestions made this book so much better, and I will always be grateful that you allowed me to tell our story in my story. I love you and am so proud of you.

Finally, to my wonderful wife, Karen, I owe the most. My wife read every word of this book, corrected facts, and was better at spotting "that doesn't sound like you" passages than anyone else. Her support, encouragement, and prayers carried me through the past two years of this project, every bit as much as they have during the thirty-seven years of our marriage. The Bible says, "Many women do noble things, but you surpass them all." Thank you for loving me through all our adventures and for being the love of my life.

And to God I give all the glory, for whatever I have been able to accomplish in my life has been only through the grace of our Lord and Savior Jesus Christ. To Him all my thanks and praise. Thank you, Jesus.

Appendix

"Confessions of a Negative Campaigner," Indiana Policy Review,
October 1991, copyright Indiana Policy Review

> *It is a trustworthy statement, deserving of full acceptance,*
> *that Christ Jesus came into the world to save sinners,*
> *among whom I am foremost of all.*
> —1 Timothy 1:15

In the wake of the 1990 election cycle, after one of the most divisive and negative campaigns in Indiana's modern congressional history, the words of Saint Paul provide an appropriate starting point for the confessions of a negative campaigner.

Negative campaigning, I now know, is wrong. That is not to say that a negative campaign is an ineffective option in a tough political race. Pollsters will attest—with great conviction—that it is the negatives that move voters. The mantra of a modern political campaign is "drive up the negatives."

That is the advice political pros give to Republican and Democratic candidates alike, even though negative ads sell better for Democrats. (My admittedly biased explanation is that Republican voters disregard a Democrat's negative ads as "predictable" while expecting a Republican to be "above that sort of thing.")

But none of that explains my conversion. It would be ludicrous to argue that negative campaigning is wrong merely because it is "unfair," or because it works better for one side than the other, or because it breaks some tactical rule.

The wrongness is not of rule violated but of opportunity lost. It is wrong, quite simply, to squander a candidate's priceless moment in history, a moment in which he or she could have brought critical issues before the citizenry, on partisan bickering.

And this wrongness is not limited to the personal but extends to the general. Yes, it was personally wrong for me to waste my moment and limited campaign dollars talking about how an opponent might or might not have financed a rural retreat. But in my party's defeat, as unaddressed issue piled upon unaddressed issue, it seems more grievous that the faithful were left with so few clues as to how I would have governed differently.

Campaigns ought to be about three simple propositions:

First, a campaign ought to demonstrate the basic human decency of the candidate. That means your First Amendment rights end at the tip of your opponent's nose—even in the matter of political rhetoric.

Second, a campaign ought to be about the advancement of issues whose success or failure is more significant than that of the candidate. Whether on the left or the right, candidates ought to leave a legacy— a foundation of arguments—in favor of policies upon which their successors can build. William Buckley carries with him a purposeful malapropism. "Don't just do something," it says, "stand there."

Third and very much last, campaigns should be about winning. A fellow member of the Failed Politician's Club told me recently, "Our only mistake was that we thought that winning was the most important thing we could do." He considers it more than a literal correction that Vince Lombardi's exact words were, "Winning isn't everything, but wanting to win is."

Negative campaigning is born of that trap. But one day soon the new candidates will step forward, faces as fresh as the morning and hearts as brave as the dawn. This breed will turn away from running "to win" and toward running "to stand." And its representatives will see the inside of as many offices as their party will nominate them to fill.

"The Presidency and the Constitution," speech delivered at
Hillsdale College, Hillsdale, Michigan, September 20, 2010

The presidency is the most visible thread that runs through the tapestry of the American government. More often than not, for good or for ill, it sets the tone for the other branches and spurs the expectations of the people. Its powers are vast and consequential, its requirements impossible for mortals to fulfill without humility and insistent attention to its purpose as set forth in the Constitution of the United States.

Isn't it amazing, given the great and momentous nature of the office, that those who seek it seldom pause to consider what they are seeking? Rather, unconstrained by principle or reflection, there is a mad rush toward something that, once its powers are seized, the new president can wield as an instrument with which to transform the nation and the people according to his highest aspirations.

But, other than in a crisis of the house divided, the presidency is neither fit nor intended to be such an instrument. When it is made that, the country sustains a wound, and cries out justly and indignantly. And what the nation says is the theme of this address. What it says—informed by its long history, impelled by the laws of nature and nature's God—is that we as a people are not to be ruled and not to be commanded. It says that the president should never forget this; that he has not risen above us, but is merely one of us, chosen by ballot, dismissed after his term, tasked not to transform and work his will upon us, but to bear the weight of decision and to carry out faithfully the design laid down in the Constitution in accordance with the Declaration of Independence.

The presidency must adhere to its definition as expressed in the Constitution, and to conduct defined over time and by tradition. While the powers of the office have enlarged, along with those of the legislature and the judiciary, the framework of the government was intended to restrict abuses common to classical empires and to the regal states of the 18th century.

Without proper adherence to the role contemplated in the Constitution for the presidency, the checks and balances in the constitutional plan become weakened. This has been most obvious in recent years when the three branches of government have been subject to the tutelage of a single party. Under either party, presidents have often forgotten that they are intended to restrain the Congress at times, and that the Congress is independent of their desires. And thus fused in unholy unity, the political class has raged forward in a drunken expansion of powers and prerogatives, mistakenly assuming that to exercise power is by default to do good.

Even the simplest among us knows that this is not so. Power is an instrument of fatal consequence. It is confined no more readily than quicksilver, and escapes good intentions as easily as air flows through mesh. Therefore, those who are entrusted with it must educate themselves in self-restraint. A republic is about limitation, and for good reason, because we are mortal and our actions are imperfect.

The tragedy of presidential decision is that even with the best choice, some, perhaps many, will be left behind, and some, perhaps many, may die. Because of this, a true statesman lives continuously with what Churchill called "stress of soul." He may give to Paul, but only because he robs Peter. And that is why you must always be wary of a president who seems to float upon his own greatness. For all greatness is tempered by mortality, every soul is equal, and distinctions among men cannot be owned; they are on loan from God, who takes them back and evens accounts at the end.

It is a tragedy indeed that new generations taking office attribute failures in governance to insufficient power, and seek more of it. In the judiciary, this has seldom been better expressed than by Justice Thurgood Marshall, who said: "You do what you think is right and let the law catch up." In the Congress, it presents itself in massive legislation, acts and codes thousands of pages long and so monstrously over-complicated that no human being can read through them—much less understand them, much less apply them justly to a people that increasingly feel like they are no longer being asked, but rather told. Our nation finds itself in the position of a dog whose duty it is not to ask why—because the "why" is too elevated for his nature—but simply to obey.

America is not a dog, and does not require a "because-I-said-so" jurisprudence; or legislators who knit laws of such insulting complexity that they are heavier than chains; or a president who acts like, speaks like, and is received as a king.

The president is not our teacher, our tutor, our guide or ruler. He does not command us; we command him. We serve neither him nor his vision. It is not his job or his prerogative to redefine custom, law, and beliefs; to appropriate industries; to seize the country, as it were, by the shoulders or by the throat so as to impose by force of theatrical charisma his justice upon 300 million others. It is neither his job nor his prerogative to shift the power of decision away from them, and to him and the acolytes of his choosing.

Is my characterization of unprecedented presumption incorrect? Listen to the words of the leader of President Obama's transition team and perhaps his next chief-of-staff: "It's important that President-Elect Obama is prepared to really take power and begin to rule day one." Or, more recently, the latest presidential appointment to avoid confirmation by the Senate—the new head of the Consumer Financial Protection Bureau—who wrote last Friday: "President Obama understands the importance of leveling the playing field again."

"Take power . . . rule . . . leveling." Though it is the model now, this has never been and should never again be the model of the presidency or the character of the American president. No one can say this too strongly, and no one can say it enough until it is remedied. We are not subjects; we are citizens. We fought a war so that we do not have to treat even kings like kings, and—if I may remind you—we won that war. Since then, the principle of royalty has, in this country, been inoperative. Who is better suited or more required to exemplify this conviction, in word and deed, than the President of the United States?

The powers of the presidency are extraordinary and necessarily great, and great presidents treat them sparingly. For example, it is not the president's job to manipulate the nation's youth for the sake of his agenda or his party. They are a potent political force when massed by the social network to which they are permanently attached. But if the president has their true interests at heart he will neither flatter them nor let them adore him, for in flattery is condescension and in adoration is direction, and youth is neither seasoned nor tested enough to direct a nation. Nor should it be the president's business to presume to direct them. It is difficult enough to do right by one's own children. No one can be the father of a whole continent's youth.

Is the president, therefore, expected to turn away from this and other easy advantage? Yes. Like Harry Truman, who went to bed before the result on election night, he must know when to withdraw, to hold back, and to forgo attention, publicity, or advantage.

There is no finer, more moving, or more profound understanding of the nature of the presidency and the command of humility placed upon it than that expressed by President Coolidge. He, like Lincoln, lost a child while he was president, a son of sixteen. "The day I became president," Coolidge wrote, "he had just started to work in a tobacco field. When one of his fellow laborers said to him, 'If my father was president I would not work in a tobacco field,' Calvin replied, 'If my father were your father you would.'" His admiration for the boy was obvious.

Young Calvin contracted blood poisoning from an incident on the South Lawn of the White House. Coolidge wrote, "What might have happened to him under other circumstances we do not know, but if I had not been president. . . ." And then he continued, "In his suffering he was asking me to make him well. I could not. When he went, the power and glory of the Presidency went with him."

A sensibility such as this, and not power, is the source of presidential dignity, and must be restored. It depends entirely upon character, self-discipline, and an understanding of the fundamental principles that underlie not only the republic, but life itself. It communicates that the president feels the gravity of his office and is willing to sacrifice himself; that his eye is not upon his own prospects but on the storm of history, through which he must navigate with the specific powers accorded to him and the limitations placed on those powers both by man and by God.

****

The modern presidency has drifted far from the great strength and illumination of its source: the Constitution as given life by the Declaration of Independence, the greatest political document ever written. The Constitution—terse, sober, and specific—does not, except by implication, address the president's demeanor. But this we can read in the best qualities of the founding generation, which we would do well to imitate. In the Capitol Rotunda are heroic paintings of the signing of the Declaration of Independence, the victory at Saratoga, the victory at Yorktown, and—something seldom seen in history—a general, the leader of an armed rebellion, resigning his commission and surrendering his army to a new democracy. Upon hearing from Benjamin West that George Washington, having won the war and been urged by some to use the army to make himself king, would instead return to his farm, King George III said: "If he does that, he will be the greatest man in the world." He did, and he was.

To aspire to such virtue and self-restraint would in a sense be difficult, but in another sense it should be easy—difficult because it would be demanding and ideal, and easy because it is the right thing to do and the rewards are immediately self-evident.

A president who slights the Constitution is like a rider who hates his horse: he will be thrown, and the nation along with him. The president solemnly swears to preserve, protect, and defend the Constitution. He does not solemnly swear to ignore, overlook, supplement, or reinterpret it. Other than in a crisis of existence, such as the Civil War, amendment should be the sole means of circumventing the Constitution. For if a president joins the powers of his office to his own willful interpretation, he steps away from a government of laws and toward a government of men.

Is the Constitution a fluctuating and inconstant document, a collection of suggestions whose purpose is to stimulate debate in a future to which the Founders were necessarily blind? Progressives tell us that even the Framers themselves could not reach agreement in its regard. But they did agree upon it. And they wrote it down. And they signed it. And they lived by it. Its words are unchanging and unchangeable except, again, by amendment. There is no allowance for a president to override it according to his supposed superior conception. Why is this good? It is good because the sun will burn out, the Ohio River will flow backwards, and the cow will jump over the moon 10,000 times before any modern president's conception is superior to that of the Founders of this nation.

Would it be such a great surprise that a good part of the political strife of our times is because one president after another, rather than keeping faith with it, argues with the document he is supposed to live by? This discontent will only be calmed by returning the presidency to the nation's first principles. The Constitution and the Declaration should be on a president's mind all the time, as the prism through which the light of all questions of governance passes. Though we have—sometimes gradually, sometimes radically—moved away from this, we can move back to it. And who better than the president to restore this wholesome devotion to limited government?

And as the president returns to the consistent application of the principles in the Constitution, he will also ensure fiscal responsibility and prosperity. Who is better suited, with his executive and veto powers, to carry over the duty of self-restraint and discipline to the idea of fiscal solvency? When the president restrains government spending, leaving room for the American people to enjoy the fruits of their labor, growth is inevitable. As Senator Robert Taft wrote: "Liberty has been the key to our progress in the past and is the key to our progress in the future. . . . If we can preserve liberty in all its essentials, there is no limit to the future of the American people."

Whereas the president must be cautious, dutiful, and deferential at home, his character must change abroad. Were he to ask for a primer on how to act in relation to other states, which no holder of the office has needed to this point, and were that primer to be written by the American people, whether of 1776 or 2010, you can be confident that it would contain the following instructions:

> You do not bow to kings. Outside our shores, the president of the United States of America bows to no man. When in foreign

lands, you do not criticize your own country. You do not argue the case against the United States, but the case for it. You do not apologize to the enemies of the United States. Should you be confused, a country, people, or region that harbors, shelters, supports, encourages, or cheers attacks upon our country or the slaughter of our friends and families are enemies of the United States. And, to repeat, you do not apologize to them.

Closely related to this, and perhaps the least ambiguous of the president's complex responsibilities, is his duty as commander-in-chief of the military. In this regard there is a very simple rule, unknown to some presidents regardless of party: If, after careful determination, intense stress of soul, and the deepest prayer, you go to war, then, having gone to war, you go to war to win. You do not cast away American lives, or those of the innocent noncombatant enemy, upon a theory, a gambit, or a notion. And if the politics of your own election or of your party intrude upon your decisions for even an instant—there are no words for this.

More commonplace, but hardly less important, are other expectations of the president in this regard. He must not stint on the equipment and provisioning of the armed forces, and if he errs it must be not on the side of scarcity but of surplus. And he must be the guardian of his troops, taking every step to avoid the loss of even a single life.

The American soldier is as precious as the closest of your kin—because he is your kin, and for his sake the president must, in effect, say to the Congress and to the people: I am the Commander-in-Chief. It is my sacred duty to defend the United States, and to give our soldiers what they need to complete the mission and come home safe, whatever the cost.

If, in fulfilling this duty, the president wavers, he will have betrayed his office, for this is not a policy, it is probity. It is written on the blood-soaked ground of Saratoga, Yorktown, Antietam, Cold Harbor, the Marne, Guadalcanal, the Pointe du Hoc, the Chosin Reservoir, Khe Sanh, Iraq, Afghanistan, and a thousand other places in our history, in lessons repeated over and over again.

****

The presidency, a great and complex subject upon which I have only touched, has become symbolic of overreaching. There are many truths that we have been frightened to tell or face. If we run from them, they will catch us with our backs turned and pull us down. Better that we should not flee but rather stop and look them in the eye.

What might our forebears say to us, knowing what they knew, and having done what they did? I have no doubt that they would tell us to channel our passions, speak the truth and do what is right, slowly and with resolution; to work calmly, steadily and without animus or fear; to be like a rock in the tide, let the water tumble about us, and be firm and unashamed in our love of country.

I see us like those in Philadelphia in 1776. Danger all around, but a fresh chapter, ready to begin, uncorrupted, with great possibilities and—inexplicably, perhaps miraculously—the way is clearing ahead. I have never doubted that Providence can appear in history like the sun emerging from behind the clouds, if only as a reward for adherence to first principles. As Winston Churchill said in a speech to Congress on December 26, 1941: "He must indeed have a blind soul who cannot see that some great purpose and design is being worked out here below, of which we have the honor to be the faithful servants."

As Americans, we inherit what Lincoln in his First Inaugural called "the mystic chords of memory stretching from every patriot grave." They bind us to the great and the humble, the known and the unknown of Americans past—and if I hear them clearly, what they say is that although we may have strayed, we have not strayed too far to return, for we are their descendants. We can still astound the world with justice, reason and strength. I know this is true, but even if it was not we could not in decency stand down, if only for our debt to history. We owe a debt to those who came before, who did great things, and suffered more than we suffer, and gave more than we give, and pledged their lives, their fortunes, and their sacred honor for us, whom they did not know. For we "drink from wells we did not dig" and are "warmed by fires we did not build," and so we must be faithful in our time as they were in theirs.

Many great generations are gone, but by the character and memory of their existence they forbid us to despair of the republic. I see them crossing the prairies in the sun and wind. I see their faces looking out from steel mills and coal mines, and immigrant ships crawling into the harbors at dawn. I see them at war, at work and at peace. I see them, long departed, looking into the camera, with hopeful and sad eyes. And I see them embracing their children, who became us. They are our family and our blood, and we cannot desert them. In spirit, all of them come down to all of us, in a connection that, out of love, we cannot betray.

They are silent now and forever, but from the eternal silence of every patriot grave there is yet an echo that says, "It is not too late; keep faith with us, keep faith with God, and do not, do not ever despair of the republic."

2016 State of the State of Indiana Address, delivered January 12, 2016

200 years ago this summer, 43 founders gathered beneath an elm tree in Corydon, to craft a constitution for a new state they would call Indiana.

Over the past two centuries, our state has seen remarkable growth. A population of some 60,000 is now more than 6.5 million. An agrarian economy bound to the great Ohio River has become a global engine of commerce, ingenuity, education and culture.

On the foundation poured beneath that historic elm, we can proudly say Indiana is not just 200 years old.

Indiana is 200 years strong.

In the past three years, we have added 139,000 new jobs to our economy, reduced the unemployment rate from over 8 percent three years ago to 4.4 percent today, and have seen 34,000 fewer Hoosiers receiving unemployment claims. Indiana consistently ranks in the top 10 best states to do business. Last year, we saw global businesses like GM, Subaru, Rolls-Royce and Raytheon invest billions of dollars in our economy. And, most significantly, last year our state set a new record for private sector employment. Today, there are more Hoosiers going to work than ever before in the 200-year history of this state.

That is 200 years Indiana strong.

And the celebration of our bicentennial has already started. Plans are underway for a new state archive and the Bicentennial Nature Trust has preserved thousands of acres of wilderness. Our Bicentennial Commission is also making sure we bring our celebration to every county of this state. I am truly grateful to all those who have worked to make this possible, but I'm especially partial to the ambassador of the bicentennial. Join me in welcoming our devoted First Lady Karen Pence back to this historic chamber.

Indiana is strong.

And our strength is nowhere more evident than in the men and women who put on the uniform to defend our families at home and abroad—our public safety community and the Indiana National Guard.

I have no higher honor than serving as commander-in-chief of the finest National Guard in America.

In the wake of the terrorist attack on a recruiting station in Chattanooga, Tennessee, I'm proud to say that Indiana was among the first states to allow our National Guard to carry firearms at all recruiting stations. Now, those who defend our freedom have the ability to defend themselves.

Hoosiers know firearms in the hands of law abiding citizens—including our National Guard—makes our communities more safe, not less safe. Indiana will always defend the right to keep and bear arms. Mr. President, please stop blaming our gun laws for violence in Chicago. Hoosiers are not the cause of crime in your hometown—criminals are.

This year, Hoosiers will be proud to know that the 122nd Fighter Wing of the Indiana Air National Guard took the fight to the enemy as they left families and homes to deploy in the Middle East. In April 2015, over 300 Blacksnakes returned from a historic deployment flying nearly 1,300 sorties, severely destroying and degrading enemy capabilities.

I am honored to be joined tonight by two Hoosier heroes.

Colonel Pat Renwick, Commander of the 122nd Fighter Wing, Indiana Air National Guard, and Captain Sarah Jones, also of the 122nd Fighter Wing.

Join me in saying welcome home to the Indiana Air National Guard Blacksnakes. Job well done.

2015 really was a year of progress on many fronts.

Last week, a fourth grader named Samantha at Forest Glen Elementary asked me, "Do you use math in your job?"

I told her, "I use math every day, and Indiana is really good at math."

Last year, we passed another balanced budget, and moved forward with a balanced budget amendment. We maintained strong budget reserves and our AAA bond rating.

We cut taxes for the third year in a row and reduced unemployment taxes on job creators this year by more than $300 million.

And, in 2015, Indiana made genuine progress in student achievement. We raised our standards and saw graduation rates go up to seventh highest in the nation. And, Indiana kids outperformed the national average in every major category on the Nation's Report Card.

We supported our goal to see 100,000 more kids in B or better schools by putting education first in this year's budget.

And when I say we, I'm talking about all of you—members of the best state legislature in America.

Hoosiers deserve to know this General Assembly passed the largest increase in K–12 education funding in Indiana history. And, with nearly $50 million in new funding, Indiana has become the first state in America to make career and vocational education a priority in every high school again.

We increased bonuses for hardworking teachers, launched the first-ever statewide pre-K program—opening doors of opportunity for disadvantaged kids—and we now have one of the largest school voucher programs in the nation. We also invested millions to make our schools safer.

And, 2015 was a great year of progress on the Crossroads of America.

Last year, we invested more than $1 billion in nearly 400 transportation projects. We finished I-69 from Evansville to Bloomington, improved US 31 to South Bend, and the new Ohio River Bridges will support growth in southern Indiana for generations.

And in 2015, Indiana made great strides to improve the health of Hoosiers.

We became the first state in America to reform traditional Medicaid for all able-bodied adults with the launch of the Healthy Indiana Plan 2.0. Unlike the mandates and taxes of Obamacare, HIP 2.0 is based on personal responsibility.

Today, more than 350,000 low-income Hoosiers have access to health insurance they can pay for and it is changing lives.

Like Jo Ann McQueen of New Castle. For years, Jo Ann was without health insurance and went without receiving routine checkups. One day, a friend mentioned HIP 2.0—said it was affordable and offered good coverage. During a routine checkup, Jo Ann had a mammogram where they discovered a lump in her breast. It was breast cancer and she had surgery and recently had her second round of chemo treatment.

She is battling every day, but she and her husband, Dale, are both optimistic. Jo Ann wanted you all to know what HIP 2.0 meant to her and her family. Thank you, Jo Ann. You and Dale will be in our prayers. Get well.

While we have much to celebrate in this bicentennial year, we have much more to do. For despite all these gains, there are still too many Hoosiers struggling to make ends meet.

To keep Indiana growing, we must focus on the challenges before us to strengthen our economy, support our schools, improve our roads and better the health of Hoosiers. For a growing economy, we have to keep taxes low and invest in infrastructure.

While the condition of our roads and bridges ranks above the national average, I propose we make $1 billion available to improve state roads and bridges in the next four years and follow the lead of Senators Long and Hershman to provide another $400 million for local roads.

There are lots of ways to pay for infrastructure, and I expect we will have a healthy debate.

I think when you have money in the bank and the best credit rating in America, the last place you should look to pay for roads and bridges is the wallets and pocketbooks of hardworking Hoosiers.

Let's invest in our roads and bridges, and let's do it without raising taxes.

But infrastructure is more than roads.

Indiana's ports have also been spectacular catalysts for job growth. That is why I have called upon the Ports of Indiana to vigorously explore the building of a fourth port in the far southeastern part of our state, which could unleash enormous economic investment throughout the southeast region of our state.

Because we need to invest in regional growth, our Regional Cities Initiative was designed to do just that, and it has been a remarkable success.

With our state investment, we are leveraging more than $2 billion in public and private investment that will support 96 projects in three regions across the state. These include revitalizing the Fort Wayne riverfront, redeveloping South Bend's Studebaker plant, and residential development in Evansville's city center.

I commend each and every region that participated, and I urge you to fully fund our Regional Cities Initiative and get Indiana growing regionally.

For our schools, with all we've done in education in recent years— higher standards and a new test—we have been asking a lot of our teachers. Teachers that make the difference.

Teachers like Jean Russell, a literacy specialist at Haverhill Elementary School in Southwest Allen County Schools. She has been an educator for 25 years. And, she is the 2016 Indiana Teacher of the Year. Join me in thanking Jean and all our teachers for the work they do every day.

This year let's find ways to make teaching more attractive and do our part to encourage more Hoosiers to pursue careers in education. That is why I am so enthusiastic about Speaker Bosma's Next Generation Scholarship that would cover up to $7,500 per year in tuition for students who are in the top 20 percent of their class and commit to teaching in Indiana for at least five years.

Accountability is important, but testing must be reliable and the results fairly applied. Let's take a step back from ISTEP and improve on the test we use to measure our kids and schools every year. Let's also take action to ensure that our teachers and schools are treated fairly with the results of the latest ISTEP test.

Leaders in both parties and the Department of Education are working with our administration, and I promise you we will make sure the 2015 test scores fairly reflect the performance of our schools and will not affect teacher bonuses or compensation.

Finally, we must support new ways to confront the growing epidemic of drug abuse and addiction that is tearing apart Hoosier families and driving much of the senseless violence impacting our major cities. We must respond with courage and compassion, just the way Reverend Charles Harrison is taking his message of peace and reconciliation to the streets of our capital city.

Our state has been leaning into the war on drugs and will continue to go hard after those who would profit from selling drugs to our kids. Last year, the Indiana State Police took down drug rings across the state and busted 1,500 meth labs.

I have a message for some who might be watching: if you are selling drugs to our kids, we are coming after you. Let's get even tougher on drug dealers in this state. Let's pass stiffer penalties on those who sell these poisons to our kids and let's do it this year.

But we cannot just arrest our way out of this problem. We have to make sure families have more options for treatment and somewhere to go when a loved one is caught up in drug addiction.

That is why I formed the Governor's Task Force on Enforcement, Treatment and Prevention. And, that is why we announced plans for the state's first new mental health hospital in a generation.

That is why, last year, we enacted two laws that were born in the tragic loss of two young Hoosiers.

Aaron Sims was described as an "athletic, red-headed charmer of a son" with a "big heart and big smile." He was a sensitive and promising young man who played football for Lawrence North who lost his dreams and his life to a heroin overdose at the age of 20 in 2013.

Jennifer Reynolds was a radiant young woman, an honor roll student, and a member of her high school cheerleading squad who battled a chronic prescription drug and heroin addiction for 13 years after experimenting with pills as a teen. She lost her life to a prescription drug overdose in 2009, at the age of 29.

Out of their tragic loss, the mothers of these two young Hoosiers worked to change the laws in Indiana in ways that will save lives for years to come with the passage of The Jennifer Act and Aaron's Law that I signed last year.

Aaron's Law allows healthcare providers to make an antidote for opioid overdoses available, and The Jennifer Act allows Medicaid to cover inpatient detoxification.

Those moms are with us tonight. Join me in thanking Sharon Blair and Justin Phillips for their courage and their devotion to the families of Indiana. We are all in your debt. God bless and comfort you both.

Jobs, the economy, schools, roads and confronting drug abuse. These are my priorities.

But, I am aware there is at least one more issue getting attention: whether to extend full civil rights protections to Hoosiers on the basis of sexual orientation and gender identity. Over the past few months, I have studied this issue carefully, and listened respectfully to people across this state. I have met with Hoosiers on every side of this debate, from pastors to LGBT activists to college presidents to business leaders.

While Hoosiers are divided over how or even whether to change our civil rights laws, I think there are two things we can all agree on: Hoosiers do not tolerate discrimination against anybody, and Hoosiers cherish faith and the freedoms enshrined in our constitution.

I was raised like most Hoosiers—on the Golden Rule. That you should do unto others as you would have them do unto you.

Our State Constitution declares that "all people are created equal," and I believe that no one should be harassed or mistreated because of who they are, who they love, or what they believe. We cherish the dignity and worth of all our citizens. We are an open and welcoming state that respects everyone. And anybody who does not know that does not know Indiana.

Hoosiers also cherish faith and the freedom to live out their faith in their daily lives. Whether you worship in a church, synagogue, temple or mosque, religion brings meaning to the daily lives of millions of Hoosiers. And, no one should ever fear persecution because of their deeply held religious beliefs.

The question before you as the elected representatives of the people of Indiana is whether it is necessary or even possible to reconcile these two values in the law without compromising the freedoms we hold dear.

But remember, we are a state with a constitution. Our constitution not only protects the "right to worship Almighty God . . . according to the dictates of (our) own consciences," but, it also provides that "No law shall, in any case whatever, control the free exercise and enjoyment of religious opinions, nor interfere with the rights of conscience."

Our Supreme Court has made it clear that our constitution protects both belief and practice.

As you go about your work on this and other issues, know that I will always give careful consideration to any bill you send me, but legislation must be consistent with the Indiana Constitution.

I will not support any bill that diminishes the religious freedom of Hoosiers or that interferes with the Constitutional rights of our citizens to live out their beliefs in worship, service or work.

Our freedoms are too precious to our people, too vital to our well-being and have been bought at too high a price to do any less.

The issues confronting our state are complex, but I believe if we will hew to our roots, stand firm on the freedoms bequeathed to us by our founders; if we confront the challenges before us with common sense and craft Indiana solutions to improve the lives of Hoosiers, we will move forward together.

We will find a way to continue to live and prosper together as neighbors and friends because that is what Hoosiers do. We solve problems and then we unite. That is how we became the heart of the heartland.

But, for all our successes and for all our challenges, I believe our best days are ahead because for all the change that has come these past two centuries, Indiana's timeless charm remains.

For the moonlight is still fair tonight along the Wabash, and from the fields still comes the breath of new mown hay. The candle lights are still gleaming, thro' the sycamores, on the banks of the Wabash, far away.

God has blessed Indiana, and I believe he will continue to shine his grace on this great state.

If we will but keep faith with the vision, ideals, character and freedoms our founders built this state upon 200 years ago, I know our third century will be the greatest Indiana century yet.

Thank you. God bless you.

And, God bless the great state of Indiana.

Let's get to work.

Address accepting the vice presidential nomination at the
Republican National Convention, July 20, 2016

Mr. Chairman, delegates, friends and my fellow Americans, thank you from the bottom of my heart. I am deeply humbled by your confidence.

And on behalf of my family, here and gone, I accept your nomination to run and serve as vice president of the United States of America.

And let me thank Speaker Paul Ryan for that gracious welcome.

Paul, you're a true friend and a great American leader.

But Paul knows me well, and he knows the introduction I prefer is just a little bit shorter: I'm a Christian, a conservative and a Republican, in that order.

You know, I'm new to this campaign and honestly I never thought I'd be standing here. I thought I'd be spending this evening with all my friends from the great state of Indiana.

Yet, there I was, a few days ago in New York City with the man who won 37 states, who faced 16 talented opponents and outlasted every one of them and along the way brought millions of new voters into the Republican Party.

You know, he's a man known for a larger personality, a colorful style and lots of charisma. And so, I guess he was just looking for some balance on the ticket.

Well, for those of you who don't know me, which is most of you . . .

. . . I grew up on the front row of the American dream. My grandfather immigrated to this country. I was raised in a small town in southern Indiana, in a big family with a cornfield in the backyard.

Although we weren't really a political family, the heroes of my youth were President John F. Kennedy and the Reverend Dr. Martin Luther King, Jr.

When I was young, I watched my mom and dad build everything that matters: a family, a business and a good name. I was raised to believe in hard work, in faith and family. My dad, Ed Pence, was a combat veteran in Korea.

Dad ran gas stations in our small town and he was a great father. If

Dad were with us today, I have a feeling he'd enjoy this moment and probably be pretty surprised.

But it's such a joy for me to tell you that my mother is here. Would you join me in welcoming the light of my life, my mom, Nancy.

You know, growing up I actually started in politics in the other party until I heard the voice and the ideals of the 40th president and I signed on for the Reagan revolution.

But the best thing that ever happened to me, even counting tonight, was that 31 years ago I married the girl of my dreams, a school teacher and artist. She is everything to me. Would you welcome my wonderful wife, Karen Pence.

And regardless of any title I'll ever hold, the most important job I'll ever have is spelled D-A-D.

Karen and I are blessed. Karen and I are blessed to be the parents of the three greatest kids in the world: a writer named Charlotte, a college student named Audrey and a second lieutenant in the United States Marine Corps Michael J. Pence.

I'm so proud of you guys.

Now, if you know anything about Hoosiers, you know we love to suit up and compete. We play to win. That's why I joined this campaign in a heartbeat. You have nominated a man for president who never quits, who never backs down, a fighter, a winner. Until now, he's had to do it all by himself against all odds, but this week, with this united party, he's got backup. And on November 8th, I know we will elect Donald Trump to be the 45th president of the United States of America!

Now, we'll win because we're running on the issues facing this country and because we're leveling with the American people about the stakes and the choice.

You know, the American people are tired of being told. They're tired of being told that this is as good as it gets. They're tired of hearing politicians in both parties tell us that we'll get to that tomorrow while we pile a mountain range of debt on our children and our grandchildren.

And as Ronald Reagan used to say, they're tired of being told that a little intellectual elite in a far-distant capital can plan our lives better for us than we can plan them for ourselves.

In the end, this election comes down to just two names on the ballot, so let's resolve here and now that Hillary Clinton will never become president of the United States of America.

Now, Hillary Clinton essentially offers a third Obama term. And the role is perfect for her. She championed "Obamacare" because years earlier she had all but invented it. The national debt has nearly doubled in these eight years and her only answer is to keep borrowing and spending. And like the president, she thinks the path to a growing economy is more taxes, more regulation and more government.

Now, they tell us this economy is the best that we can do. It's nowhere near the best that we could do, it's just the best that they can do.

Now, let me tell you, I know firsthand it doesn't have to be like this. In my home state of Indiana we prove every day that you can build a growing economy on balanced budgets, low taxes, even while making record investments in education and roads and health care.

You know, Indiana is a state that works because conservative principles work every time you put them into practice.

Now, today, while the nation suffers under the weight of $19 trillion in a national debt, we in Indiana have a $2 billion surplus, the highest credit rating in the nation, even though we've cut taxes every year since I became governor four years ago.

We have fewer state employees than when I took office, and businesses large and small have created nearly 150,000 new jobs, and there's more Hoosiers going to work than ever before. That's what you can do with common sense Republican leadership and that's exactly what the no-nonsense leadership of Donald Trump will bring to the White House.

You know, Donald Trump gets it, he's the genuine article. He's a doer in a game usually reserved for talkers. And when Donald Trump does his talking, he doesn't tiptoe around the thousand new rules of political correctness.

He's his own man, distinctly American. And where else would an independent spirit like his find a following than in the land of the free and the home of the brave.

The funny thing is . . .

You know, the funny thing is the party in power seems helpless to figure out our nominee. The media has the same problem.

They all keep telling each other that the usual methods will work against him. They keep thinking they've done him in, only to wake up the next morning and find that Donald Trump is still standing and running stronger than ever before. The man just doesn't quit.

He's tough. He perseveres. He's gone about as far as you can go in business, but he's never turned his back on the working men and women who make this country grow.

And Donald Trump will never turn his back on those who serve and protect us at home and abroad.

You know, it's been a heartbreaking time for the women and men in our law enforcement community. And in this time of great testing for them, let's let them know here and now, all across this country, we will always stand with those who stand on the thin blue line of law enforcement in America.

Now, you know, while Donald Trump was taking my measure as a possible running mate, I did some observing myself. I've seen the way he deals with people who work for him at every level. And I've seen the way they feel about working for him.

Now, I'll grant you he can be a little rough with politicians on the stage, and I'll bet we see that again.

But I've seen this good man up close, his utter lack of pretense, his respect for the people who work for him and his devotion to his family.

And if you still doubt what I'm saying, remember, as we say back home, you can't fake good kids. How about his amazing children, aren't they something?

These are the true measures of our nominee, chosen by the voters as the right man for these times. This is the outsider, my running mate, who turned a long-shot campaign into a movement.

Now, over in the other party, you know, if the idea was to present the exact opposite of a political outsider, the exact opposite of an uncalculating truth-teller, then on that score you've got to hand it to the Democratic establishment, they outdid themselves this time!

I mean, at the very moment when America is crying out for something new and different, the other party has answered with a stale agenda and the most predictable of names. People in both parties are restless for change, ready to break free of old patterns in Washington. And Democrats are about to anoint someone who represents everything this country is tired of.

You know, Hillary Clinton wants a better title and I would, too, if I was already America's secretary of the status quo.

You know, the choice couldn't be more clear. Americans can elect someone who literally personifies the failed establishment in Washington, D.C., or we can choose a leader who will fight every day to make America great again. It's change versus status quo. And my fellow Republicans, when Donald Trump becomes president of the United States of America, the change will be huge.

You know, for years we've had fundamental problems in America that get talked to death in Washington, D.C., but they never get solved and they even get worse. We've seen entire stretches of our country written off by bad economic policies in ways that are deeply unfair to American workers. We've seen relentless mandates from the executive branch. It seems like no aspect of our lives is too small for the present administration to supervise and no provision of the Constitution is too large for them to ignore.

Meanwhile, we've seen borders that go unrespected, a military that's been diminished, and promise after ringing promise to our veterans, promptly forgotten.

Then Donald Trump came along and started saying what practically everybody was thinking anyway, that our leaders need to be stronger. Under Donald Trump, our deals will be smarter, our soldiers will have what they need and our veterans will have what they earned. We will secure our borders, protect our nation. In all this, we will be more serious. And when we do, this nation will start winning again.

You know, that's the message that men and women in both parties have been longing to hear. But none of us should think for one second that this will be easy. The outcome of this election depends on us and how we contend with an incredible onslaught that's coming our way.

You know, this won't be America's first glimpse of the Clinton machine in action, as Bernie Sanders can tell you.

And this time around, she'll have the press doing half her work for her.

The good news is it won't be nearly enough, not against a candidate who's captured the attention of the country the way Donald Trump has.

On issue by issue, he and I will take our case to the voters, pointing out the failures of the Obama/Clinton agenda and showing a better way. We will win the hearts and minds of the American people with an agenda for a stronger and more prosperous America.

Now, the establishment in Washington, D.C. thinks it's only a narrow range of voters who are giving Donald Trump a serious look. But I can tell you firsthand there's a lot of Americans out there who feel like Democrat politicians have taken them for granted.

It's union members who don't want a president who promises to put a lot of coal miners and coal companies out of business.

Those miners want an American energy policy and they know that Donald Trump digs coal.

It's African Americans, who remember generations of hollow promises about safe streets and better schools, and they know Donald Trump will fight for equal opportunity. And he loves educational choice.

And it's Hispanic Americans, who respect the law, want jobs and opportunities for their families, who know that Donald Trump will uphold the law and get this economy moving for every American.

You know, the party of Lincoln was founded on equality of opportunity. And during these difficult days, it will be our party and our agenda that opens the doors for every American to succeed and prosper in this land.

You know, in so many ways the Democratic Party has abandoned those it used to protect. Maybe they've become too entrenched in power, so comfortable at times that they lose patience with the normal legislative process. It's so much simpler to impose their values by executive order or court action. And make no mistake about it, Hillary Clinton has some big ideas along those lines, too.

As this election approaches, every American should know that while we're filling the presidency for the next four years, this election will define the Supreme Court for the next 40.

We all better think very carefully—very carefully—about what this means for our Constitution and limited government. Elect Hillary Clinton and you better get used to being subject to unelected judges using unaccountable power to take unconstitutional actions.

So let me say, for the sake of the rule of law, for the sake of the sanctity of life, for the sake of our Second Amendment and for the sake of all our other God-given liberties, we must ensure that the next president appointing justices to the Supreme Court is Donald Trump.

And Hillary Clinton's record on foreign affairs gets even worse. You know, it was Hillary Clinton who helped undo all the gains of the troop surge, a staggering failure of judgment that set ISIS on the loose.

It was Hillary Clinton who instigated the president's disastrous agreement with the radical mullahs in Iran. And it was Hillary Clinton who left Americans in harm's way in Benghazi and after four Americans fell said, what difference at this point does it make?

As the proud father of a United States Marine, let me say from my heart, anyone who said that, anyone who did that should be disqualified from ever serving as commander in chief of the armed forces of the United States of America!

Seven-and-a-half years of Barack Obama and Hillary Clinton's policies have weakened America's place in the world. Terrorist attacks at home and abroad, grim and heartbreaking scenes from France just a few short days ago, and the attempted coup in Turkey all attest to a world spinning apart.

History teaches us that weakness arouses evil. Hillary Clinton and Barack Obama's foreign policy of leading from behind, moving red lines, feigning resets with Russia, and the rise, rule and reign of ISIS are a testament to this truth of history. We cannot have four more years apologizing to our enemies and abandoning our friends.

America needs to be strong for the world to be safe, and on the world stage Donald Trump will lead from strength.

Donald Trump will rebuild our military and stand with our allies. Donald Trump will confront radical Islamic terrorism at its source and destroy the enemies of our freedom.

And if the world knows nothing else, it will know this: America stands with Israel!

You know, if you looked at the calendar this morning you might have noticed the presidency of Barack Obama ends exactly six months from today.

And this much is certain, this much is certain of the Obama years. They're not ending well. There seems to be so many things that divide us and so few great purposes that unite us as they once did. And it's at moments like this, moments when politics fail, that I believe we'd do well to remember that what unites us far exceeds anything that sets us apart in America.

That we are, as we have always been, one nation under God, indivisible, with liberty and justice for all.

Should I have the awesome privilege to serve as your vice president, I promise to keep faith with that conviction, to pray daily for a wise and discerning heart, for who is able to govern this great people of yours without it.

My fellow Americans, I believe we have come to another rendezvous with destiny. And I have faith, faith in the boundless capacity of the American people and faith that God can still heal our land.

But we have a choice to make. This is another time for choosing. If you want a president who will protect this nation, confront radical Islamic terrorism and rid the world of ISIS, if you want a president who will restore law and order to this country and give law enforcement the support and resources they deserve, if you want a president who will cut taxes, grow our economy and squeeze every nickel out of the federal bureaucracy . . .

if you want a president who will build strong borders and enforce our laws, and if you want a president who will upend the status quo in Washington, D.C. and appoint justices to the Supreme Court who will uphold the Constitution . . .

. . . we have but one choice and that man is ready, this team is ready, our party is ready. And when we elect Donald Trump the 45th president of the United States, together we will make America great again!

Thank you, and God bless you, and God bless the United States of America!

Letter to Congress, January 6, 2021

Dear Colleague:

Today, for the 59th time in our Nation's history, Congress will convene in Joint Session to count the electoral votes for President of the United States. Under our Constitution, it will be my duty as Vice President and as President of the Senate to serve as the presiding officer.

After an election with significant allegations of voting irregularities and numerous instances of officials setting aside state election law, I share the concerns of millions of Americans about the integrity of this election. The American people choose the American President, and have every right under the law to demand free and fair elections and a full investigation of electoral misconduct. As presiding officer, I will do my duty to ensure that these concerns receive a fair and open hearing in the Congress of the United States. Objections will be heard, evidence will be presented, and the elected representatives of the American people will make their decision.

Our Founders created the Electoral College in 1787, and it first convened in 1789. With the advent of political parties, the Electoral College was amended in 1804 to provide that Electors vote separately for President and Vice President. Following a contentious election in 1876, with widespread allegations of fraud and malfeasance, Congress spent a decade establishing rules and procedures to govern the counting of electoral votes and the resolution of any objections.

During the 130 years since the Electoral Count Act was passed, Congress has, without exception, used these formal procedures to count the electoral votes every four years.

Given the controversy surrounding this year's election, some approach this year's quadrennial tradition with great expectation, and others with dismissive disdain. Some believe that as Vice President, I should be able to accept or reject electoral votes unilaterally. Others believe that electoral votes should never be challenged in a Joint Session of Congress.

After a careful study of our Constitution, our laws, and our history, I believe neither view is correct.

The President is the chief executive officer of the Federal Government under our Constitution, possessing immense power to impact the lives of the American people. The Presidency belongs to the American people, and to them alone. When disputes concerning a presidential election arise, under Federal law, it is the people's representatives who review the evidence and resolve disputes through a democratic process.

Our Founders were deeply skeptical of concentrations of power and created a Republic based on separation of powers and checks and balances under the Constitution of the United States.

Vesting the Vice President with unilateral authority to decide presidential contests would be entirely antithetical to that design. As a student of history who loves the Constitution and reveres its Framers, I do not believe that the Founders of our country intended to invest the Vice President with unilateral authority to decide which electoral votes should be counted during the Joint Session of Congress, and no Vice President in American history has ever asserted such authority. Instead, Vice Presidents presiding over Joint Sessions have uniformly followed the Electoral Count Act, conducting the proceedings in an orderly manner even where the count resulted in the defeat of their party or their own candidacy.

As Supreme Court Justice Joseph Bradley wrote following the contentious election of 1876, "the powers of the President of the Senate are merely ministerial . . . He is not invested with any authority for making any investigation outside of the Joint Meeting of the two Houses . . . [I]f any examination at all is to be gone into, or any judgment exercised in relation to the votes received, it must be performed and exercised by the two Houses." More recently, as the former U.S. Court of Appeals Judge J. Michael Luttig observed, "[t]he only responsibility and power of the Vice President under the Constitution is to faithfully count the Electoral College votes as they have been cast," adding "[t]he Constitution does not empower the Vice President to alter in any way the votes that have been cast, either by rejecting certain votes or otherwise."

It is my considered judgment that my oath to support and defend the Constitution constrains me from claiming unilateral authority to determine which electoral votes should be counted and which should not.

While my role as presiding officer is largely ceremonial, the role of the Congress is much different, and the Electoral Count Act of 1887 establishes a clear procedure to address election controversies when they arise during the count of the vote of the Electoral College. Given the voting irregularities that took place in our November elections and the disregard of state election statutes by some officials, I welcome the efforts of Senate and House members who have stepped forward to use their authority under the law to raise objections and present evidence.

As presiding officer, I will ensure that any objections that are sponsored by both a Representative and a Senator are given proper consideration, and that all facts supporting those objections are brought before the Congress and the American people. Those who suggest that raising objections under the Electoral Count Act is improper or undemocratic ignore more than 130 years of history, and fail to acknowledge that Democrats raised objections in Congress each of the last three times that a Republican candidate for President prevailed.

Today it will be my duty to preside when the Congress convenes in Joint Session to count the votes of the Electoral College, and I will do so to the best of my ability. I ask only that Representatives and Senators who will assemble before me approach this moment with the same sense of duty and an open mind, setting politics and personal interests aside, and do our part to faithfully discharge our duties under the Constitution. I also pray that we will do so with humility and faith, remembering the words of John Quincy Adams, who said, "Duty is ours; results are God's."

Four years ago, surrounded by my family, I took an oath to support and defend the Constitution, which ended with the words, "So help me God." Today I want to assure the American people that I will keep the oath I made to them, and I will keep the oath I made to Almighty God. When the Joint Session of Congress convenes today, I will do my duty to see to it that we open the certificates of the Electors of the several states, we hear objections raised by Senators and Representatives, and we count the votes of the Electoral College for President and Vice President in a manner consistent with our Constitution, laws, and history. So Help Me God.

Michael R. Pence
Vice President of the United States

Letter to Speaker Nancy Pelosi on the Twenty-Fifth
Amendment, January 12, 2021

The Honorable Nancy Pelosi
Speaker of the House of Representatives
Washington, D.C. 20515

Every American was shocked and saddened by the attack on our Nation's Capitol last week, and I am grateful for the leadership that you and other congressional leaders provided in reconvening Congress to complete the people's business on the very same day. It was a moment that demonstrated to the American people the unity that is still possible in Congress when it is needed most.

But now, with just eight days left in the President's term, you and the Democratic Caucus are demanding that the Cabinet and I invoke the 25th Amendment. I do not believe that such a course of action is in the best interest of our Nation or consistent with our Constitution. Last week, I did not yield to pressure to exert power beyond my constitutional authority to determine the outcome of the election, and I will not now yield to efforts in the House of Representatives to play political games at a time so serious in the life of our Nation.

As you know full well, the 25th Amendment was designed to address Presidential incapacity or disability. Just a few months ago, when you introduced legislation to create a 25th Amendment Commission, you said, "[a] President's fitness for office must be determined by science" and you said then that we must be "[v]ery respectful of not making a judgment on the basis of a comment or behavior that we don't like, but based on a medical decision." Madam Speaker, you were right. Under our Constitution, the 25th Amendment is not a means of punishment or usurpation. Invoking the 25th Amendment in such a manner would set a terrible precedent.

After the horrific events of this last week, our Administration's energy is directed to ensuring an orderly transition. The Bible says that "for everything there is a season, and a time for every purpose under heaven . . . a time to heal, . . . and a time to build up." That time is now.

In the midst of a global pandemic, economic hardship for millions of Americans, and the tragic events of January 6th, now is the time for us to come together, now is the time to heal.

I urge you and every member of Congress to avoid actions that would further divide and inflame the passions of the moment. Work with us to lower the temperature and unite our country as we prepare to inaugurate President-elect Joe Biden as the next President of the United States. I pledge to you that I will continue to do my part to work in good faith with the incoming administration to ensure an orderly transition of power. So help me God.

Index

About the Author

Michael R. Pence was born and raised in Columbus, Indiana. He graduated with a BA from Hanover College and received his JD from the Indiana University School of Law. He was elected to the US Congress in 2000, where he represented Indiana's Second and then Sixth District for twelve years. From 2013 to 2017, he served as Indiana's fiftieth governor and then served as the forty-eighth vice president of the United States from 2017 to 2021. He and his wife, Karen, have three married children and one granddaughter. The Pences live in Zionsville, Indiana.